Contingency Views of Organization and Management

Contingency Views of Organization and Management

Fremont E. Kast, *University of Washington*

James E. Rosenzweig, *University of Washington*

SRA Consulting Editors in Management

SCIENCE RESEARCH ASSOCIATES, INC.

Chicago, Palo Alto, Toronto, Henley-on-Thames, Sydney, Paris

A Subsidiary of IBM

658.4
K 191

Acknowledgments

In this project we have relied on contributions from many sources. First and foremost are the authors of the seventeen readings presented in Part 2. Without their pioneering conceptual and research endeavors, this book would not have been possible. Many other readings might have been included; space limitations made the selection process very difficult. Unquestionably ideas from authors not included in the readings have contributed to our analysis and interpretation of contingency views.

Several reviewers have provided objective insight at several stages of the project; we have benefited from their incisive comments. We are also indebted to our colleagues at the University of Washington for a climate of continuing debate and refinement of ideas.

Nona Pedersen shepherded the manuscript from beginning to end, making the project more palatable than it might have been.

Foreword

Introduction

A major achievement of modern man is the creation of a large number of diverse social organizations for accomplishing specific purposes. A vast array of business enterprises provides a multitude of products and services. Millions of students are active participants in educational organizations. Complex hospitals and related health service agencies have been created to meet national needs. Man's space exploration and lunar landings are symbols of organizational and managerial ingenuity.

Past successes in designing and managing complex organizations might suggest that we already know "everything there is to know" and that all that remains is the application of current knowledge to new situations. *This is not the case.* In many ways managerial success has been based on trial and error—learning through experience. Comprehensive understanding of how organizations really function (organization theory) and astute guidelines for improving their performance (the art of management) are still in the developmental stage.

Early efforts in organization and management theory came primarily from manager-philosophers who drew on their own experience to develop universal principles. Then came empirical researchers who engaged in detailed investigations of specific dimensions and issues in organizations. These complementary approaches reinforced each other and provided deeper insights into organizations and their management.

Because of the pervasiveness and diversity of organizations, the related theory and scientific study have come from many sources. It is an eclectic theory comprised of subsystems of many disciplines; certain aspects of sociology, psychology, anthropology, economics, political science, philosophy, and quantitative analysis are applicable. Organizations have received increasing attention from these areas in the twentieth century and the study of organizations has evolved as an important, visible field. Research in a variety of disciplines provides a theoretical base for propositions which are useful in understanding organizations and for managing them.

Experience gained in management practice is also an important input to organization theory. In short, the art of management is based on information generated by both practical experience and scientific research concerning organizations—individual behavior, group dynamics, intergroup relations, and total organizational phenomena, including environmental relationships.

As various disciplines have become interested in organizations and their management, researchers have begun to reflect on their own traditional preoccupation with certain selected subject matter. Even though some theorists (or cults) espouse simplicity and monistic views of organizations, the attempt to synthesize a variety of efforts has led to greater overall complexity and the necessary inclusion of more variables. The development of a general theory has (and will continue to) become even more difficult. Rather than facilitating integration of the various theories, modern developments in the relevant sciences have contributed to their divergence.

Furthermore, there is evidence of increasing divergence between organization theory and management practice. Management scientists (both behaviorally and quantitatively oriented) become impatient when managers do not seem to understand or to recognize the value of their findings. Managers in turn are frequently suspicious of untried theories and recommendations which do not seem to fit the reality of their own organizations. Is there any hope of greater convergence within the theories themselves and between theory and practice? We think there is; in this book we address this question and explore models or constructs which can be useful both conceptually and operationally.

This project has really only begun. Much research and conceptualization remains to be done. Indeed, we see it as an open-ended task requiring continual refinement as we learn more about organization theory and management practice. Because organizations (including their individual participants and societal environments) will continue to evolve, the related body of knowledge must keep pace in order to be relevant. Hopefully, this book will be a useful step in this continuing process.

Purpose

The purpose of this book is to facilitate the understanding and development of contingency views of organizations and their management. These views are based on systems concepts and stress the relevancy of theory to practice in specific situations. The central theme can be stated as follows:

The contingency view of organizations and their management suggests that an organization is a system composed of subsystems and delineated by identifiable boundaries from its environmental suprasystem. The contingency view seeks to understand the interrelationships within and among subsystems as well as between the organization and its environment and to define patterns of relationships or configurations of variables. It emphasizes the multivariate nature of organizations and attempts to understand how organizations operate under varying conditions and in specific circumstances. Contingency views are ultimately directed toward suggesting organizational designs and managerial practices most appropriate for specific situations.

This is primarily a book of readings, not a basic text. It assumes some prior knowledge about organization theory and management practice. We have selected seventeen articles or sections of books which reflect the development of contingency views in a variety of ways. Our objective has been to present these readings within a framework which will facilitate their understanding and integration. Although we attempt to interpret the conclusions of the various authors, our own perception of the contingency view underlies such endeavors. It is therefore essential that the reader examine the individual readings in depth for a more complete understanding of their content.

The central theme of this book is based on the assumption that there is a middle ground between (1) the view that there are universal principles of organization and management and (2) the view that each organization is unique and that each situation must be analyzed separately. The contingency view is a mid-range concept which recognizes the complexity involved in managing modern organizations but uses patterns of relationships and/or configurations of subsystems in order to facilitate improved practice.

The contingency view suggests that there are definable patterns of relationships for different types of organizations and that we can improve our understanding of how the relevant variables interact. For example, certain principles of organization and/or management might be appropriate for uniform operations in a relatively stable environment. A mass production organization such as an automobile assembly line might operate most efficiently under a rather rigid hierarchy with precise planning and control, as well as routinization of activities. Such an approach might also apply to a routine service organization such as the post office. In contrast, other organizations, operating in an uncertain environment and with nonroutine technology, may operate most efficiently under a very different set of principles. A research and development laboratory or a university graduate program, for example, might be characterized by a flexible structure, nonroutine activities, and adaptive planning and control processes.

Moreover, the contingency view suggests that different approaches may be appropriate in subparts of the same organization. Managing the campus police is not the same as managing the history department. Authority relationships, leadership styles, and other variables are likely to be quite different. Also, the production, sales, and engineering departments within a corporation may need differential management approaches in order to perform their specific functions effectively.

With organizations, as with individuals, there are similarities and differences. In terms of basic components and fundamental relationships all organizations are alike. For example, they are subsystems of their broader environment and goal-oriented or purposeful. All organizations are comprised of subsystems—technical, structural, and psychosocial—and coordinated by a managerial subsystem designed to plan and control the overall endeavor. Within this framework certain fundamental or universal principles apply to all organizations. For example, the interrelatedness of the structural and psychosocial subsystems suggests that changes in one (a new pattern of authority) will affect the other (interpersonal relationships).

However, the specifics of organization design and managerial approaches should be adapted to the particular situation. An organization structure appropriate for the history department probably will not be effective in the campus police department. The sales group may need a different type of compensation system than engineering or production departments. Information-decision systems have fundamental processes (collect, process, compare, and decide); however, banks and hospitals have vastly different purposes and and must adapt the system to their specific needs.

Thus, there should be continual tradeoffs between universal principles and specific situational analysis. Systems concepts provide a framework for contingency views which in turn allow us to find a middle ground between "universal principles" and "it all depends."

Plan of the Book

The book is divided into four parts. Part 1 traces the evolution of organization and management theory, providing historical perspective for current conditions and future prospects. Increasingly, organizations are being considered as open, adaptive, problem-solving, socio-technical systems. Of particular importance is the concept of inter-relationships among systems and subsystems. This approach blends into contingency views which have received increasing attention by researchers and writers in recent years. The brief review of the development of systems concepts and contingency views provides a basic background for the readings and interpretations that follow. However, it is an overview and should not be considered to be comprehensive.*

Part 2 is comprised of seventeen readings which exemplify contingency views. They have been selected in terms of (1) relating organizations to complex, dynamic environments, and (2) comprehending interrelated organizational subsystems—goals and values, technical, structural, psychosocial, and managerial.

Part 3 is a synthesis of the various views expressed in the readings along with our appraisal of their relevance for organization theory. The focus is the development of a conceptual model of contingency views of organization and management. It is important to recognize that this model represents our ideas of "the state of the art" and that it is open for additions, deletions, and modifications.

Part 4 focuses on the application of contingency views to management practice. Our purpose is to evaluate and illustrate their usefulness. Of particular importance are suggestions for operationalizing contingency views in a way which will facilitate managerial effectiveness and efficiency.

A comprehensive bibliography is included for the reader who may wish to explore the concept of contingency views in more depth than is possible within the scope of this book.

---

*For more detail, see, for example, Fremont E. Kast and James E. Rosenzweig, *Organization and Management: A Systems Approach* (New York: McGraw-Hill, 1970), pp. 57-137.

Contents

Contingency Views of Organization and Management

Part 1

Evolution of Organization and Management Theory

A phenomenon of modern industrial society is the evolution of large-scale organizations for the accomplishment of specific purposes. This relatively new development has been pervasive over the past century. Throughout most of man's history his social relationships were primarily on a family or small-group basis. The Industrial Revolution, with its demand for concentration of resources and greater scale, fostered the development of large economic and other organizational units. Modern governmental and educational institutions, corporations, and hospitals, for example, have emerged as complex systems.

This evolution is not restricted to Western culture. The trend toward more complex organizations is moving as a wave through many cultures. Societies are not static; they are continually changing. "New social forms emerge, old ones modify their forms, change their traditional functions, and acquire new meanings. One of the most significant and important of these developments is the emergence of many varieties of large-scale organizations on which the society increasingly depends." [1, p. vii] * As other countries pass through the phases of industrialization, they also find it advantageous to

---

* References in brackets refer to works cited at the end of each section of the text. References in parentheses refer to the articles reprinted in Part 2.

develop larger organizational units. People can no longer accomplish their objectives individually or in small groups. In order to function effectively and efficiently, human activities must be integrated into more encompassing systems.

The growth of complex organizations has led to another major phenomenon—the emergence of the managerial or administrative function. With primitive and informal means of social organization, the administrative functions of goal establishment, planning, and integration were relatively simple and were usually based upon established traditions of behavior. Now, however, a distinct managerial role has become vital. Witness the increased emphasis during the twentieth century in the educational preparation of managers/administrators—for business, government, education, correctional institutions, and many other fields of endeavor. The growth and development of organizations and the increasing importance of management have given impetus to (1) scientific research in many related disciplines, (2) the generation of an underlying body of knowledge, and (3) the interaction between theory and practice.

The attempts to codify organization and management knowledge as a separate and identifiable field of study is relatively recent. Only during the twentieth century have attempts been made to develop a general theory. However, there is a rich heritage of ideas from the past. Throughout recorded history men have pondered the problems of human organization and the administration of governments, churches, armies, and other social groups. Yet the beginning of a systematic body of knowledge is closely associated with the Industrial Revolution and the rise of large-scale economic enterprises which required the development of new organizational forms and managerial practices.

Traditional Organization and Management Theory

There are three primary pillars to the traditional theory: (1) scientific management, (2) the bureaucratic model, and (3) administrative management theory. (Thompson, pp. 26-36) Taken collectively, they provide the major concepts for the design and management of organizations during the first part of this century.

The early contributors represent a heterogeneous group of practitioners as well as academic generalists and specialists. Much of management thought came from practicing executives who recorded their observations and experiences and set them forth as general guidelines for others. Scientific management focused on empirical observation and advocated use of the scientific method in the development of more efficient operations. The bureaucratic model was conceived in

large part by Max Weber who made significant contributions to
organization theory. Henri Fayol gave direction to the development
of administrative management theory. By no means have the traditional views formulated by these men been totally abandoned.
They still provide an appropriate and fundamental part of our current
knowledge.

Scientific management. Many of our basic ideas concerning the
management of organizations are derived from early scientific management theory. The movement was given its original impetus by
Frederick W. Taylor and was strongly influenced by the Protestant
ethic. He emphasized the value of hard work, economic rationality,
individualism, and the view that each man had a role in society. His
primary aim was to increase worker efficiency.

He felt that work could be analyzed scientifically and that it was
management's responsibility to provide the specific guidelines for
worker performance. This logically led to (1) the development of
the one best method to accomplish a given task, (2) the standardization of this method (usually through time-and-motion studies), (3)
the selection of workers best suited to performing the specific task,
and (4) the training of those workers in the most efficient method
for performing the work. It was an engineering approach and viewed
the worker as an adjunct to the equipment. Basic assumptions about
the nature of man are implicit in the scientific management approach,
including the assumption that employees will be motivated by the
greater economic rewards which would come from increased productivity. A pessimistic view of man prevails; workers are considered to
be basically indifferent and unreliable, and tight control over them
must be maintained by those in authority (managers). Workers are
primarily motivated by economic self-interest. (Knowles and Saxberg,
pp. 101-19).

Although there was much criticism of scientific management, the
principles spread rapidly throughout industry and applications were
soon found in other areas. Pragmatically, the theory worked to increase the efficiency of operations and all resistance could therefore
be brushed aside in the drive for greater producivity.

Bureaucratic model. The second major pillar in the development of
classical organization theory was provided by Max Weber's bureaucratic model. He was one of the founders of modern sociology and
was a significant contributor to economic, social, and administrative
thought. Writing during the first part of the twentieth century, he
was contemporary with the scientific management movement. However, he was interested in the broad economic and political structure
of society as well as the administration of the single organization. His

ideas concerning the bureaucratic organization were only part of a total social theory. In his various writings he traced the changes in religious views, discussed their impact upon the growth of capitalism, and examined the effect of industrialization upon organization structure. His discussions of bureaucracy were a natural evolution stemming from broader considerations of historical and social factors which led to the development of complex organizations.

The term *bureaucracy* as developed by Weber and his followers is not used in the popularized, emotionally charged sense of red tape and inefficiency. Weber viewed bureaucracy as the most efficient form, one that could be used most effectively for complex organizations—business, government, military, for example—arising out of the needs of modern society. His model had a strong flavor of depersonalization—an explicit attempt to offset nepotism, political favoritism, and general capriciousness in decision making. The ideal bureaucracy had the following characteristics: (1) a division of labor based upon functional specialization, (2) a well-defined hierarchy of authority, (3) a system of rules governing the rights and duties of positional incumbents, (4) a system of procedures for dealing with work situations, (5) impersonality of interpersonal relations, and (6) promotion and selection for employment based upon technical competence [2, p. 33].

Appraisal of any large-scale organization suggests that these dimensions are present in varying degrees. Students of bureaucracy have analyzed Weber's ideal model to determine both its functional and dysfunctional consequences. Merton, Selznick, Gouldner, and others have critically evaluated the bureaucratic form and have suggested that while it may describe an ideal type in terms of formal relationships, it does not take into account consequences dysfunctional to organizational effectiveness. However, the modern view is to utilize the Weberian bureaucratic model when appropriate for a particular situation, yet to recognize the limitations and consequences of this highly structured approach.

Administrative management theory. Scientific management was concerned with optimizing effort at the shop or operating level and thus was a micro approach. A complementary body of knowledge, which placed primary emphasis on broad administrative principles applicable to higher organization levels, was also developing. March and Simon refer to this body of knowledge as "administrative management theory." [3, p. 22] Other writers call it the traditional or classical theory of management. It focuses on formal organization structure and the delineation of universal principles of management.

Henri Fayol was one of the earliest exponents of a general theory of administration. Many other writers, primarily those actively engaged in management or consulting practices, set forth their views following his pattern. Although serious questions have been raised regarding the appropriateness of the approach and the universal application of the administrative management theories, many of the concepts from this school are apparent in the administration of organizations today. The pyramidal form, the scalar principle, unity of command, the exception principle, the delegation of authority, limited span of control, and departmentalization principles are currently being applied in the design and operation of many organizations. Although the administrative management theorists have been criticized for their rigid approach (there is, for example, little recognition of psychological and sociological factors), their ideas still have some validity in the structuring of organizations and in providing general managerial guidelines.

Appraisal of traditional views. In addition to these foundations of traditional organization and management theory there were supporting views. The value system of classical economics and the "ideal competitive model" strongly influenced managerial thought and action, and provided a rationale for the operation of the business firm within society. Classical economic theory and traditional organization theory shared many common viewpoints, particularly with regard to their assumptions about the entrepreneurial role and human motivation. It was a basic premise of both that the entrepreneur or manager had the legitimate right to exercise authority based on the ownership of private property. Employees had the duty to follow orders and were motivated by economic incentives. They had to be directed and controlled by the managerial elites.

A number of readings included here provide insight into the weaknesses of traditional views (Leavitt, pp. 57-73; Lombard, p. 255-72; Lorsch, pp. 179-94; and Thompson, pp. 26-36). Taken together, traditional theories provided a rather narrow view of organizations. The primary emphasis was upon increasing efficiency through structuring and controlling human participants. People were assumed to be motivated primarily by economic incentives. It was necessary to specialize tasks and to provide detailed instructions and controls. In order to ensure cooperation in meeting organizational goals, the participants had to be closely supervised. Administration was the primary integrative force and the formal hierarchy was the mechanism for achieving coordination. Traditional views evolved universal "principles of management" which the originators viewed as appropriate for all organizations.

One of the major criticisms of the traditional view is that it employed relatively closed-system assumptions about organizations which failed to consider many of the environmental influences upon the organization, as well as many important internal aspects.

It seems clear that the rational-model approach uses a closed-system strategy. It also seems clear that the developers of the several schools using the rational model have been primarily students of performance or efficiency, and only incidentally students of organizations. Having focused on control of the organization as a target, each employs a closed system of logic and conceptually closes the organization to coincide with that type of logic, for this elimination of uncertainty is the way to achieve determinateness. The rational model of an organization results in everything being functional—making a positive, indeed an optimum, contribution to the overall result. All resources are appropriate resources, and their allocation fits a master plan. All action is appropriate action, and its outcomes are predictable. (Thompson, p. 28)

The traditional view envisioned the organization as a closed, mechanistic system which was isolated from environmental forces. Also, it made unrealistic assumptions about human behavior. The universal principles of management which were developed were frequently vague and contradictory.

While recognizing these limitations, we cannot reject the traditional views entirely. They, and the derived principles of management, do have applicability in some circumstances [4, pp. 241-257]. One of the major tasks of this book is to determine the circumstances, patterns, or contingencies under which the different views of organizations and their management are appropriate.

Modifications: Behavioral and Quantitative Sciences

Many forces, both within organizations and in the external environment, have stimulated change in theory and practice. The growth in size and complexity of organizations has been unparalleled. Technological change and improvement have forced many adaptations. Specialization has increased and the generally higher level of education has provided people with more advanced intellectual skills. Participants usually have diverse objectives and more refined inducements have been designed in order to ensure loyalty to the organization. The rising aspiration levels for satisfaction of economic and other needs have been important factors in creating change.

Over the past several decades these and other environmental and internal changes have caused major modification in traditional theories. It is difficult to review all of them; however, two broad categories emerge as being fundamental influences: (1) the behavioral sciences, which emphasize the psychosocial system and the human aspects of administration; and (2) the quantitative sciences which emphasize quantification, mathematical models, and the application of computer technology.

Behavioral sciences. The behavioral sciences are relatively new academic and intellectual disciplines. Much of the work in psychology, sociology, and anthropology is a product of this century, particularly with respect to empirical research. Contributions to organization theory and management practice began with the human relationists. The Hawthorne studies highlight these efforts.

Many concepts from the behavioral sciences underlie the advocacy of organization change through "people approaches." (Leavitt, pp. 57-73) Accordingly, methods based on behavioral science premises seek to facilitate growth and change in individuals, groups, and organizations. (Harrison, pp. 238-54)

In their study of organizations, the behavioral scientists emphasize the *psychosocial system* and its human components. Whereas traditional management concepts were concerned with structure and tasks, the emphasis of the behavioral scientists is on human factors and the way people behave in actual organizations. Typically they have a "humanistic" view which differs substantially from the mechanistic orientation of traditionalists and quantitative scientists. They are primarily concerned with studying and describing behavior in actual organizations, and less interested in establishing normative models. They try to open the system and to consider many variables which were excluded from the traditional views.

They tend to take a more optimistic view of the basic nature of man. (Knowles and Saxberg, pp. 101-19) While traditional theorists emphasized control of human behavior, the writings of many of the behavioral scientists indicate the higher value placed on more democratic, less authoritarian, less hierarchically structured organizations. They tend to advocate a "power equalization" system which emphasizes morale, sensitivity, and psychological security—one which values human growth and fulfillment. These approaches share a normative belief that power in organizations should be distributed more equally than in most traditional authoritarian hierarchies. (Leavitt, pp. 57-73)

The behavioral sciences have had a profound influence on organization theory and management practices. However, as with traditional theories, many concepts have been suggested as universal views which apply to all organizations. Although they may be highly useful in organization design and management practice, these viewpoints are undoubtedly more appropriate in some situations than in others. The behavioral sciences often take a partial systems view which tends to overemphasize the human or psychosocial system. In the open system and contingency view, the psychosocial subsystem must be considered in terms of its *interaction* with the environment and with other subsystems in the organization.

Quantitative sciences. Another major influence came about through the application of quantitative methods to decision making. This post-World War II development has variously been called *operations research, management science,* or *quantitative science.* In many ways the approach is a descendent of the scientific management movement with the addition of more sophisticated (primarily mathematical) methods, computer technology, and an orientation toward more comprehensive problems. (Leavitt, pp. 57-73)

Most of the quantitative scientists come from mathematics, statistics, engineering, and economics and have an economic-technical orientation. They use the scientific method as a framework for problem solving with emphasis upon objective analysis rather than subjective judgment.

Operations researchers are dedicated to the utilization of scientific method for the solution of organizational problems and emphasize normative approaches designed to aid managerial decision making. Given a sense of economic-technical rationality and the objectives to be achieved, operations research (OR) techniques prescribe optimal courses of action. Many assumptions about organizational and participant behavior have to be made initially by the operations researchers. These assumptions often differ significantly from those made by behavioral scientists.

The quantitative sciences typically have been directed less toward strategic problems and more toward tactical decisions. For the most part, they have not been engaged in problem solving for those types of ill-structured problems which are the concern of top management and which generally have not been amenable to precise mathematical and statistical approaches. The emphasis has been on lower- to middle-level problems where quantification is possible. Recently, however, there has been a growing interest in dealing with ill-structured problems with approaches such as computer simulation and heuristic decision making. Greater emphasis on heuristic problem solving will move the quantitative scientist away from his concentration on mathematical techniques and will require the integration of knowledge from the behavioral sciences as well as traditional theories.

Operations researchers have become increasingly concerned about the implementation of their recommendations. There is growing awareness of the necessity to view the organization as a social as well as an economic-technical system. The quantitative scientist, like the behavioral scientist, has become an agent for change in organizations. Often he develops new concepts and ideas which challenge traditional management approaches. But, just as with the knowledge developed from the behavioral sciences, we must look critically at the concepts being generated. Under what circumstances are certain techniques or approaches useful? What are the contingencies which affect their appropriateness?

Divergence in theory. Behavioral and quantitative science endeavors have done much to modify traditional organization theory and management practice. Ideally, these two approaches would be integrated with traditional views to provide a unified and clearly delineated modern theory. This has not happened for many reasons. There are basic differences in values and ideologies; diverse academic disciplines are involved; differential emphasis on descriptive and normative points of view are evident. As many disciplines have become interested in organization and management, researchers have brought into consideration their own traditional preoccupations with certain selected subject matters which necessarily restricts their perspective. Rather than developing a simplified, less complex organization theory, the tendency has been in quite the opposite direction—toward greater complexity and the inclusion of more variables. Thus the development of a simplified "general theory" is becoming increasingly more difficult.

Traditional theory, as modified by the behavioral and quantitative sciences, has evolved into highly fragmented and diverse concepts concerning organization theory and management practice. This diversity should not be considered undesirable, however, because it is an indication of active intellectual involvement in the study of organizations and their administration. Organizations are complex systems comprised of psychological, sociological, technical, and economic elements and require intensive investigation. The suggestion that we wrap it all up neatly in one bundle and tie it together with a ribbon of simplified theory is unrealistic. Attempts to restrict this field of study to a limited perspective would reduce our flexibility and opportunity for continued investigation. Additional progress is tied closely with the development of these varied approaches. We agree with Herbert Simon that

The progress of management theory today is inextricably interwoven with techniques of observation and experiment, with sociology, psychology, and economics, and with the sharp tools of mathematics. In this respect, there is no more confusion than exists in any other area of scientific endeavor that has its observational techniques, its bodies of general theory, and its tools of analysis. Confusion, by another name, is progress to which we have not yet become accustomed. [5, p. 82]

However, in recent years there has emerged an approach which does offer an opportunity for some convergence in organization and management theory. The systems approach provides a basis for integration, by giving us a way to view the total organization in interaction with its environment and for conceptualizing the relationships between internal components or subsystems. Furthermore, systems concepts provide the basic frame of reference for the development of contingency views of organizations and their management.

Emergence of Systems Concepts

A *system* is generally defined as *an organized, unitary whole composed of two or more interdependent parts, components, or subsystems and delineated by identifiable boundaries from its environmental suprasystem.* The term system covers a broad spectrum of our physical, biological, and social world. The concepts involved in systems thinking provide a foundation for refining contingency views (understanding patterns of relationships and interactions) and applying this knowledge in designing and managing organizations.

General systems theory. The emergence of the systems approach in the study of organizations is a reflection of an even broader theoretical development. General systems theory provides a basis for understanding and integrating knowledge from a wide variety of highly specialized fields. While traditional knowledge has often been compartmentalized along well-defined subject-matter lines, von Bertalanffy suggests that various fields of modern science have evolved toward a parallelism of ideas. This parallelism provides an opportunity to formulate and develop principles which hold for systems in general. "In modern science, dynamic interaction is the basic problem in all fields, and its general principles will have to be formulated in General System Theory." [6, p. 201]

The general systems perspective has had a major impact upon the various physical, biological, and social sciences. As Buckley suggests:

> The development and contagion of the modern systems perspective can be traced in part to the concern of several disciplines to treat their subject matter—whether the organism, the species, or the social group—as a whole, an entity in its own right, with unique properties understandable only in terms of the whole, especially in the face of a more traditional reductionistic or mechanistic focus on the separate parts and a simplistic notion of how these parts fit together. [7, p. xxiii]

With the adoption of the systems perspective in most of the sciences, it is little wonder that many organization and management theorists were anxious to be members of this movement and to contribute to the development of an approach which purports to offer the ultimate—the unification of all science into one grand conceptual model. General systems theory seems to provide a relief from the limitations of more mechanistic approaches and a rationale for rejecting principles based upon relatively closed-system thinking. It provides a way for organization and management theorists to include in their systems model all of the diverse knowledge from relevant underlying disciplines.

However, difficulties are encountered when applying general systems theory to organizations and their management. (For a discussion of some of these problems see: Kast and Rosenzweig, pp. 37-56.) Many of the concepts are very abstract because general systems theorists have tried to develop broad concepts which are applicable to all types of systems—natural, biological, mechanical, and social. We can make use of these concepts but need to refine them for use at a practical level of organization theory and management practice. In spite of the limitations, systems theory does provide a useful approach for the study of social organizations. The key concepts of general systems theory have been set forth by many writers and used by many organization and management theorists [8]. (This is readily apparent in the readings in Part 2.) It is not our purpose here to elaborate on these concepts in great detail but rather to look briefly at those which are most relevant to social organizations and the development of contingency views.

Essential features of open systems. General systems theorists have attempted to develop a broad definition of a system in order to include all types. For example, "A system is a set of components, interacting with each other, and a boundary which selects both the kind and rate of flow of inputs and outputs to and from the system." [9, p. 32] This simple definition emphasizes the three essential features of systems: (1) they are composed of components or subsystems; (2) they have boundaries which delineate them from some broader suprasystem; and (3) they receive inputs, transform them in some way, and return outputs to their environment.

The open system can be viewed as a transformation model which exchanges information, energy, or materials with its environment. (Hunt, pp. 160-78) For example, the business organization is an open system which receives inputs of money, people, and other resources, transforms these through its production processes, and exports products or services. The university imports new students, financial and other resources, transforms them, and exports trained graduates and new knowledge. There are many elaborations on this concept of an open system. (Kast and Rosenzweig, pp. 37-56) However, the essentials are interactive components, openness to environment, and transformation of inputs into outputs.

The organization as an open subsystem in society. The distinction between open and closed, although not absolute, is important in organization theory. Closed-system perspectives stem primarily from the physical sciences and are applicable to mechanistic systems. Many of the earlier concepts in the social sciences and in organization theory were based on relatively closed-system perspectives that considered the system under study as self-contained and deterministic.

Traditional management theories were primarily closed-system views concentrating on the internal operations of the organization and adopting highly rationalistic approaches taken from the physical science models. The open-system view suggests a more uncertain, less deterministic pattern of internal relationships with the organization. (Thompson, pp. 26-36)

The historical roots of systems concepts related to organization and management go back many years. Mary Parker Follett, writing at the time of the classical management theorists, expressed many views indicative of the systems approach. She considered the psychological and sociological aspects of management; described management as a social process; and viewed the organization as a social system [10]. Chester Barnard was also influential in setting the stage for the systems approach. He was among the first to consider the organization as a social system, as indicated by his definition:

> It is the central hypothesis of this book that the most useful concept for the analysis of experience of coöperative systems is embodied in the definition of a formal organization as *a system of consciously coordinated activities or forces of two or more persons.* [11, p. 73]

These and other writers prepared the way for considering the organization not only as an economic-technical system, but as a social system as well.

The organization as a sociotechnical system. In addition to considering the organization as an open system in interaction with its environment, it should also be thought of as more than simply a technical or social system. It is in fact a sociotechnical system with a structuring and integration of human activities around various technologies toward the accomplishment of certain goals. The technologies affect the types of inputs to and outputs from the organization. It is the social system, however, that determines the effectiveness and efficiency of the utilization of the technology. Leavitt supports this view of organizations. He sees them "as multivariate systems, in which at least four interacting variables loom especially large: the variables of task, structure, technology, and actors (usually people)." (Leavitt, p. 57)

Burns and Stalker and their associates at the Tavistock Institute in England also share this concept. (Burns and Stalker, pp. 74-80) The technological and subsystem is based upon the tasks to be performed and includes the equipment, tools, facilities, and operating techniques, while the social subsystem consists of the relationships among the participants in the organization. These two subsystems interact with each other and are interdependent.

The concept of the socio-technical system arose from the consideration that any production system requires both a technological organization—equipment and process layout—and a work organization—relating those who carry out the necessary tasks to each other. Technological demands limit the kinds of work organization possible, but a work organization has social and psychological properties of its own that are independent of technology. [12, p. 182]

An integrated systems view of organizations. The various views expressed here are best summarized by saying that an organization is:

(1) a subsystem of its broader environment; and
(2) goal-oriented—people with a purpose; comprised of
(3) a technical subsystem—people using knowledge, techniques, equipment, and facilities;
(4) a structural subsystem—people working together on integrated activities;
(5) a psychosocial subsystem—people in social relationships; and coordinated by
(6) a managerial subsystem—planning and controlling the overall endeavor.

As illustrated by figure 1-1, a basic premise is that the organization, as a *subsystem of the society,* must accomplish its goals within limitations which are an integral part of the suprasystem. The organization performs a function for society; if it is to be successful in receiving inputs, it must conform to social constraints and requirements. Conversely, the organization influences its environmental suprasystem. (Terreberry, pp. 81-100) For example, the automobile companies perform a transformation function in turning raw materials, energy, information, and financial resources into cars. The output is accepted because it meets a societal need (within prescribed constraints) to which the companies have responded. However, the production and distribution of cars has had a tremendous effect upon the environment. It has led to the development of complex highways, altered living patterns, and affected the very air we breath. Certainly, there has been a major interactive effect—the society influences the organization but the organization also influences the society.

The internal organization can be viewed as composed of several major subsystems. Organizational *goals and values* represent one of the more important subsystems. (Knowles and Saxberg, pp. 101-19; Simon, pp. 120-37) While the organization takes many of its values from its broader sociocultural environment, it also influences societal values.

The *technical subsystem* refers to the knowledge required for the performance of tasks. By organizational technology we mean the

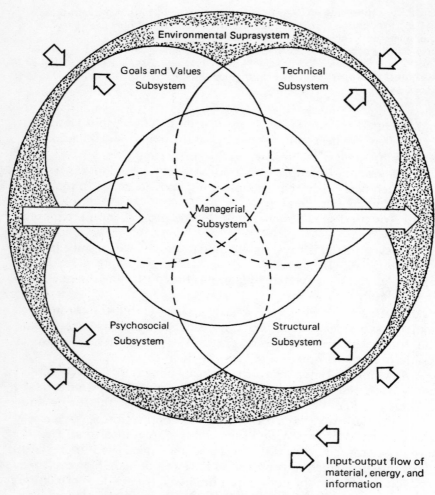

FIGURE 1-1: The Organizational System

techniques, equipment, processes, and facilities used in the transformation of inputs into outputs. The technical subsystem is determined by the purposes of the organization and will vary according to
the task requirements. The technology frequently prescribes the
type of organization structure and psychosocial system. (Hunt,
pp. 160-78; Perrow, pp. 138-59)

Every organization has a *psychosocial subsystem* which consists of
individual behaviors and motivations, status and role hierarchies,
group dynamics, and influence systems. This subsystem is, of course,

affected by external environmental forces as well as the technology, tasks, and structure of the internal organization. (Fiedler, pp. 229-37; Harrison, pp. 238-54; Morse, pp. 213-28)

Intermeshed with the technical and the psychosocial subsystem is the organization *structure*. Structure is concerned with the ways in which the tasks of the organization are divided (differentiation) and with the coordination of these activities (integration). In a formal sense, structure can be set forth by organization charts, job descriptions, and by rules and procedures. It is concerned with patterns of authority, communication, and work flow. (Lorsch, pp. 179-94; Pugh, Hickson, and Hinings, pp. 195-212) The organization's structure provides for formalization of relationships between the technical and psychosocial subsystems. However, it should be emphasized that the linkage between these subsystems is by no means complete; many interactions and relationships occur between the technical and psychosocial subsystems which bypass the formal structure.

The *managerial subsystem* plays a central role in establishing goals, planning, organizing, and controlling activities, and in relating the organization to its environment. (Lombard, pp. 225-72; Newman, pp. 287-303; Thompson, pp. 273-86) As we will discuss in more detail in Part 4, the managerial system itself is composed of subsystems with significantly different tasks and perspectives.

An example. It is obvious that these various organizational subsystems are interdependent. Major modifications in any one of these subsystems create waves of interaction and change in other subsystems. An example illustrates this point. The community general hospital has undergone substantial transformation over the past century. The basic goals of the hospital for instance, have reflected major changes. Until the twentieth century the primary role of the hospital was to serve as a refuge for the ill and needy rather than a place for medical treatment. It was the "charitable last resort of the ill pauper " [13, p. 69]. Medical technology was in its infancy and hospitals were geared toward making the ill more comfortable rather than dispensing effective treatment. Because of the unsanitary conditions and high mortality rate among patients, hospitals typically were utilized only by the poor. The more affluent ill received treatment in their own homes by private physicians.

The dramatic developments in medical science and technology in the late nineteenth and early twentieth centuries revolutionized the goals and functions of the hospital. The boundaries of the hospital's activities have expanded and it has taken on a much greater role in providing medical treatment and related services.

These changes have had tremendous impact on the hospital's structural, psychosocial, and managerial systems. The diversity of activities and specialization of skills in the hospital required changes in structure to provide for integration and coordination. Furthermore, the psychosocial system of the hospital has changed significantly because of the growing professionalism of various technical personnel. For example, the roles and status of the medical staff, nurses, and other participants have been modified.

The managerial system of the hospital has also changed substantially. With the increased complexity of the hospital, the managerial functions of planning and controlling activities have become more important. These functions were originally performed by the medical staff. Now the hospital administrator, a specialized professional, has emerged as the primary coordinator within the hospital unit.

Toward Contingency Views

One of the consequences of accepting systems concepts is a rejection of simplistic statements of universal principles for organization or management. Modern organization theory reflects a search for patterns of relationships, configurations among subsystems, and a contingency view. Lorsch and Lawrence say:

> During the past few years there has been evident a new trend in the study of organizational phenomena. Underlying this new approach is the idea that the internal functioning of organizations must be consistent with the demands of the organization task, technology, or external environment, and the needs of its members if the organization is to be effective. Rather than searching for the panacea of the one best way to organize under all conditions, investigators have more and more tended to examine the functioning of organizations in relation to the needs of their particular members and the external pressures facing them. Basically, this approach seems to be leading to the development of a "contingency" theory of organization with the appropriate internal states and processes of the organization contingent upon external requirements and member needs. [14, p. 1]

Numerous others have stressed this same idea. Thompson suggests that the essence of administration lies in understanding the basic patterns which exist between the various subsystems and with the environment. "The basic function of administration appears to be co-alignment, not merely of people (in coalitions) but of institutionalized action—of technology and task environment into a viable domain, and of organizational design and structure appropriate to it." (Thompson, p. 285)

The systems approach provides us with the macro paradigm for the study of social organizations. It emphasizes a very high level of abstraction and attempts to develop comprehensive concepts appropriate for all types of biological, physical, and social systems. Traditional bureaucratic theory provided the first major macro view of organizations. Administrative management theorists concentrated upon the development of macro principles of management which were applicable to all organizations. As with other sciences, when macro views seem incomplete and unable to explain important phenomena, attention turns to the micro level—more detailed analyses of components or parts of the organization such as human relations, technology, or structure.

We are now ready to move toward a modified micro analysis. By doing so, we will be able to deal in more operational terms and with more specific mid-range concepts. The ideas may be based on the broad paradigm of systems theory but are more concrete and emphasize specific characteristics and relationships in social organizations. Such a mid-range level of analysis is a contingency view, a study of relationships, and a search for configurations among subsystems. If organization theory is to advance and make contributions to managerial practice, it must define more explicit patterns of relationships among organizational variables.

As figure 1-2 indicates, organization and management theory has evolved continually. And, as in biological evolution, there has never been a radical transformation which eliminated the old and substituted the new. Rather, the resulting theories at each stage have been mutations of the old, retaining many of the more enduring concepts. Furthermore, the most appropriate models are those which best fit the environment of modern organizations (an extension of Darwin's theme—survival of the fittest). We can attempt to take the best of the existing theory, develop new insights about organizational relationships, and refine the body of knowledge accordingly. This process is basic to the development of theory which is applicable to a variety of organizations in specific situations—the essence of a contingency view.

There are many examples of attempts to develop concepts concerning patterns of interactive relationships among various organizational subsystems. The readings in Part 2 were selected to reflect several of the current and most cogent perceptions of those interrelationships. Using the readings to focus the direction of our discussion, we will consider the relevancy of the contingency view to understanding organizations and their management.

Notes

1. W. Lloyd Warner, editor, *The Emergent American Society: Large-Scale Organizations* (New Haven: Yale University Press, 1967).
2. Richard H. Hall, "The Concept of Bureaucracy: An Empirical Assessment," *Amer. J. Sociology*, July, 1963.

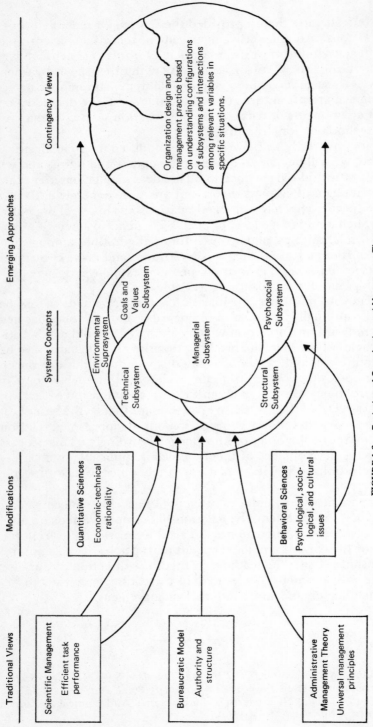

Traditional Views

Scientific Management
Efficient task performance

Bureaucratic Model
Authority and structure

Administrative Management Theory
Universal management principles

Modifications

Quantitative Sciences
Economic-technical rationality

Behavioral Sciences
Psychological, socio-logical, and cultural issues

Emerging Approaches

Systems Concepts

Environmental Suprasystem

Goals and Values Subsystem

Technical Subsystem

Managerial Subsystem

Psychosocial Subsystem

Structural Subsystem

Contingency Views

Organization design and management practice based on understanding configurations of subsystems and interactions among relevant variables in specific situations.

FIGURE 1-2: Evolution of Organization and Management Theory

3. James G. March and Herbert A. Simon, *Organizations* (New York: Wiley, 1958).

4. Joan Woodward, *Industrial Organization: Theory and Practice* (London: Oxford University Press, 1965).

5. Herbert A. Simon, "Approaching the Theory of Management," in *Toward a Unified Theory of Management,* edited by Harold Koontz (New York: McGraw, 1964).

6. Ludwig von Bertalanffy, *Problems of Life* (New York: Wiley, 1952).

7. Walter Buckley, editor, *Modern Systems Research for the Behavioral Scientist* (Chicago: Aldine, 1968).

8. For background reading on general systems theory, see: F. Kenneth Berrien, *General and Social Systems* (New Brunswick, N.J.: Rutgers University Press, 1968); Kenneth E. Boulding, "General Systems Theory: The Skeleton of Science," *Management Science,* April 1956, pp. 197-208; Buckley, op. cit.; James G. Miller, "Living Systems: Basic Concepts," *Behavioral Science,* July 1965, pp. 193-237; and Ludwig von Bertalanffy, *General System Theory* (New York: George Braziller, 1968).

9. Berrien, op. cit., note 8.

10. H. C. Metcalf and Lyndall Urwick, editors, *Dynamic Administration: The Collected Papers of Mary Parker Follett* (New York: Harper & Row, 1941).

11. Chester I. Barnard, *The Functions of the Executive* (Cambridge, Mass.: Harvard University Press, 1938).

12. A. K. Rice, *The Enterprise and Its Environment* (London: Tavistock, 1963).

13. Robert N. Wilson, "The Social Structure of a General Hospital," *Annals of the American Academy of Political and Social Science,* March 1963.

14. Jay W. Lorsch and Paul R. Lawrence, *Studies in Organization Design* (Homewood, Ill.: Richard D. Irwin and Dorsey Press, 1970).

Part 2

Selected Readings on Contingency Views

Many writers have contributed to the development of contingency views. We could have selected a hundred or more readings, but the seventeen readings included here reflect the essence of the contingency view as well as current research and conceptual thinking. Although we have provided the background material, the student is encouraged to seek out additional material. A number of references are included in the bibliography to facilitate further study.

We begin this section with several readings which provide a general overview; the others are classified according to the systems model set forth in Part 1:

> Environmental Suprasystem
> Goals and Values
> Technical Subsystem
> Structural Subsystem
> Psychosocial Subsystem
> Managerial Subsystem

We have attempted to place the readings in an appropriate sequence. The reader, however, should recognize their relevancy to other subsystems. It is essential that the student have a thorough familiarity with these readings in order to understand the importance of contingency views to organization theory as presented in Part 3 and to management practice as presented in Part 4.

General Overview

Four readings were selected to provide the foundation for contingency concepts. They reflect the view that there are various appropriate ways to design and manage organizations, depending upon a number of variables such as environmental influences, nature of the technology, and goals. Patterns of relationships and/or configurations of variables as a basis for deciding on appropriate organizational designs and attendant managerial approaches are emphasized.

James D. Thompson *(Strategies for Studying Organizations)* reviews the evolution of organization theory and makes the important distinction between closed- and open-system strategies in the study of organizations. He provides a conceptual framework for the integration of these two strategies by considering three levels present in an organization—technical, managerial, and institutional.

In our article entitled *General Systems Theory: Applications for Organization and Management,* we provide an overview of the key concepts of general systems theory and how they relate to organization theory and management practice. The article includes a discussion of some of the problems associated with applying general systems theory to organizations and suggests the need for further refinement of systems concepts to reflect contingency views. Intensive comparative investigation of many organizations is advocated since such study is essential before general systems theory can be translated into appropriate midrange models relevant for organization theory and management practice.

Harold J. Leavitt *(Applied Organization Change in Industry: Structural, Technical, and Human Approaches)* gives another general overview of the interrelationships between organizational variables. He focuses upon the change process and four interacting variables: task, structure, technology, and people. He stresses that change in any of these variables most probably results in compensatory changes in the others.

Tom Burns and G. M. Stalker *(Mechanistic and Organic Systems)* distinguish between two different organizational forms, the mechanistic and the organic. They suggest that the mechanistic organization is appropriate for stable conditions while the organic form is more appropriate to changing conditions. The characteristics of mechanistic and organic systems indicate many of the important varibles for consideration in a contingency view.

Environmental Suprasystem

A number of the articles emphasize that environmental influences affect the design and management of organizations.

Shirley Terreberry *(The Evolution of Organizational Environments)* suggests that the environments of organizations are becoming more turbulent and that organizations are becoming less autonomous. She feels that change is caused increasingly by environmental forces and that organizations must learn to adapt their behavior according to conditions in the environment.

Goals and Values

The goals of an organization will determine to a great extent its activities and internal relationships. They also are influenced by certain societal and internally defined values. Two articles consider the relevance of goals and values to organizations.

Henry P. Knowles and Borje O. Saxberg *(Human Relations and the Nature of Man)* focus on the influence that assumptions about human nature have on interpersonal relations in our society and in our organizations. Managerial practices are fundamentally affected by such views.

Herbert A. Simon *(On the Concept of Organizational Goal)* views the goals of an organization as a whole set of constraints which organizational actions must satisfy; they are seldom unitary. In this view, the decision-making mechanism in organizations is a loosely-coupled, partially-decentralized structure in which different sets of constraints may impinge on decisions in various organizational settings.

Technical Subsystem

There is increasing evidence and growing awareness that the nature of the technology required to accomplish the transformation task has a fundamental bearing upon other components; for instance, the structural and the psychosocial subsystems.

Charles Perrow *(A Framework for the Comparative Analysis of Organizations)* argues that complex organizations can be conceptualized in terms of their technologies. Technology, or how the work is done, is considered the defining characteristic of organizations. He suggests various dimensions of technology which can provide a basis for the comparative analysis of different organizations.

Raymond G. Hunt *(Technology and Organization)* indicates a number of ways in which organizations might be classified and then appraises the current knowledge on the relationship between technology and the design or organizations. He concludes his article with a suggestion that there are two fundamentally different models

for organizations—performance and problem solving—and sets forth
the characteristics of each.

Structural Subsystem

A great deal of attention has been given to the appropriate design of
the organizational structure. Two of the readings provide insights
into this issue.

Jay W. Lorsch *(Introduction to the Structural Design of Organizations)* suggests that the structure of an organization is not an immutable given, but rather a set of complex variables about which
managers can exercise considerable choice. He provides a systemic
approach to the design of organization structure and relates structure
to other organizational subsystems.

D. S. Pugh, D. J. Hickson, and C. R. Hinings *(An Empirical Taxonomy of Structures of Work Organizations)* base their conclusions
on an empirical study of 52 organizations in England. Three dimensions are utilized: (1) structuring of activities; (2) concentration of
authority; and (3) line control of workflow. On the basis of these
three dimensions, a sevenfold classification of organization structures
is developed—ranging from full bureaucracy to implicitly structured
organizations. The results indicate that the concept of a single
bureaucratic type is no longer useful because bureaucracy takes on
different forms in different settings.

Psychosocial Subsystem

Several of the articles deal with psychological and sociological factors
in organizations. In some cases the psychosocial system is considered
to be a dependent variable in relation to other subsystems. Three
articles in this section emphasize the psychosocial system in its overall context.

John J. Morse *(Organizational Characteristics and Individual
Motivation)* believes that designing and developing an organization
to fit the demands of its environment and technology may also provide important psychological rewards for the members of the organization. This study follows closely from the research reported by
Jay W. Lorsch in his article.

Fred E. Fiedler *(Style or Circumstance: the Leadership Enigma)*
suggests a contingency view in which different circumstances call
for different leadership styles. He provides a framework for determining which style of leadership is appropriate in which situations.
Fiedler's theory of leadership effectiveness suggests that a leader's

performance can be improved by engineering or fitting the job to the style of the leader.

Roger Harrison *(Choosing the Depth of Organizational Intervention)* discusses some of the most current issues facing behavioral scientists and managers. He feels that there are numerous change strategies available in organizational development (such as operations analysis, management by objective, the managerial grid, the T-group, and task group therapy). The behavioral scientist-consultant should orient himself to the client's needs with a broad understanding of the importance of constraints imposed by technology, structure, environment, etc. Lasting change in the psychosocial system can be accomplished only in relationship to the other subsystems.

Managerial Subsystem

We have suggested previously that the managerial subsystem is superimposed on the other subsystems. Therefore, it is obvious that many of the readings have some significance for management. We have selected three articles which deal specifically with the impact of contingency views upon the managerial task.

George F. Lombard *(Relativism in Organizations)* suggests that the philosophy of relativism is growing in all aspects of life and has important implications for management. He sees a trend from absolutism toward multiple values. In this view the manager recognizes the different goals and values within his organization and deemphasizes simple, unitary concepts of formal organizations. Rather than retaining a single-minded, closed view of principles of management, we are moving toward relativistic views which consider how the various system components are interrelated in specific situations. Lombard discusses some of the problems involved in training managers to take a relativistic view.

James D. Thompson *(The Administrative Process)* identifies many of the elements which should be incorporated in a new and fuller understanding of management or administration. He suggests that the nature of the administrative process is contingent upon many variables and emphasizes that the basic function of administration is co-alignment of environmental, technical, structural, and human factors.

William H. Newman *(Strategy and Management Structure)* discusses how corporate strategy is influenced by the organizational structure and the technological environment. He emphasizes the importance of a contingency view in the matching of strategy and the design of the managerial system. He stresses appropriate design in order to foster a synergistic effect among the management processes of organizing, planning, leading, and controlling.

Strategies
for Studying
Organizations

James D. Thompson

Complex organizations—manufacturing firms, hospitals, schools, armies, community agencies—are ubiquitous in modern societies, but our understanding of them is limited and segmented.

The fact that impressive and sometimes frightening consequences flow from organizations suggests that some individuals have had considerable insight into these social instruments. But insight and private experiences may generate private understandings without producing a public body of knowledge adequate for the preparation of a next generation of administrators, for designing new styles of organizations for new purposes, for controlling organizations, or for appreciation of distinctive aspects of modern societies.

What we know or think we know about complex organizations is housed in a variety of fields or disciplines, and communication among them more nearly resembles a trickle than a torrent [1]. Although each of the several schools has its unique terminology and special heroes, Gouldner was able to discern two fundamental models underlying most of the literature [2]. He labeled these the "rational" and "natural-system" models of organizations, and these labels are indeed descriptive of the results.

To Gouldner's important distinction we wish to add the notion that the rational model results from a *closed-system strategy* for studying organizations, and that the natural-system model flows from an *open-system strategy*.

Closed-System Strategy

The search for certainty.   If we wish to predict accurately the state a system will be in presently, it helps immensely to be dealing with a *determinate system.* As Ashby observes, fixing the present circumstances of a determinate system will determine the state it moves to next, and since such a system cannot go to two states at once, the transformation will be unique [3].

Fixing the present circumstances requires, of course, that the variables and relationships involved be few enough for us to comprehend and that we have control over or can reliably predict all of the variables and relations. In other words, it requires that the system be closed or, if closure is not complete, that the outside forces acting on it be predictable.

Now if we have responsibility for the future states or performance of some system, we are likely to opt for a closed system. Bartlett's research on mental processes, comparing "adventurous thinking" with "thinking in closed systems," suggests that there are strong human tendencies to reduce various forms of knowledge to the closed-system variety, to rid them of all ultimate uncertainty [4]. If such tendencies appear in puzzle-solving as well as in everyday situations, we would especially expect them to be emphasized when responsibility and high stakes are added.

Since much of the literature about organizations has been generated as a by-product of the search for improved efficiency or performance, it is not surprising that it employs closed-system assumptions —employs the rational model—about organizations. Whether we consider *scientific management, administrative management, or bureaucracy,* the ingredients of the organization are deliberately chosen for their necessary contribution to a goal, and the structures established are those deliberately intended to attain highest efficiency [5].

Three schools in caricature. Scientific management, focused primarily on manufacturing or similar production activities, clearly employs economic efficiency as its ultimate criterion, and seeks to maximize efficiency by planning procedures according to a technical logic, setting standards, and exercising controls to ensure conformity with standards and thereby with the technical logic. Scientific management achieves conceptual closure of the organization by assuming that goals are known, tasks are repetitive, output of the production process somehow disappears, and resources in uniform qualities are available.

Administrative-management literature focuses on structural relationships among production, personnel, supply, and other service units of the organization; and again employs as the ultimate criterion economic efficiency. Here efficiency is maximized by specializing tasks and grouping them into departments, fixing responsibility according to such principles as span of control or delegation, and controlling action to plans. Administrative management achieves closure by assuming that ultimately a master plan is known, against which specialization, departmentalization, and control are determined. (That this master plan is elusive is shown by Simon [6].) Administrative management also assumes that production tasks are known, that output disappears, and that resources are automatically available to the organization.

Bureaucracy also follows the pattern noted above, focusing on staffing and structure as means of handling clients and disposing of cases. Again the ultimate criterion is efficiency, and this time it is maximized by defining offices according to jurisdiction and place in a hierarchy, appointing experts to offices, establishing rules for categories of activity, categorizing cases or clients, and then motivating proper performance of expert officials by providing salaries and patterns for career advancement. (The extended implications of the assumptions made by bureaucratic theory are brought out by Merton's discussion of "bureaucratic personality" [7].) Bureaucratic theory also employs the closed system of logic. Weber saw three holes through which empirical reality might penetrate the logic, but in outlining his "pure type" he quickly plugged these holes. Policymakers, somewhere above the bureaucracy, could alter the goals, but the implications of this are set aside. Human components—the expert officeholders—might be more complicated than the model describes, but bureaucratic theory handles this by divorcing the individual's private life from his life as an officeholder through the use of rules, salary, and career. Finally, bureaucratic theory takes note of outsiders—clientele—but nullifies their effects by depersonalizing and categorizing clients.

It seems clear that the rational-model approach uses a closed-system strategy. It also seems clear that the developers of the several schools using the rational model have been primarily students of performance or efficiency, and only incidentally students of organizations. Having focused on control of the organization as a target, each employs a closed system of logic and conceptually closes the organization to coincide with that type of logic, for this elimination of uncertainty is the way to achieve determinateness. The rational model of an organization results in everything being functional —making a positive, indeed an optimum, contribution to the overall result. All resources are appropriate resources, and their allocation fits a master plan. All action is appropriate action, and its outcomes are predictable.

It is no accident that much of the literature on the management or administration of complex organizations centers on the concepts of *planning* or *controlling*. Nor is it any accident that such views are dismissed by those using the open-system strategy.

Open-System Strategy

The expectation of uncertainty.   If, instead of assuming closure, we assume that a system contains more variables than we can comprehend at one time, or that some of the variables are subject to influences we cannot control or predict, we must resort to a different sort of logic. We can, if we wish, assume that the system is determinate by nature, but that it is our incomplete understanding which forces us to expect surprise or the intrusion of uncertainty. In this case we can employ a natural-system model.

Approached as a natural system, the complex organization is a set of interdependent parts which together make up a whole because each contributes something and receives something from the whole, which in turn is interdependent with some larger environment. Survival of the system is taken to be the goal, and the parts and their relationships presumably are determined through evolutionary processes. Dysfunctions are conceivable, but it is assumed that an offending part will adjust to produce a net positive contribution or be disengaged, or else the system will degenerate.

Central to the natural-system approach is the concept of homeostasis, or self-stabilization, which spontaneously, or naturally, governs the necessary relationships among parts and activities and thereby keeps the system viable in the face of disturbances stemming from the environment.

Two examples in caricature.   Study of the *informal organization* constitutes one example of research in complex organizations using the natural-system approach. Here attention is focused on variables which are not included in any of the rational models—sentiments, cliques, social controls via informal norms, status and status striving, and so on. It is clear that students of informal organization regard these variables not as random deviations or errors, but as patterned, adaptive responses of human beings in problematic situations [8]. In this view the informal organization is a spontaneous and functional development, indeed a necessity, in complex organizations, permitting the system to adapt and survive.

A second version of the natural-system approach is more global but less crystallized under a label. This school views the organization as a unit in interaction with its environment, and its view was perhaps most forcefully expressed by Chester Barnard and by the empirical studies of Selznick and Clark [9]. This stream of work leads to the conclusion that organizations are not autonomous entities; instead, the best laid plans of managers have unintended consequences and are conditioned or upset by other social units—other complex organizations or publics—on which the organization is dependent.

Again it is clear that in contrast to the rational-model approach, this research area focuses on variables not subject to complete control by the organization and hence not contained within a closed system of logic. It is also clear that students regard interdependence of organization and environment as inevitable or natural, and as adaptive or functional.

Choice or Compromise?

The literature about organizations, or at least much of it, seems to fall into one of the two categories, each of which at best tends to ignore the other and at worst denies the relevance of the other. The logics associated with each appear to be incompatible, for one avoids uncertainty to achieve determinateness, while the other assumes uncertainty and indeterminateness. Yet the phenomena treated by each approach, as distinct from the explanations of each, cannot be denied.

Viewed in the large, complex organizations are often effective instruments for achievement, and that achievement flows from planned, controlled action. In every sphere—educational, medical, industrial, commercial, or governmental—the quality or costs of goods or services may be challenged and questions may be raised about the equity of distribution within the society of the fruits of complex organizations. Still millions live each day on the assumption that a reasonable degree of purposeful, effective action will be forthcoming from the many complex organizations on which they depend. Planned action, not random behavior, supports our daily lives. Specialized, controlled, patterned action surrounds us.

There can be no question but that the rational model of organizations directs our attention to important phenomena—to important "truth" in the sense that complex organizations viewed in the large exhibit some of the patterns and results to which the rational model attends, but which the natural-system model tends to ignore. But it is equally evident that phenomena associated with the natural-system approach also exist in complex organizations. There is little room to doubt the universal emergence of the informal organization. The daily news about labor-management negotiations, interagency jurisdictional squabbles, collusive agreements, favoritism, breeches of contract, and so on, is impressive evidence that complex organizations are influenced in significant ways by elements of their environments, a phenomenon addressed by the natural-system approach but avoided by the rational. Yet most versions of the natural-system approach treat organizational purposes and achievements as peripheral matters.

It appears that each approach leads to some truth, but neither alone affords an adequate understanding of complex organizations. Gouldner calls for a synthesis of the two models but does not provide the synthetic model.

Meanwhile, a serious and sustained elaboration of Barnard's work has produced a newer tradition which evades the closed- versus open-system dilemma [6; 10].

A Newer Tradition

What emerges from the Simon-March-Cyert stream of study is the organization as a problem-facing and problem-solving phenomenon. The focus is on organizational processes related to choice of courses of action in an environment which does not fully disclose the alternatives available or the consequences of those alternatives. In this view, the organization has limited capacity to gather and process information or to predict consequences of alternatives. To deal with situations of such great complexity, the organization must develop processes for *searching* and *learning*, as well as for *deciding*. The complexity, if fully faced, would overwhelm the organization, hence it must set limits to its definitions of situations; it must make decisions in *bounded rationality* [11]. This requirement involves replacing the maximum-efficiency criterion with one of satisfactory accomplishment, decision-making now involving *satisficing* rather than *maximizing* [11].

These are highly significant notions, and it will become apparent that this book seeks to extend this "newer tradition." The assumptions it makes are consistent with the open-system strategy, for it holds that the processes going on within the organization are significantly affected by the complexity of the organization's environment. But this tradition also touches on matters important in the closed-system strategy: performance and deliberate decisions.

But despite what seem to be obvious advantages, the Simon-March-Cyert stream of work has not entirely replaced the more extreme strategies, and we need to ask why so many intelligent men and women in a position to make the same observations we have been making should continue to espouse patently incomplete views of complex organizations.

The cutting edge of uncertainty.   Part of the answer to that question undoubtedly lies in the fact that supporters of each extreme strategy have had different purposes in mind, with open-system strategists attempting to understand organizations per se, and closed-system strategists interested in organizations mainly as vehicles for rational achievements. Yet this answer does not seem completely satisfactory, for these students could not have been entirely unaware of the challenges to their assumptions and beliefs.

We can suggest now that rather than reflecting weakness in those who use them, the two strategies reflect something fundamental about the cultures surrounding complex organizations—the fact that our culture does not contain concepts for simultaneously thinking about rationality and indeterminateness. These appear to be incompatible concepts, and we have no ready way of thinking about something as half-closed, half-rational. One alternative, then, is the closed-system approach of ignoring uncertainty to see rationality; another is to ignore rational action in order to see spontaneous processes. The newer tradition with its focus on organizational coping with uncertainty is indeed a major advance. It is notable that a recent treatment by Crozier starts from the bureaucratic position but focuses on coping with uncertainty as its major topic [12].

Yet in directing our attention to processes for meeting uncertainty, Simon, March, and Cyert may lead us to overlook the useful knowledge amassed by the older approaches. If the phenomena of rational models are indeed observable, we may want to incorporate some elements of those models; and if natural-system phenomena occur, we should also benefit from the relevant theories. For purposes of this volume, then, *we will conceive of complex organizations as open systems, hence indeterminate and faced with uncertainty, but at the same time as subject to criteria of rationality and hence needing determinateness and certainty.*

The Location of Problems

As a starting point, we will suggest that the phenomena associated with open- and closed-system strategies are not randomly distributed through complex organizations, but instead tend to be specialized by location. To introduce this notion we will start with Parsons' suggestion that organizations exhibit three distinct levels of responsibility and control—*technical, managerial,* and *institutional* [13].

In this view, every formal organization contains a suborganization whose "problems" are focused around effective performance of the technical function—the conduct of classes by teachers, the processing of income tax returns and the handling of recalcitrants by the bureau, the processing of material and supervision of these operations in the case of physical production. The primary exigencies to which the technical suborganization is oriented are those imposed by the nature of the technical task, such as the materials which must be processed and the kinds of cooperation of different peopl required to get the job done effectively.

The second level, the managerial, *services* the technical suborganization by (1) mediating between the technical suborganization and those who use its products—the customers, pupils, and so on—and (2) procuring the resources necessary for carrying out the technical functions. The managerial level *controls*, or administers, the technical suborganization (although Parsons notes that its control is not unilateral) by deciding such matters as the broad technical task which is to be performed, the scale of operations, employment and purchasing policy, and so on.

Finally, in the Parsons formulation, the organization which consists of both technical and managerial suborganizations is also part of a wider social system which is the source of the "meaning," legitimation, or higher-level support which makes the implementation of the organization's goals possible. In terms of "formal" controls, an organization may be relatively independent; but in terms of the meaning of the functions performed by the organization and hence of its "rights" to command resources and to subject its customers to discipline, it is never wholly independent. This overall articulation of the organization and the institutional structure and agencies of the community is the function of the third, or institutional, level of the organization.

Parson's distinction of the three levels becomes more significant when he points out that at each of the two points of articulation between them there is a *qualitative* break in the simple continuity of "line" authority because the functions at each level are qualitatively different. Those at the second level are not simply lower-order spellings-out of the top-level functions. Moreover, the articulation of levels and of functions rests on a two-way interaction, with each side, by withholding its important contribution, in a position to interfere with the functioning of the other and of the larger organization.

If we now reintroduce the conception of the complex organization as an open system subject to criteria of rationality, we are in a position to speculate about some dynamic properties of organizations. As we suggested, the logical model for achieving complete technical rationality uses a closed system of logic—closed by the elimination of uncertainty. In practice, it would seem, the more variables involved, the greater the likelihood of uncertainty, and it would therefore be advantageous for an organization subject to criteria of rationality to remove as much uncertainty as possible from its *technical core* by reducing the number of variables operating on it. Hence if both resource-acquisition and output-disposal problems—which are in part controlled by environmental elements and hence to a degree uncertain or problematic—can be removed from the technical core, the logic can be brought closer to closure, and the rationality increased.

Uncertainty would appear to be greatest, at least potentially, at the other extreme, the institutional level. Here the organization deals largely with elements of the environment over which it has no formal authority or control. Instead, it is subjected to generalized norms, ranging from formally codified law to informal standards of good practice, to public authority, or to elements expressing the public interest.

At this extreme the closed system of logic is clearly inappropriate. The organization is open to influence by the environment (and vice versa) which can change independently of the actions of the organization. Here an open system of logic, permitting the intrusion of variables penetrating the organization from outside and facing up to uncertainty, seems indispensable.

If the closed-system aspects of organizations are seen most clearly at the technical level, and the open-system qualities appear most vividly at the institutional level, it would suggest that a significant function of the managerial level is to mediate between the two extremes and the emphases they exhibit. If the organization must approach certainty at the technical level to satisfy its rationality criteria, but must remain flexible and adaptive to satisfy environmental requirements, we might expect the managerial level to mediate between them, ironing out some irregularities stemming from external sources, but also pressing the technical core for modifications as conditions alter. One exploration of this notion was offered in Thompson [14].

Possible sources of variation.   Following Parsons' reasoning leads to the expectation that differences in technical functions, or *technologies,* cause significant differences among organizations, and since the three levels are interdependent, differences in technical functions should also make for differences at managerial and institutional levels of the organization. Similarly, differences in the institutional structures in which organizations are imbedded should make for significant variations among organizations at all three levels.

Relating this back to the Simon-March-Cyert focus on organizational processes of searching, learning, and deciding, we can also suggest that while these adaptive processes may be generic, the ways in which they proceed may well vary with differences in technologies or in environments.

Recapitulation

Most of our beliefs about complex organizations follow from one or the other of two distinct strategies. The closed-system strategy seeks certainty by incorporating only those variables positively associated with goal achievement and subjecting them to a monolithic control network. The open-system strategy shifts attention from goal achievement to survival, and incorporates uncertainty by recognizing organizational interdependence with environment. A newer tradition enables us to conceive of the organization as an open system, indeterminate and faced with uncertainty, but subject to criteria of rationality and hence needing certainty.

With this conception the central problem for complex organizations is one of coping with uncertainty. As a point of departure, we suggest that organizations cope with uncertainty by creating certain parts specifically to deal with it, specializing other parts in operating under conditions of certainty or near certainty. In this case, articulation of these specialized parts becomes significant.

We also suggest that technologies and environments are major sources of uncertainty for organizations, and that differences in those dimensions will result in differences in organizations.

Notes

1. William R. Dill, "Desegregation or Integration? Comments about Contemporary Research on Organizations," in *New Perspectives in Organization Research,* edited by W. W. Cooper et al. (New York: Wiley, 1964); James G. March, "Introduction" to *Handbook of Organizations,* edited by James G. March (Chicago: Rand, 1965).
2. Alvin W. Gouldner, "Organizational Analysis," in *Sociology Today,* edited by Robert K. Merton, Leonard Broom, and Leonard S. Cottrell, Jr. (New York: Basic Books, 1959).
3. W. Ross Ashby, *An Introduction to Cybernetics* (London: Chapman, 1956).
4. Sir Frederic Bartlett, *Thinking: An Experimental and Social Study* (New York: Basic Books, 1958).
5. Frederick W. Taylor, *Scientific Management* (New York: Harper, 1911); Luther Gulick and L. Urwick, editors, *Papers on the Science of Administration* (New York: Institute of Public Administration, 1937); Max Weber, *The Theory of Social and Economic Organization,* edited by Talcott Parsons, translated by A. M. Henderson and Talcott Parsons (New York: Free Press of Glencoe, 1947).
6. Herbert A. Simon, *Administrative Behavior,* 2d ed. (New York: Macmillan, 1957).
7. Robert K. Merton, "Bureaucratic Structure and Personality," in *Social Theory and Social Structure,* edited by Robert K. Merton, rev. ed. (New York: Free Press of Glencoe, 1957).
8. Fritz J. Roethlisberger and W. J. Dickson, *Management and the Worker* (Cambridge: Harvard University Press, 1939).
9. Chester I. Barnard, *The Functions of the Executive* (Cambridge: Harvard University Press, 1938); Philip Selznick, *TVA and the Grass Roots* (Berkeley: Univ. of California Press, 1949); Burton R. Clark, *Adult Education in Transition* (Berkeley: Univ. of California Press, 1956).

10. James G. March and Herbert A. Simon, *Organizations* (New York: Wiley, 1958); Richard M. Cyert and James G. March, *A Behavioral Theory of the Firm* (Englewood Cliffs, N.J.: Prentice-Hall, 1963).
11. Herbert A. Simon, *Models of Man: Social and Rational* (New York: Wiley, 1957).
12. Michel Crozier, *The Bureaucratic Phenomenon* (Chicago: Univ. of Chicago Press, 1964).
13. Talcott Parsons, *Structure and Process in Modern Societies* (New York: Free Press of Glencoe, 1960).
14. James D. Thompson, "Decision-making, the Firm, and the Market," in *New Perspectives in Organization Research*, edited by W. W. Cooper et al. (New York: Wiley, 1964).

General Systems Theory: Applications for Organization and Management

Fremont E. Kast   *James E. Rosenzweig*

Biological and social scientists generally have embraced systems concepts. Many organization and management theorists seem anxious to identify with this movement and to contribute to the development of an approach which purports to offer the ultimate— the unification of all science into one grand conceptual model. Who possibly could resist? General systems theory seems to provide a relief from the limitations of more mechanistic approaches and a rationale for rejecting "principles" based on relatively "closed-system" thinking. This theory provides the paradigm for organization and management theorists to crank into their systems model all of the diverse knowledge from relevant underlying disciplines. It has become almost mandatory to have the word "system" in the title of recent articles and books (many of us have compromised and placed it only in the subtitle).*

But where did it all start? This question projects us back into history and brings to mind the long-standing philosophical arguments between mechanistic and organismic models of the 19th and early 20th centuries. As Deutsch says:

Both mechanistic and organismic models were based substantially on experiences and operations known before 1850. Since then, the experience of almost a century of scientific and technological progress has so far not been utilized for any significant new model for the study of organization, and in particular of human thought. [1, *p. 389*]

---

*An entire article could be devoted to a discussion of ingenious ways in which the term "systems approach" has been used in the literature pertinent to organization theory and management practice.

From *Academy of Management Journal*, December 1972, 447-465. Copyright © 1972 by Academy Management.

General systems theory even revives the specter of the "vitalists" and their views on "life force" and most certainly brings forth renewed questions of teleological or purposeful behavior of both living and nonliving systems. Philips and others have suggested that the philosophical roots of general systems theory go back even further, at least to the German philosopher Hegel (1770-1831) [2, *p. 56*]. Thus we should recognize that in the adoption of the systems approach for the study of organizations we are not dealing with newly discovered ideas—they have a rich genealogy.

Even in the field of organization and management theory, systems views are not new. Chester Barnard used a basic systems framework.

A cooperative system is a complex of physical, biological, personal, and social components which are in a specific systematic relationship by reason of the cooperation of two or more persons for at least one definite end. Such a system is evidently a subordinate unit of larger systems from one point of view; and itself embraces subsidiary systems—physical, biological, etc.—from another point of view. One of the systems within a cooperative system, the one which is implicit in the phrase "cooperation of two or more persons," is called an "organization." [3, *p. 65*]

And Barnard was influenced by the "systems views" of Vilfredo Pareto and Talcott Parsons. Certainly this quote (dressed up a bit to give the term "system" more emphasis) could be the introduction to a 1972 book on organizations.

Miller points out that Alexander Bogdanov, the Russian philosopher, developed a theory of tektology or universal organization science in 1912 which foreshadowed general systems theory and used many of the same concepts as modern systems theorists [4, *pp. 249-50*].

However, in spite of a long history of organismic and holistic thinking, the utilization of the systems approach did not become the accepted model for organization and management writers until relatively recently. It is difficult to specify the turning point exactly. The momentum of systems thinking was identified by Scott in 1961 when he described the relationship between general systems theory and organization theory.

The distinctive qualities of modern organization theory are its conceptual-analytical base, its reliance on empirical research data, and above all, its integrating nature. These qualities are framed in a philosophy which accepts the premise that the only meaningful way to study organization is to study it as a system.... . Modern organization theory and general system theory are similar in that they look at organization as an integrated whole. [5, *pp. 15-21*]

Scott said explicitly what many in our field had been thinking and/or implying—he helped us put into perspective the important writings of Herbert Simon, James March, Talcott Parsons, George Homans, E. Wight Bakke, Kenneth Boulding, and many others.

But how far have we really advanced over the past decade in applying general systems theory to organizations and their management? Is it still a "skeleton," or have we been able to "put some meat on the bones?" The systems approach has been touted because of its potential usefulness in understanding the complexities of "live" organizations. Has this approach really helped us in this endeavor or has it compounded confusion with chaos? Herbert Simon describes the challenge for the systems approach:

In both science and engineering, the study of "systems" is an increasingly popular activity. Its popularity is more a response to a pressing need for synthesizing and analyzing complexity than it is to any large development of a body of knowledge and technique for dealing with complexity. If this popularity is to be more than a fad, necessity will have to mother invention and provide substance to go with the name. [6, *p.114*]

In this article we will explore the issue of whether we are providing substance for the term *systems approach* as it relates to the study of organizations and their management. There are many interesting historical and philosophical questions concerning the relationship between the mechanistic and organistic approaches and their applicability to the various fields of science, as well as other interesting digressions into the evolution of systems approaches. However, we will resist those temptations and plunge directly into a discussion of the key concepts of general systems theory, the way in which these ideas have been used by organization theorists, the limitations in their application, and some suggestions for the future.

Key Concepts of General Systems Theory

The key concepts of general systems theory have been set forth by many writers [7] and have been used by many organization and management theorists [8]. It is not our purpose here to elaborate on them in great detail because we anticipate that most readers will have been exposed to them in some depth. Figure I provides a very brief review of those characteristics of systems which seem to have wide acceptance. The review is far from complete. It is difficult to identify a complete list of characteristics derived from general systems theory; moreover, it is merely a first-order classification. There are many derived second- and third-order characteristics which could be considered. For example, James G. Miller sets forth 165 hypotheses, stemming from open systems theory, which might be applicable to

FIGURE I
Key Concepts of General Systems Theory

Subsystems or Components: A system by definition is composed of interrelated parts or elements. This is true for all systems—mechanical, biological, and social. Every system has at least two elements, and these elements are interconnected.

Holism, Synergism, Organicism, and Gestalt: The whole is not just the sum of the parts; the system itself can be explained only as a totality. Holism is the opposite of elementarism, which views the total as the sum of its individual parts.

Open Systems View: Systems can be considered in two ways: (1) closed or (2) open. Open systems exchange information, energy, or material with their environments. Biological and social systems are inherently open systems; mechanical systems may be open or closed. The concepts of open and closed systems are difficult to defend in the absolute. We prefer to think of open–closed as a dimension; i.e., systems are relatively open or relatively closed.

Input-Transformation-Output Model: The open system can be viewed as a transformation model. In a dynamic relationship with its environment, it receives various inputs, transforms these inputs in some way, and exports outputs.

System Boundaries: It follows that systems have boundaries which separate them from their environments. The concept of boundaries helps us understand the distinction between open and closed systems. The relatively closed system has rigid, impenetrable boundaries; whereas, the open system has permeable boundaries between itself and a broader suprasystem. Boundaries are relatively easily defined in physical and biological systems but are very difficult to delineate in social systems such as organizations.

Negative Entropy: Closed, physical systems are subject to the force of entropy which increases until eventually the entire system fails. The tendency toward maximum entropy is a movement to disorder, complete lack of resource transformation, and death. In a closed system, the change in entropy must always be positive; however, in open biological or social systems, entropy can be arrested and may even be transformed into negative entropy—a process of more complete organization and ability to transform resources—because the system imports resources from its environment.

Steady State, Dynamic Equilibrium, and Homeostasis: The concept of steady state is closely related to that of negative entropy. A closed system eventually must attain an equilibrium state with maximum entropy—death or disorganization. However, an open system may attain a state where the system remains in dynamic equilibrium through the continuous inflow of materials, energy, and information.

Feedback: The concept of feedback is important in understanding how a system maintains a steady state. Information concerning the outputs or the process of the system is fed back as an input into the system, perhaps leading to changes in the transformation process and/or future outputs. Feedback can be both positive and negative, although the field of cybernetics is based upon negative feedback. Negative feedback is informational input which indicates that the system is deviating from a prescribed course and should readjust to a new steady state.

FIGURE I (Continued)

Hierarchy: A basic concept in systems thinking is that of hierarchical relationships between systems. A system is composed of subsystems of a lower order and is also part of a suprasystem. Thus, there is a hierarchy of the components of the system.

Internal Elaboration: Closed systems move toward entropy and disorganization. In contrast, open systems appear to move in the direction of greater differentiation, elaboration, and a higher level of organization.

Multiple Goal Seeking: Biological and social systems appear to have multiple goals or purposes. Social organizations seek multiple goals, if for no other reason than that they are composed of individuals and subunits with different values and objectives.

Equifinality of Open Systems: In mechanistic systems there is a direct cause-and-effect relationship between the initial conditions and the final state. Biological and social systems operate differently. Equifinality suggests that certain results may be achieved with different initial conditions and in different ways. This view suggests that social organizations can accomplish their objectives with diverse inputs and with varying internal activities (conversion processes).

---

two or more levels of systems [9]. He suggests that they are *general* systems theoretical hypotheses and qualifies them by suggesting that they are propositions applicable to general systems *behavior* theory and would thus exclude nonliving systems. He does not limit these propositions to individual organisms, but considers them appropriate for social systems as well. His hypotheses are related to such issues as structure, process, subsystems, information, growth, and integration. It is obviously impossible to discuss all of these hypotheses; we only want to indicate the extent to which many interesting propositions are being posed which might have relevance to many different types of systems. It will be a very long time (if ever) before most of these hypotheses are validated; however, we are surprised at how many of them can be agreed with intuitively, and we can see their possible verification in studies of social organizations.

We turn now to a closer look at how successful or unsuccessful we have been in utilizing these concepts in the development of "modern organization theory."

A Beginning: Enthusiastic but Incomplete

We have embraced general systems theory but, really, how completely? We could review a vast literature in modern organization theory which has explicitly or implicitly adopted systems theory as a frame of reference, and we have investigated in detail a few examples of the literature in assessing the "state of the art" [10]. It was found that most of these books professed to utilize general systems theory. Indeed, in the first few chapters, many of them did an excellent job of presenting basic systems concepts and showing their relationship to organizations; however, when they moved further into the discussion of more specific subject matter, they departed substantially from systems theory. The studies appear to use a "partial systems approach" and leave for the reader the problem of integrating the various ideas into a systemic whole. It also appears that many of the authors are unable, because of limitations of knowledge about subsystem relationships, to carry out the task of using general systems theory as a conceptual basis for organization theory.

Furthermore, it is evident that each author had many "good ideas" stemming from the existing body of knowledge or current research on organizations which did not fit neatly into a "systems model." For example, they might discuss leadership from a relatively closed-system point of view and not consider it in relationship to organizational technology, structure, or other variables. Our review of the literature suggests that much remains to be done in applying general systems theory to organization theory and management practice.

Some Dilemmas in Applying GST to Organizations

Why have writers embracing general systems theory as a basis for studying organizations had so much difficulty in following through? Part of this difficulty may stem from the newness of the paradigm and our inability to operationalize "all we think we know" about this approach. Or it may be because we know too little about the systems under investigation. Both of these possibilities will be covered later, but first we need to look at some of the more specific conceptual problems.

Organizations as organisms. One of the basic contributions of general systems theory was the rejection of the traditional close-system, or mechanistic view of social organizations. But did general systems theory free us from this constraint only to impose another, less obvious one? General systems theory grew out of the organismic views of Von Bertalanffy and other biologists; thus, many of the characteristics are relevant to the living organism. It is conceptually easy to draw the analogy between living organisms and social organizations. "There is, after all, an intuitive similarity between the organization of the human body and the kinds of organizations men create. And so, undaunted by the failures of the human-social analogy through time, new theorists try afresh in each epoch." [11, *p. 660*]. General systems theory would have us accept this analogy between organism and social organization. Yet, we have a hard time swallowing it whole. Katz and Kahn warn us of the danger:

> There has been no more pervasive, persistent, and futile fallacy handicapping the social sciences than the use of the physical model for the understanding of social structures. The biological metaphor, with its crude comparison of the physical parts of the body to the parts of the social system, has been replaced by more subtle but equally misleading analogies between biological and social functioning. This figurative type of thinking ignores the essential difference between the socially contrived nature of social systems and the physical structure of the machine or the human organism. So long as writers are committed to a theoretical framework based upon the physical model, they will miss the essential social-psychological facts of the highly variable, loosely articulated character of social systems. [12, *p. 31*]

In spite of this warning, Katz and Kahn do embrace much of the general systems theory concepts which are based on the biological metaphor. We must be very cautious about trying to make this analogy too literal. We agree with Silverman, who says, "It may, therefore, be necessary to drop the analogy between an organisation and organism: organisations may be systems but not necessarily *natural* systems." [13, *p. 31*]

Distinction between organization and an organization. General systems theory emphasizes that systems are organized—they are composed of interdependent components in some relationship. The social organization would then follow logically as just another system. But we are perhaps being caught in circular thinking. It is true that all systems (physical, biological, and social) are by definition organized, but are all systems organizations? Rapoport and Horvath distinguish "organization theory" and "the theory of organizations" as follows:

> We see organization theory as dealing with general and abstract organizational principles; it applies to any system exhibiting organized complexity. As such, organization theory is seen as an extension of mathematical physics or, even more generally, of mathematics designed to deal with organized systems. The theory of organizations, on the other hand, purports to be a social science. It puts real human organizations at the center of interest. It may study the social structure of organizations and so can be viewed as a branch of sociology; it can study the behavior of individuals or groups as members of organizations and can be viewed as a part of social psychology; it can study power relations and principles of control in organizations and so fits into political science [14, *pp. 74-5*].

Why make an issue of this distinction? It seems to us that there is a vital matter involved. All systems may be considered to be organized, and more advanced systems may display differentiation in the activities of component parts—such as the specialization of human organs. However, all systems *do not* have purposeful entities. Can the heart or lungs be considered as purposeful entities in themselves or are they only components of the larger purposeful system, the human body? By contrast, the social organization is composed of two or more purposeful elements. "An organization consists of elements that have and can exercise their own wills" [15, *p. 669*]. Organisms, the foundation stone of general systems theory, do not contain purposeful elements which exercise their own will. This distinction between the organism and the social organization is of importance. In much of general systems theory, the concern is primarily with the way in which the *organism* responds to environmentally generated inputs. Feedback concepts and the maintenance of a steady state are based on internal adaptations to environmental forces. (This is particularly true of cybernetic models.) But what about those changes and adaptations which occur from *within* social organizations? Purposeful elements within the social organization may initiate activities and adaptations which are difficult to subsume under feedback and steady state concepts.

Open and closed systems.   Another dilemma stemming from general systems theory is the tendency to dichotomize all systems as open or closed. We have been led to think of physical systems as closed, subject to the laws of entropy, and to think of biological systems as open to their environment and, possibly, becoming ne-gentropic. But applying this strict polarization to social organizations creates many difficulties. In fact, most social organizations and their subsystems are "partially open" and "partially closed." Open and closed are a matter of degree. Unfortunately, there seems to be a widely held view (often more implicit than explicit) that *open-system thinking is good and closed-system thinking is bad.* We have not become sufficiently sophisticated to recognize that both are appropriate under certain conditions. For example, one of the most useful conceptualizations set forth by Thompson is that the social organization *must seek* to use closed-system concepts (particularly at the technical core) to reduce uncertainty and to create more effective performance at this level.

Still subsystems thinking.   Even though we preach a general systems approach, we often practice subsystems thinking. Each of the academic disciplines and each of us personally has limited perspective of the system we are studying. While proclaiming a broad systems viewpoint, we often dismiss variables outside our interest or competence as being irrelevant, and open our system only to those inputs which we can handle with our disciplinary bag of tools. We are hampered because each of the academic disciplines has taken a narrow, "partial systems view" and find comfort in the relative certainty which this creates. Of course, this is not a problem unique to modern organization theory. Under the more traditional process approach to the study of management we were able to do an admirable job of delineating and discussing planning, organizing, and controlling as separate activities. We were much less successful in discussing them as integrated and interrelated activities.

How does our knowledge fit? One of the major problems in utilizing general systems theory is that we know (or think we know) more about certain relationships than we can fit into a general systems model. For example, we are beginning to understand the two-variable relationship between technology and structure. But when we introduce another variable, say psychosocial relationships, our models become too complex. Consequently, in order to discuss all the things we know about organizations, we depart from a systems approach. Perhaps it is because we know a great deal more about the elements or subsystems of an organization than we do about the interrelationships and interactions between these subsystems. And general systems theory forces us to consider those relationships about which we know the least—a true dilemma. So we continue to elaborate on those aspects of the organization which we know best—a partial systems view.

Failure to delineate a specific system. When the social sciences embraced general systems theory, the total system became the focus of attention and terminology tended toward vagueness. In the utilization of systems theory, we should be more precise in delineating the specific system under consideration. Failure to do this leads to much confusion. As Murray suggests:

> I am wary of the word "system" because social scientists use it very frequently without specifying which of several possible different denotations they have in mind; but more particularly because, today, "system" is a highly cathected term, loaded with prestige; hence, we are all strongly tempted to employ it even when we have nothing definite in mind and its only service is to indicate that we subscribe to the general premise respecting the interdependence of things— basic to organismic theory, holism, field theory, interactionism, transactionism, etc. . . . When definitions of the units of a system are lacking, the term stands for no more than an article of faith, and is misleading to boot, in so far as it suggests a condition of affairs that may not actually exist. [16, *pp. 50-51*]

We need to be much more precise in delineating both the boundaries of the system under consideration and the level of our analysis. There is a tendency for current writers in organization theory to accept general systems theory and then to move indiscriminately across systems boundaries and between levels of systems without being very precise (and letting their readers in on what is occurring). James Miller suggests the need for clear delineation of levels in applying systems theory: "It is important to follow one procedural rule in systems theory in order to avoid confusion. Every discussion should begin with an identification of the level of reference, and the discourse should not change to another level without a specific statement that this is occurring" [9, *p. 216*]. Our field is replete with these confusions about systems levels. For example, when we use the term "organizational behavior" are we talking about the way the organization behaves as a system or are we talking about the behavior of the individual participants? By goals, do we mean the goals of the organization or the goals of the individuals within the organization? In using systems theory we must become more precise in our delineation of systems boundaries and systems levels if we are to prevent confusing conceptual ambiguity.

Recognition that organizations are "contrived systems." We have a vague uneasiness that general systems theory truly does not recognize the "contrived" nature of social organizations. With its predominate emphasis on natural organisms, it may understate some characteristics which are vital for the social organization. Social organizations do not occur naturally in nature; they are contrived by man. They have structure; but it is the structure of events rather than of physical components, and it cannot be separated from the processes of the system. The fact that social organizations are contrived by human beings suggests that they can be established for an infinite variety of purposes and do not follow the same life-cycle patterns of birth, growth, maturity, and death as biological systems. As Katz and Kahn say:

Social structures are essentially contrived systems. They are made of men and are imperfect systems. They can come apart at the seams overnight, but they can also outlast by centuries the biological organisms which originally created them. The cement which holds them together is essentially psychological rather than biological. Social systems are anchored in the attitudes, perceptions, beliefs, motivations, habits, and expectations of human beings. [12, *p. 33*]

Recognizing that the social organization is contrived, again cautions us against making an exact analogy between it and physical or biological systems.

Questions of systems effectiveness. General systems theory with its biological orientation would appear to have an evolutionary view of system effectiveness. That living system which best adapts to its environment prospers and survives. The primary measure of effectiveness is perpetuation of the organism's species. Teleological behavior is therefore directed toward survival. But is survival the only criterion of effectiveness of the social system? It is probably an essential but not all-inclusive measure of effectiveness.

General systems theory emphasizes the organism's survival goal and does not fully relate to the question of the effectiveness of the system in its suprasystem—the environment. Parsonian functional-structural views provide a contrast. "The *raison d'etre* of complex organizations according to this analysis, is mainly to benefit the society in which they belong, and that society is, therefore, the appropriate frame of reference for the evaluation of organizational effectiveness." [*17, p. 896*]

But this view seems to go to the opposite extreme from the survival view of general systems theory—the organization exists to serve the society. It seems to us that the truth lies somewhere between these two viewpoints. And it is likely that a systems viewpoint (modified from the species survival view of general systems theory) will be most appropriate. Yuchtman and Seashore suggest:

The organization's success over a period of time in this competition for resources—i.e., its bargaining position in a given environment—is regarded as an expression of its overall effectiveness. Since the resources are of various kinds, and the competitive relationships are multiple, and since there is interchangeability among classes of resources, the assessment of organizational effectiveness must be in terms not of any single criterion but of an open-ended multidimensional set of criteria. [*17, p. 891*]

This viewpoint suggests that questions of organizational effectiveness must be concerned with at least three levels of analysis. The level of the environment, the level of the social organization as a system, and the level of the subsystems (human participants) within the organization. Perhaps much of our confusion and ambiguity concerning organizational effectiveness stems from our failure to clearly delineate the level of our analysis and even more important, our failure really to understand the relationships among these levels.

Our discussion of some of the problems associated with the application of general systems theory to the study of social organizations might suggest that we completely reject the appropriateness of this model. On the contrary, we see the systems approach as the new paradigm for the study of organizations; but, like all new concepts in the sciences, one which has to be applied, modified, and elaborated in order to make it as useful as possible.

Systems Theory Provides the New Paradigm

We hope the discussion of GST and organizations provides a realistic appraisal. We do not want to promote the value of the systems ap-

proach as a matter of faith; however, we do see systems theory as
vital to the study of social organizations and as providing the major
new paradigm for our field of study.

Thomas Kuhn provides an interesting interpretation of the nature
of scientific revolution [18]. He suggests that major changes in all
fields of science occur with the development of new conceptual
schemes or "paradigms." These new paradigms do not represent just
a step-by-step advancement in "normal" science (the science generally accepted and practiced) but rather a revolutionary change in the
way the scientific field is perceived by the practioners. Kuhn says:

> The historian of science may be tempted to exclaim that when paradigms
> change, the world itself changes with them. Led by a new paradigm, scientists
> adopt new instruments and look in new places. Even more important, during
> revolutions scientists see new and different things when looking with familiar
> instruments in places they have looked before. It is rather as if the professional
> community has been suddenly transported to another planet where familiar
> objects are seen in a different light and are joined by unfamiliar ones as well . . . .
> Paradigm changes do cause scientists to see the world of their research-
> engagement differently. Insofar as their only recourse to that world is through
> what they see and do, we may want to say that after a revolution scientists are
> responding to a different world. [18, *p. 110*]

New paradigms frequently are rejected by the scientific community.
(At first they may seem crude and limited—offering very little more
than older paradigms.) They frequently lack the apparent sophistication of the older paradigms which they ultimately replace. They
do not display the clarity and certainty of older paradigms which
have been refined through years of research and writing. But a new
paradigm does provide for a "new start" and opens up new directions
which were not possible under the old. "We must recognize how very
limited in both scope and precision a paradigm can be at the time of
its first appearance. Paradigms gain their status because they are
more successful than their competitors in solving a few problems
that the group of practitioners has come to recognize as acute.
To be more successful is not, however, to be either completely successful with a single problem or notably successful with any large
number." [18, *p. 23*]

Systems theory does provide a new paradigm for the study of
social organizations and their management. At this stage it is obviously crude and lacking in precision. In some ways it may not be
much better than older paradigms which have been accepted and used
for a long time (such as the management process approach). As in
other fields of scientific endeavor, the new paradigm must be applied,
clarified, elaborated, and made more precise. But it does provide a
fundamentally different view of the reality of social organizations
and can serve as the basis for major advancements in our field.

We see many exciting examples of the utilization of the new systems paradigm in the field of organization and management. Several of these have been referred to earlier [19], and there have been many others. Burns and Stalker made substantial use of systems views in setting forth their concepts of mechanistic and organic managerial systems [20]. Their studies of the characteristics of these two organization types lack precise definition of the variables and relationships, but their colleagues have used the systems approach to look at the relationship of organizations to their environment and also among the technical, structural, and behavioral characteristics within the organization [21]. Chamberlain used a system view in studying enterprises and their environment which is substantially different from traditional microeconomics [22]. The emerging field of "environmental sciences" and "environmental administration" has found the systems paradigm vital.

Thus, the systems theory paradigm is being used extensively in the investigation of relationships between subsystems within organizations and in studying the environmental interfaces. But it still has not advanced sufficiently to meet the needs. One of the major problems is that the practical need to deal with comprehensive systems of relationships is overrunning our ability to fully understand and predict these relationships. *We vitally need the systems paradigm but we are not sufficiently sophisticated to use it appropriately.* This is the dilemma. Do our current failures to fully ultilize the systems paradigm suggest that we reject it and return to the older, more traditional and time-tested paradigms? Or do we work with systems theory to make it more precise, to understand the relationships among subsystems, and to gather the informational inputs which are necessary to make the systems approach really work? We think the latter course offers the best opportunity.

Thus, we prefer to accept current limitations of systems theory, while working to reduce them and to develop more complete and sophisticated approaches for its application. We agree with Rapoport who says:

The system approach to the study of man can be appreciated as an effort to restore meaning (in terms of intuitively grasped understanding of wholes) while adhering to the principles of *disciplined* generalizations and rigorous deduction. It is, in short, an attempt to make the study of man both scientific and meaningful. [23, *p. xxii*]

We are sympathetic with the second part of Rapoport's comment, the need to apply the systems approach but to make disciplined generalizations and rigorous deductions. This is a vital necessity and yet a major current limitation. We do have some indication that progress (although very slow) is being made.

What Do We Need Now?

Everything is related to everything else—but how? General systems
theory provides us with the macro paradigm for the study of social
organizations. As Scott and others have pointed out, most sciences
go through a macro-micro-macro cycle or sequence of emphasis [5].
Traditional bureaucratic theory provided the first major macro view
of organizations. Administrative management theorists concentrated
on the development of macro "principles of management" which
were applicable to all organizations. When these macro views seemed
incomplete (unable to explain important phenomena), attention
turned to the micro level—more detailed analysis of components or
parts of the organization, thus the interest in human relations, technology, or structural dimensions.

The systems approach returns us to the macro level with a new
paradigm. General systems theory emphasizes a very high level of
abstraction. Phillips classifies it as a third-order study [2] that attempts to develop macro concepts appropriate for all types of biological, physical, and social systems.

In our view, we are now ready to move down a level of abstraction
to consider second-order systems studies or midrange concepts.
These will be based on general systems theory but will be more concrete and will emphasize more specific characteristics and relationships in social organizations. They will operate within the broad
paradigm of systems theory but at a less abstract level.

What should we call this new midrange level of analysis? Various
authors have referred to it as a "contingency view," a study of
"patterns of relationships," or a search for "configurations among
subsystems." Lawrence and Lorsch reflect this view:

During the past few years there has been evident a new trend in the study of
organizational phenomena. Underlying this new approach is the idea that the
internal functioning of organizations must be consistent with the demands of
the organization task, technology, or external environment, and the needs of its
members if the organization is to be effective. Rather than searching for the
panacea of the one best way to organize under all conditions, investigators have
more and more tended to examine the functioning of organizations in relation
to the needs of their particular members and the external pressures facing them.
Basically, this approach seems to be leading to the development of a "contingency" theory of organization with the appropriate internal states and processes of
the organization contingent upon external requirements and member needs.
[24, p.1]

Numerous others have stressed a similar viewpoint. Thompson suggests that the essence of administration lies in understanding basic
configurations which exist between the various subsystems and with

the environment. "The basic function of administration appears to be coalignment, not merely of people (in coalitions) but of institutionalized action—of technology and task environment into a viable domain, and of organizational design and structure appropriate to it." [25, *p. 157*]

Bringing these ideas together we can provide a more precise definition of the contingency view:

The contingency view of organizations and their management suggests that an organization is a system composed of subsystems and delineated by identifiable boundaries from its environmental suprasystem. The contingency view seeks to understand the interrelationships within and among subsystems as well as between the organization and its environment and to define patterns of relationships or configurations of variables. It emphasizes the multivariate nature of organizations and attempts to understand how organizations operate under varying conditions and in specific circumstances. Contingency views are ultimately directed toward suggesting organizational designs and managerial systems most appropriate for specific situations.

But it is not enough to suggest that a "contingency view" based on systems concepts of organizations and their management is more appropriate than the simplistic "principles approach." If organization theory is to advance and make contributions to managerial practice, it must define more explicitly certain patterns of relationships between organizational variables. This is the major challenge facing our field.

Just how do we go about using systems theory to develop these midrange or contingency views? We see no alternative but to engage in intensive comparative investigation of many organizations following the advice of Blau:

A theory of organization, whatever its specific nature, and regardless of how subtle the organizational processes it takes into account, has as its central aim to establish the constellations of characteristics that develop in organizations of various kinds. Comparative studies of many organizations are necessary, not alone to test the hypotheses implied by such a theory, but also to provide a basis for initial exploration and refinement of the theory by indicating the conditions on which relationships, originally assumed to hold universally are contingent. . . . Systematic research on many organizations that provides the data needed to determine the interrelationships between several organizational features is, however, extremely rare. [26, *p. 332*]

Various conceptual designs for the comparative study of organizations and their subsystems are emerging to help in the development of a contingency view. We do not want to impose our model as to what should be considered in looking for these patterns of relationships. However, the tentative matrix shown in Figure II suggests this

FIGURE II

Matrix of Patterns of Relationships between Organization Types and Systems Variables

Organizational Supra- and Subsystems	Continuum of Organization Types	
	Closed/Stable/Mechanistic	Open/Adaptive/Organic
Environmental relationships		
General nature	Placid	Turbulent
Predictability	Certain, determinate	Uncertain, indeterminate
Boundary relationships	Relatively closed; limited to few participants (sales, purchasing, etc.); fixed and well defined	Relatively open; many participants have external relationships; varied and not clearly defined
Goals and values		
Organizational goals in general	Efficient performance, stability, maintenance	Effective problem solving, innovation, growth
Goal set	Single, clear-cut	Multiple, determined by necessity to satisfy a set of constraints
Stability	Stable	Unstable
Technical		
Structural		
Psychosocial		
Managerial		

approach. We have used as a starting point the two polar organization types which have been emphasized in the literature—closed/stable/mechanistic and open/adaptive/organic.

We would consider the environmental suprasystem and organizational subsystems (goals and valus, technical, structural, psychosocial, and managerial) plus various dimensions or characteristics of each of these systems. By way of illustration we have indicated several specific subcategories under the Environmental Suprasystem as well as the Goals and Values Subsystem. This process would have to be completed and extended to all of the subsystems. The next step would be the development of appropriate descriptive language (based on research and conceptualization) for each relevant characteristic across the continuum of organization types. For example, on the "stability" dimension for Goals and Values we would have High, Medium, and Low at appropriate places on the continuum. If the entire matrix were filled in, it is likely that we would begin to see discernible patterns of relationships among subsystems.

We do not expect this matrix to provide *the* midrange model for everyone. It is highly doubtful that we will be able to follow through with the field work investigations necessary to fill in all the squares. Nevertheless, it does illustrate a possible approach for the translation of more abstract general systems theory into an appropriate midrange model which is relevant for organization theory and management practice. Frankly, we see this as a major long-term effort on the part of many researchers, investigating a wide variety of organizations. In spite of the difficulties involved in such research, the endeavor has practical significance. Sophistication in the study of organizations will come when we have a more complete understanding of organizations as total systems (configurations of subsystems) so that we can prescribe more appropriate organizational designs and managerial systems. Ultimately, organization theory should serve as the foundation for more effective management practice.

Application of Systems Concepts to Management Practice

The study of organizations is an applied science because the resulting knowledge is relevant to problem-solving in on-going institutions. Contributions to organization theory come fom many sources. Deductive and inductive research in a variety of disciplines provides a theoretical base of propositions which are useful for understanding organizations and for managing them. Experience gained in management practice is also an important input to organization theory. In short, management is based on the body of knowledge generated by

practical experience *and* electric scientific research concerning organizations. The body of knowledge developed through theory and
research should be translatable into more effective organizational
design and managerial practices.

Do systems concepts and contingency views provide a panacea
for solving problems in organizations? The answer is an emphatic
no; this approach does not provide "ten easy steps" to success in
management. Such cookbook approaches, while seemingly applicable and easy to grasp, are usually shortsighted, narrow in perspective,
and superficial—in short, unrealistic. Fundamental ideas, such as
systems concepts and contingency views, are more difficult to comprehend. However, they facilitate more thorough understanding of
complex situations and increase the likelihood of appropriate action.

It is important to recognize that many managers have used and
will continue to use a systems approach and contingency views intuitively and implicitly. Without much knowledge of the underlying
body of organization theory, they have an intuitive "sense of the
situation," are flexible diagnosticians, and adjust their actions and
decisions accordingly. Thus, systems concepts and contingency views
are not new. However, if this approach to organization theory and
management practice can be made more explicit, we can facilitate
better management and more effective organizations.

Practicing managers in business firms, hospitals, and government
agencies continue to function on a day-to-day basis. Therefore, they
must use whatever theory is available; they cannot wait for the
ultimate body of knowledge (there is none!). Practitioners should be
included in the search for new knowledge because they control access
to an essential ingredient—organizational data—and they are the ones
who ultimately put the theory to the test. Mutual understanding
among managers, teachers, and researchers will facilitate the development of a relevant body of knowledge.

Simultaneous with the refinement of the body of knowledge, a
concerted effort should be directed toward applying what we do
know. We need ways of making systems and contingency views more
useable. Without oversimplication, we need some relevant guidelines for practicing managers.

The general tenor of the contingency view is somewhere between
simplistic, specific principles and complex, vague notions. It is a mid-
range concept which recognizes the complexity involved in managing
modern organizations but uses patterns of relationships and/or configurations of subsystems in order to facilitate improved practice.
The art of management depends on a reasonable success rate for
actions in a probabilistic environment. Our hope is that systems concepts and contingency views, while continually being refined by
scientists/researchers/theorists, will also be made more applicable.

Notes

1. Karl W. Deutsch, "Toward a Cybernetic Model of Man and Society," in *Modern Systems Research for the Behavioral Scientist*, edited by Walter Buckley (Chicago: Aldine Publishing, 1968).
2. D. C. Phillips, "Systems Theory—A Discredited Philosophy," in *Management Systems*, edited by Peter P. Schoderbek (New York: Wiley, 1971).
3. Chester I. Barnard, *The Functions of the Executive* (Cambridge: Harvard Univ. Press, 1938).
4. Robert F. Miller, "The New Science of Administration in the USSR," *Admin. Sci. Quart.*, Sept. 1971.
5. William G. Scott, "Organization Theory: An Overview and an Appraisal," *Acad. Management J.*, April 1961.
6. Herbert A. Simon, "The Architecture of Complexity," in *Organizations: Systems Control and Adaptation*, Vol. 2, by Joseph A. Litterer (New York: Wiley, 1969).
7. Kenneth E. Boulding, "General Systems Theory: The Skeleton of Science," *Management Science*, April 1956; Walter Buckley, editor, *Modern Systems Research for the Behavioral Scientist* (Chicago: Aldine, 1968); David Easton, *A Systems Analysis of Political Life* (New York: Wiley, 1965); A. D. Hall and R. E. Eagen, "Definition of System," *General Systems, Yearbook for the Society for the Advancement of General Systems Theory*, Vol. 1, 1956; James G. Miller, "Living Systems: Basic Concepts," *Behav. Sci.*, July 1965; Talcott Parsons, *The Social System* (New York: Free Press of Glencoe, 1951); Ludwig von Bertalanffy, *General Systems Theory* (New York: Braziller, 1968).
8. C. West Churchman, *The Systems Approach* (New York: Dell Publishing, 1968); F. E. Emery and E. L. Trist, "Socio-technical Systems," in *Management Sciences: Models and Techniques*, edited by C. W. Churchman and Michele Verhulst (New York: Pergamon, 1960); Fremont E. Kast and James E. Rosenzweig, *Organization and Management Theory: A Systems Approach* (New York: McGraw, 1970); Daniel Katz and Robert L. Kahn, *The Social Psychology of Organizations* (New York: Wiley, 1966); Joseph A. Litterer, *Organizations: Structure and Behavior*, Vol. 1 (New York: Wiley, 1969); Joseph A. Litterer, *Organizations: Systems, Control and Adaptation*, Vol. 2 (New York: Wiley, 1969); E. J. Miller and A. K. Rice, *Systems of Organizations* (London: Tavistock, 1967); Edgar Schein, *Organizational Psychology*, rev. ed. (Englewood Cliffs: Prentice-Hall, 1970).
9. James G. Miller, op. cit., note 7.
10. Fremont E. Kast and James E. Rosenzweig, op. cit., note 8; Daniel Katz and Robert L. Kahn, op. cit., note 8; Joseph A. Litterer, op. cit., note 8; A. K. Rice, *The Modern University* (London: Tavistock, 1970); James D. Thompson, *Organizations in Action* (New York: McGraw, 1967).
11. Kurt W. Back, "Biological Models of Social Change," *Amer. Sociological Review*, August 1971.
12. Daniel Katz and Robert L. Kahn, op. cit., note 8.
13. David Silverman, *The Theory of Organisations* (New York: Basic Books, 1971).
14. Anatol Rapoport and William J. Horvath, "Thoughts on Organization Theory," in *Modern Systems Research for the Behavioral Scientist*, edited by Walter Buckley (Chicago: Aldine, 1968).
15. Russell L. Ackoff, "Towards a System of Systems Concepts," *Management Science*, July 1971.

16. Henry A. Murray, "Preparation for the Scaffold of a Comprehensive System," in *Psychology: A Study of the Science,* Vol. 3, edited by Sigmund Koch (New York: McGraw, 1959).
17. Ephraim Yuchtman and Stanley E. Seashore, "A System Resource Approach to Organizational Effectiveness," *Amer. Sociological Review,* Dec. 1967.
18. Thomas S. Kuhn, *The Structure of Scientific Revolutions* (Chicago: Univ. of Chicago Press, 1962).
19. David Easton, op. cit., note 7; Daniel Katz and Robert L. Kahn, op. cit., note 8; Joseph A. Litterer, op. cit., note 8; E. J. Miller and A. K. Rice, op. cit., note 8; A. K. Rice, op. cit., note 10; James D. Thompson, op. cit., note 10.
20. Tom Burns and G. M. Stalker, *The Management of Innovation* (London: Tavistock, 1961).
21. E. J. Miller and A. K. Rice, op. cit., note 8.
22. Neil W. Chamberlain, *Enterprise and Environment: The Firm in Time and Place* (New York: McGraw, 1968).
23. Walter Buckley, editor, *Modern Systems Research for the Behavioral Scientist* (Chicago: Aldine, 1968).
24. Jay W. Lorsch and Paul R. Lawrence, *Studies in Organizational Design* (Homewood, Ill.: Irwin-Dorsey, 1970).
25. James D. Thompson, op. cit., note 10.
26. Peter M. Blau, "The Comparative Study of Organizations," *Industrial and Labor Relations Review,* April 1965.

Additional Reading

1. DeGreene, Kenyon, editor, *Systems Psychology* (New York: McGraw, 1970).
2. Emshoff, James R., *Analysis of Behavioral Systems* (New York: Macmillan, 1971).
3. Gross, Bertram M., "The Coming General Systems Models of Social Systems," *Human Relations,* Nov. 1967.
4. Berrien, F. Kenneth, *General and Social Systems* (New Brunswick, N.J.: Rutgers University Press, 1968).
5. Springer, Michael, "Social Indicators, Reports, and Accounts: Toward the Management of Society," *Annals of American Academy of Political and Social Science,* March 1970.
6. Terreberry, Shirley, "The Evolution of Organizational Environments," *Admin. Sci. Quart.,* March 1969.
7. Von Bertalanffy, Ludwig, "The Theory of Open Systems in Physics and Biology," *Science,* Jan. 13, 1950.

Applied Organization Change in Industry: Structural, Technical, and Human Approaches

Harold J. Leavitt

This is a mapping chapter. It is a part of a search for perspective on complex organizations, in this instance, through consideration of several classes of efforts to change ongoing organizations. Approaches to change provide a kind of sharp caricature of underlying beliefs and prejudices about the important dimensions of organizations. Thereby, perhaps, they provide some insights into areas of real or apparent difference among perspectives on organization theory.

To classify several major approaches to change, I have found it useful, first, to view organizations as multivariate systems, in which at least four interacting variables loom especially large: the variables of task, structure, technology, and actors (usually people). (Figure 1)

Roughly speaking, task refers to organizational *raisons d'être*—manufacturing, servicing, etc., including the large numbers of different, but operationally meaningful, subtasks which may exist in complex organizations.

By actors I mean mostly people, but with the qualification that acts usually executed by people need not remain exclusively in the human domain.

By technology, I mean technical tools—problem-solving inventions—like work measurement, computers, or drill presses. Note that I include both machines and programs in this category, but with some uncertainty about the line between structure and technology.

Finally by structure, I mean systems to communication, systems of authority (or other roles), and systems of work flow.

These four are highly interdependent, so that change in any one

From *New Perspectives in Organization Research*, edited by W. W. Cooper, H. J. Leavitt, and M. W. Shelly II. Copyright © 1964 by John Wiley & Sons, Inc. Reprinted by permission.

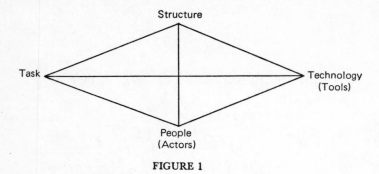

FIGURE 1

will most probably result in compensatory (or retaliatory) change in others. In discussing organizational change, therefore, I shall assume that it is one or more of these variables that we seek to change. Sometimes we may aim to change one of these as an end in itself, sometimes as a mechanism for effecting some changes in one or more of the others.

Thus, for example, structural change toward, say, decentralization should change the performance of certain organizational tasks (indeed, even the selection of tasks), the technology that is brought to bear (e.g., changes in accounting procedures), and the nature, numbers, and/or motivation and attitudes of people in the organization. Any of these changes could presumably be consciously intended; or they could occur as unforeseen and often troublesome outcomes of efforts to change only one or two of the variables.

Similarly, the introduction of new technological tools—computers, for example—may effect changes in structure (e.g., in the communication system or decision map of the organization), changes in people (their numbers, skills, attitudes, and activities), and changes in task performance or even task definition, since some tasks may now become feasible of accomplishment for the first time.

Changes in the people and task variables could presumably branch out through the system to cause similar changes in other variables.

We can turn now to the central focus of this chapter, namely, a categorization and evaluation of several approaches to organizational change—approaches that differ markedly in their degree of emphasis and their ordering of these four variables.

Clearly most efforts to effect change, whether they take off from people, technology, structure or task, soon must deal with the others. Human relators must invent technical devices for implementing their ideas, and they must evaluate alternative structures, classing some as consonant and some as dissonant with their views of the world. Structuralists must take stands on the kinds of human interaction that are supportive of their position, and the kinds that threaten to undermine it, etc.

Although I differentiate structural from technical from human approaches to organizational tasks, the differentiation is in points of origin, relative weightings, and underlying conceptions and values, not in the exclusion of all other variables.

This categorization must be further complicated by the fact that the objectives of the several approaches to organizational change are not uniform. All of them do share a considerable interest in improved solutions to tasks. But while some of the technical approaches focus almost exclusively on task solutions, that is, on the *quality* of decisions, some of the people approaches are at least as interested in performance of task subsequent to decisions. Although improved task solution serves as a common goal for all of these approaches, several carry other associated objectives that weigh almost as heavily in the eyes of their proponents. Thus some of the early structural approaches were almost as concerned with maintaining a power status quo as with improving task performance, and some of the current people approaches are at least as interested in providing organizations that fulfill human needs as they are in efficacious performance of tasks.

The several approaches are still further complicated by variations in the causal chains by which they are supposed to bring about their intended changes. Some of the structural approaches, for example, are not aimed directly at task but at people as mediating intervening variables. In these approaches, one changes structure to change people to improve task performance. Similarly, some of the people approaches seek to change people in order to change structure and tools, to change task performance, and also to make life more fulfilling for people. We can turn now to the several varieties of efforts themselves.

The Structural Approaches

Applied efforts to change organizations by changing structure seem to fall into four classes. First, structural change has been the major mechanism of the "classical" organization theorist. Out of the deductive, logical, largely military-based thinking of early non-empirical organization theory, there evolved the whole set of now familiar "principles" for optimizing organizational performance by optimizing structure. These are deductive approaches carrying out their analyses from task backwards to appropriate divisions of labor and appropriate systems of authority. These early structural approaches almost always mediated their activities through people to task. One improves task performance by clarifying and defining the jobs of people and setting up appropriate relationships among these jobs. Operationally one worried about modifying spans of control, defining nonoverlapping areas of responsibility and authority, and logically defining necessary functions.

In retrospect, most of us think of these early approaches as abstractions, formal and legalistic, and poorly anchored in empirical data. They were also almost incredibly naive in their assumptions about human behavior. In fact, almost the only assumptions that were made were legalistic and moralistic ones: that people, having contracted to work, would then carry out the terms of their contract; that people assigned responsibility would necessarily accept that responsibility; that people when informed of the organization's goals would strive wholeheartedly to achieve those goals.

The values underlying these early approaches were thus probably more authoritarian and puritanical than anything else. Order, discipline, system, and acceptance of authority seemed to be dominant values. The objective, of course, was optimal task performance, but within the constraints imposed by the hierarchy of authority.

In one variation or another, such structural approaches are still widely applied. It is still commonplace for consultants or organization planning departments to try to solve organizational problems by redefining areas of responsibility and authority, enforcing the chain of command, and so on.

A second widespread approach to structural change, allied to the first, somewhat more modern and sophisticated and somewhat narrower, too, is the idea of decentralization. The idea of changing organizations by decentralizing their structure was probably more an invention of the accounting profession than anyone else, though it has been widely endorsed by structuralists and by human relators too. Almost nobody is against it. Not too long ago, I heard the senior officer of one of the nation's largest consulting firms remind his large staff of young consultants that their firm was founded on the "bedrock principle of decentralization."

Decentralization affects the performance of tasks partially through its intervening effects on people. By creating profit centers, one presumably increases the motivation and goal-oriented behavior of local managers. One also adds flexibility so that variations in technology appropriate to the different tasks of different decentralized units now become more possible; so do subvariations in structure, and local variations in the use of people. Decentralization can be thought of as a mechanism for changing organizations at a meta level, providing local autonomy for further change. Thus, within limits, decentralized units may further change themselves through the use of any one of the many alternatives available, and perhaps for this reason no group has questioned it, at least until the last couple of years.

Recently, two other structural approaches have shown up, but they have not yet reached a widespread level of application. One of them is best represented by Chapple and Sayles [1]. Theirs is a form of social engineering aimed at task, but via people. They seek to modify the behavior of people in order to improve task performance, but they do it by modifying structure, in this case, the flow of work. Out of the tradition of applied anthropology, they argue that planning of work flows and groupings of specialties will directly affect the morale, behavior, and output of employees. One of the failings of earlier structural models, in their view, is that the design of work was almost entirely determined by task and technical variables, and failed to take account of human social variables. They provide illustrative cases to show that appropriate redesigning of work, in a social engineering sense, affects both human attitudes and output.

I cannot overlook in this discussion of structure the implications of a second approach—the research on communication networks [2]. I know of no *direct* applications of this laboratory research to the real world, though it has had some indirect influence on structural planning. In that research, variations in communication nets affect both routine and novel task performance rather significantly. The results suggest that appropriate communication structures might vary considerably within a complex organization, depending upon the type of task that any subunit of the organization undertakes. Thus for highly programmed repetitive tasks, highly centralized communication structures seem to operate most efficiently, but with some human costs. For more novel, ill-structured tasks, more wide-open communication nets with larger numbers of channels and less differentiation among members seem to work more effectively.

Technological Approaches to Organizational Change

My first entry in this technological category is Taylor's *Scientific Management* [3]. Its birth date was around 1910, its father, Frederick W. Taylor. Its tools were work measurement tools. It bore none of the abstract deductive flavor of the structural approaches. From the classic programming of the labors of Schmidt, the immigrant pig-iron handler at Bethlehem, on to the more sophisticated forms of work measurement and analysis of succeeding decades, Taylorism has constituted a significant force in influencing task performance in American organizations.

Scientific management, almost from its inception, took a position outside of the task, not of it. Taylor created a new technical skill— industrial engineering—and a new class of specialized practitioners— the industrial engineers. Theirs was a staff skill, a planning skill. They were the organizers and designers of work. The Schmidts were the doers.

Like the early structural approaches, scientific management was thus to a great extent ahuman, perhaps even inhuman. For in creating the separate planning specialist, it removed planning from its old location—the head of the doer of work. Many observers, both contemporary and subsequent, saw this phase of scientific management as downright demeaning of mankind. Taylor put his foot deeply into his mouth by saying things like this:

> Now one of the very first requirements for a man who is fit to handle pig iron . . . is that he shall be so stupid and so phlegmatic that he more nearly resembles . . . the ox than any other type . . . . He must consequently be trained by a man more intelligent than himself. [3]

But despite the flurry of Congressional investigations and active counterattack by Taylor's contemporaries, scientific management grew and prospered, and radically changed structure, people, and the ways jobs got done. Indeed, it spread and flourished until no self-respecting manufacturing firm was without time-study men, methods engineers, work standards, piece rates, and job classification schemes.

The range of scientific management, however, was limited by its relatively simple tools largely to the programming of eye-hand and muscle jobs. Though Taylor and his fellows were ready to generalize their methods to almost any organizational problem, the methods themselves fell pretty short when applied to judgment and think-type jobs.

If one asks why scientific management flourished, several reasonable answers appear. The environment of the day, despite counterattacks by Upton Sinclair and others, was probably supportive. It was an environment of growth, expansiveness, and muscle flexing. Work in associated disciplines was supportive, too. Psychology, for example, was physiologically oriented, concerned with individual differences and anxious to be treated as a science. Hence it, too, was measurement happy.* Finger dexterity tests meshed neatly with Taylor's motion study.

But most of all, Taylorism, like many other ideas, seemed to be carried by its own operational gimmicks—by its cheap, workable, easily-taught techniques and methods.

---

*See, for example, Bendix's account of the early enthusiasm of industrial psychologists. He quotes Hugo Munsterberg appraising the promise of industrial psychology in 1913: ". . . still more important than the valued commercial profit on both sides is the cultural gain which will come to the total economic life of the nation, as soon as everyone can be brought to the place where his best energies may be unfolded and his greatest personal satisfaction secured. The economic experimental psychology offers no more inspiring idea than this adjustment of work and psyche by which mental dissatisfaction with the work, mental depression, and discouragement may be replaced in our social community by overflowing joy and perfect inner harmony." [4]

Scientific management receded into a relatively stable and undramatic background in the late 1930's and 1940's and has never made a real comeback in its original form. But the technological approaches were by no means dead. The development of operations research and the more or less contemporaneous invention and exploitation of computers have more than revived them.

I submit that operational operations research methods for changing organizational problem solving can be reasonably placed in the same category with scientific management. They have both developed a body of technical methods for solving work problems. They both are usually *external* in their approach, essentially separating the planning of problem-solving programs from the routine acting out of solutions. Operations research, too, is quickly developing in its operational form a new class of hot-shot staff specialists, in many ways analogous to the earlier staff efficiency man. What is *clearly* different, of course, is the nature of the techniques, although there may be larger differences that are not yet so clear.

The operations research and information-processing techniques are turning out to be, if not more general, at least applicable to large classes of tasks that scientific management could not touch [5]. Now armed with linear programming methods, one can approach a task like media selection in an advertising agency, though it would have been nonsense to time study it.

But note the overall similarity: change the setting of the movie from Bethlehem, Pa., to Madison Avenue; the time from 1910 to 1962; the costuming from overalls to gray flannel suits; and the tasks from simple muscular labor to complex judgmental decisions. Turn worried laborer Schmidt into worried media executive Jones. Then replace Taylor with Charnes and Cooper and supplant the stopwatch with the computer. It is the same old theme either way—the conflict between technology and humanity.

A distinction needs to be drawn, of course, between operational operations research and other computer-based information-processing approaches, although they are often closely allied. "Management science" hopefully will mean more than highly operational applications of specific techniques, and organizations are also being changed by simulation techniques and by heuristic problem-solving methods. Their impact has not yet been felt in anything like full force; but tasks, people, and structures are already being rather radically modified by them. In fact, one wonders if these task-directed efforts will not end up having at least as radical an impact on structure and on the role of humans as on task solutions themselves. For out of new information-processing methods we now begin to reconsider the bedrock issue of decentralization and to reconsider the permanency and primacy of human judgments for making certain classes of decisions. All the way round the organization, visible changes are being generated out of technical innovations.

Without delving further into the substance of these more recent technological approaches, it may be worth pointing up one other characteristic that they share with many of their predecessors—a kind of faith in the ultimate victory of *better* problem solutions over less good ones. This faith is often perceived by people-oriented practitioners of change as sheer naïveté about the nature of man. They ascribe it to a pre-Freudian fixation on rationality; to a failure to realize that human acceptance of ideas is the real carrier of change; and that emotional human resistance is the real road block. They can point, in evidence, to a monotonously long list of cases in which technological innovations, methods changes, or operations research techniques have fallen short because they ignored the human side of the enterprise. It is not the logically better solutions that get adopted, this argument runs, but the more humanly acceptable, more feasible ones. Unless the new technologist wises up, he may end up a miserable social isolate, like his predecessor, the unhappy industrial engineer.

Often this argument fits the facts. Operations research people can be incredibly naive in their insensitivity to human feelings. But in another, more gracious sense, one can say that the technological approaches have simply taken a more macroscopic, longer view of the world than the people approaches. Better solutions do get accepted in the long run, because deeper forces in the economy press them upon the individual organization—competitive forces, mainly. Macroscopically these ahuman or people-last approaches may encounter bumps and grinds in the microcosms of the individual firm; but sooner or later, in the aggregate, human resistances will be allayed or displaced or overcome, and the steam drill must inevitably defeat John Henry.

The technological approaches assume some communication among firms, and between firms and the world; and they assume further that the demonstration of more economic solutions will eventually result in their adoption, though the road may be rough.

The technological approaches seem not only to predict the victory of cleaner, more logical, and more parsimonious solutions but also to *value* them. Failure of human beings to search for or use more efficient solutions is a sign, from this perspective, of human weakness and inadequacy. People must be teased or educated into greater logic, greater rationality. Resistance to better solutions is proof only of the poverty of our educational system; certainly it is not in any way an indication that "optimal" solutions are less than optimal.

The People Approaches

The people approaches try to change the organizational world by changing the behavior of actors in the organization. By changing people, it is argued, one can cause the creative invention of new tools, or one can cause modifications in structure (especially power structure). By one or another of these means, changing people will cause changes in solutions to tasks and performance of tasks as well as changes in human growth and fulfillment.

In surveying the people approaches, one is immediately struck by the fact that the literature dealing directly with organizational change is almost all people-oriented. Just in the last four or five years, for example, several volumes specifically concerned with organizational change have been published. All of them are people-type books. They include Lippitt, Watson, and Westley's *The Dynamics of Planned Change*; Lawrence's *The Changing of Organizational Behavior Patterns*; Ginsberg and Reilly's *Effecting Change in Large Organizations;* Bennis, Benne, and Chin's *The Planning of Change;* and Guest's *Organizational Change* [6].

This tendency to focus on the process of change itself constitutes one of the major distinguishing features of the people approaches. The technological and structural approaches tend to focus on problem solving, sliding past the microprocesses by which new problem-solving techniques are generated and adopted.

Historically, the people approaches have moved through at least two phases: the first was essentially manipulative, responsive to the primitive and seductive question, "How can we get people to do what we want them to do?"

Although most of us identify such questions with borderline workers like Dale Carnegie, much of the early work (immediately post-World War II) by social scientists on "overcoming resistance to change" dealt with the same issues.

Carnegie's *How to Win Friends and Influence People* was first published in 1936, a few years ahead of most of what we now regard as psychological work in the same area [7]. Like the social scientists that followed, Carnegie's model for change focused on the relationship between changer and changee, pointing out that changes in feelings and attitudes were prerequisites to voluntary changes in overt behavior. Carnegie proposes that one changes others first by developing a valuable (to the other person) relationship, and then using that relationship as a lever for bringing about the change one seeks. One does not attack with logic and criticism and advice. *A* offers *B* support, approval, a permissive atmosphere; and having thus established warm, affective bonds (invariably "sincere" bonds, too) *A* then requests of B that he change in the way A wishes, while A holds the relationship as collateral.

Though social scientists have tended to reject it out of hand, current research on influence processes suggests that the Carnegie model is not technically foolish at all, although we have disavowed it as manipulative, slick, and of questionable honesty.

The Carnegie model, moreover, has some current social scientific parallels. Thus Martin and Sims, for example, directly attack the issue of how to be a successful power politician in industrial organizations [8]. They argue that dramatic skill, capacity to withhold certain kinds of information, the appearance of decisiveness, and a variety of other calculatedly strategic behaviors, appear to be effective in influencing behavior in organizational hierarchies.

In fact, Carnegie-like interest in face-to-face influence has finally become a respectable area of social scientific research. Several works of Hovland et al. on influence and persuasion provide experimental support for the efficacy of certain behavioral techniques of influence over others [9].

But if we move over into the traditionally more "legitimate" spheres of social science, we find that much of the work after World War II on "overcoming resistance to change" was still responsive to the same manipulative question. Consider, for example, the now classic work by Kurt Lewin and his associates on changing food habits, or the later industrial work by Coch and French [10]. In both cases, A sets out to bring about a predetermined change in the behavior of B. Lewin sets out to cause housewives to purchase and consume more variety meats—a selling problem. Coch and French set out to gain acceptance of a preplanned methods change by hourly workers in a factory. In both cases the methodology included large elements of indirection, with less than full information available to the changees.

But whereas Dale Carnegie built warm personal relationships and then bargained with them, neither Lewin nor Coch and French are centrally concerned about intimate relationships between changer and changee. Their concern is much more with warming up the interrelationships among changees.

Thus 32% of Lewin's test housewives exposed to a group-decision method served new variety meats, as against only 3% of the women exposed to lectures. Lewin accounts for these results by calling upon two concepts: "involvement" and "group pressure." Lectures leave their audiences passive and unpressed by the group, whereas discussions are both active and pressing. Similarly, Coch and French, causing the girls in a pajama factory to accept a methods change, emphasize *group* methods, seeing resistance to change as a function partially of individual frustration and partially of strong group-generated forces. Their methodology, therefore, is to provide opportunities for need satisfaction and quietly to corner the group forces and re-direct them toward the desired change.

But it is this slight thread of stealth that was the soft spot (both ethically and methodologically) of these early people approaches to change, and this is the reason I classify them as manipulative. For surely no bright student has ever read the Coch and French piece without wondering a little bit about what *would* have hap-pened if the change being urged by management just did not seem like a good idea to the "smaller, more intimate" work groups of Coch and French's "total participation" condition.

One might say that these early studies wrestled rather effectively with questions of affect and involvement, but ducked a key variable —power. Coch and French modified behavior by manipulating par-ticipation while trying to hold power constant. In so doing, the artistry of the "discussion leader" remained an important but only vaguely controlled variable, causing difficulties in replicating results and generating widespread discomfort among other social scientists.

Other contemporary and subsequent people approaches also avoided the power problem and encountered similar soft spots. The Western Electric counseling program that emerged out of the Haw-thorne researches sought for change through catharsis, with a spe-cific prohibition against any follow-up action by counselors—a "power-free" but eminently human approach [11]. Later, users of morale and attitude surveys sought to effect change by feeding back anonymous aggregate data so that the power groups might then mo-dify their own behavior. But the very anonymity of the process represented an acceptance of the power status quo.

It was to be expected, then, that the next moves in the develop-ment of people approaches would be toward working out the power variable. It was obvious, too, that the direction would be toward power equalization rather than toward power differentiation. The theoretical underpinnings, the prevalent values, and the initial re-search results all pointed that way.

But though this is what happened, it happened in a complicated and mostly implicit way. Most of the push has come from work on individuals and small groups, and has then been largely extrapolated to organizations. Client-centered therapy [12] and applied group dynamics [13] have been prime movers. In both of those cases, the-ory and technique explicitly aimed at allocating at least equal pow-er to the changee(s), a fact of considerable importance in later dev-elopment of dicta for organizational change.

Thus Carl Rogers describes his approach to counseling and therapy:

This newer approach differs from the older one in that it has a genuinely different goal. It aims directly toward the greater independence and integration of the individual rather than hoping that such results will accrue if the counsellor assists in solving the problem. The individual and not the problem is the focus. The aim is not to solve one particular problem, but to assist the individual to grow. [12, *pp. 28-29*]

At the group level, a comparable development was occurring, namely the development of the T (for training) group (or sensitivity training or development group). The T-group is the core tool of programs aimed at teaching people how to lead and change groups. It has also become a core tool for effecting organizational change. T-group leaders try to bring about changes in their groups by taking extremely permissive, extremely nonauthoritarian, sometimes utterly nonparticipative roles, thus encouraging group members not only to solve their own problems but also to define them. The T-group leader becomes, in the language of the profession, a "resource person," not consciously trying to cause a substantive set of changes but only changes in group processes, which would then, in turn, generate substantive changes.

Though the T-group is a tool, a piece of technology, an invention, I include it in the people rather than the tool approaches, for it evolved out of those approaches as a mechanism specifically designed for effecting change in people.

In contrast to earlier group discussion tools, the T-group deals with the power variable directly. Thus Bennis and Shepard comment:

The core of the theory of group development is that the principle obstacles to the development of valid communication are to be found in the orientations toward authority and intimacy that members bring to the group. Rebelliousness, submissiveness or withdrawal as the characteristic responses to authority figures . . . prevent consensual validation of experience. The behaviors determined by these orientations are directed toward enslavement of the other in the service of the self, enslavement of the self in the service of the other, or disintegration of the situation. Hence, they prevent the setting, clarification of, and movement toward, group shared goals. [14]

I offer these quotes to show the extent to which the moral and methodological soft spots of the early manipulative models were being dealt with directly in group training situations. These are not wishy-washy positions. They deal directly with the power variable. Their objective is to transfer more power to the client or the group.

But these are both nonorganizational situations. For the therapist, the relationship with the individual client bounds the world. For the T-group trainer, the group is the world. They can both deal more easily with the power variable than change agents working in a time-constrained and work-flow-constrained organizational setting.

At the organizational level, things therefore are a little more vague.

The direction is there, in the form of movement toward power equalization, but roadblocks are many and maps are somewhat sketchy and undetailed. McGregor's development of participative Theory Y to replace authoritarian Theory X is a case in point. McGregor's whole conception of Theory Y very clearly implies a shift from an all powerful superior dealing with impotent subordinates to something much more like a balance of power:

> People today are accustomed to being directed and manipulated and controlled in industrial organizations and to finding satisfaction for their social, egoistic and self-fulfillment needs away from the job. This is true of much of management as well as of workers. Genuine "industrial citizenship"—to borrow a term from Drucker—is a remote and unrealistic idea, the meaning of which has not even been considered by most members of industrial organizations.
>
> Another way of saying this is that Theory "X" places exclusive reliance upon external control of human behavior, while Theory "Y" [the theory McGregor exposits] relies heavily on self-control and self-direction. It is worth noting that this difference is the difference between treating people as children and treating them as mature adults. [15]

Bennis, Benne, and Chin specifically set out power equalization (PE) as one of the distinguishing features of the deliberate collaborative process they define as planned change: "A power distribution in which the client and change agent have equal, or almost equal, opportunities to influence" is part of their definition [6].

In any case, power equalization has become a key idea in the prevalent people approaches, a first step in the theoretical causal chain leading toward organizational change. It has served as an initial subgoal, a necessary predecessor to creative change in structure, technology, task solving, and task implementation. Although the distances are not marked, there is no unclarity about direction—a more egalitarian power distribution is better.

It is worth pointing out that the techniques for causing redistribution of power in these models are themselves power-equalization techniques—techniques like counseling and T-group training. Thus both Lippitt et al. and Bennis et al. lay great emphasis on the need for collaboration between changer and changee in order for change to take place [6]. But it is understandable that neither those writers nor most other workers in power equalization seriously investigate the possibility that power may be redistributed unilaterally or authoritatively (e.g., by the creation of profit centers in a large business firm or by coercion).

If we examine some of the major variables of organizational behavior, we will see rather quickly that the power-equalization approaches yield outcomes that are very different from those produced by the structural or technological approaches.

Thus in the PE models, *communication* is something to be maximized. The more channels the better, the less filtering the better, the more feedback the better. All these because power will be more equally distributed, validity of information greater, and commitment to organizational goals more intense.

Contrast these views with the earlier structural models which argued for clear but limited communication lines, never to be circumvented; and which disallowed the transmission of affective and therefore task-irrelevant information. They stand in sharp contrast, too, to some current technical views which search for optimal information flows that may be far less than maximum flows.

The PE models also focus much of their attention on issues of *group pressure, cohesiveness,* and *conformity.* The more cohesiveness the better, for cohesiveness causes commitment. The broader the group standards, the better. The more supportive the group, the freer the individual to express his individuality.

These, of course, are issues of much current popular debate. But as factors in effecting change, they are almost entirely ignored by the technical and most of the structural models. In their faith that best solutions will be recognized and in their more macroscopic outlook, until very recently at least, the technical and structural models did not concern themselves with questions of human emotionality and irrationality. If these were treated at all, they were treated as petty sources of interference with the emergence of Truth.

Evidence on this last question—the question of whether or not truth is obscured or enhanced by group pressures—is not yet perfectly clear. On the one hand, Asch has shown in his classic experiments that group pressures may indeed cause individuals to deny their own sense data [16]. On the other hand, Asch himself has warned against interpreting this denial as an entirely emotional non-cognitive process [17]. When ten good men and true announce that line A is longer than line B, and when the eleventh man, still seeking truth, but himself seeing B as longer than A, still goes along with the group, he may do so not because he is overwhelmed by emotional pressure but because "rationally" he decides that ten other good sets of eyes are more likely to be right than his own.

Moreover, some data from some recent experiments being conducted at Carnegie Tech and elsewhere suggest that in-fighting and debate will cease rather rapidly within a group when a solution that is prominently better than other alternatives is put forth [18]. This is to say that people use their heads as well as their guts; though at times in our history we have vociferously denied either one or the other.

Consider next the *decision-making* variable. Decision making, from the perspective of power equalization, is viewed not from a cognitive perspective, nor substantively, but as a problem in achieving committed agreement. The much discussed issues are commitment and consensual validation, and means for lowering and spreading decision-making opportunities.

Contrast this with the technical emphasis on working out optimal decision rules, and with the structuralist's emphasis on locating precise decision points and assigning decision-making responsibility always to individuals.

Summary

If we view organizations as systems of interaction among task, structural, technical, and human variables, several different classes of efforts to change organizational behavior can be grossly mapped.

Such a view provides several entry points for efforts to effect change. One can try to change aspects of task solution, task definition, or task performance by introducing new tools, new structures, or new or modified people or machines. On occasion we have tried to manipulate only one of these variables and discovered that all the others move in unforeseen and often costly directions.

We have more than once been caught short by this failing. The scientific management movement, for example, enamored of its measurement techniques, worked out efficient task solutions only to have many of them backfire because the same methods were also evoking human resistance and hostility. The human relations movement, I submit, is only now bumping into some of the unforeseen costs of building a theory of organization exclusively of human bricks, only to find that technological advances may obviate large chunks of human relations problems by obviating large chunks of humans or by reducing the need for "consensual validation" by programming areas formerly reserved to uncheckable human judgment.

Approaches with strong structural foci have also on occasion fallen into the one-track trap, changing structure to facilitate task solution, only then to find that humans do not fit the cubby holes or technology does not adapt to the new structure.

On the positive side, however, one can put up a strong argument that there is progress in the world; that by pushing structural or human or technical buttons to see what lights up, we are beginning gropingly to understand some of the interdependencies among the several variables.

What we still lack is a good yardstick for comparing the relative costs and advantages of one kind of effort or another. We need, as Likert has suggested, an economics of organizational change [19].

If we had one, we could more effectively evaluate the costs of movement in one direction or another. Likert urges an economics of change because he believes the presently unmeasured costs of human resistance, if measured, would demonstrate the economic utility of organizational designs based on PE models. But such an economics might also pinpoint some of the as yet unmeasured costs of PE-based models. For the present state of unaccountability provides a protective jungle that offers quick cover to the proponents of any current approach to organizational change.

If I may conclude with a speculation, I will bet long odds that, as we develop such an economics, as we learn to weigh costs and advantages, and to predict second and third order changes, we will not move uniformly toward one of these approaches or another, even within the firm. We will move instead toward a mélange, toward differentiated organizations in which the nature of changes becomes largely dependent on the nature of task. We have progressed, I submit; we have not just oscillated. We have learned about people, about structure, about technology; and we will learn to use what we know about all three to change the shape of future organizations.

Notes

1. E. D. Chapple and L. R. Sayles, *The Measure of Management* (New York: Macmillan, 1961).
2. M. Glanzer and R. Glaser, "Techniques for the Study of Group Structure and Behavior," *Psychol. Bul.*, 58 (Jan. 1961), 1:1-27.
3. F. W. Taylor, *Scientific Management* (New York: Harper, 1947).
4. R. Bendix, *Work and Authority in Industry* (New York: Wiley, 1956).
5. G. P. Shultz and T. L. Whister, editors, *Management Organization and the Computer* (Glencoe: Free Press, 1960).
6. R. Lippitt, J. Watson, and B. Westley, *The Dynamics of Planned Change* (New York: Harcourt, 1958); P. R. Lawrence, *The Changing of Organizational Behavior Patterns* (Boston: Harvard University, Graduate School of Business Administration, Division of Research, 1958); E. Ginsberg and E. Reilley, *Effecting Change in Large Organizations* (New York: Columbia University Press, 1957); W. G. Bennis, K. D. Benne, and R. Chin, editors, *The Planning of Change* (New York: Holt, Rinehart & Winston, 1961); R. H. Guest, *Organizational Change: The Effect of Successful Leadership* (Homewood, Ill.: Dorsey Press, 1962).
7. Dale Carnegie, *How to Win Friends and Influence People* (New York: Simon & Schuster, 1936).
8. N. H. Martin and J. R. Sims, "The Problem of Power," in *Industrial Man*, edited by W. L. Warner and N. H. Martin (New York: Harper, 1959).
9. C. E. Hovland, I. L. Janis, and H. H. Kelley, *Communication and Persuasion* (New Haven: Yale University Press, 1953).
10. Kurt Lewin, "Group Decision and Social Change," in *Readings in Social Psychology*, 2d ed., edited by G. E. Swanson, T. M. Newcomb, and E. L. Hartley (New York: Holt, 1952); L. Coch and J. R. P. French, "Overcoming Resistance to Change," *Hum. Relations*, 1 (1948), 4:512-32.
11. F. J. Roethlisberger and W. J. Dickson, *Management and the Worker* (Cambridge: Harvard University Press, 1939).

12. C. R. Rogers, *Counseling and Psychotherapy* (Boston: Houghton, 1942).
13. M. B. Miles, *Learning to Work in Groups* (New York: Bureau of Publications, Teachers College, Columbia University, 1959).
14. W. G. Bennis and H. A. Shepard, "A Theory of Group Development," in *The Planning of Change*, edited by W. G. Bennis, K. D. Benne, and R. Chin (New York: Holt, Rinehart & Winston, 1961).
15. D[ouglas] McGregor, *The Human Side of Enterprise* (New York: McGraw, 1960).
16. S. E. Asch, *Social Psychology* (Englewood Cliffs, N.J.: Prentice-Hall, 1952).
17. ———, "Issues in the Study of Social Influences on Judgment," in *Conformity and Deviation*, edited by I. A. Berg and B. M. Bass (New York: Harper, 1961).
18. As reported in a personal communication from T. C. Schelling, 1961.
19. R[ensis] Likert, *New Patterns of Management* (New York: McGraw, 1961).

Mechanistic and Organic Systems

Tom Burns   *G. M. Stalker*

We are now at the point at which we may set down the outline of the two management systems which represent for us the two polar extremities of the forms which such systems can take when they are adapted to a specific rate of technical and commercial change. The case we have tried to establish from the literature . . . is that the different forms assumed by a working organization do exist objectively and are not merely interpretations offered by observers of different schools.

Both types represent a "rational" form of organization in that they may both, in our experience, be explicitly and deliberately created and maintained to exploit the human resources of a concern in the most efficient manner feasible in the circumstances of the concern. Not surprisingly, however, each exhibits characteristics which have been hitherto associated with different kinds of interpretation. For it is our contention that empirical findings have usually been classified according to sociological ideology rather than according to the functional specificity of the working organization to its task and the conditions confronting it.

We have tried to argue that these are two formally contrasted forms of management system. These we shall call the mechanistic and organic forms.

A *mechanistic* management system is appropriate to stable conditions. It is characterized by:

(a) the specialized differentiation of functional tasks into which the problems and tasks facing the concern as a whole are broken down;

(b) the abstract nature of each individual task, which is pursued with techniques and purposes more or less distinct from those of the concern as a whole, i.e., the functionaries tend to pursue the technical improvement of means, rather than the accomplishment of the ends of the concern;

(c) the reconciliation, for each level in the hierarchy, of these distinct performances by the immediate superiors who are also, in turn, responsible for seeing that each is relevant in his own special part of the main task;

(d) the precise definition of rights and obligations and methods attached to each functional role;

(e) the translation of rights and obligations and methods into the responsibilities of a functional position;

(f) hierarchic structure of control, authority, and communication;

(g) a reinforcement of the hierarchic structure by the location of knowledge of actualities exclusively at the top of the hierarchy, where the final reconciliation of distinct tasks and assessment of relevance is made,*

(h) a tendency for interaction between members of the concern to be vertical, i.e., between superior and subordinate;

(i) a tendency for operations and working behaviour to be governed by the instructions and decisions issued by superiors;

(j) insistence on loyalty to the concern and obedience to superiors as a condition of membership;

(k) a greater importance and prestige attaching to internal (local) than to general (cosmopolitan) knowledge, experience, and skill.

The *organic* form is appropriate to changing conditions, which give rise constantly to fresh problems and unforeseen requirements for action which cannot be broken down or distributed automatically arising from the functional roles defined within a hierarchic structure. It is characterized by:

(a) the contributive nature of special knowledge and experience to the common task of the concern;

(b) the "realistic" nature of the individual task, which is seen as set by the total situation of the concern;

(c) the adjustment and continual redefinition of individual tasks through interaction with others;

(d) the shedding of "responsibility" as a limited field of rights, obligations, and methods. (Problems may not be posted upwards,

---

*This functional attribute of the head of a concern often takes on a clearly expressive aspect. It is common enough for concerns to instruct all people with whom they deal to address correspondence to the firm (i.e., to its formal head) and for all outgoing letters and orders to be signed by the head of the concern. Similarly, the printed letter heading used by government departments carries instructions for the replies to be addressed to the secretary, etc..These instructions are not always taken seriously, either by members of the organization or their correspondents, but in one company this practice was insisted upon and was taken to somewhat unusual lengths; *all* correspondence was delivered to the managing director, who would thereafter distribute excerpts to members of the staff, synthesizing their replies into the letter of reply which he eventually sent. Telephone communication was also controlled by limiting the number of extensions, and by monitoring incoming and outgoing calls.

downwards, or sideways as being someone else's responsibility.)

(e) the spread of commitment to the concern beyond any technical definition;

(f) a network structure of control, authority, and communication. The sanctions which apply to the individual's conduct in his working role derive more from presumed community of interest with the rest of the working organization in the survival and growth of the firm, and less from a contractual relationship between himself and a nonpersonal corporation, represented for him by an immediate superior;

(g) omniscience no longer imputed to the head of the concern; knowledge about the technical or commercial nature of the here-and-now task may be located anywhere in the network; this location becoming the *ad hoc* centre of control authority and communication [1];

(h) a lateral rather than a vertical direction of communication through the organization, communication between people of different rank, also, resembling consultation rather than command;

(i) a content of communication which consists of information and advice rather than instructions and decisions [2];

(j) commitment to the concern's tasks and to the "technological ethos" of material progress and expansion is more highly valued than loyalty and obedience;

(k) importance and prestige attach to affiliations and expertise valid in the industrial and technical and commercial milieux external to the firm.

One important corollary to be attached to this account is that while organic systems are not hierarchic in the same sense as are mechanistic, they remain stratified. Positions are differentiated according to seniority, i.e., greater expertise. The lead in joint decisions is frequently taken by seniors, but it is an essential presumption of the organic system that the lead, i.e. "authority," is taken by whoever shows himself most informed and capable, i.e., the "best authority." The location of authority is settled by consensus.

A second observation is that the area of commitment to the concern—the extent to which the individual yields himself as a resource to be used by the working organization—is far more extensive in organic than in mechanistic systems. Commitment, in fact, is expected to approach that of the professional scientist to his work, and frequently does. One further consequence of this is that it becomes far less feasible to distinguish "informal" from "formal" organization.

Thirdly, the emptying out of significance from the hierarchic command system, by which cooperation is ensured and which serves to monitor the working organization under a mechanistic system, is countered by the development of shared beliefs about the values and goals of the concern. The growth and accretion of institutionalized values, beliefs, and conduct, in the form of commitments, ideology, and manners, around an image of the concern in its industrial and commercial setting make good the loss of formal structure.

Finally, the two forms of system represent a polarity, not a dichotomy; there are, as we have tried to show, intermediate stages between the extremities empirically known to us. Also, the relation of one form to the other is elastic, so that a concern oscillating between relative stability and relative change may also oscillate between the two forms. A concern may (and frequently does) operate with a management system which includes both types.

The organic form, by departing from the familiar clarity and fixity of the hierarchic structure, is often experienced by the individual manager as an uneasy, embarrassed, or chonically anxious quest for knowledge about what he should be doing, or what is expected of him, and similar apprehensiveness about what others are doing. Indeed . . . this kind of response is necessary if the organic form of organization is to work effectively. Understandably, such anxiety finds expression in resentment when the apparent confusion besetting him is not explained. In these situations, all managers some of the time, and many managers all the time, yearn for more definition and structure.

On the other hand, some managers recognize a rationale of nondefinition, a reasoned basis for the practice of those successful firms in which designation of status, function, and line of responsibility and authority has been vague or even avoided.

The desire for more definition is often in effect a wish to have the limits of one's task more neatly defined—to know what and when one doesn't have to bother about as much as to know what one does have to. It follows that the more definition given, the more omniscient the management must be, so that no functions are left wholly or partly undischarged, no person is overburdened with undelegated responsibility, or left without the authority to do his job properly. To do this, to have all the separate functions attached to individual roles fitting together and comprehensively, to have communication between persons constantly maintained on a level adequate to the needs of each functional role, requires rules or traditions of behaviour proved over a long time and an equally fixed, stable task. The omniscience which may then be credited to the head of the concern is expressed throughout its body through the lines of command, extending in a clear, explicitly titled hierarchy of officers and subordinates.

The whole mechanistic form is instinct with this twofold principle of definition and dependence which acts as the frame within which action is conceived and carried out. It works, unconsciously,

almost in the smallest minutiae of daily activity. "How late is late?"
The answer to this question is not to be found in the rule book, but
in the superior. Late is when the boss thinks it is late. Is he the
kind of man who thinks 8:00 is the time, and 8:01 is late? Does
he think that 8:15 is all right occasionally if it is not a regular thing?
Does he think that everyone should be allowed a 5-minutes grace
after 8:00 but after that they are late? [3]

Settling questions about how a person's job is to be done in this
way is nevertheless simple, direct, and economical of effort. . . .

One other feature of mechanistic organization needs emphasis.
It is a necessary condition of its operation that the individual "works
on his own," functionally isolated; he "knows his job," he is "responsible for seeing it's done." He works at a job which is in a sense
artificially abstracted from the realities of the situation the concern
is dealing with, the accountant "dealing with the costs side," the
works manager "pushing production," and so on. As this works out
in practice, the rest of the organization becomes part of the problem
situation the individual has to deal with in order to perform successfully; i.e., difficulties and problems arising from work or information
which has been handed over the "responsibility barrier" between two
jobs or departments are regarded as "really" the responsibility of the
person from whom they were received. As a design engineer put it,
"When you get designers handing over designs completely to production, it's 'their responsibility' now. And you get tennis games
played with the responsibility for anything that goes wrong. What
happens is that you're constantly getting unsuspected faults arising
from characteristics which you didn't think important in the design.
If you get to hear of these through a sales person, or somebody to
whom the design was handed over in the dim past, then, instead
of being a design problem, it's an annoyance caused by that particular person, who can't do his own job—because you'd thought you
were finished with that one, and you're on to something else now."

When the assumptions of the form of organization make for preoccupation with specialized tasks, the chances of career success, or
of greater influence, depend rather on the relative importance which
may be attached to each special function by the superior whose task
it is to reconcile and control a number of them. And, indeed, to
press the claims of one's job or department for a bigger share of the
firm's resources is in many cases regarded as a mark of initiative, of
effectiveness, and even of "loyalty to the firm's interests." The
state of affairs thus engendered squares with the role of the superior,
the man who can see the woods instead of just the trees, and gives it
the reinforcement of the aloof detachment belonging to a court of
appeal. The ordinary relationship prevailing between individual
managers "in charge of" different functions is one of rivalry, a rivalry

which may be rendered innocuous to the persons involved by personal friendship or the norms of sociability, but which turns discussion about the situations which constitute the real problems of the concern—how to make products more cheaply, how to sell more, how to allocate resources, whether to curtail activity in one sector, whether to risk expansion in another, and so on—into an arena of conflicting interests.

The distinctive feature of the second, organic system is the pervasiveness of the working organization as an institution. In concrete terms, this makes itself felt in a preparedness to combine with others in serving the general aims of the concern. Proportionately to the rate and extent of change, the less can the omniscience appropriate to command organizations be ascribed to the head of the organization; for executives, and even operatives, in a changing firm it is always theirs to reason why. Furthermore, the less definition can be given to status, roles, and modes of communication, the more do the activities of each member of the organization become determined by the real tasks of the firm as he sees them than by instruction and routine. The individual's job ceases to be self-contained; the only way in which "his" job can be done is by his participating continually with others in the solution of problems which are real to the firm, and put in a language of requirements and activities meaningful to them all. Such methods of working put much heavier demands on the individual.

We have endeavoured to stress the appropriateness of each system to its own specific set of conditions. Equally, we desire to avoid the suggestion that either system is superior under all circumstances to the other. In particular, nothing in our experience justifies the assumption that mechanistic systems should be superseded by organic in conditions of stability.* The beginning of administrative wisdom is the awareness that there is no one optimum type of management system.

---

*A recent instance of this assumption is contained in H. A. Shepard's paper addressed to the Symposium on the Direction of Research Establishments, 1956. "There is much evidence to suggest that the optimal use of human resources in industrial organizations requires a different set of conditions, assumptions, and skills from those traditionally present in industry. Over the past twenty-five years, some new orientations have emerged from organizational experiments, observations, and inventions. The new orientations depart radically from doctrines associated with scientific management and traditional bureaucratic patterns.
"The central emphases in this development are as follows:
  1. Wide participation in decision-making, rather than centralized decision-making.
  2. The face-to-face group, rather than the individual, as the basic unit of organization.
  3. Mutual confidence, rather than authority, as the integrative force in organization.
  4. The supervisor as the agent for maintaining intragroup and intergroup communication, rather than as the agent of higher authority.
  5. Growth of members of the organization to greater responsibility, rather than external control of the member's performance or their tasks." [4]

Notes

1. J. Klein, *The Study of Groups* (London: Routledge, 1956), Chap. 2.
2. Tom Burns, "The Directions of Activity and Communication in a Departmental Executive Group," *Human Relations*, 7 (1954), 73-97.
3. M. Haire, *Psychology in Management* (New York: McGraw, 1956), p. 54.
4. H. A. Shepard, "Superiors and Subordinates in Research," Paper 12 of Symposium on the Direction of Research Establishments (H.M.S.O.: Dept. of Scientific and Industrial Research).

The Evolution of Organizational Environments

Shirley Terreberry

This paper argues that evolutionary processes occur in the environments of organizations. Ideal types of environment, originally conceptualized by Emery and Trist, are elaborated and extended. A review of recent literature gives evidence of the decreasing autonomy and the increasing interdependence of organizations.

Four approaches to interorganizational analysis are reviewed and found inadequate to deal with present-day conditions. This paper then outlines a perspective which allows any organization, its transactions, and the environment itself to be viewed in a common conceptual framework.

Two hypotheses are discussed: (1) that organizational change is increasingly externally induced; and (2) that organizational adaptability is a function of ability to learn and to perform, according to changes in the environment.

Shirley Terreberry is a Ph.D. candidate in the Doctoral Program in Social Work and Social Science at The University of Michigan.

Darwin published *The Origin of Species by Means of Natural Selection* in 1859. Modern genetics has vastly altered our understanding of the variance upon which natural selection operates. But there has been no conceptual breakthrough in understanding *environmental* evolution which, alone, shapes the direction of change. Even today most theorists of change still focus on *internal* interdependencies of systems—biological, psychological, or social—although the external environments of these sytems are changing more rapidly than ever before.

From *Administrative Science Quarterly*, 12 (March 1968), 590-613. Copyright ©1968 by Graduate School of Business and Public Administration, Cornell University.

Introduction

Von Bertalanffy was the first to reveal fully the importance of a system being open or closed to the environment in distinguishing living from inanimate systems [1, 1-10]. Although von Bertalanffy's formulation makes it possible to deal with a system's exchange processes in a new perspective, it does not deal at all with those processes in environment *itself* that are among the determining conditions of exchange.

Emery and Trist have argued the need for one additional concept, "the causal texture of the environment." [2, 21-31] Writing in the context of formal organizations, they offer the following general proposition:

> That a comprehensive understanding of organizational behaviour requires some knowledge of each member of the following set, where L indicates some potentially lawful connection, and the suffix 1 refers to the organization and the suffix 2 to the environment:

$$L_{11} L_{12}$$
$$L_{21} L_{22}$$

> L_{11} here refers to processes within the organization—the area of internal interdependencies; L_{12} and L_{21} to exchanges between the organization and its environment—the area of transactional interdependencies, from either direction; and L_{22} to processes through which parts of the environment become related to each other—i.e., its causal texture—the area of interdependencies that belong within the environment itself.

We have reproduced the above paragraph in its entirety because, in the balance of this paper, we will use Emery and Trist's symbols (i.e., L_{11}, L_{21}, L_{12}, and L_{22}) to denote intra-, input, output, and extra-system interdependencies, respectively. Our purpose in doing so is to avoid the misleading connotations of conventional terminology.

Purpose. The theses here are: (1) that contemporary changes in organizational environments are such as to increase the ratio of externally induced change to internally induced change; and (2) that *other* formal organizations are, increasingly, the important components in the environment of any focal organization. Furthermore, the evolution of environments is accompanied—among viable systems—by an increase in the system's ability to learn and to perform according to changing contingencies in its environment. An integrative framework is outlined for the concurrent analysis of an organization, its transactions with environmental units, and interdependencies among those units. Lastly, two hypotheses are presented, one about organizational *change* and the other about organizational *adaptability*; and some problems in any empirical test of these hypotheses are discussed.*

Concepts of organizational environments. In Emery and Trist's terms, L_{22} relations (i.e., interdependencies within the environment itself) comprise the "causal texture" of the field. This causal texture of the environment is treated as a quasi-independent domain, since the environment cannot be conceptualized except with respect to some focal organization. The components of the environment are identified in terms of that system's actual and *potential* transactional interdependencies, both input (L_{21}) and output (L_{12}).

Emery and Trist postulate four "ideal types" of environment, which can be ordered according to the degree of *system connectedness* that exists among the components of the environment (L_{22}). The first of these is a "placid, randomized" environment: goods and bads are relatively unchanging in themselves and are randomly distributed (e.g., the environments of an amoeba, a human foetus, a nomadic tribe). The second is a "placid, clustered" environment: goods and bads are relatively unchanging in themselves but clustered (e.g., the environments of plants that are subjected to the cycle of seasons, of human infants, of extractive industries). The third ideal type is "disturbed-reactive" environment and constitutes a significant qualitative change over simpler types of environments: an environment characterized by similar systems in the field. The extinction of dinosaurs can be traced to the emergence of more complex environments on the biological level. Human beings, beyond infancy, live in disturbed-reactive environments in relation to one another. The theory of oligopoly in economics is a theory of this type of environment [3, 24-26].

These three types of environment have been identified and described in the literature of biology, economics, and mathematics [4]. "The fourth type, however, is new, at least to us, and is the one that for some time we have been endeavouring to identify." [2, 24] This fourth ideal type of environment is called a "turbulent field." Dynamic processes "arise from the *field itself*" and not merely from the interactions of components; the actions of component organizations and linked sets of them "are both persistent and strong enough to induce autochthonous processes in the environment." [2, 26]

An alternate description of a turbulent field is that the accelerat-

*I am particularly grateful to Kenneth Boulding for inspiration and to Eugene Litwak, Rosemary Sarri, and Robert Vinter for helpful criticisms. A Special Research Fellowship from the National Institutes of Health has supported my doctoral studies and, therefore, has made possible the development of this paper.

ing rate and complexity of interactive effects exceeds the component systems' capacities for prediction and, hence, control of the compounding consequences of their actions.

Turbulence is characterized by complexity as well as rapidity of change in causal interconnections in the environment. Emery and Trist illustrate the transition from a disturbed-reactive to a turbulent-field environment for a company that had maintained a steady 65 percent of the market for its main product—a canned vegetable—over many years. At the end of World War II, the firm made an enormous investment in a new automated factory that was set up exclusively for the traditional product and technology. At the same time postwar controls on steel strip and tin were removed, so that cheaper cans were available; surplus crops were more cheaply obtained by importers; diversity increased in available products, including substitutes for the staple; the quick-freeze technology was developed; home buyers became more affluent; supermarkets emerged and placed bulk orders with small firms for retail under supermarket names. These changes in technology, international trade, and affluence of buyers gradually interacted (L_{22}) and ultimately had a pronounced effect on the company: its market dwindled rapidly. "The changed texture of the environment was not recognized by an able but traditional management until it was too late." [2, 24]

Sociological, social psychological, and business management theorists often still treat formal organizations as closed systems. In recent years, however, this perspective seems to be changing. Etzioni asserts that interorganizational relations need intensive empirical study [5, 223-28]. Blau and Scott present a rich but unconceptualized discussion of the "social context of organizational life." [6, *pp. 194-221*]. Parsons distinguishes three distinct levels of organizational responsibility and control: technical, managerial, and institutional [7, *pp. 63-64*]. His categories can be construed to parallel the intraorganizational (i.e., technical or L_{11}), the interorganizational (i.e., managerial or L_{21} and L_{12}), and the extra-organizational levels of analysis (i.e., the institutional or L_{22} areas). Perhaps in the normal developmental course of a science, intrasystem analysis necessarily precedes the intersystem focus. On the other hand, increasing attention to interorganizational relations may reflect a real change in the phenomenon being studied. The first question to consider is whether there is evidence that the environments of formal organizations are evolving toward turbulent-field conditions.

Evidence for turbulence. Ohlin argues that the sheer rapidity of social change today requires greater organizational adaptability [8, 63]. Hood points to the increasing complexity, as well as the accelerating rate of change, in organizational environments [9, 73]. In business circles there is growing conviction that the future is unpredictable. Drucker and Gardner both assert that the kind and extent of present-day change precludes prediction of the future [10]. Increasingly, the rational strategies of planned-innovation and long-range planning are being undermined by unpredictable changes. McNulty found no association between organization adaptation and the introduction of purposeful change in a study of 30 companies in fast-growing markets [11, 1-21]. He suggests that built-in flexibility may be more efficient than the explicit reorganization implicit in the quasi-rational model. *Dun's Review* questions the effectiveness of long-range planning in the light of frequent failures, and suggests that error may be attributable to forecasting the future by extrapolation of a noncomparable past. The conclusion is that the rapidity and complexity of change may increasingly preclude effective long-range planning [12, 42]. These examples clearly suggest the emergence of a change in the environment that is suggestive of turbulence.

Some writers with this open-system perspective derive implications for interorganizational relations from the changing environment. Blau and Scott argue that the success of a firm increasingly depends upon its ability to establish symbiotic relations with other organizations, in which extensive advantageous exchange takes place [6, *p. 217*]. Lee Adler proposes "symbiotic marketing" [13, 59-71]. Dill found that the task environments of two Norwegian firms comprised four major sectors: *customers*, including both distributors and users; *suppliers* of materials, labor, capital, equipment, and work space; *competitors* for both markets and resources; and *regulatory groups*, including governmental agencies, unions, and interfirm associations [14, 409-43]. Not only does Dill's list include many more components than are accommodated by present theories, but all components are themselves evolving into formal organizations. In his recent book, Thompson discusses "task environments," which comprise the units with which an organization has input and output transactions (L_{21} and L_{12}), and postulates two dimensions of such environments: homogeneous-heterogeneous, and stable-dynamic. When the task environment is *both* heterogeneous and dynamic (i.e., probably turbulent), he expects an organization's boundary-spanning units to be functionally differentiated to correspond to segments of the task environment and each to operate on a decentralized basis to monitor and plan responses to fluctuations in its sector of the task environment. He does not focus on other organizations as components of the environment, but he provides a novel perspective on structural implications (L_{11}) for organizations in turbulent fields [15, *pp. 27-28*].

Selznick's work on TVA appears to be the first organizational case

study to emphasize transactional interdependencies [16]. The next
study was Ridgway's study of manufacturer-dealer relationships [17,
464-83]. Within the following few years the study by Dill [14] and
others by Levine and White [18, 583-601], Litwak and Hylton [19,
395-420], Elling and Halebsky [20, 185-209] appeared, and in recent years, the publication of such studies has accelerated.

The following are examples from two volumes of the *Administrative Science Quarterly* alone. Rubington argues that structural
changes in organizations that seek to change the behavior of "prison-
ers, drug addicts, juvenile delinquents, parolees, alcoholics [are] . . .
the result of a social movement whose own organizational history
has yet to be written" [21,350-69]. Rosengren reports a similar
phenomenon in the mental health field whose origin he finds hard
to explain: "In any event, a more symbiotic relationship has come
to characterize the relations between the [mental] hospitals and
other agencies, professions, and establishments in the community."
He ascribes changes in organizational goals and technology to this
interorganizational evolution [22, 70-90]. In the field of education,
Clark outlines the increasing influence of private foundations, national associations, and divisions of the federal government. He, too,
is not clear as to how these changes have come about, but he traces
numerous changes in the behavior of educational organizations to
interorganizational influences [23, 224-37]. Maniha and Perrow
analyze the origins and development of a city youth commission.
The agency had little reason to be formed, no goals to guide it, and
was staffed by people who sought a minimal, no-action role in the
community. By virtue of its existence and broad province, however,
it was seized upon as a valuable weapon by other organizations for
the pursuit of their own goals. "But in this very process it became
an organization with a mission of its own, in spite of itself." [24,
238-57]

Since uncertainty is the dominant characteristic of turbulent
fields, it is not surprising that emphasis in recent literature is away
from algorithmic and toward heuristic problem-solving models [25,
pp. 48-82]; that optimizing models are giving way to satisficing models
[26, *pp. 140-41*]; and that rational decision making is replaced by "dis-
jointed incrementalism" [27]. These trends reflect *not* the ignorance
of the authors of earlier models, but a change in the causal texture of
organizational environments and, therefore, of appropriate strategies
for coping with the environment. Cyert and March state that "so
long as the environment of the firm is unstable—and predictably unstable—the heart of the theory [of the firm] must be the process of
short-run adaptive reactions." [28, *p. 100*]

In summary, both the theoretical and case study literature on organizations suggests that these systems are increasingly finding them-

selves in environments where the complexity and rapidity of change in external interconnectedness (L_{22}) gives rise to increasingly unpredictable change in their transactional interdependencies $(L_{21}$ and $L_{12})$. This seems to be good evidence for the emergence of turbulence in the environments of many formal organizations.

Interorganizational Environment

Evidence for increasing dependence on environment. Elsewhere the author has argued that Emery and Trist's concepts can be extended to *all* living systems; furthermore, that this evolutionary process gives rise to conditions—biological, psychological, and social—in which the rate of evolution of environments exceeds the rate of evolution of component systems [29, *pp. 1-37*].

In the short run, the openness of a living system to its environment enables it to take in ingredients from the environment for conversion into energy or information that allows it to maintain a steady state and, hence, to violate the dismal second law of thermodynamics (i.e., of entropy). In the long run, "the characteristic of living systems which most clearly distinguishes them from the nonliving is their property of progressing by the process which is called evolution from less to more complex states of organization." [30, 90] It then follows that to the extent that the environment of some living system X is comprised of *other living systems*, the environment of X is *itself* evolving from less to more complex states of organization. A major corollary is that the evolution of environments is characterized by an increase in the ratio of externally induced change over internally induced change in a system's transactional interdependencies $(L_{21}$ and $L_{12})$.

For illustration, let us assume that at some given time, each system in some set of interdependent systems is equally likely to experience an internal (L_{11}) change that is functional for survival (i.e., improves its L_{21} or L_{12} transactions). The greater the number of other systems in that set, the greater the probability that some system other than X will experience that change. Since we posit interdependence among members of the set, X's viability over time depends upon X's capacity (L_{11}) for adaptation to environmentally induced (L_{22}) changes in its transactive position, or else upon control over these external relations.

In the case of formal organizations, disturbed-reactive or oligopolistic environments require some form of accommodation between like but competitive organizations whose fates are negatively correlated to some degree. A change in the transactional position of one system in an oligopolistic set, whether for better or worse, automàtically affects the transactional position of all other members of the set, and in the opposite direction (i.e., for worse or better, as the case may be).* On the other hand, turbulent environments require relationships between dissimilar organizations whose fates are independent or, perhaps, positively correlated.† A testable hypothesis that derives from the formal argument is that the evolution of environments is accompanied, in viable systems, by an increase in ability to learn and to perform according to changing contingencies in the environment.

The evolution of organizational environments is characterized by a change in the important constituents of the environment. The earliest formal organizations to appear in the United States (e.g., in agriculture, retail trade, construction, mining) operated largely under placid-clustered conditions [31, *p. 156*]. Important inputs, such as natural resources and labor, as well as consumers, comprised an environment in which strategies of optimal location and distinctive competence were critical organizational responses [2, 29]. Two important attributes of placid-clustered environments are: (1) the environment is itself *not* formally organized; and (2) transactions are largely initiated and controlled by the organization (i.e., L_{12}).

Later developments, such as transport technology and derivative overlap in loss of strength gradients, and communication and automation technologies that increased economies of scale, gave rise to disturbed reactive (oligopolistic) conditions in which similar formal organizations become the important actors in an organization's field. They are responsive to its acts (L_{12}) *and* it must be responsive to theirs (L_{21}). The critical organizational response now involves complex operations, requiring sequential choices based on the calculated actions of others, and counteractions [2, 25-26].

When the environment becomes turbulent, however, its constituents are a multitude of other formal organizations. Increasingly, an organization's markets consist of other organizations; suppliers of material, labor, and capital are increasingly organized; and regulatory groups are more numerous and powerful. The critical response of organizations under these conditions will be discussed later. It should be noted that *real* environments are often mixtures of these ideal types.

The evolution from placid-clustered environments to turbulent environments†† can be summarized as a process in which formal or-

---

* Assuming a nonexpanding economy, in the ideal instance.

† Emery and Trist argue that fates, here, are positively correlated. This writer agrees if an expanding economy is assumed.

†† The author does not agree with Emery and Trist that *formal* (as distinct from social) organization will emerge in placid-random environments.

ganizations evolve: (1) *from* the status of systems within environments not formally organized; (2) *through* intermediate phases (e.g., Weberian bureaucracy); and (3) *to* the status of subsystems of a larger social system.

Clark Kerr traces this evolution for the university in the United States [32]. In modern industrial societies, this evolutionary process has resulted in the replacement of individuals and informal groups by organizations as *actors* in the social system. Functions that were once the sole responsibility of families and communities are increasingly allocated to formal organizations; child-rearing, work, recreation, education, health, and so on. Events which were long a matter of chance are increasingly subject to organizational control, such as population growth, business cycles, and even the weather. One wonders whether Durkheim, if he could observe the current scene, might speculate that the evolution from "mechanical solidarity" to "organic solidarity" is now occurring on the *organizational level*, where the common values of organizations in oligopolies are replaced by functional interdependencies among specialized organizations [33].

Interorganizational analysis. It was noted that survival in disturbed-reactive environments depends upon the ability of the organization to anticipate and counteract the behavior of similar systems. The analysis of interorganizational behavior, therefore, becomes meaningful only in these and more complex environments. The interdependence of organizations, or any kind of living systems, at less complex environmental levels is more appropriately studied by means of ecological, competitive market, or other similar models.

The only systematic conceptual approach to interorganizational analysis has been the theory of oligopoly in economics. This theory clearly addresses only disturbed-reactive environments. Many economists admit that the theory, which assumes maximization of profit and perfect knowledge, is increasingly at odds with empirical evidence that organizational behavior is characterized by satisficing and bounded rationality. Boulding comments that "it is surprisingly hard to make a really intelligent conflict move in the economic area simply because of the complexity of the system and the enormous importance of side effects and dynamic effects." [34, *p. 189*]

A fairly comprehensive search of the literature has revealed only four conceptual frameworks for the analysis of interorganizational relations outside the field of economics. These are briefly reviewed, particular attention being given to assumptions about organization environments, and to the utility of these assumptions in the analysis of interorganizational relations in turbulent fields.

William Evan has introduced the concept of "organization-set," after Merton's "role-set" [35, *pp. 175-80*]. Relations between a focal organization and members of its organization-set are mediated by the role-sets of boundary personnel. "Relations" are conceived as the flow of information, products or services, and personnel [35, *pp. 175-76*]. Presumably, monetary, and legal, and other transactions can be accommodated in the conceptual system. In general, Evan offers a conceptual tool for identifying transactions at a given time. He makes no explicit assumptions about the nature of environmental dynamics, nor does he imply that they are changing. The relative neglect of interorganizational relations, which he finds surprising, is ascribed instead to the traditional intraorganizational focus, which derives from Weber, Taylor, and Barnard [35]. His concepts, however, go considerably beyond those of conventional organization and economic theory (e.g., comparative versus reference organizations and overlap in goals and values). If a temporal dimension were added to Evan's conceptual scheme, then, it would be a very useful tool for describing the "structural" aspects of transactional interdependencies (L_{21} and L_{12} relations) in turbulent fields.

Another approach is taken by Levine and White who focus specifically on relations among community health and welfare agencies. This local set of organizations "may be seen as a system with individual organizations or system parts varying in the kinds and frequencies of their relationships with one another." [18, 586] The authors admit that interdependence exists among these local parts only to the extent that relevant resources are not available from *outside* the local region, which lies beyond their conceptual domain. Nor do we find here any suggestion of turbulence in these local environments. If such local sets of agencies are increasingly interdependent with other components of the local community and with organizations outside the locality, as the evidence suggests, then the utility of Levine and White's approach is both limited and shrinking.

Litwak and Hylton provide a third perspective. They too are concerned with health and welfare organizations, but their major emphasis is on coordination [19]. The degree of interdependence among organizations is a major variable; low interdependence leads to *no* coordination and high interdependence leads to merger, therefore they deal only with conditions of moderate interdependence. The type of coordinating mechanism that emerges under conditions of moderate interdependence is hypothesized to result from the interaction of three trichotomized variables: the *number* of interdependent organizations; the degree of their *awareness* of their interdependence; and the extent of *standardization* in their transactions. The attractive feature of the Litwak and Hylton scheme is the possibility it offers of making different predictions for a great variety of environments. Their model also seems to have predictive power beyond the class of organizations to which they specifically address themselves. If environments are becoming turbulent, however, then increasingly fewer of the model's cells (a 3 X 3 X 3 space) are relevant. In the one-cell turbulent corner of their model, where a large number of organizations have low awareness of their complex and unstandardized interdependence, "there is little chance of coordination," according to Litwak and Hylton [19, 417]. If the level of awareness of interdependence increases, the model predicts that some process of arbitration will emerge. Thus the model anticipates the interorganizational implications of turbulent fields, but tells us little about the emerging processes that will enable organizations to adapt to turbulence.

The fourth conceptual framework available in the literature is by Thompson and McEwen [36, 23-31]. They emphasize the interdependence of organizations with the larger society and discuss the consequences that this has for goal setting. "Because the setting of goals is essentially a problem of defining desired relationships between an organization and its environment, change in either requires review and perhaps alteration of goals." [36, 23] They do not argue that such changes are more frequent today, but they do assert that reappraisal of goals is "a more constant problem in an unstable environment than in a stable one," and also "more difficult as the 'product' of the enterprise becomes less tangible" [36, 24].

Thompson and McEwen outline four organizational strategies for dealing with the environment. One is competition; the other three are subtypes of a cooperative strategy: bargaining, co-optation, and coalition. These cooperative strategies all require direct interaction among organizations and this, they argue, increases the environment's potential control over the focal organization [36, 27]. In bargaining, to the extent that the second party's support is necessary, that party is in a position to exercise a veto over the final choice of alternative goals, and thus takes part in the decision. The co-optation strategy makes still further inroads into the goal-setting process. From the standpoint of society, however, co-optation, by providing overlapping memberships, is an important social device for increasing the likelihood that organizations related to each other in complicated ways will in fact find compatible goals. Co-optation thus aids in the integration of heterogeneous parts of a complex social system. Coalition refers to a combination of two or more organizations for a common purpose and is viewed by these authors as the ultimate form of environmental conditioning of organization goals [36, 25-28].

The conceptual approaches of Levine and White and of Litwak and Hylton therefore appear to be designed for nonturbulent conditions. Indeed, it may well be that coordination *per se*, in the static sense usually implied by that term, is dysfunctional for adaptation to turbulent fields. (This criticism has often been leveled at local "councils of social agencies" [37].) On the other hand, Evan's concept of organization-set seems useful for describing static aspects of inter-organizational relations in either disturbed-reactive *or* turbulent-field environments. Its application in longitudinal rather than static studies might yield data on the relationship between structural aspects of transactional relations and organizational adaptability. Lastly, Thompson and McEwen make a unique contribution by distinguishing different *kinds* of interorganizational relations.

As an aside, note that Evan's extension of the role-set concept to organizations suggests still further analogies, which may be heuristically useful. A role is a set of acts prescribed for the occupant of some position. The role accrues to the position; its occupants are interchangeable. If formal organizations are treated as social actors, then one can conceive of organizations as occupants of positions in the larger social system. Each organization has one or more roles in its behavioral repertoire (these are more commonly called functions or goals). The organization occupants of these social positions, however, are also interchangeable.

Integrative Framework

Model. It is assumed that the foregoing arguments are valid: (1) that organizational environments are increasingly turbulent; (2) that organizations are increasingly less autonomous; and (3) that other formal organizations are increasingly important components of organizational environments. Some conceptual perspective is now needed, which will make it possible to view any formal organization, its transactional interdependencies, and the environment itself within a common conceptual framework. The intent of this section is to outline the beginnings of such a framework.

A formal organization is a system primarily oriented to the attainment of a specific goal, which constitutes an output of the system and which is an input for some other system [38, *p. 33*]. Needless to say, the output of any living system is dependent upon

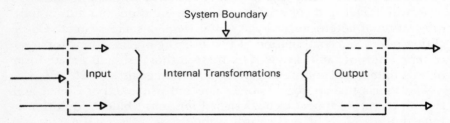

FIGURE 1   Structure of Living Systems such as a Formal Organization.

input into it. Figure 1 schematically illustrates the skeletal structure of a living system. The input and output regions are partially permeable with respect to the environment, which is the region outside the system boundary. Arrows coming into a system represent input and arrows going out of a system represent output. In Figure 2, rectangles represent formal organizations and circles represent individuals and *non*formal social organizations. Figure 2 represents the *statics* of a system X and its turbulent environment. Three-dimensional illustration would be necessary to show the *dynamics* of a turbulent environment schematically. Assume that a third, temporal dimension is imposed on Figure 2 and that this reveals an increasing number of elements and an increasing rate and complexity of change in their interdependencies over time. To do full justice to the concept of turbulence we should add other sets of elements even in Figure 2, although these are not yet linked to X's set. A notion that is integral to Emery and Trist's conception of turbulence is that changes outside of X's set, and hence difficult for X to predict and impossible for X to control, will have impact on X's transaction-

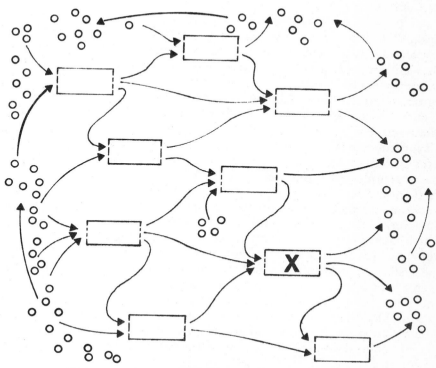

FIGURE 2   Illustration of System X in Turbulent Environment.

al interdependencies in the future. The addition of just one link at some future time may not affect the supersystem but may constitute a system break for X.

This schematization shows only one-way directionality and is meant to depict energic inputs (e.g., personnel and material) and output (e.g., product). The organization provides something in exchange for the inputs it receives, of course, and this is usually informational in nature—money, most commonly. Similarly the organization receives money for its product from those systems for whom its product is an input. Nor does our framework distinguish different kinds of inputs, although the analysis of interorganizational exchange requires this kind of taxonomic device. It seems important to distinguish energic inputs and outputs from informational ones. Energic inputs include machinery, personnel, clientele in the case of service organizations, electric power, and so on. Informational inputs are not well conceptualized although there is no doubt of their increasing importance in environments which are more complex and changeable. Special divisions of organizations and whole firms devoted to information collecting, processing, and distributing are also rapidly proliferating (e.g., research organizations, accounting firms, the Central Intelligency Agency).

An input called "legitimacy" is popular in sociological circles but highly resistant to empirical specification. The view taken here is that legitimacy is mediated by the exchange of other resources. Thus the willingness of firm A to contribute capital to X, and of agency B to refer personnel to X and firm C to buy X's product testifies to the legitimacy of X. This "willingness" on the part of organizations A, B, and C, however, can best be understood in terms of informational exchange. For example, A provides X with capital on the basis of A's information about the market for X's product. Or B refuses to refer skilled workmen to X since B has information on X's discriminatory employment practices and also knows of consequences to itself from elsewhere if it is party to X's practice. Technology is also sometimes treated as an input to organizations. We use the term, however, to refer to the complex set of interactions among inputs which takes place in the internal region shown in Figure 1. It is technology which transforms the inputs to the system into the output of the system. Transportation and communication technologies, however, are of a uniquely different order; the former constitutes an energic and the latter an informational transcendence of space-time that enabled the evolution of the more complex environments (L_{22}) which concern us here. Automation and computer technologies are roughly equivalent (i.e., energic and informational, respectively) but on an intraorganizational (L_{11}) level.

Our attention to "legitimacy" and "technology" was tangential to our main theme, to which we now return. Our simplistic approach to an integrative framework for the study of organizations (L_{11}), their transactional interdependencies (L_{21} and L_{12}), and the connectedness within their environments (L_{22}), gives the following conceptual ingredients: (1) units that are mainly formal organizations, and (2) relationships between them that are the directed flow [39] of (3) energy and information. The enormous and increasing importance of informational transaction has not been matched by conceptual developments in organization theory. The importance of information is frequently cited in a general way, however, especially in the context of organizational change or innovation. Dill has made a cogent argument on the need for more attention to this dimension [40, 94-109].

The importance of communication for organizational change has been stressed by Ohlin, March and Simon, Benne, Lippitt, and others [41]. Diversity of informational input has been used to explain the creativity of individuals as well as of social systems [42, *pp. 662-70*]. The importance of boundary positions as primary sources of innovative inputs from the environment has been stressed by March and Simon [26, 165-66, 189] and by Kahn et al. [43, *pp. 101-26*]. James Miller hypothesizes that up to a maximum, which no living system has yet reached, the more energy a system devotes to information processing (as opposed to productive and maintenance activity), the more likely the system is to survive [44, 530].

Evolution on the biological level is accompanied by improvement in the ability of systems to discover and perform according to contingencies in their environments. The random walk which suffices in a placid-randomized environment must be replaced by stochastic processes under placid-clustered conditions, and by cybernetic processes in disturbed-reactive fields. Among biological/psychological systems, only man appears to have the capacity for the purposeful behavior that may permit adaptation to or control of turbulent environments. There is some question, of course, as to whether man actually *has* the capacity to cope with the turbulence that he has introduced into the environment.

Analogous concepts are equally applicable to the evolution of social systems in general and to formal organizations in particular. The capacity of *any* system for adapting to changing contingencies in its environment is inversely related to its dependence upon instinct, habit, or tradition. Adaptability exists, by definition, to the extent that a system (L_{11}) can survive externally induced (L_{22}) change in its transactional interdependencies (L_{21} and L_{12}); therefore viability equals adaptability.

Hypotheses.   HYPOTHESIS 1.   Organizational change is largely externally induced.

Any particular change may be adaptive or maladaptive, and it may be one of these in the short run and the other in the long run.   There is *no* systematic empirical evidence on the relative influence of internal versus environmental antecedents to organizational change. The empirical task here is to identify organizational changes, and the internal or external origins of each change.

It is crucial to distinguish change on the organizational level from the multitude of changes that may occur in or among subsystems, only some of which give rise to change on the system level. Many social psychologists, for example, study change in individuals and groups *within* organizations, but with no reference to variables of organizational level. Likert's book is one noteworthy exception [45]. The important point is that change on the organizational level is analytically distinct from change on other levels.

Organizational change means any change in the kind or quantity of output. Ideally, output is treated as a function of inputs and of transfer functions (i.e., intraorganizational change is inferred from change in input-output relations). Haberstroh illustrates the use of these general system concepts in the organization context [46, 1171-1211]. An excellent discussion of the efficiency and effectiveness of organizations, in an open-systems framework, is given in Katz and Kahn [47].

However, the input-output functions in diversified industries and the outputs of many service organizations are resistant to objective specification and measurement. An empirical test of this hypothesis, with presently available tools, may have to settle for some set of input and internal change that seems to be reasonably antecedent to output change.

The identification of the origin of change is also beset by difficulties. An input change may indeed have external antecedents, but external events may also be responses to some prior internal change in the focal organization . And internal change may be internally generated, but it may also be the result of an informational input from external sources. Novel informational inputs, as well as novel communication channels, often derive from change in personnel inputs. Increasingly, organizations seek personnel who bring specialized information rather than "man power" to the organization. The presence of first, second, and higher order causation poses a problem for any empirical test of this hypothesis.

HYPOTHESIS 2.   System adaptability (e.g., organizational) is a function of ability to learn and to perform according to changing environmental contingencies.

Adaptability exists by definition, to the extent that a system can survive externally induced change in its transactional interdependencies in the long run. Diversity in a system's input (L_{21}) and output (L_{12}) interdependencies will increase adaptability. The recent and rapid diversification in major industries illustrates this strategy. Flexible structure $(L_{11}$, e.g., decentralized decision making) will facilitate adaptation. Beyond this, however, adaptability would seem to be largely a function of a system's perceptual and information-processing capacities.* The following variables appear crucial: (1) *advance information* of impending externally induced (L_{22}) change in L_{21} or L_{12} transactions; (2) *active search* for, and activation of, more advantageous input and output transactions; and (3) *available memory store* (L_{11}) of interchangeable input and output components in the environment.

Advance information and active search might be empirically handled with Evan's concept of the role-sets of boundary personnel, along with notions of channel efficiency. For example, overlapping memberships (e.g., on boards) would constitute a particularly efficient channel. Likewise, direct communication between members of separate organizations, while less effective than overlapping memberships, would be a more efficient channel between agencies A and B than instances where their messages must be mediated by a third agency, C. Efficiency of interorganizational communication channels should be positively associated with access to advance information, and be facilitative of search, for example. The members of an organization's informational set may become increasingly differentiated from its energic set. Communication channels to research and marketing firms, universities, governmental agencies and other important information producing and distributing agencies would be expected to increase long-run viability. The third variable, memory store, is probably a function of the efficiency of past and present informational channels, but it involves internal (L_{11}) information processing as well.

Lastly, *any* internal change that improves an organization's transactional advantage (e.g., improved technology) will also be conducive to adaptability. Since organizational innovation is more often imitation than invention [48, 63-70], these changes are usually also the product of information input and can be handled within the same integrative framework.

---

*Igor Ansoff speaks of the "wide-open windows of perception" required of tomorrow's firms, and offers a perspective on the future that is fully compatible with that presented here; see "The Firm of the Future," *Harv. Bus. Review*, 43 (Sept. 1965), 162.

Summary

The lag between evolution in the real world and evolution in theorists' ability to comprehend it is vast, but hopefully shrinking. It was only a little over one hundred years ago that Darwin identified natural selection as the mechanism of evolutionary process. Despite Darwin's enduring insight, theorists of change, including biologists, have continued to focus largely on internal aspects of systems.

It is our thesis that the selective advantage of one intra- or interorganizational configuration over another cannot be assessed apart from an understanding of the dynamics of the environment itself. It is the environment which exerts selective pressure. "Survival of the fittest" is a function of the fitness of the environment. The dinosaurs *were* impressive creatures, in their day.

Notes

1. Ludwig von Bertalanffy, "General System Theory," *General Systems,* 1 (1956).
2. F. E. Emery and E. L. Trist, "The Causal Texture of Organizational Environments," *Human Relations,* 18 (1965).
3. The concepts of ideal types of environment, and one of the examples in this paragraph, are from Emery and Trist, ibid.
4. The following illustrations are taken from Emery and Trist, ibid.: For random-placid environment, see Herbert A. Simon, *Models of Man* (New York: Wiley, 1957), p. 137; W. Ross Ashby, *Design for A Brain,* 2d ed. (London: Chapman, 1960), sec. 15/4; the mathematical concept of random field; and the economic concept of classical market.

   For random-clustered environment, see Edward C. Tolman and Egon Brunswick, "The Organism and the Causal Texture of the Environment," *Psychol. Review,* 42 (1935), 43-72; Ashby, op. cit., sec. 15/8; and the economic concept of imperfect competition.

   For distrubed-reactive environment, see Ashby, op. cit., sec. 7; the concept of "imbrication" from I. Chein, "Personality and Typology," *J. Social Psychol.,* 18 (1943), 89-101; and the concept of oligopoly.
5. Amitai Etzioni, "New Directions in the Study of Organizations and Society," *Social Research,* 27 (1960).
6. Peter M. Blau and Richard Scott, *Formal Organizations* (San Francisco: Chandler, 1962).
7. Talcott Parsons, *Structure and Process in Modern Societies* (New York: Free Press, 1960).
8. Lloyd E. Ohlin, "Conformity in American Society Today," *Social Work,* 3 (1958).
9. Robert C. Hood, "Business Organization as a Cross Product of Its Purposes and of Its Environment," in *Organizational Theory in Industrial Practice,* edited by Mason Haire (New York: Wiley, 1962).
10. Peter F. Drucker, "The Big Power of Little Ideas," *Harv. Bus. Review,* 42 (May 1964), 6-8; John W. Gardner, *Self-Renewal* (New York: Harper & Row, 1963), p. 107.

11. James E. McNulty, "Organizational Change in Growing Enterprises," *Admin. Sci. Quart.*, 7 (1962).
12. "Long-Range Planning and Cloudy Horizons," *Dun's Review*, 81 (Jan. 1963).
13. Lee Adler, "Symbiotic Marketing," *Harv. Bus. Review*, 44 (Nov. 1966).
14. W. R. Dill, "Environment as an Influence on Managerial Autonomy," *Admin. Sci. Quart.*, 2 (1958).
15. James D. Thompson, *Organizations in Action* (New York: McGraw, 1967).
16. Philip Selznick, *TVA and the Grass Roots* (Berkeley: Univ. of Calif., 1949).
17. V. F. Ridgway, "Administration of Manufacturer-Dealer Systems," *Admin. Sci. Quart.*, 2 (1957).
18. Sol Levine and Paul E. White, "Exchange as a Conceptual Framework for the Study of Interorganizational Relationships," *Admin. Sci. Quart.*, 5 (1961).
19. Eugene Litwak and Lydia Hylton, "Interorganizational Analysis: A Hypothesis on Coordinating Agencies," *Admin. Sci. Quart.*, 6 (1962).
20. R. H. Elling and S. Halebsky, "Organizational Differentiation and Support: A Conceptual Framework," *Admin. Sci. Quart.*, 6 (1961).
21. Earl Rubington, "Organizational Strain and Key Roles," *Admin. Sci. Quart.* 9 (1965).
22. William R. Rosengren, "Communication, Organization, and Conduct in the 'Therapeutic Milieu,'" *Admin. Sci. Quart.*, 9 (1964).
23. Burton R. Clark, "Interorganizational Patterns in Education," *Admin. Sci. Quart.*, 10 (1965).
24. John Maniha and Charles Perrow, "The Reluctant Organization and the Aggressive Environment," *Admin. Sci. Quart.*, 10 (1965).
25. Donald W. Taylor, "Decision Making and Problem Solving," in *Handbook of Organizations*, edited by James G. March (Chicago: Rand, 1965).
26. James G. March and Herbert A. Simon, *Organizations* (New York: Wiley, 1958).
27. David Braybrooke and C. E. Lindholm, *A Strategy of Decision* (Glencoe: Free Press, 1963), esp. Chaps. 3, 5.
28. Richard M. Cyert and James G. March, *A Behavioral Theory of the Firm* (Englewood Cliffs, N.J.: Prentice-Hall, 1963).
29. Shirley Terreberry, "The Evolution of Environments," mimeographed course paper (1967).
30. J. W. S. Pringle, "On the Parallel Between Learning and Evolution," *General Systems*, 1 (1956).
31. Arthur L. Stinchcombe, "Social Structure and Organizations," in *Handbook of Organizations*, edited by James G. March (Chicago: Rand, 1965).
32. Clark Kerr, *The Uses of the University* (New York: Harper Torchbooks, 1963).
33. Emile Durkheim, *The Division of Labor in Society*, translated by George Simpson (Glencoe: Free Press, 1947).
34. Kenneth E. Boulding, "The Economies of Human Conflict," in *The Nature of Human Conflict*, edited by Elton B. McNeil (Englewood Cliffs, N.J.: Prentice-Hall, 1965).
35. William M. Evan, "The Organization-Set: Toward a Theory of Interorganizational Relations," in *Approaches to Organizational Design*, edited by James D. Thompson (Pittsburgh, Pa.: Univ. of Pittsburgh Press, 1966).
36. James D. Thompson and William J. McEwen, "Organizational Goals and Environment," *Amer. Sociol. Review*, 23 (1958).
37. Examples include: Robert Morris and Ollie A. Randall, "Planning and Organization of Community Services for the Elderly," *Social Work*, 10 (1965), 96-103; Frank W. Harris, "A Modern Council Point of View," *Social Work*, 9 (1964), 34-41; Harold L. Wilensky and Charles N. Lebeaux, *Industrial*

Society and Social Welfare (New York: Russell Sage Foundation, 1958), esp. pp. 263-65.

38. Talcott Parsons, "Suggestions for a Sociological Approach to the Theory of Organizations," in *Complex Organizations,* edited by Amitai Etzioni (New York: Holt, Rinehart & Winston, 1962).

39. Dorwin Cartwright, "The Potential Contribution of Graph Theory to Organization Theory," in *Modern Organization Theory,* edited by Mason Haire (New York: Wiley, 1959), pp. 254-71.

40. William R. Dill, "The Impact of Environment in Organizational Development," in *Concepts and Issues in Administrative Behavior,* edited by Sidney Mailick and Edward H. Van Ness (Englewood Cliffs, N.J.: Prentice-Hall, 1962).

41. Ohlin, op. cit., note 8, 63; March and Simon, op. cit., note 26, pp. 173-83; Kenneth D. Benne, "Deliberate Changing as the Facilitation of Growth," in *The Planning of Change,* edited by Warren G. Bennis et al. (New York: Holt, Rinehart & Winston, 1962), p. 232; Ronald Lippitt, *The Dynamics of Planned Change* (New York: Harcourt, 1958), p. 52.

42. For example: Floyd H. Allport, *Theories of Perception and the Concept of Structure* (New York: Wiley, 1955), p. 76; William F. Ogburn and Meyer F. Nimkoff, *Sociology,* 4th ed. (Boston: Houghton, 1964).

43. Robert L. Kahn et al., *Organizational Stress* (New York: Wiley, 1964).

44. James G. Miller, "Toward a General Theory for the Behavioral Sciences," *American Psychologist,* 10 (1955).

45. Rensis Likert, *New Patterns of Management* (New York: McGraw, 1961).

46. Chadwick J. Haberstroh, "Organization Design and Systems Analysis," in *Handbook of Organizations,* edited by James G. March (Chicago: Rand, 1965).

47. Daniel Katz and Robert L. Kahn, *The Social Psychology of Organizations* (New York: Wiley, 1966), esp. pp. 149-70.

48. Theodore Levitt, "Innovative Imitation," *Harv. Bus. Review,* 44 (Sept. 1966).

Human Relations
and the
Nature of Man

Henry P. Knowles   Borje O. Saxberg

This article deals with the influence that assumptions about human nature have on human relations in our society—not only in organizations, but also across a wide range of institutions and forms of social control. No other variable weighs more heavily on the ultimate form and quality of organizational interpersonal relations. For this reason, managers need to know more about the fundamental relationship between how they value man and their own organizational lives. The authors are Henry P. Knowles, Associate Professor of Organizational Behavior, and Borje O. Saxberg, Associate Professor of Business Policy and Organizational Behavior, both in the Graduate School of Business Administration, University of Washington.

We all know how little boys love fighting. They get their heads punched. But they have the satisfaction of having punched the other fellow's head. [1, *p. 284*]

The principle of co-operation is the most dominant and biologically the most important. [2, *p. 50*]

The point is constantly made that traditional organizations work on the assumption that people are essentially opposed to work and lack the capacity for self-direction and personal responsibility. Modern theories of organization take the opposite view; i.e., people do have the capacity to become psychologically involved in cooperative activity and, under certain conditions, to be virtually self-motivated and self-controlled.

   Douglas McGregor, among others, has noted how these implicit assumptions about the nature of man influence organization and leadership in his now classic discussion of Theory X and Theory Y. The former assumes that man is innately lazy and unreliable, and

---

From *Harvard Business Review*, March-April, 1967, 20-44ff. Copyright © 1967 by the President and Fellows of Harvard College; all rights reserved.

leads to organization and control based on external or imposed authority. The latter assumes that man can be basically self-directed and creative at work if properly motivated; this assumption is said to lead toward an integrative organizational strategy.

However, neither McGregor nor other writers in this field have undertaken to reveal how deeply the roots of these assumptions about man penetrate our culture and thus how powerfully they influence human relations in our society. Not only are these assumptions important in theories of human organization, but they are also crucial in every system of thought involved with human and social control. Whether concerned with organizational strategy, the ancient social order of the Zuni, or the political theories of a Machiavelli or a Locke, one cannot escape the underlying relatedness and importance of what is assumed about man himself.

Managers need to know more about the nature, sources, and effects of one assumption or the other in order (1) to sort out and understand their own ideas about the nature of humanity, and (2) to evaluate the fundamental influence of these ideas on managerial decisions. It may be asserted that no other variable weighs more heavily on the ultimate form and quality of organizational and interpersonal relations.

The question of the basic nature of man is, of course, as old as history and probably as old as society itself. The argument, in its many forms, stems from the ancient philosophical debate as to whether man is an end or a means. Reducing the argument to its simplest terms, and considering only the extremities of the spectrum, we treat a person as an *end* when we permit him to establish his own purposes and to choose and decide for himself. Contrariwise, we treat a person as a *means* when we limit his choices and utilize him primarily as an instrument for our own ends and purposes.

Implicit in these values are central assumptions concerning (1) whether man is "good" or "evil," (2) whether he has the ability to cooperate voluntarily or must be forced to cooperate, [and] (3) whether he is a "pilot" capable of choosing or a "robot" imprisoned by circumstances and incapable of choice [3, *p. 595 ff.*]. Values such as these lie at the very core of philosophies of religion, politics, education, organization, and human relations.

It is our intention in this article to describe how the choice of one or the other of these sets of values has influenced a number of systems of thought concerned with questions of human regulation and control. We do not intend to emphasize the growing body of empirical evidence which indicates that the quality of individual and group performance varies from one kind of assumption and system to the other. This area is adequately covered in the writings of such men as Chris Argyris, Rensis Likert, and, of course, McGregor. Rather, we shall explore some of the cultural roots and branches of optimistic-pessimistic assumptions about human nature in order to show that an underlying unit exists along this dimension in a variety of human-social control systems.

Man: Pessimistic View

In their polar aspects, attitudes about human nature range from pessimism to optimism—from assumptions that evilness, predatory competition, and aggression on the one hand, to goodness, cooperation, and virtue on the other, constitute the central predispositions of men and, therefore, of the social order. Let us begin our discussion by examining how certain ideas about human-social control have been affected by the pessimistic of "means" view of man. This is the attitude that man is essentially evil and driven by aggressive and uncooperative motives and drives.

Fear versus love.   As early giants in the history of Western idea makers, Niccolo Machiavelli and Thomas Hobbes—a pair of political scientists—provide us with a suitable starting point. It will be recalled that Machiavelli in *The Prince* (1515) urged that, because of man's rebellious and uncooperative behavior, he must be strictly and ruthlessly controlled by anyone who aspires to gain or maintain a position of power. A ruler, in his view, must put aside any question of morality and must achieve control at any price and by whatever means he can find: "It is much safer to be feared than loved. . . . For it may be said of men in general that they are ungrateful, voluble, dissemblers, anxious to avoid dangers, and covetous of gain." [4, *p. 61*]

In all fairness, however, it must be made clear that he did not advocate his "end justifies the means" philosophy to benefit the prince or the ruler but to benefit the people. He assumed that only the ruler is competent to judge what the necessary ends are and must be. In furtherance of these ends, then, the ruler must resort to means which appear ruthless and deceitful.

Hobbes in the *Leviathan* (1651) outlined a theory of social relationships which makes him a direct intellectual descendant of Machiavelli. According to Hobbes, since men covet prestige, material goods, and power, and expect to attain these at their discretion, they live in perpetual fear of their neighbors: "And therefore if any two men desire the same thing, which nevertheless they cannot both enjoy, they become enemies." [5, *p. 105*]

Law must therefore define what is honest and virtuous. But, in order for law to be applicable, a common authority must exist to enforce it. Man recognizes this need out of fear of loss of life and property. As a consequence, he enters into a social contract in which he gives up to a central authority whatever rights he has had in nature. In this way, he brings about the creation of a commonwealth ruled by a sovereign. Each man is individually bound to this authority, or Leviathan, and the latter's powers are irrevocable. The sovereign is a despot; whatever he wills becomes the people's will. As the Leviathan, he represents the supremacy of law, absolute authority and power, and the bureaucracy of the state.

Survival of the fittest. Both Machiavelli and Hobbes viewed human nature primarily as a product of experience. They perceived in mankind a predominance of aggressive and selfish motives as a result of socialization rather than biological inheritance, and they designed political systems in order to constrain and control human behavior and thus create order in society.

Such orderliness in nature as a whole was also evident to Charles Darwin, who, through his research into the causes of variations in species and the contribution of these variations to the survival of species in nature, became convinced that survival was assured through a process of natural selection.

Darwin thought that survival was guaranteed only to those who were the best representatives of the species and best adapted to the conditions of the environment. The survivors were those who through physical prowess and mental agility were able to win in the competition for food and mate. The suggestion here is clear, that nature is a never-ending struggle—a competition—and that a permanent state of war exists among and between all species and the natural environment.

Darwin's interpreters suggested that as with animals so with man. Herbert Spencer, who was quick to find social implications in Darwin's biological theory, argued that among men the fittest survive; indeed, they are the only ones entitled to survive. In this, the process of natural selection in man's world favors the aggressive and the strong. Man, in this scheme, is a predatory creature. Spencer's interpretations of Darwinian theory underlie much of the creed of many nineteenth century U.S. industrialists and their philosophy of the "stewardship" of the rich and the "gospel of wealth."

(It is to be noted that Darwin himself was not willing to accept Spencer's theory that the law of natural selection applied to the human race. Actually, he turned the argument around. Man's weakness, Darwin thought, becomes his greatest strength; it forces man to establish cooperative relationships with others for protection and maintenance. In addition, Darwin attributed to man a moral feeling—one of sympathy and compassion—rather than indifference toward the weak and defective. Unhappily, it has been his fate to become associated with "survival of the fittest" as a scientific theory which is applied to man as well as other natural species.)

The invisible hand.   Often associated with Darwin as a supporter of the idea of self-regulation in human society is Adam Smith. A century earlier, he placed his special emphasis on the automaticity of economic affairs. Under his doctrine of the invisible hand, there is a just allocation of a nation's scarce resources through the price mechanism which reflects supply and demand conditions of the market. By pursuing his self-interest, each individual can further not only his own fortune but also that of society as a whole.

It is this idea of self-interest as prime mover which has led many to assume that Smith considered man to possess a basically selfish, rather than a virtuous, nature. The economic doctrine of laissez-faire which Smith originated has meant "permission to do or make what you choose"; hence, noninterference with personal indulgence. This, when combined with self-interest as motivator, would seem, ergo, to support the notion that man is by nature self-seeking, predatory, and interested only in his own good at the expense of his weaker and less fortunate fellows. For example: "It is not from the benevolence of the butcher, the brewer, or the baker that we expect our dinner, but from their regard of their own interest. We address ourselves not to their humanity, but to their self-love, and never talk to them of our own necessities, but of their advantage." [6, *p .14*]

Though there is ample evidence to indicate that Smith, like Darwin, recognized that morality and government must and do govern the actions of men, he has nevertheless become, with Darwin, a symbol of individualism.

(Smith, at one time, occupied a professorial chair in moral philosophy and in *The Theory of Moral Sentiment* [1759] made it clear that he relied on natural law and, as a reflection of that, on a natural morality which prescribed three cardinal virtues: justice, prudence, and benevolence. Though he recognized some truth in the aphorism that private vices become public virtues, he clearly assumed that, as a reflection of a natural state of equality, men in pursuit of enlightened self-interest are characterized by adherence to justice—"a scrupulous refusal ever to hurt or injure anyone else, in the pursuit of one's own interest or advantage." Smith was not concerned with production and the accumulation of goods per se, but rather with the ends served thereby. In effect, the welfare of the ordinary man was on his mind to such an extent that he implicitly took the side of the underdog, which he perceived the ordinary laboring man to be.)

Sex and aggression.   Sigmund Freud, the father of psychoanalysis and the first to explore man's unconscious mind, took a clearer position on human nature than did Machiavelli, Hobbes, Darwin, or

Smith. According to Freud, man is motivated by innate instincts and drives that he constantly struggles to pacify in ways which are antithetical to the norms of society. (These instincts and drives have been identified with sex and aggression but were really intended by Freud to refer to nature's and man's hankering to stay alive.) To the extent that society succeeds in curbing these animal forces, man becomes civilized and his energies can be turned toward socially acceptable goals. But, said Freud pessimistically: "Psychoanalysis has concluded . . . that the primitive, savage, and evil impulses of mankind have not vanished in any individual, but continue their existence, although in repressed state . . . and . . . they wait for opportunities to display their activity." [7, *p. 368*]

Freud further observed, in his *Civilization and Its Discontents* (1930), that society, itself, is perpetually threatened by the underlying hostilities which exist between human beings. Periodically, these feelings explode into open aggression which persists until the participants can once more be brought under control. However, society's attempts to neutralize destructive impulses through a "cultural superego," which defines for man what is "good" and what is "bad," create feelings of guilt. This, Freud said, is man's most urgent and important problem [8,*p. 81*]. The anxieties generated by this constant clash between man's basic nature and the demands and needs of society increase human unhappiness and lead to mental illness. Thus, Freud seems to suggest, man is essentially doomed: "From his [Freud's] point of view, society, by its very nature, forces man to repress his inborn aggression more and more. The outlook for the future is that the more civilized he becomes, the more potentially destructive he becomes." [9, *p. 151*]

Warrior and weaponmaker.   Recent evidence has been uncovered which seems to support the idea that man has been an aggressor and warrior since the beginning of his existence. Under the direction of L. S. B. Leakey, excavations conducted in South Africa—among what now appear to be the earliest remnants of man's ancestors —have uncovered man's earliest tools and have established that among them weapons occupied the most important place. The indications are that these were used not only for killing in the acquisition of food but also against man—for protection, in the defense of mate or of territory, and in the conduct of war. While the evidence is mixed, it has led some to theorize that a warlike, aggressive nature is a part of every man's inheritance.

As a consequence, it can be argued that Darwin's law of nature, survival of the fittest, also applies to man. Such an emphasis on aggression over a span of hundreds of thousands of years, Robert Ardrey has argued, must have had a permanent effect on his hereditary structure: "Man is a predator with an instinct to kill and a genetic cultural affinity for the weapon." [10, *p. 166*]

In this view the urge to aggression, the desire to dominate others, is an instinct or drive transmitted from generation to generation through the genes.

The predisposition of men toward aggression has also been noted by one of the most renowned philosophers of our own time, Henri Bergson, who wrote:

> But no matter the thing taken, the motive adduced: the origin of war is ownership, individual or collective, and since humanity is predestined to ownership by its structure, war is natural. So strong, indeed, is the war instinct, that it is the first to appear when we scratch below the surface of civilization in search of nature. We all know how little boys love fighting.

> They get their heads punched. But they have the satisfaction of having punched the other fellow's head. [1, *p. 284*]

Bergson clearly joins with those who take a pessimistic view of man. By assuming that innate, predatory, and selfish instincts are first causes, he cannot conceive of a human society—with its dependence on material possessions—as capable of avoiding conflict through the processes of reason and self-control.

Manager and managed. The underlying ideas about human nature which have been previously outlined will also be found among some thinkers whose work focuses on the relationship between the manager and the managed in business and industry. These are the writers who are generally associated with the scientific management movement and who date from about 1900.

At this time, Frederick W. Taylor, who pioneered this movement in the United States, saw a need for management to exert close control over the indifferent behavior of workmen in order to ensure their adherence to the objectives and goals of business enterprise. In spite of all the human values which have been imputed to his writings, it seems clear that Taylor and his followers made these six basic assumptions about human nature:

1. The employee is a "constant" in the production equation. The implication here is that man has a fixed nature.
2. The employee is an inert adjunct of the machine, prone to inefficiency and waste unless properly programmed.
3. The employee is by nature lazy; only managers honor the "hard work" creed of the Protestant Ethic.
4. The employee's main concern is self-interest. At work, this is always expressed in economic values.
5. Given appropriate expression, these values will make man fiercely competitive among his peers as an accumulator of financial rewards.

6. Man (at least the working man) must therefore be tightly controlled and externally motivated in order to overcome his natural desire to avoid work unless the material gains available to him are worth his effort.

In accordance with these assumptions, Taylor thought that management must assume the responsibility for specifying in detail the method to be followed by the employee in order to gain an approximation of his full output potential. In addition, a piece-rate plan would have to be included as a financial incentive to ensure maximum performance.

At about the same time, a contemporary of Taylor was developing a similar pattern of thought in Europe regarding the relationship between manager and managed. While Taylor concerned himself mainly with the shop environment, Max Weber designed the features of his ideal bureaucracy viewing the organization from the top downward.

Again, in the elements of Weber's bureaucracy—specialization of personnel, impersonality, a hierarchy of authority relationships, entry and advancement by competitive examination, written policies, rules and procedures, and others—we find the Weberian image of man as a reluctant cog in an organizational machine. Thus the great majority of employees are confined to tightly controlled and dependent relationships with their superiors.

The pervasiveness of the Taylor-Weber approach to organization and management is evident throughout industrial organization today. Management scholars such as Urwick, Mooney, and Brown, as well as important business executives like Cordiner of General Electric, Greenwalt of DuPont, and Kappel of AT&T, have generally adhered to this model of managerial control and the underlying values which emphasize the need to minimize employee resistance to work—to support the Protestant Ethic—and a consequent need for autocratic rule and the traditional bureaucratic hierarchy.

Man: Optimistic View

Now let us turn from the foregoing cynical view of the nature of man to the view which emphasizes man's strength as a potentially creative, social being. As in dealing with the opposite view discussed earlier, we shall examine how an assumption that human beings have worth and goodness influences a wide-ranging sample of systems of social control. The examples used are not intended to be other than illustrative, straddling such divergent systems of human thought as political government, psychoanalysis, sociology, and business organization.

Social instinct and reason.   Although separated in time by sixteen centuries, Marcus Tullius Cicero and John Locke shared remarkably similar ideas about the governing of men. Cicero in *On the Commonwealth* (51 B.C.) argued that men by nature believe in goodness and well-doing, and abhor savagery and baseness. On the assumption of mutual advantage, they come together in obedience to a social instinct and enough individuals are involved to form a democratic association or commonwealth for the benefit of all. Out of this emerges a leader who governs voluntary subjects through a moral claim to their allegiance rather than through regulation based on force.

Locke, in *The Second Treatise of Government*, contended that men of reason are inherently disposed toward mutual support and cooperation: "The state of nature has a law of nature to govern it, which obliges everyone; and reason, which is that law, teaches all mankind who will but consult it that, being all equal and independent, no one ought to harm another in his life, health, liberty, or possessions." [11, *p. 5*]

In other words, Locke argued that man's fundamental potential is reason and *reason itself* establishes cooperation as the basis for human relationships.

Under Locke's concept of the social contract, agreement is reached between free men to entrust to the community the authority to protect the common welfare. This custodianship is continued through tacit consent and is subject to the rule of majority. For Locke, man is naturally disposed toward doing good, and government is essentially a convenience. The sovereign is assumed to will what the people will. Locke believed that man's mind at birth is a *tabula rasa*, a blank sheet of paper, and, therefore, that man becomes a person through sense impressions, mediated by reason, which he derives from social experience.

Thus the human mind and character are shaped by interaction with the world; whatever man becomes is a function of reason and social interaction. The function of government, therefore, is not to create its own laws as a controlling force but to discover what natural forces bring man to a state of reason *in which he can control himself.*

Cooperation and survival.   Two men of science, W. C. Allee, a biologist, and Ashley Montagu, a cultural anthropologist, have advanced ideas from their own fields about human nature which correspond in important respects with those of Cicero and Locke. They have argued that nature, from a biological standpoint, supports the concept of survival through cooperation rather than competition.

Allee reported in his *Cooperation Among Animals* the results of a wealth of research which provides evidence that cooperative, social relationships increase the probability of survival for any single individual as well as for a species as a whole. One of his simple experiments showed that it takes proportionately less toxic colloidal silver to kill a single goldfish in an aquarium than if the aquarium holds a number of goldfish. He suggested that the ability of a group of goldfish to neutralize a poison appears to increase faster than that of a single goldfish. He concluded his discussion of complex animal life in this way: "The conclusion seems inescapable that the more closely knit societies arose from some sort of simple aggregation . . . such an evolution could come about most readily with the existence of an underlying pervasive element of unconscious proto-cooperation, or automatic tendency toward mutual aid among animals." [12, *p. 29*]

As Allee explored further evidences of cooperation in higher animals, he came to this conclusion: "All through the animal kingdom—from amoeba to insects, or to man—animals show automatic unconscious proto-cooperation or even true cooperation. There is much evidence that the drift toward natural cooperation is somewhat stronger than the opposing tendency toward disoperation [among crowded animals]." [12, *p. 203*]

However, in spite of his argument that a cooperative social instinct is readily found in nature, Allee also recognized a counter-principle. This principle was that threat or force will be employed on the part of individuals, animal or man, to dominate others in a group in order to establish a hierarchy or pecking order. And he felt impelled to add that "much can be said for an established order of dominance and subordination" [12, *p. 204*].

Allee pointed to evidences from the animal world which seem to reveal that any single individual thrives better where the pecking order is firmly established than where constant reorganization is in progress. He also saw evidence for this on the world scene. However, in all cases, Allee believed there will finally appear a subordinate to challenge the existing order. Thus he concluded that a pecking order brings peace and stability for the *short* run, but that an integrated unit characterized by natural cooperation promises stability for the *long* run.

Montagu agreed in all essential respects with Allee. He argued that from a biological point of view men prefer to survive through cooperation rather than competition: "The principle of co-operation is the most dominant and biologically the most important." [2, *p. 50*]

Montagu, of course, was particularly concerned with man rather than with the animal world. He believed that man from infancy on must rely on others for the satisfaction of his needs, and therefore affinity for interdependence is a fundamental reflection of the social state: "All of man's natural inclinations are toward the development of goodness, toward the continuance of states of goodness and the discontinuance of unpleasant states." [2, *p. 57*]

Thus warfare is considered by Montagu, as it was by Allee, as a human invention derived from economic or materialistic, rather than biological, considerations.

"Blank page" concept. On the basis of their more sanguine views of man's nature, these men, from Cicero through Montagu, have set forth behavioral concepts which support the idea of cooperation over aggression in the human relationships and the need for strengthening these relationships through a constructive process of learning. Much of modern thought in psychoanalysis and psychotherapy, in sociology and social psychology, and in the field of organizational studies is also based on an optimistic view of man's nature. It resists Descartes' assumption that men are born with innate ideas and a more or less given nature.

Thus many modern behavioral scientists tend, like Locke, to think of man as entering life with a mind like a blank page on which experience is then impressed, and out of which the form and content of his personality are molded. To this way of thought, man's behavior is acquired in life and changes with experience. It is not solely predetermined by the genes, nor is it fixed and irrevocable. Out of these views have emerged new ways of perceiving man as an individual and as a member of a group.

Earlier, we outlined the pessimistic view of man on which Freud based his psychoanalytic theory. Freud's assumption about man's innate nature affected his theories in the same way as Hobbes's assumptions about man influenced his theories of government and society—man, left to his own devices, will prey on other men to satisfy his desires and must, in the interests of all, be restrained by forces in society.

The psychoanalysts who followed Freud have made distinctive contributions to modern view of the nature of man. From among them has emerged a group which broke with Freud on the issue of the basic nature of man, the so-called neo-Freudians, represented in this discussion by Harry Stack Sullivan, Erich Fromm, and Karen Horney. The neo-Freudians base their theories of human behavior on the assumption that the development of personality is influenced primarily by external societal forces and events rather than by biogenetically determined, innate instincts or drives.

Freud, of course, assumed that man and society are basically divided—on the one hand, a set of drives in man (sex and aggression) which are at the root of man's evil and, on the other, a set of rules in the human culture which inhibit and control the individual. The neo-Freudians argue that there is no dichotomy between man and society. According to Fromm: "The most beautiful as well as the most ugly inclinations of man are not a part of a fixed and biologically given human nature but result from the social process." [13, *p. 12*]

Necessarily, then, if man is to be understood, major attention must be given to those forces in his environment which influence the molding of his personality.

J. A. C. Brown in *The Social Psychology of Industry* has described the difference between Freudian and neo-Freudian ideas about the nature of man as the difference between thinking of man as being "pushed from behind" or "drawn from in front." This, in a rough way, is the difference between psychological determinism or behaviorist psychology—with its focus on drives, instincts, or the conditioned reflex as a source of behavior—and subjectivist theories of psychology, which perceive psychic energy as being derived from personal goals and personal perceptions of reality. Sullivan's theory of personality development, like those of Fromm and Horney, belongs in this latter category.

According to Sullivan, the individual begins life with certain potentials and two basic goals: satisfaction and security. The extent to which he realizes his potential and achieves his goals depends on his experiences with other people. The pursuit of "satisfaction" has to do with satisfying physical needs like sleep, hunger, and sex.

However, the manner in which such needs are satisfied does not depend on the innate characteristics of an individual but reflects behavior patterns which are the product of interpersonal relations. It is in relation to other people that an individual seeks "security" —that is, in the avoidance of anxiety caused by feelings of disapproval or inadequacy in a social situation. Thus the matter of psychological security is culture-bound, and the form and content of the human personality is a product of specific cultural forces.

Sullivan defines the anxiety-free condition of "euphoria" as a tensionless state similar to that experienced by a new-born and sleeping child who has yet to discover that he has arrived in a threatening environment. Such an infant is at peace with the world or, in Rousseau's terms, in a state of oneness and harmony with nature. Only exposure to the anxieties which arise out of human relationships can change this profound sense of well-being into a state of tension. This state of tension then promotes education and learning through which the self-system of an individual finally emerges.

The self-system, as Sullivan defines it, represents that portion of an individual's potential which is realized, while the "true self" contains the maximum potentialities which could have, under ideal conditions of experience, been developed. Since it is an unfortunate fact of life in our culture that interpersonal experience is far from ideal, Sullivan felt that most people are "inferior caricatures of what they might have been" [14, *p. 167*].

Cultural determination.   Fromm does not accept the "blank page" concept of Locke but, nevertheless, strongly rejects the idea that instincts are the primary source of human behavior. Fromm concedes that man comes into existence with a set of drives and instincts. However, he argues that their particular patterns of development and their manifestation in the behavior of individuals are culturally determined: "Any given social order does not create these fundamental strivings but it determines which of the limited number of potential passions are to become manifest or dominant." [15, *p. 14*]

From this, it is clear that Fromm considers that human potentialities depend to a very large extent on the *will to productiveness which society succeeds in bringing to man.* The individual is shaped by society. The environment in which the individual exists, therefore, becomes a primary factor in the way he responds to life and work.

Fromm emphasizes in his theory that man is faced with a desire to be part of nature. Animals, through their instinctual equipment, seem able to accommodate themselves to the external environment through what appears to be an automatic process and, therefore, to achieve close ties with nature. Man, in contrast, through self-awareness and reason is alienated from nature.

In fact, in industrial society he is often alienated from himself, from meaningful human relationships, and from his work. In this process man is caught in a tug-of-war between self-reliance, power, control over nature, independence, and escape from isolation, competition, hostility, and insecurity. He must find his path by relating to things and to people. Ideally, he should succeed in establishing a productive relationship in which he is able to feel and act in accordance with his potential for contributing to constructive human life.

Pilot or robot?   As our final example of modern psychoanalytic thought, we consider Karen Horney. In her writings Horney agrees with Sullivan and Fromm in the view that Freud gave biological and genetic factors an excessive role in character formation. Taking the position that man's nature is not instinctive but learned, she was one of the first analysts to emphasize the importance of interpersonal relations in behavior development. What an individual learns—that is, how he reacts to life with others—is influenced most by the way he is treated by others.

It was Horney's view that all individuals in their natural development seek sentiments of liking and approval from others. Where interpersonal relationships do not have such support, anxiety develops and begins to interfere with the growth of a healthy personality. In such cases people respond to others in three basic ways: (1) by "moving toward people"—feeling inadequate, they become attached and dependent; (2) by "moving against people"—rejected, they become rebellious and aggressive; or (3) by "moving away from people" —they seek comfort for rejection in symbolic substitutes and fantasy. Neurotic behavior occurs when there is conflict over which response pattern to adopt in a given situation. Various defense mechanisms help solve such conflicts but at the expense of genuineness in human relationships and of needed problem-solving behavior.

Because of her emphasis on the importance of situational factors in personality development, Horney tended to look to a person's present interpersonal involvements for the causes and solutions to neurotic problems. She did not deny that a connection exists between an individual's current responses and his early life—a connection which was so important a part of Freud's thinking—but she argued that one must look to the present situation for clues as to what triggered these responses.

Man is not, therefore, doomed by a set of prenatally determined instincts, nor are his patterns of behavior eternally established by early life experience. Horney's concept of man is cheerful and optimistic, not gloomy and pessimistic. Man is born neither a devil nor a saint; he simply reflects in his behavior the nature of relationships developed since the time of his birth with people who were important to him.

The insights into human nature which have been outlined above and which summarize the thinking of an important school of modern psychotherapy are based on the confident viewpoint that man is not doomed by a fixed and evil nature from which he cannot escape. Rather, they would seem to suggest just the opposite: man has within himself the potential to grow and develop significantly in cooperation with others. Man is a pilot not a robot. What is needed is not a method of controlling innately selfish or even predatory drives toward war with other men, but a means of tapping man's potential for joining in productive relationships with others.

Individual or environment?   One of the first social scientists to apply this concept of man to analysis of industrial organizations was Elton May of Harvard University. Mayo's view of human nature was optimistic and anti-Freudian. To illustrate: "The concealed assumption of the doctrine of original sin invalidates the psychoanalytic findings. The theory that life is a strenuous fight to subdue perversion, that the human mind is by nature 'pathogenic' (i.e., predisposed to the pathological) is not a starting point for biological observation." [16, *p. 152*]

In other words, the concept that life on earth is an atonement for original transgressions of God's laws, and that man is cursed with a set of evil instincts which must be curbed by society, is inadequate as a base for observing and understanding man's behavior in daily life.

Mayo argued that too much attention was being given in industrial settings to *individuals* as the source of noncooperative and unproductive relationships between the leadership of the organization and those who are employed to accomplish the work. He pointed out that developments in sociology and in social anthropology had already opened to serious question whether a merely psychological study of individuals in an organization is a logical approach to a comprehension of their behavior as workers.

On the contrary, Mayo said, such individuals constitute a group which develops responses to the total organizational environment. On the basis of this, the research interview program at the Hawthorne Works, originally consisting of isolated interviews, was restructured so that interviewers were assigned to study individuals over extended periods in relation to their jobs, the informal social organization in which they worked, and company policy.

The original isolated interviewing method was based on the premise that personal behavior or misbehavior was a result of personal rationality or irrationality; the second method assumed that the individual was only one of a number of interdependent variables relating to behavior. These other variables were part of the working environment and included such factors as leadership, working conditions, and working group membership. Science, inspired by the work of early sociologists and anthropologists, was at last beginning to show, contrary to Hobbesian theory, that man was more victim than antagonist in his environment.

Behavioral science man. While the initial thrust toward change in managerial philosophy and practice can be traced back to the origin of the human relations movement in the 1930's, it has continued through the present time in two somewhat divergent directions: (1) toward the fusion of the scientific organizational behavior approach with a new, more humanistic management philosophy, and (2) toward organizational reeducation and change through sensitivity or laboratory training. In both cases the importance of the roles played by behavioral and other social scientists in defining the relationship between the manager and the managed is becoming more and more evident.

While Mayo's work resulted in increasing the emphasis on human relations mainly in normative terms, much of the subsequent direction of this work is based on the research and findings of the behavioral sciences of sociology, psychology, social psychology, and cultural anthropology. Research workers such as Argyris, McGregor, and Likert have identified themselves with A. H. Maslow's theory of the need hierarchy as an aspect of human nature. Given the assumption that a satisfied need does not motivate, man is seen as satisfying in ascending order the needs of hunger in an extended sense, safety, social affection, esteem, and finally self-actualization or self-fulfillment.

The challenge for management today is seen by these authors as one of providing man at work with the opportunity to grow and mature continually into a human being who, because of a favorable working climate, is able to realize his own goals best by working for the success of the organization of which he is a member. Implicit in their assumptions is the idea that man has an essential nature which is defined by the broad spectrum of his needs, capacities, and tendencies. These needs, as expressed by Maslow, "are on their face good or neutral rather than evil" [17, *p. 340*].

In a continuing reflection of the neo-Freudian view of man, we find McGregor stating, "If employees are lazy, indifferent, unwilling to take responsibility, intransigent, uncreative, uncooperative," this is due to the traditional bureaucratic assumptions and methods of organization and control [18, *p. 48*]. Argyris, in a similar vein suggests, "Mutal understanding, trust, self-esteem, openness, internal commitment, fully functioning human beings who aspire to excellence . . . these values can not only be protected, but indeed increased, in an industrial setting." [19, *p. 5*]

In the world of work, therefore, man is seen by the behavioral scientists as responding to the influences of his organizational environment. Given the opportunity, he will participate creatively in furthering the objectives of the organization. If frustrated, his behavior will characteristically revert to the basic need level of hunger; he will turn apathetic, slovenly, and totally alienated from an orientation toward work as a central life interest.

Such a basic underlying belief in man as a creative human being oriented toward constructive rather than destructive activities is even more clearly represented in the sensitivity training movement. Through this process of reeducation and skill development, Warren G. Bennis and his collaborators see the way to democratization of management—a condition which they view as essential in the face of accelerating technological change, the increasing proportion of professionals in the work force, and the consequent necessity of the organization to accept the values of science and scientific inquiry in order to survive in the future.

("Democracy" is here defined not as permissiveness or laissez-faire but as a system of values by which people in organizations are assumed to feel "internally compelled" to live. These include free communication, the consensus principle, influence based on competence rather than position, acceptance of emotion as fact, and a "basically human bias" in dealing with conflict.) [20, 51]

In Bennis' terms, the "organization man" becomes a signpost on the road pointing the way to the kinds of flexibility and adaptability which are essential if the democratic environment in which science and scientists can flourish is to be realized. Whether one agrees or not, it is well known among men of science that personalities are only of passing interest compared to the contribution they hope to make to the accumulation of new knowledge.

Where Do You Stand?

We have confined the discussion to the pessimistic-optimistic views for the sake of simplicity and clarity, although it is, of course, a matter of common observation that all of the possible social processes are located along a continuum whose polar extremities are mutual cooperation and predatory competition.

As opposite ends of a spectrum, cooperation and competition are closely related to love and hate, friendship and enmity, harmony and discord, collaboration and opposition. They may therefore be used to describe a person's *basic* or *characteristic* propensity toward his fellowman. In terms of his attitudes toward others, every man will find himself at some point on this spectrum depending on the particular situation in which he is involved.

However, each man is drawn by the force of his own history and experience toward some primary tendency, some central quality of being, which determines the general pattern of his social behavior. Peripheral changes occur in this pattern to accommodate the demands of the various roles he plays, but there would seem to be a core pattern which represents his basic beliefs concerning the nature of man. Man is evil or man is good, depending on man's experience with mankind.

The examples from the history of human thought that we have cited illustrate this concept of the *primary tendency* in the kind of view one man takes of another. They also clearly indicate that cooperation and competition, or goodness and evilness, as human characteristics, are not discrete activities or qualities but rather exist in various mixtures in human nature.

Hobbes's *primary tendency*, for example, was to view man as evil. Nevertheless, his idea of the "social contract" contains the implicit assumption of *cooperative* activity among men by which they give up their rights to a ruling Leviathan to gain protection from one another. Bergson said that war in a materialistic society is natural, but he noted that collective ownership leads to cooperation within groups to protect members from outsiders. Even Freud, who comes closest to a concept of innately evil men straining against societal constraints to satisfy their needs, conceded that man may become "good" because of his dependency on others; he will, in short, *cooperate* when he finds helping behavior in other men.

Among those whose primary tendency is to view man as good, we find similar ambivalences:

- Locke argued that reason evoked cooperation among men. However, he implied that the "social contract" exists between ruler and ruled to control man's acquired *competitive*, aggressive nature.
- The neo-Freudians believed that man's goodness or evilness was a product of experience—that is, competitive (hating) experiences lead to malfunctioning by societal standards, but cooperative (loving) experiences lead to satisfaction and to development.

The psychoanalytic assumptions and clinical findings of the neo-Freudians to the effect that man has basic worth and is capable of constructive psychic responses in an environment of understanding and encouragement have received scientific support among modern experimenters. Behavioral Science Man, whether the setting has been in the laboratory or in the field—in a business, education, or government organization—is a "good" man whose potential for productive growth and self-actualization has too often been stunted by his superiors' outmoded assumptions that he is "bad." Therefore, for their purposes, he must be manipulated like a puppet on a string.

Conclusion

The quality of human relations in any organization, from the political state to the business enterprise, reflects first of all its members', and particularly its leaders', views of the essential character of humanity itself. It makes a great deal of difference in systems of social control whether those involved tend to view man, in general, as good or evil. If we assume that man is good, we can believe that misbehavior is a reactive response rather than a manifestation of character. This will lead to a search for causes in his experience rather than in his nature. If we are to find a cause for behavioral failure, we are more apt to look outside the offender than inside and thus consider a whole new range of variables and contributory circumstances.

If, on the other hand, we assume that man himself is bad, a priori, then we are prone to assume that misbehavior is caused by something within him which we cannot alter directly. Accordingly, our attention will focus on limiting his freedom to choose and to act through external curbs or controls. In limiting the causes of behavior, we exclude ourselves from powerful internal sources of control.

Thus the underlying human value which predominates is readily perceived in (1) the way social relationships are structured; (2) the kinds of rewards and penalties that are used; (3) the character of the communication process which links people together, and (4) the other elements of social control that characterize a relationship or an organization.

Notes

1. Henri Bergson, *The Two Sources of Morality and Religion* (Garden City, N.Y.: Doubleday, Anchor Books, 1935).
2. Ashley Montagu, *Man in Process* (New York: New American Library, Mentor, 1962).
3. The terms "pilot" and "robot" have been borrowed from Donald H. Ford and Hugh B. Urban, *Systems of Psychotherapy* (New York: Wiley, 1965).
4. Niccolo Machiavelli, *The Prince and the Discourses* (New York: Random House, Modern Library, 1950).
5. Thomas Hobbes, *Leviathan* (Indianapolis: Bobbs, Library of Liberal Arts, 1958).
6. Adam Smith, *An Inquiry into the Nature and Causes of the Wealth of Nations* (New York: Random House, Modern Library, 1937).
7. Letter from Freud to Dr. van Eeden, quoted in Ernest Jones, *The Life and Work of Sigmund Freud*, Vol. II (New York: Basic Books, 1957).
8. Sigmund Freud, *Civilization and Its Discontents*, translated by James Strachey (New York: Norton, 1961).
9. Clara Thompson, *Psychoanalysis: Its Evolution and Development*, 1st ed. (New York: Grove Press, Evergreen, 1957).
10. Robert Ardrey, *African Genesis* (New York: Dell, 1961).
11. John Locke, *The Second Treatise of Government* (New York: Liberal Arts Press, 1952).
12. W. C. Allee, *Cooperation Among Animals* (New York: Henry Schuman, 1951).
13. Erich Fromm, *Escape from Freedom* (New York: Farrar & Rinehart, 1941).
14. J. A. C. Brown, *Freud and the Post-Freudians* (Baltimore: Penguin Books, 1961).
15. Erich Fromm, *The Sane Society* (New York: Holt, Rinehart & Winston, 1955).
16. Elton Mayo, *The Human Problems of an Industrial Civilization* (New York: Viking Press, 1960).
17. A. H. Maslow, *Motivation and Personality* (New York: Harper, 1954).
18. Douglas McGregor, *The Human Side of Enterprise* (New York: McGraw, 1960).
19. Chris Argyris, *Interpersonal Competence and Organizational Effectiveness* (Homewood, Ill.: Dorsey Press and Richard D. Irwin, Inc., 1962).
20. See Philip E. Slater and Warren G. Bennis, "Democracy Is Inevitable," *Harv. Bus. Rev.*, (March-April 1964).

On the
Concept of
Organizational Goal

Herbert A. Simon

It is difficult to introduce the concept of organizational goal without reifying the organization—treating it as something more than a system of interacting individuals. On the other hand, the concept of a goal appears indispensable to organization theory. This paper proposes a definition of "organizational goal" that resolves this dilemma.

The goal of an action is seldom unitary, but generally consists of a whole set of constraints the action must satisfy. It appears convenient to use the term "organizational goal" to refer to constraints, or sets of constraints, imposed by the organizational role, that have only an indirect relation with the personal motives of the individual who fills the role. More narrowly, "organizational goal" may be used to refer particularly to the constraint sets that define roles at the upper levels of the administrative hierarchy.

In actual organizations, the decision-making mechanism is a loosely coupled, partially decentralized structure in which different sets of constraints may impinge on decisions at different organizational locations. Although the description of organizational goals is consequently complex, the concept of goal can still be introduced in an entirely operational manner.

Herbert A. Simon is professor of administration and psychology in the Graduate School of Industrial Administration, Carnegie Institute of Technology. [1]

Few discussions of organization theory manage to get along without introducing some concept of "organization goal." In the classical economic theory of the firm, where no distinction is made between an organization and a single entrepreneur, the organization's goal—the goal of the firm—is simply identical with the goal of the real or hypothetical entrepreneur. In general, it is thought not to be

From *Administrative Science Quarterly*, 9 (June 1964), 1-22. Copyright © 1964 by Graduate School of Business and Public Administration, Cornell University.

problematical to postulate that individuals have goals. If it is not, this solution raises no difficulties.

When we are interested in the internal structure of an organization, however, the problem cannot be avoided in this way. Either we must explain organizational behavior in terms of the goals of the individual members of the organization, or we must postulate the existence of one or more organization goals, over and above the goals of the individuals.*

The first alternative is an attractive one. It protects us from the danger of reifying the organization, of treating it as a superindividual entity having an existence and behavior independent of the behavior of its members. The difficulty with this alternative is that it is hard to carry off. The usual way it is attempted is by identifying the phrase "organization goals" with "goals of the firm's owners" or, alternatively, "goals of the firm's top management," or "goals of those who hold legitimate authority to direct the organization."

But this solution raises new difficulties, for we often have occasion to observe that the goals that actually underlie the decisions made in an organization do not coincide with the goals of the owners, or of top management, but have been modified by managers and employees at all echelons. Must we conclude, then, that it is the goals of the latter—of subordinate managers and employees—that are governing organizational behavior? Presumably not, because the kinds of behavior taking place are not those we would expect if the managers and employees were consulting only their personal goals. The whole concept of an informal organization, modified by, but not identical with, the goals either of management or of individual employees, becomes hazy and ambiguous if we follow this path.

Let us see if we can find a way between this Scylla and the Charybdix of reification. The first step toward clarification is to maintain a distinction between goals, on the one hand, and motives, on the other. By *goals* we shall mean value premises that can serve as inputs to decisions. By *motives* we mean the causes, whatever they are, that lead individuals to select some goals rather than others as premises for their decisions. In the next section we shall develop the concept of goal, defined as above. In subsequent sections we shall undertake to explicate the notion of *organization goal* and to clarify the relations between organization goals and personal motives.

Before we can define "organization goals" we shall have to be clear on what we mean by "goals of an individual." We shall begin by considering the latter question.

---

*The present discussion is generally compatible with, but not identical to, that of my colleagues, R. M. Cyert and J. G. March, who discuss organizational goals in ch. iii of *A Behavioral Theory of the Firm* (Englewood Cliffs, N.J.: Prentice-Hall, 1963). Their analysis is most germane to the paragraphs of this paper that treat of motivation for goals and organizational survival.

Goals and Decisions: Multiple Criteria

Our discussion of goals will be much simplified if we have a definite model before us of the situation we are considering. In recent years in the field of management science or operations research, we have learned to build formal models to characterize even quite elaborate and complex decision situations, and to use these models to reach "optimal" decisions. Since many of these models make use of the tool of linear programming, we will employ a linear programming framework to describe the decision situation. No mathematical knowledge will be assumed beyond the ability to read algebraic notation [2].

The optimal diet problem is a typical simple linear programming problem. We are given a list of foods, and for each item on the list its price, its calory content, and its proportions of each of the minerals and vitamins relevant to nutrition. Then we are given a set of nutritional requirements, which may include statements about minimum daily intake of minerals, vitamins, and calories, and may also put limits on maximum intake of some or all of these components.

The diet problem is to find that sublist of foods and their quantities that will meet the nutritional requirements at least cost. The problem can be formalized as follows:

Let the various foods be numbered from *1* through N, and the various nutritional components from *1* through M. Let x_i be the quantity of the ith food in the diet, y_j be the total quantity of the jth nutritional component in the diet, and p_i the price of the ith food. Let a_{ij} be the amount of the jth nutritional component in a unit quantity of the ith food; let b_j be the minimum requirement of the jth nutritional component, and c_j the maximum allowance. (Some of the b_j's may be zero, and some of the c_j's infinite.) Then:

(1) $\sum_i a_{ij}x_i = y_j$,   for $j = 1, \ldots, M$;

i.e., the total consumption of the jth nutritional element is the sum of the quantities of that element for each of the foods consumed. The nutritional requirements can be stated:

(2) $c_j \geqslant y_j \geqslant b_j$,   for $j = 1, \ldots, M$;

i.e., the total quantity of the jth element must lie between b_j and c_j. The quantity of each food consumed must be non-negative, although it may be zero:

(3) $x_i \geqslant 0$, $i = 1, \ldots, N$.

Finally, the total cost of the diet is to be minimized; we are to find:

(4) $\underset{x}{\text{Min}} \sum_i x_i p_i$

A diet (the solution is not necessarily unique) that satisfies all the relations (2), (3), (4) is called an *optimal* diet. A diet that satisfies the inequalities (2) and (3) (called *constraints*), but which is not necessarily a minimum cost diet, is called a *feasible* diet.

What is the goal of the diet decision? It would be an appropriate use of ordinary language to say that the goal is to minimize the cost of obtaining an adequate diet, for the condition (4) is the criterion we are minimizing. This criterion puts the emphasis on economy as the goal.

Alternatively, we might direct our attention primarily to the constraints, and in particular to the nutritional requirements (2). Then we might say that the goal is to find a nutritionally satisfactory diet that is economical. Although we still mention costs in this statement, we have clearly shifted the emphasis to the adequacy of the diet from a nutritional standpoint. The primary goal has now become good nutrition.

The relation between the criterion function (4) and the constraints (2) can be made even more symmetrical. Let us replace the criterion (4) with a new constraint:

(5) $\Sigma\, x_i p_i \leqslant k,$

that is to say, with the requirement that the total cost of the diet not exceed some constant, k. Now the set of feasible diets has been restricted to those that satisfy (5) as well as (2) and (3). But since the minimization condition has been removed, there is apparently no basis for choosing one of these diets over another.

Under some circumstances, we can, however, restrict the set of diets that deserve consideration to a subset of the feasible set. Suppose that all the nutritional constraints (2) are minimal constraints, and that we would always prefer, *ceteris paribus*, a greater amount of any nutritional factor to a smaller amount. We will say that diet A is dominated by diet B if the cost of diet B is no greater than the cost of diet A, and if diet B contains at least as much of each nutritional factor as does diet A, and more of at least one factor. We will call the set of diets in the feasible set that is undominated by other diets in that set the Pareto optimal set.

Our preference for one or the other of the diets in the Pareto optimal set will depend on the relative importance we assign to cost in comparison with amounts of nutritional factors, and to the amounts of these factors in relation with each other. If cost is the most important factor, then we will again choose the diet that is selected by criterion (4). On the other hand, if we attach great importance to nutritional factor j, we will generally choose a quite different feasible diet—one in which the quantity of factor j is as great as possible. Within the limits set by the constraints, it would

be quite reasonable to call whatever criterion led us to select a particular member of the Pareto optimal set our goal. But if the constraints are strong enough, so that the feasible set and, *a fortiori*, the
Pareto optimal set is very small, then the constraints will have as
much or more influence on what diet we finally select than will
the goal, so defined. For example, if we set one or more of the
nutritional requirements very high, so that only a narrow range of
diets also satisfy the budget constraint (5), then introducing the
cost minimization criterion as the final selection rule will have
relatively little effect on what diet we choose.

Under such circumstances it might be well to give up the idea
that the decision situation can be described in terms of a simple
goal. Instead, it would be more reasonable to speak of a whole
set of goals—the whole set, in fact, of nutritional and budgetary
constraints—that the decision maker is trying to attain. To para-
phrase a familiar epigram: "If you allow me to determine the
constraints, I don't care who selects the optimization criterion."

Multiple Criteria in Organizations

To show the organizational relevance of our example it is only
necessary to suppose that the decision we are discussing has arisen
within a business firm that manufactures commercial stock feeds,
that the nutritional requirements are requirements for hogs and
the prices those of available feed ingredients, and that the finished
feed prices facing the firm are fixed. Then minimizing the cost of
feed meeting certain nutritional standards is identical with maximizing the profit from selling feed meeting those standards. Cost
minimization represents the profit-maximizing goal of the company.

We can equally well say that the goal of the feed company is to
provide its customers with the best feed possible, in terms of nutritional standards, at a given price, i.e., to produce feeds that are in
the Pareto optimal set. Presumably this is what industry spokesmen
mean when they say that the goal of business is not profit but efficient production of goods and services. If we had enlarged our model
to give some of the prices that appear in it the status constraints, instead of fixing them as constants, we could have introduced other
goals, for example, the goal of suppliers' profits, or, if there were a
labor input, the goal of high wages [3].

We may summarize the discussion to this point as follows. In the
decision-making situations of real life, a course of action, to be acceptable, must satisfy a whole set of requirements, or constraints.
Sometimes one of these requirements is singled out and referred to
as the goal of the action. But the choice of one of the constraints,
from many, is to a large extent arbitrary. For many purposes it is

more meaningful to refer to the whole set of requirements as the (complex) goal of the action. This conclusion applies both to individual and organizational decision making.

Search for a Course of Action

Thus far, we have assumed that the set of possible actions is known in advance to the decision maker. In many, if not most, real-life situations, possible courses of action must be discovered, designed, or synthesized. In the process of searching for a satisfactory solution, the goals of the action—that is, the constraints that must be satisfied by the solution—may play a guiding role in two ways. First, the goals may be used directly to synthesize proposed solutions (*alternative generation*). Second, the goals may be used to test the satisfactoriness of a proposed solution (*alternative testing*) [4].

We may illustrate these possibilities by considering what goes on in the mind of a chess player when he is trying to choose a move in a game. One requirement of a good move is that it put pressure on the opponent by attacking him in some way or by preparing an attack. This requirement suggests possible moves to an experienced player (alternative generation). For example, if the opponent's king is not well protected, the player will search for moves that attack the king, but after a possible move has been generated in this way (and thus automatically satisfies the requirement that it put pressure on the opponent), it must be tested against other requirements (alternative testing). For example, it will not be satisfactory if it permits a counterattack that is more potent than the attack or that can be carried out more quickly.

The decisions of everyday organizational life are similar to these decisions in chess. A bank officer who is investing trust funds in stocks and bonds may, because of the terms of the trust document, take as his goal increasing the capital value of the fund. This will lead him to consider buying common stock in firms in growth industries (alternative generation). But he will check each possible purchase against other requirements: that the firm's financial structure be sound, its past earnings record satisfactory, and so on (alternative testing). All these considerations can be counted among his goals in constructing the portfolio, but some of the goals serve as generators of possible portfolios, others as checks [5].

The process of designing courses of action provides us, then, with another source of asymmetry between the goals that guide the actual synthesis and the constraints that determine whether possible courses of action are in fact feasible. In general, the search will continue until one decision in the feasible set is found, or, at most, a very few alternatives. Which member of the feasible set is discovered and selected may depend considerably on the search process, that is, on which requirements serve as goals or generators, in the sense just defined, and which as constraints or tests.

In a multiperson situation, one man's goals may be another man's constraints. The feed manufacturer may seek to produce feed as cheaply as possible, searching, for example, for possible new ingredients. The feed, however, has to meet certain nutritional specifications. The hog farmer may seek the best quality of feed, searching, for example, for new manufacturers. The feed, however, cannot cost more than his funds allow; if it is too expensive, he must cut quality or quantity. A sale will be made when a lot of feed is feasible in terms of the requirements of both manufacturer and farmer. Do manufacturer and farmer have the same goals? In one sense, clearly not, for there is a definite conflict of interest between them: the farmer wishes to buy cheap, the manufacturer to sell dear. On the other hand, if a bargain can be struck that meets the requirements of both—if the feasible set that satisfies both sets of constraints is not empty—then there is another sense in which they do have a common goal. In the limiting case of perfect competition, the constraints imposed by the market and the technology actually narrow down the feasible set to a single point, determining uniquely the quantity of goods they will exchange and the price.

The neatness and definiteness of the limiting case of perfect competition should not blind us to the fact that most real-life situations do not fit this case exactly. Typically, the generation of alternatives (e.g., product invention, development, and design) is a laborious, costly process. Typically, also, there is a practically unlimited sea of potential alternatives. A river valley development plan that aims at the generation of electric power, subject to appropriate provision for irrigation, flood control, and recreation will generally look quite different from a plan that aims at flood control, subject to appropriate provision for the other goals mentioned. Even though the plans generated in both cases will be examined for their suitability along all the dimensions mentioned, it is almost certain that quite different plans will be devised and proposed for consideration in the two cases, and that the plans finally selected will represent quite distinct points in the feasible set.

In later paragraphs we shall state some reasons for supposing that the total sets of constraints considered by decision makers in different parts of an organization are likely to be quite similar, but that different decision makers are likely to divide the constraints between generators and tests in quite different ways. Under these circumstances, if we use the phrase organization goals broadly to denote the constraint sets, we will conclude that organizations do, indeed, have goals (widely shared constraint sets). If we use the phrase organization goals narrowly to denote the generators, we will conclude that there is little communality of goals among the several parts of large organizations and that subgoal formation and goal conflict are prominent and significant features of organizational life. The distinction we have made between generators and tests helps resolve this ambiguity, but also underlines the importance of always making explicit which sense of goal is intended.

Motivation for Goals

If by motivation we mean whatever it is that causes someone to follow a particular course of action, then every action is motivated —by definition. But in most human behavior the relation between motives and action is not simple; it is mediated by a whole chain of events and surrounding conditions.

We observe a man scratching his arm. His motive (or goal)? To relieve an itch.

We observe a man reaching into a medicine cabinet. His motive (or goal)? To get a bottle of lotion that, his wife has assured him, is very effective in relieving the itch of mosquito bites. Or have we misstated his motive? Is it to apply the lotion to his arm? Or, as before, to relieve the itch? But the connection between action and goal is much more complex in this case than in the previous one. There intervenes between them a means-end chain (get bottle, apply lotion, relieve itch), an expectation (that the lotion will relieve the itch), and a social belief supporting the expectation (that the wife's assurance is a reliable predictor of the lotion's efficacy). The relation between the action and the ultimate goal has become highly indirect and contingent, even in this simple case. Notice that these new complications of indirectness are superimposed on the complications we have discussed earlier—that the goal is pursued only within limits imposed by numerous side constraints (don't knock over the other bottles in the medicine cabinet, don't brush against the fresh paint, and so on).

Our point is identical with the point of the venerable story of the three bricklayers who were asked what they were doing. "Laying bricks," "Building a wall," "Helping to erect a great cathedral," were their respective answers. The investment trust officer whose behavior we considered earlier could answer in any of these modes, or others. "I am trying to select a stock for this investment portfolio." "I am assembling a portfolio that will provide retirement income for my client." "I am employed as an investment trust officer." Now it is the step of indirectness between the second and third answers that has principal interest for organization theory. The investment trust officer presumably has no "personal" interest in the retirement income of his client, only a "professional" interest in his role as trust officer and bank employee. He does have, on the other hand, a personal interest in maintaining that role and that employment status.

Role Behavior

Of course, in real life the line of demarcation between personal and professional interests is not a sharp one, for personal satisfactions may arise from the competent performance of a professional role, and both personal satisfactions and dissatisfactions may result from innumerable conditions that surround the employment. Nevertheless, it is exceedingly important, as a first approximation, to distinguish between the answers to two questions of motive: "Why do you keep (or take) this job?" and "Why do you make this particular investment decision?" The first question is properly answered in terms of the personal motives or goals of the occupant of the role, the second question in terms of goals that define behavior appropriate to the role itself.

Corresponding to this subdivision of goals into personal and role-defined goals, organization theory is sometimes divided into two subparts: (1) a theory of motivation explaining the decisions of people to participate in and remain in organizations; and (2) a theory of decision making within organizations comprised of such people [6]

In the motivational theory formulated by Barnard and me, it is postulated that the motives of each group of participants can be divided into *inducements* (aspects of participation that are desired by the participants) and *contributions* (aspects of participation that are inputs to the organization's production function but that generally have negative utility to participants). Each participant is motivated to maximize, or at least increase, his inducements while decreasing his contributions, and this motivation is a crucial consideration in explaining the decision to join (or remain). But "joining" means accepting an organizational role, and hence we do not need any additional motivational assumptions beyond those of inducements-contributions theory to explain the ensuing role-enacting behavior.

I hasten to repeat the caveat, introduced a few paragraphs above, that in thus separating our consideration of organizational role-enacting behavior from our consideration of personal motivation —allowing the decision to join as the only bridge between them —we are proposing an abstraction from the complexities of real life. A good deal of the significant research on human relations and informal organization, which has contributed heavily in the last generation to our understanding of organizational behavior, has been concerned specifically with the phenomena that this abstraction excludes. Thus, desire for power and concern for personal advancement represent an intrusion of personal goals upon organizational role, as do the social and craft satisfactions and dissatisfactions associated with work.

To say that the abstraction is sometimes untenable is not to deny that there may be many situations in which it is highly useful. There are, first of all, many organizational decisions that simply do not affect personal motives at all—where organizational goals and personal goals are orthogonal, so to speak. As a trivial example, the secretary's inducement-contribution balance is generally in no whit affected by the choice between typing a letter to A or a letter to B or by the content of the letter. Second, personal motives may enter the decision process as fixed constraints (only courses of action that satisfy the constraints are considered, but the constraints have no influence on the choice of action within the set). Thus, the terms of the employment contract may limit work to a forty-hour week but may have little to say about what goes on during the forty hours [7].

The abstraction of organizational role from personal goals turns out to be particularly useful in studying the cognitive aspects of organizational decision making, for the abstraction is consonant with some known facts about human cognitive processes. Of all the knowledge, attitudes, and values stored in a human memory, only a very small fraction are evoked in a given concrete situation. Thus, an individual can assume a wide variety of roles when these are evoked by appropriate circumstances, each of which may interact only weakly with the others. At one time he may be a father, at another a machinist, at another a chess player. Current information processing theories of human cognition postulate that there is only modest overlap of the subsets of memory contents—information and programs—that are evoked by these several roles. Thus, we might postulate that the day-to-day organizational environment evokes quite different associations out of the memory of the participant from those evoked when he is considering a change of jobs. To the extent this is so, it provides a further explanation of why his "personal" system of inducements and contributions, i.e., the utilities that enter into the latter decisions, will have no effect on his "organizational" decisions, i.e., those that are made while the first set is evoked.

The ability of a single individual to shift from one role to another as a function of the environment in which he finds himself thus helps explain the extent to which organizational goals become internalized, that is, are automatically evoked and applied during performance of the role. By whatever means the individual was originally motivated to adopt the role in the first place, the goals and constraints appropriate to the role become a part of the decision-making program, stored in his memory, that defines his role behavior.

Interpersonal Differences

Although the considerations introduced in the last section show
that the uncoupling of organizational role from personal goals need
not be complete, it may be useful to indicate a little more specifically how differences among individuals can affect their behavior in
roles that are identical from an organizational standpoint.

A role must be understood not as a specific, stereotyped set of
behaviors, but as a *program* (as that word is understood in computer
technology) for determining the courses of action to be taken over
the range of circumstances that arise. In previous sections we have
given examples of such programs and have shown that they can be
highly complex; for instance, a single decision may be a function of
a large number of program instructions or premises.

Thus, while we may conceive of an ideal type of role that incorporates only organizational goals among its premises, the roles that
members of organizations actually enact invariably incorporate both
organizational and personal goals. We have already seen how both
can be part of the total system of constraints.

But interpersonal differences in the enactment of roles go far beyond the incorporation of personal goals in the role. Role behavior
depends on means-end premises as well as goal premises. Thus,
particular professional training may provide an individual with specific techniques and knowledge for solving problems (accounting
techniques, legal techniques, and so on), which are then drawn upon
as part of the program evoked by his role. In this way, a chief executive with an accounting background may find different problem
solutions from a chief executive, in the same position, with a legal
background.

An individual may incorporate in his role not only a professional
style but also a personal style. He may bring to the role, for example, habits and beliefs that provide him with crucial premises for his
handling of interpersonal relations. Thus, an authoritarian personality will behave quite differently from a more permissive person
when both are in the same organizational role and pursuing the same
organizational goals.

The leeway for the expression of individual differences in role behavior is commonly narrowest in the handling of those matters that
come to the role occupant at the initiative of others and is commonly
broadest in his exercise of initiative and in selecting those discretion-
ary matters to which he will attend and give priority. In terms used
in earlier paragraphs, premises supplied by the organizational environment generally control alternative selection more closely than alternative generation.

The Organizational Decision-Making System

Let us limit ourselves for the present to situations where occupational roles are almost completely divorced from personal goals and pursue the implications of this factoring of the behavior of organizational participants into its personal and organizational components. If we now consider the organizational decision-making programs of all the participants, together with the connecting flow of communication, we can assemble them into a composite description of the organizational decision-making system—a system that has been largely abstracted from the individual motives that determine participation.

In the simplest case, of a small, relatively unspecialized organization, we are back to a decision-making situation not unlike that of the optimal diet problem. The language of "goals," "requirements," "constraints," that we applied there is equally applicable to similarly uncomplicated organizational situations.

In more complicated cases, abstracting out the organizational decision-making system from personal motives does not remove all aspects of interpersonal (more accurately, interrole) difference from the decision-making process. For when many persons in specialized roles participate in making an organization's decisions, the total system is not likely to be monolithic in structure. Individual roles will differ with respect to the number and kinds of communications they receive and the parts of the environment from which they receive them. They will differ with respect to the evaluative communications they receive from other roles. They will differ in their search programs. Hence, even within our abstraction, which neglects personal motives, we can accommodate the pheonmena of differential perception and subgoal formation.

To make our discussion more specific, let us again consider a specific example of an organizational decision-making system—in this case a system for controlling inventory and production. We suppose a factory in which decisions have to be made about (1) the aggregate rate of production, that is, the work force that will be employed and the hours employees will work each week, (2) the allocation of aggregate production facilities among the several products the factory makes, and (3) the scheduling of the sequence in which the individual products will be handled on the production facilities. Let us call these the aggregate production decision, item allocation decision, and scheduling decision, respectively. The three sets of decisions may be made by different roles in the organization; in general, we would expect the aggregate decision to be handled at more central levels than the others. The real world situation will

always include complications beyond those we have described, for
it will involve decisions with respect to shipments to warehouses,
decisions as to which products to hold in warehouse inventories,
and many others.

Now we could conceive of an omniscient Planner (the entrepreneur
of classical economic theory) who, by solving a set of simultaneous
equations, would make each and all of these interrelated decisions.
Decision problems of this kind have been widely studied during the
past decade by management scientists, with the result that we now
know a great deal about the mathematical structures of the problems
and the magnitude of the computations that would be required to
solve them. We know, in particular, that discovery of the optimal
solution of a complete problem of this kind is well beyond the powers of existing or prospective computational equipment.

In actual organizational practice, no one attempts to find an optimal solution for the whole problem. Instead, various particular
decisions, or groups of decisions, within the whole complex are
made by specialized members or units of the organization. In making
these particular decisions, the specialized units do not solve the
whole problem, but find a "satisfactory" solution for one or more
subproblems, where some of the effects of the solution on other
parts of the system are incorporated in the definition of "satisfactory."

For example, standard costs may be set as constraints for a manufacturing executive. If he finds that his operations are not meeting
those constraints, he will search for ways of lowering his costs.
Longer production runs may occur to him as a means for accomplishing this end. He can achieve longer production runs if the number of
style variations in product is reduced, so he proposes product standardization as a solution to his cost problem. Presumably he will not
implement the solution until he has tested it against constraints introduced by the sales department—objections that refusal to meet special requirements of customers will lose sales.

Anyone familiar with organizational life can multiply examples of
this sort, where different problems will come to attention in different parts of the organization, or where different solutions will be
generated for a problem, depending on where it arises in the organization. The important point to be noted here is that we do not have
to postulate conflict in personal goals or motivations in order to
explain such conflicts or discrepancies. They could, and would,
equally well arise if each of the organizational decision-making roles
were being enacted by digital computers, where the usual sorts of
personal limits on the acceptance of organizational roles would be
entirely absent. The discrepancies arise out of the cognitive inability
of the decision makers to deal with the entire problem as a set of

simultaneous relations, each to be treated symmetrically with the others [8].

An aspect of the division of decision-making labor that is common to virtually all organizations is the distinction between the kinds of general, aggregative decisions that are made at high levels of the organization, and the kinds of specific, item-by-item decisions that are made at low levels. We have already alluded to this distinction in the preceding example of a system for controlling inventory and production. When executives at high levels in such a system make decisions about "aggregate inventory," this mode of factoring the decision-making problem already involves radical simplification and approximation. For example, there is no single, well-defined total cost associated with a given total value of aggregate inventories. There will generally be different costs associated with each of the different kinds of items that make up the inventory(for example, different items may have different spoilage rates or obsolescence rates), and different probabilities and costs associated with stockouts of each kind of item. Thus, a given aggregate inventory will have different costs depending on its composition in terms of individual items.

To design a system for making decisions about the aggregate work force, production rate, and inventories requires an assumption that the aggregate inventory will never depart very far from a typical composition in terms of individual item types. The assumption is likely to be tolerable because subsidiary decisions are continually being made at other points in the organization about the inventories of individual items. These subsidiary decisions prevent the aggregate inventory from becoming severely unbalanced, hence make averages meaningful for the aggregate.

The assumption required for aggregation is not unlike that made by an engineer when he controls the temperature of a tank of water, with a single thermometer as indicator, knowing that sufficient mixing of the liquid in the tank is going on to maintain a stable pattern of temperature relations among its parts. Without such a stable pattern it would be infeasible to control the process by means of a measurement of the average temperature.

If one set of decisions is made, on this approximate basis, about aggregate work force, production rate, and inventories, then these decisions can be used as constraints in making detailed decisions at subsidiary levels about the inventory or production of particular items. If the aggregate decision has been reached to make one million gallons of paint next month, then other decisions can be reached as to how much paint of each kind to make, subject to the constraint that the production quotas for the individual items should, when added together, total one million gallons [9].

This simple example serves to elucidate how the whole mass of decisions that are continually being made in a complex organization can be viewed as an organized system. They constitute a system in which (1) particular decision-making processes are aimed at finding courses of action that are feasible or satisfactory in the light of multiple goals and constraints, and (2) decisions reached in any one part of the organization enter as goals or constraints into the decisions being made in other parts of the organization.

There is no guarantee that the decisions reached will be optimal with respect to any overall organizational goal. The system is a loosely coupled one. Nevertheless, the results of the overall system can be measured against one or more organizational goals, and changes can be made in the decision-making structure when these results are adjudged unsatisfactory.

Further, if we look at the decision-making structure in an actual organization, we see that it is usually put together in such a way as to insure that the decisions made by specialized units will be made in cognizance of the more general goals. Individual units are linked to the total system by production schedules, systems of rewards and penalties based on cost and profit goals, inventory limits, and so on. The loose coupling among the parts has the positive consequence of permitting specific constraints in great variety to be imposed on subsystems without rendering their decision-making mechanisms inoperative.

The Decision-Making System and Organizational Behavior

In the previous sections great pains were taken to distinguish the goals and constraints (inducements and contributions) that motivate people to accept organizational roles from the goals and constraints that enter into their decision making when they are enacting those organizational roles. On the one hand, the system of personal inducements and contributions imposes constraints that the organization must satisfy if it is to survive. On the other hand, the constraints incorporated in the organizational roles, hence in what I have called here the organizational decision-making system, are the constraints that a course of action must satisfy in order for the organization to adopt it.

There is no necessary *logical* connection between these two sets of constraints. After all, organizations sometimes fail to survive, and their demise can often be attributed to failure to incorporate all the important motivational concerns of participants among the constraints in the organizational decision-making system. For example, a major cause of small business failure is working capital shortage, a result of failure to constrain actions to those that are consistent with creditors' demands for prompt payment. Similarly new products often fail because incorrect assumptions about the inducements important to consumers are reflected in the constraints that guide product design. (It is widely believed that the troubles of the Chrysler Corporation stemmed from the design premise that car purchasers were primarily interested in buying a good piece of machinery.)

In general, however, there is a strong empirical connection between the two sets of constraints, for the organizations we will usually observe in the real world—those that have succeeded in surviving for some time—will be precisely those which have developed organizational decision-making systems whose constraints guarantee that their actions maintain a favorable balance of inducements to contributions for their participants. The argument, an evolutionary one, is the same one we can apply to biological organisms. There is no logical requirement that the temperatures, oxygen concentrations, and so on, maintained in the tissues of a bird by its physiological processes should lie within the ranges required for its survival. It is simply that we will not often have opportunities for observing birds whose physiological regulators do not reflect these external constraints. Such birds are soon extinct.*

Thus, what the sociologist calls the functional requisites for survival can usually give us good clues for predicting organizational goals; however, if the functional requisites resemble the goals, the similarity is empirical, not definitional. What the goals are must be inferred from observation of the organization's decision-making processes, whether these processes be directed toward survival or suicide.

Conclusions

We can now summarize our answers to the question that introduced this paper: What is the meaning of the phrase "organizational goal"? First, we discovered that it is doubtful whether decisions are generally directed toward achieving *a* goal. It is easier, and clearer, to view decisions as being concerned with discovering courses of action that satisfy a whole set of constraints. It is this set, and not any one of its members, that is most accurately viewed as the goal of the action.

---

*The relation between the functional requisites for survival and the actual constraints of the operating system is a central concept in W. R. Ashby's notion of a multistable system. See his *Design for a Brain*, 2d ed. (London: Chapman, 1960).

If we select any of the constraints for special attention, it is (a) because of its relation to the motivations of the decision maker, or (b) because of its relation to the search process that is generating or designing particular courses of action. Those constraints that motivate the decision maker and those that guide his search for actions are sometimes regarded as more "goal-like" than those that limit the actions he may consider or those that are used to test whether a potential course of action he has designed is satisfactory. Whether we treat all the constraints symmetrically or refer to some asymmetrically as goals is largely a matter of linguistic or analytic convenience.

When we come to organizational decisions, we observe that many, if not most, of the constraints that define a satisfactory course of action are associated with an organizational role and hence only indirectly with the personal motives of the individual who assumes that role. In this situation it is convenient to use the phrase organization goal to refer to constraints, or sets of constraints, imposed by the organizational role, which has only this indirect relation to the motives of the decision makers.

If we examine the constraint set of an organizational decision-making system, we will generally find that it contains constraints that reflect virtually all the inducements and contributions important to various classes of participants. These constraints tend to remove from consideration possible courses of action that are inimical to survival. They do not, of course, by themselves often fully determine the course of action.

In view of the hierarchical structure that is typical of most formal organizations, it is a reasonable use of language to employ organizational goal to refer particularly to the constraint sets and criteria of search that define roles at the upper levels. Thus it is reasonable to speak of conservation of forest resources as a principal goal of the U.S. Forest Service, or reducing fire losses as a principal goal of a city fire department. For high-level executives in these organizations will seek out and support actions that advance these goals, and subordinate employees will do the same or will at least tailor their choices to constraints established by the higher echelons with this end in view.

Finally, since there are large elements of decentralization in the decision making in any large organization, different constraints may define the decision problems of different positions or specialized units. For example, "profit" may not enter directly into the decision making of most members of a business organization. Again, this does not mean that it is improper or meaningless to regard profit as a principal goal of the business. It simply means that the decision-making mechanism is a loosely coupled system in which the profit constraint is only one among a number of constraints and enters into most subsystems only in indirect ways. It would be both legitimate and realistic to describe most business firms as directed toward profit making—subject to a number of side constraints—operating through a network of decision-making processes that introduces many gross approximations into the search for profitable courses of action. Further, the goal ascription does not imply that any employee is motivated by the firm's profit goal, although some may be.

This view of the nature of organization goals leaves us with a picture of organizational decision making that is not simple. But it provides us with an entirely operational way of showing, by describing the structure of the organizational decision-making mechanism, how and to what extent over-all goals, like "profit" or "conserving forest resources" help to determine the actual courses of action that are chosen.

Notes

1. This inquiry has been pursed under a grant from the Carnegie Corporation as part of a larger study on complex information processes. I am deeply indebted to Herbert Kaufman for persuading me of the need for the kind of clarification attempted here and for his helpful comments on a first draft.
2. There are now a substantial number of elementary discussions of linear programming in the management science literature. For a treatment that develops the point of view proposed here, see A. Charnes and W. W. Cooper, *Management Models and Industrial Applications of Linear Programming* (New York: Wiley, 1961), ch. i. See also Charnes and Cooper, "Deterministic Equivalents for Optimizing and Satisfying under Chance Constraints," *Operations Research,* 11 (1963), 18-39.
3. See "A Comparison of Organization Theories," in my *Models of Man* (New York: Wiley, 1957), pp. 170-182.
4. For further discussion of the role of generators and tests in decision making and problem solving, see A. Newell and H. A. Simon, "The Processes of Creative Thinking," in H. E. Gruber, G. Terrell, and M. Wertheimer, editors, *Contemporary Approaches to Creative Thinking* (New York: Atherton, 1962), particularly pp. 77-91.
5. G. P. E. Clarkson, "A Model of Trust Investment Behavior," R. M. Cyert and J. G. March, *A Behavioral Theory of the Firm* (Englewood Cliffs, N.J.: Prentice-Hall, 1963).
6. For further discussion and references, see J. G. March and H. A. Simon, *Organizations* (New York: Wiley, 1958), ch. iv.
7. See "A Formal Theory of Employment Relations," *Models of Man,* op. cit., note 3.
8. For some empirical evidence, see D. C. Dearborn and H. A. Simon, "Selective Perception: A Note on the Departmental Identification of Executives," *Sociometry,* 21 (1958), 140-44.
9. A system of this kind is developed in detail in "Determining Production Quantities under Aggregate Constraints," C. Holt, F. Modigliani, J. Muth, and H. A. Simon, *Planning Production, Inventories, and Work Force* (Englewood Cliffs, N.J.: Prentice-Hall, 1960).

A Framework
for the
Comparative Analysis
of Organizations

Charles Perrow

Complex organizations are conceptualized in terms of their technologies, or the work done on raw materials. Two aspects of technology vary independently: the number of exceptions that must be handled, and the degree to which search is an analyzable or unanalyzable procedure. If there is a large number of exceptions and search is not logical and analytic, the technology is described as nonroutine. Few exceptions and analyzable search procedures describe a routine technology. Two other types result from other combinations—craft and engineering technologies. Task structures vary with the technology utilized, and are analyzed in terms of control and coordination and three levels of management. Social structure in turn is related to technology and task structure. Finally, the variations in three types of goals are weakly related to the preceding variables in this conceptualization. The perspective provides a basis for comparing organizations which avoids many problems found in other schemes utilizing structure, function, or goals as the basis for comparison. Furthermore, it allows one to selectively utilize competing organizational theories once it is understood that their relevance is restricted to organizations with specific kinds of technologies. The scheme makes apparent some errors in present efforts to compare organizations. [1]

This paper presents a perspective on organizations that hopefully will provide a basis for comparative organizational analysis, and also allow one to utilize selectively the existing theories of organizational behavior. There are four characteristics of this perspective.

First, technology, or the work done in organizations, is considered the defining characteristic of organizations. That is, organizations

From *American Sociological Review*, April, 1967, 194-208. Copyright © 1967 by American Sociological Association.

are seen primarily as systems for getting work done, for applying techniques to the problem of altering raw materials—whether the materials be people, symbols, or things. This is in contrast to other perspectives which see organizations as, for example, cooperative systems, institutions, or decision-making systems.

Second, this perspective treats technology as an independent variable, and structure—the arrangements among people for getting work done—as a dependent variable. Goals are conceived of as being in part a dependent variable. What is held to be an independent and dependent variable when one abstracts general variables from a highly interdependent and complex social system is less of an assertion about reality than a strategy of analysis. Thus, no claim is made that for all purposes technology need be an independent variable.

Third, this perspective attempts to conceptualize the organization as a whole, rather than to deal only with specific processes or subparts. Thus, while the importance of technology has often been demonstrated within work groups or for particular organizational processes, here it will be used as a basis for dealing with the organization as an organization.

Finally, and in the long run perhaps most importantly, the perspective holds that technology is a better basis for comparing organizations than the several schemes which now exist.*

None of these points in itself is new, and the last section of this article discusses the uses to which the concept of technology has been put by others. However, the attempt to deal with all four points simultaneously, or, to put it differently, to pay systematic attention to the role of technology in analyzing and comparing organizations as a whole, is believed to be distinctive.

Technology and Raw Materials

By technology is meant the actions that an individual performs upon an object, with or without the aid of tools or mechanical devices, in order to make some change in that object. The object, or "raw material," may be a living being, human or otherwise, a symbol, or an inanimate object. People are raw materials in people-changing or people-processing organizations; symbols are materials in banks, advertising agencies, and some research organizations; the interactions of people are raw materials to be manipulated by administra-

---

*E.g., social function (schools, business firms, hospitals, etc.), as used by Talcott Parsons in *Structure and Process in Modern Society* (Glencoe, Ill.: Free Press, 1960), pp. 44-7; who benefits, proposed by Peter M. Blau and William R. Scott in *Formal Organizations* (San Francisco: Chandler, 1962), pp. 42-5; or compliance structure, as used by Amitai Etzioni, *A Comparative Analysis of Complex Organizations* (New York: Free Press, 1961).

tors in organizations; boards of directors, committees, and councils are usually involved with the changing or processing of symbols and human interactions, and so on.

In the course of changing this material in an organizational setting, the individual must interact with others. The form that this interaction takes we will call the structure of the organization. It involves the arrangements or relationships that permit the coordination and control of work. Some work is actually concerned with changing or maintaining the structure of an organization. Most administrators have this as a key role, and there is a variety of technologies for it. The distinction between technology and structure has its gray areas, but basically it is the difference between an individual acting directly upon a material that is to be changed and an individual interacting with other individuals in the course of trying to change that material. In some cases the material to be changed and the "other individuals" he interacts with are the same objects, but the relationships are different in each case.

There are a number of aspects of technology which are no doubt important to consider in some contexts, such as the environment of the work (noise, dirt, etc.) or the possibilities of seductive or exploitative relationships with clients, patients or customers. For our purposes, however, we are concerned with two aspects of technology that seem to be directly relevant to organizational structure. The first is the number of exceptional cases encountered in the work,* that is, the degree to which stimuli are perceived as familiar or unfamiliar. This varies on a scale from low to high.

The second is the nature of the search process that is undertaken by the individual when exceptions occur. We distinguish two types of search process. The first type involves a search which can be conducted on a logical, analytical basis. Search processes are always exceptional actions undertaken by the individual. They are nonroutine. No programs exist for them. If a program exists, only a very trivial search is involved in switching from one program to another program when the stimuli change [2, *p. 142*]. But though nonroutine, one type of search may be logical, systematic, and analytical. This is exemplified by the mechanical engineering unit of a firm building large machinery, or by programmers writing individual programs for slow readers in a special school. The second type of search process occurs when the problem is so vague and poorly conceptualized as to make it virtually unanalyzable. In this case, no

---

*Cf. James March and Herbert Simon, *Organizations* (New York: Wiley, 1958), pp. 141-42, where a related distinction is made on the basis of search behavior. In our view the occurrence of an exceptional case is prior to search behavior, and various types of search behavior can be distinguished.

"formal" search is undertaken, but instead one draws upon the residue of unanalyzed experience or intuition, or relies upon chance and guesswork. Examples would be work with exotic metals or nuclear fuels, psychiatric casework, and some kinds of advertising. We can conceive of a scale from analyzable to unanalyzable problems.

If we dichotomize these two continua into the presence or absence of exceptional cases and into the presence or absence of analyzable problems, we have a four-fold table as in Figure 1. The upper right-hand quadrant, cell 2, where there are many exceptional cases and a few analytic techniques for analyzing them, is one extreme to which we will refer as nonroutine. In the lower left-hand quadrant, cell 4, we have the routine extreme, where there are few exceptions and there are analytic techniques for handling those that occur. A one-dimensional scheme would follow the dotted line from routine to nonroutine. But note that the other two quadrants may represent viable cases in themselves and they have been labeled with some industrial examples. Few cases would probably fall in the upper left-hand corner of cell 1, or lower right-hand corner of cell 3, but otherwise many organizations are expected to appear in these two cells.

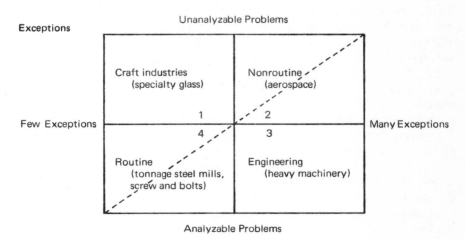

Technology Variable
(Industrial Example)

Search

Unanalyzable Problems

FIGURE 1

Techniques are performed upon raw materials. The state of the art of analyzing the characteristics of the raw materials is likely to determine what kind of technology will be used. (Tools are also necessary, of course, but by and large, the construction of tools is a simpler problem than the analysis of the nature of the material and generally follows the analysis.) To understand the nature of the material means to be able to control it better and achieve more predictability and efficiency in transformation. We are not referring here to the "essence" of the material, only to the way the organization itself perceives it.

The other relevant characteristic of the raw material, besides the understandability of its nature, is its stability and variability; that is, whether the material can be treated in a standardized fashion or whether continual adjustment to it is necessary. Organizations uniformly seek to standardize their raw material in order to minimize exceptional situations. This is the point of de-individualizing processes found in military academies, monasteries and prisons, or the superiority of the synthetic shoe material Corfam over leather.

These two characteristics interact, or course. On the one hand, increased knowledge of the nature of the material may lead to the perception of more varieties of possible outcomes or products, which in turn increases the need for more intimate knowledge of the nature of the material. Or the organization, with increased knowledge of one type of material, may begin to work with a variety of related materials about which more needs to be known, as when a social service agency or employment agency relaxes its admission criteria as it gains confidence, but in the process sets off more search behavior, or when a manufacturing organization starts producing new but related products. On the other hand, if increased knowledge of the material is gained but no expansion of the variety of output occurs, this permits easier analysis of the sources of problems that may arise in the transformation process. It may also allow one to prevent the rise of such problems by the design of the production process.

A recent analysis of a public defender system by Sudnow highlights the twin characteristics of the material variable [3, 255-76]. On the one hand, offenders are distributed into uniform categories by means of the conception of the "normal crime," and on the other hand, control over the individual offender is insured because the public defender well understands the offender's "nature"—that is, his low status, limited understanding and intellectual resources, and his impecunious condition. The technology, then, can be routine because there are few exceptions (and these are handled by a different set of personnel) and no search behavior on the public defender's part is required. The lawyer in private practice, of course, is a contrasting case [4].

It will readily be seen that these two characteristics of the raw material are paralleled in the four-fold table of technology (Figure 2). If the technology of an organization is going to move from cell 2 to

Raw Material Variables
(People-Changing Examples)

Perceived Nature of Raw Material

Variability of Material

Not Well Understood

	Socializing institutions (e.g. some schools)	Elite psychiatric agency
Perceived as uniform and stable	1	2
	4	3
	Custodial institutions, vocational training	Programmed learning school

Perceived as non-uniform and stable

Well Understood

FIGURE 2

any of the other cells, it can only do so either by reducing the variability of the material and thus the number of exceptional cases that occur, or by increasing the knowledge of the material and thus allowing more analytic techniques to be used, or both. One may move from cell 2 to cell 1 with increasing production runs, clients served, accounts handled, research projects underway, agency programs administered and so forth, since this allows more experience to be gained and thus reduces the number of stimuli seen as exceptions. If technical knowledge increases, increasing the reliability of search procedures, one may move from cell 2 to cell 3. If both things happen—and this is the aim of most organizations—one may move from cell 2 to cell 4.*

Task and Social Structure

For our purpose, the task structure of an organization is conceived of as consisting of two dimensions, control and coordination. Control itself can be broken up into two components. They are the degree of discretion an individual or group possesses in carrying out its tasks, and the power of an individual or group to mobilize scarce resources and to control definitions of various situations, such as the definition of the nature of the raw material. Discretion here does not mean freedom from supervision or freedom simply to vary task

---

*Some organizations, such as mental hospitals, perceive that their technology is inadequate to their goals, and try to move from cell 4 to cell 2 in the search for a new technology.

sequences or pace of work. Both of these are compatible with routine activities, and some nonroutine tasks must be closely supervised or have precise sequences of tasks, once a program is selected, because of their critical nature. Nor does the length of time between performance reviews necessarily indicate discretion [5]. Rather, discretion involves judgments about whether close supervision is required on one task or another, about changing programs, and about the interdependence of one's task with other tasks.* Discretion and power may often be correlated,† but there is an important distinction. Power affects outcomes directly because it involves choices regarding basic goals and strategies. Discretion relates to choices among means and judgments of tasks. The consequences of decisions in the case of discretion have no direct influence on goals and strategies; these decisions are formed within the framework of accepted goals and strategies.

Coordination, on the other hand, can be achieved through planning or feedback, to use the terms proposed by March and Simon [2, *p. 160*]. Coordination by planning refers to the programmed interaction of tasks, which interaction is clearly defined by rules or by the very tools and machinery or the logic of the transformation process. Coordination by feedback, on the other hand, refers to negotiated alterations in the nature or sequence of tasks performed by two different units.

It is now necessary to distinguish three functional or task areas within management in organizations. Area One, the design and planning function, entails such major decisions as what goods or services are to be produced, who the customers will be, the technology employed, and the source of legitimacy and capital. Area Two, the

---

*This raises serious operationalization problems. In my own work, first-line supervisors were said to have considerable independence in some routine production situations, and to have little in some nonroutine situations, according to a questionnaire, though it was observed that the former had little discretion and the latter a good deal. Kovner found the same kind of responses with a similar question regarding control of job and pace of work among nurses in routine and nonroutine nursing units. See Anthony Kovner, "The Nursing Unit: A Technological Perspective," unpublished Ph.D. dissertation (University of Pittsburgh, 1966). See also the discrepancy between scores on a similar matter resulting from different interpretations of discretion in two studies: Rose L. Coser, "Authority and Decision-Making in a Hospital," *Amer. Sociological Review*, 23 (Feb. 1958), 56-64, and James L. Hawkins and Eugene Selmanoff, "Authority Structure, Ambiguity of the Medical Task, Absence of Doctor from the Ward, and Behavior of Nurses," mimeo (Indiana University).

† See, for example, a developmental scheme which holds that critical tasks requiring considerable discretion are the basis for group domination in hospitals and other organizations, in Charles Perrow, "Analysis of Goals in Complex Organizations," *Amer. Sociological Review*, 26 (April 1961), 335-41. See also the compelling illustration presented in the discussion of maintenance personnel in a thoroughly routinized cigarette factory by Michel Crozier, *The Bureaucratic Phenomenon* (Chicago: Univ. of Chicago Press, 1964), Chap. 4.

technical control and support of production and marketing, includes such functions (to use industrial terms) as accounting, product and process research, quality control, scheduling, engineering, plant management, purchasing, customer service, advertising, market research, and general sales management. (Not all are important, or even existent, of course, in all industrial organizations.) This is distinguished as a function, though not necessarily in terms of actual persons or positions, from Area Three, the supervision of production and marketing. This area involves the direct supervision of those dealing with the basic raw materials and those doing direct selling.* In the subsequent discussion we shall ignore marketing, and, for a time, Area One.

Figure 3 shows crudely the kinds of values that might be expected to appear in the task structure, considering only Areas Two and Three—technical control and support of production, and the supervision of production. Some global organizational characterizations of structure are given at the bottom of each cell. Those familiar with Burns and Stalker's work will recognize cell 2 as closest to the organic structure and cell 4 as closest to the mechanistic structure [6].

In cell 2, we have nonuniform raw materials in both areas which are not well understood, and thus present many occasions for exceptional handling. However, the search required cannot be logically

Task Structure
(*Task-Related Interactions*)

	Discretion	Power	Coord. w/in gp.	Interdependence of groups		Discretion	Power	Coord. w/in gp.	Interdependence of groups
Technical Supervision	Low	Low	Plan	Low		High	High	Feed	High
	High	High	Feed			High	High	Feed	
	Decentralized			1	2	Flexible, Polycentralized			
	Low	High	Plan	Low	3	High	High	Feed	Low
	Low	Low	Plan	4		Low	Low	Plan	
	Formal, Centralized					Flexible, Centralized			

FIGURE 3

---

*The distinction between Areas Two and Three is based upon a more limited distinction used by Joan Woodward in her brilliant study, *Industrial Organization* (London: Oxford University Press, 1965).

conducted, but must involve a high degree of experimentation and "feel." In such a technological situation, the discretion of both those who supervise the transformation of the basic raw material, and those who provide technical help for this process, must be high. The supervisors will request help from technical personnel rather than receive orders from them, or there may not even be a clear line of distinction between the two in terms of persons. That is, the clinical psychologist or the quality control engineer will find himself "on the line" so to speak, dealing directly with patients or exotic metals and working side by side with the supervisors who are nominally of lower status. The power of both groups will be high, and not at the expense of each other. The coordination will be through feedback—that is, considerable mutual adjustment must be made. The interdependence of the two groups will be high. The development of product groups and product managers in industry provides an example, as does the somewhat premature attempt of one correctional institution to utilize a cottage system bringing both clinical and line personnel together with joint responsibility for running autonomous cottages [7].

In the case of cell 4, uniform stable materials whose relevant nature is perceived as well understood can be handled with few exceptions occurring, and those that do occur can be taken care of with analytical search processes. In such a situation the discretion of both groups is likely to be low. This is a well-programmed production process and there is no need to allow much discretion. Indeed, there is danger in doing so. However, the power of the technical group over the supervisory group is high, for they direct the activities of the supervisors of production on the basis of routine reports generated by the supervisors. Those in Area Three are likely to see those in Area Two as hindrances to their work rather than aides. Coordination can be through planning in both groups, and the interdependence of the two groups is low; it is a directive rather than an interdependent relationship.

Cell 3 represents a variation from either of these extremes, for here, in contrast to cell 2, the existence of many exceptions which require search procedures increases both the power and the discretion of the technical group, which handles these exceptions, at the expense of the supervisory group. The supervisors of production respond to the results of these search processes rather than undertake search themselves. In the case of cell 1, the situation is reversed. Because search cannot be logical and analytical, when the infrequent exceptions occur they are handled by those in closest contact with the production process such as teachers and skilled craftsmen, and there is minimal development of administrative services. Of course, in schools that attempt to do little socialization but simply offer instruction and provide custody, technical (administrative) services grow and we move to cell 2.

Having thus related technology to task structure, let us turn to another aspect of structure—the non-task-related but organizationally relevant interactions of people. We call this the social structure.

Figure 4 follows our previous four-fold classification and indicates the variety of bases for non-task-related interactions. All are present in all organizations, but the saliency varies. In cell 2, these interactions are likely to revolve more around the mission, long-range goals, and direction of development of the organizations than around the other three bases. This is because of the task structure characteristic of a flexible, polycentric organization, or at least is related to it. The category "social identity" in cell 1 is meant to convey that the non-task-related interactions of personnel that are organizationally relevant revolve around communal or personal satisfactions born of long tenure and close working relationships. This is true especially at the supervisory level, which is a large management group in this type of structure. However, it is very possible, as Blauner and others have shown, for communal relations to develop in cell 4 types of organizations if the organization is located in a rural area where kinship and rural ties are strong [8]. The basis of interaction in cell 3 is instrumental identity and in cell 4, work or task identification. These would also be predicted upon the basis of the technology.

Social Structure
[The Bases of Non-task-related Interaction]

Social identity (communal)		Goal identification (mission, "character" of organization, distinctive competence, etc.)
	1	2
	4	3
Instrumental identity (job security, pay, protection from arbitrary power)		Work or task identification (technical satisfactions)

FIGURE 4

So far we have ignored Area One—design and planning. This area receives more inputs from the environment than the other areas, and thus its tasks and technologies are derived from both internal and external stimuli. If the product environment of the organization —a term meant to cover competitors, customers, suppliers, unions, and regulatory agencies—were the same in all four cells of Figure 3, we would expect the design and planning areas in cell 4 to have routine tasks and techniques, and nonroutine ones in cell 2. This is because the occasions for design and long-range planning would be few in the one and many in the other. For example, at least until very recently, the decisions that executives in the primary metals industries, railroads and surface mining had to make were probably rather routine, while those of executives in new industries such as electronics and aerospace were probably nonroutine.* One would expect that cell 1 would also be routine, and cell 3 somewhat nonroutine. But the product environment can alter all this. Organizations in cell 4 can be in a rapidly changing market situation even though the technical control and the supervision of production are fairly routine. Consumer goods industries probably deal with many decisions where the search behavior confronts unanalyzable problems such as the hemline of women's clothes, fads in the toy industry, or the length of time that tail fins or the boxy look in autos will last. Generally speaking, however, though the intrinsic characteristics of the product remain the same, rapid changes in the extrinsic characteristics will introduce nonroutine tasks in the design and planning area, even though it hardly alters the routine character of the technical control and the supervision of production.†

These are industrial examples, but it also seems likely that the tasks of Area One in custodial mental hospitals are quite different from those in treatment-oriented hospitals. Relations with the regulatory agencies, supplying agencies, the consumers such as courts and families, and the other agencies that compete for funds or clients, will be rather routine in the first, while they will be quite nonroutine and sensitive in the second. This would not be true, of course, if the latter have the means of isolating themselves from their environment [4, *Chap. 4*]. Similarly, the market situation of vocational training institutions may change rather quickly as industrial technologies change, requiring changes in the design and planning of the institution, while the market of a public school that attempts to socialize youths will not change as often.

---

*On the former see Alfred D. Chandler, Jr., *Strategy and Structure* (Cambridge: MIT Press, 1962), pp. 329-30, and Chap. 7 in general. The discussion of social structure and time periods by Stinchcombe can be interpreted in this manner also. Those exceptions that occur in his data appear to be examples of nonroutine technologies established in periods of predominantly routine technologies, or vice versa. See Arthur Stinchcombe, "Social Structure and Organizations," in *Handbook of Organizations,* edited by James March (Chicago: Rand, 1965), pp. 142-69, esp. p. 158.

† On the distinction between intrinsic and extrinsic prestige, see Charles Perrow, "Organizational Prestige: Some Functions and Dysfunctions," *Amer. J. Sociology,* 66 (Jan. 1961).

Goals

Finally, let us turn to the last major variable, goals. Three categories of goals can be distinguished for present purposes [9]. These are system goals, which relate to the characteristics of the system as a whole, independent of its products; product characteristic goals, which relate to the characteristics of the products the organization decides to emphasize; and derived goals, which refer to the uses to which power generated by organizational activities can be put, independent of system or product goals.

We would expect completely routinized organizations to stress those "system" goals of organizational stability, low risk, and perhaps high profits or economical operations rather than growth. (See Figure 5.) In terms of "product characteristic" goals, they would be more likely to emphasize quantity than quality, stable lines over unstable or diversified lines, superficial transformations (e.g., instilling discipline in deviant clients) over basic transformation (such as character restructuring), and so forth. Their "derived" goals are likely to emphasize conservative attitudes towards the government, conservative political philosophies, conservative forms of corporate giving. Also, they are perhaps more likely to have individuals who exploit, for their own benefit, relations with suppliers, and who have collusive arrangements with competitors and devious and excessive forms of management compensation. Obviously, these comments upon possible goals are open to serious question. For one thing, we lack such data on goals for a large number of organizations. Furthermore, personalities and the environment may shape goals more than the other variables of technology and structure. Finally, the link between structure and goals is an intuitive one, based upon unproven

Goals

System	Product	Derived	System	Product	Derived
Stability Few risks Moderate to low profit emphasis	Quality No innovations	Conserv.	High growth High risks Low emphasis on profit	High quality Innovative	Liberal
1					2
Stability Few risks High profit emphasis	Quantity No innovations	Conserv.	Moderate growth Some risks Moderate profit emphasis	Reliability Moderate innovations	Liberal
4					3

FIGURE 5

assumptions regarding attitudes generated by task relations. But the comments are meant to suggest how goals may be shaped or constrained, though hardly specified, through the influence of technology and structure.

Some Cautions

This truncated perspective ignores the role of the cultural and social environment in making available definitions of raw material, providing technologies, and restricting the range of feasible structures and goals.* It also ignores, for the most part, the role of the product environment—customers, competitors, suppliers, unions and regulatory agencies—and the material and human resources. These will have their independent effect upon the major variables.

In addition, it is not proposed here that there are four types of organizations. The two-dimensional scheme is conceived of as consisting of two continua. Nor are the dimensions and the specifications of the variables necessarily the best. It is argued, however, that the main variables—raw materials, technology, task and social structure, goals, and some differentiation of task areas within organizations, are critical ones. As to the assignment of independent and dependent variables, occasions can be readily cited where changes in goals, for example those brought about by changes in the market place or the personalities of top executives, have brought about changes in the technology utilized. The argument is somewhat more subtle than one of temporal priorities. Rather, it says that structure and goals must adjust to technology or the organization will be subject to strong strains. For a radical change in goals to be a successful one, it may require a change in technology, and thus in structure, or else there will be a large price paid for the lack of fit between these variables.† Furthermore, as one proceeds, analytically, from technology through the two kinds of structure to goals, increasingly the prior variable only sets limits upon the range of possible variations in the next variable. Thus, technology may predict task struc-

---

*The role of the cultural and social environment is developed in somewhat more detail in a review of studies of general and mental hospitals in Charles Perrow, Hospitals: Technology, Structure, and Goals," in *Handbook of Organizations,* edited by James G. March (Chicago: Rand, 1965), Chap. 22.

†This is argued in detail in Perrow [9, pp. 926-46]. Kovner finds those nursing units with the greatest divergence between technology and structure to have the lowest scores on a dimension of goal realization (Anthony Kovner, "The Nursing Unit: A Technological Perspective," unpublished Ph.D. dissertation [University of Pittsburgh, 1966].)

ture quite well in a large number of organizations,* but these two predict social structure less well, and these three only set broad limits upon the range of possible goals.

Comparative Analyses

If all this is at all persuasive, it means that we have a powerful tool for comparing organizations. The first implication of this for comparative studies is that we cannot expect a particular relationship found in one organization to be found in another unless we know these organizations are in fact similar with respect to their technology. Thus, the fact that the cosmopolitan-local relationship that worked so well in Antioch College was not found in the outpatient department of a hospital should not surprise us; the work performed by the professionals in each case was markedly different [10]. That morale was associated with bureaucracy in fairly routine public schools, but not in research organizations, is understandable.† Less obvious, however, is the point that types of organization—in terms of their function in society—will vary as much within each type as between types. Thus, some schools, hospitals, banks, and steel companies may have more in common, because of their routine character, than routine and nonroutine schools, routine and nonroutine hospitals, and so forth. To assume that you are holding constant the major variable by comparing several schools or several steel mills is unwarranted until one looks at the technologies employed by various schools or steel mills. In fact, the variations within one type of organization may be such that some schools are like prisons, some prisons like churches, some churches like factories, some factories

---

*Unfortunately, verification of the predicted relationships would require a large sample of organizations since there are bound to be many examples of incompatibility between the variables. However, even in a small sample, those whose structure was appropriate to their technology should have fewer "strains" than those whose structure was inappropriate. Joan Woodward, using a similar approach with 100 industrial firms, found strong relationships between production systems and certain aspects of structure, though the rudimentary information and analysis on the 100 firms leaves one in doubt as to how strong. See Joan Woodward, *Industrial Organization* (London: Oxford University Press, 1965).

†Gerald H. Moeller and W.W. Charters, "Relation of Bureaucratization to Sense of Power Among Teachers," *Admin. Sci. Quart.*, 10 (Dec. 1966), 444-65. In addition, for this reason one becomes wary of propositional inventories that fail to make sufficient distinctions among organizations, but attempt to support the propositions by illustrations that are likely to restrict the scope of the proposition to the particular type of organization used in the illustration. For the most recent example, see William A. Rushing, "Organizational Rules and Surveillance: Propositions in Comparative Organizational Analysis," *Admin. Sci. Quart.*, 10 (Dec. 1966), 423-43.

like universities, and so on.* Once this is recognized, of course, analysis of the differences between churches or whatever can be a powerful tool, as witness the familiar contrast of custodial and treatment-oriented people-changing institutions.

Another implication is that there is little point in testing the effect of a parameter variable, such as size, age, auspices, geographical dispersion, or even national culture, unless we control for technology. For example, in the case of size, to compare the structure of a small R and D lab where the tasks of all three areas are likely to be quite nonroutine with the structure of a large bank where they are likely to be quite routine is fruitless. The nature of their tasks is so different that the structures must vary independently of their different sizes.† A meaningful study of the effect of size on structure can be made only if we control for technology, and compare, say, large and small banks all of which have similar services, or large and small R and D labs. Similarly, though the brilliant work of Crozier on French culture is very suggestive, many of his conclusions may stem from the fact that only very routine organizations were studied, and even those lacked many critical elements of the bureaucratic mode [11, *Chap. 4*]. Equally routine organizations in a protected product environment in the U.S. might have displayed the same characteristics.

Finally, to call for decentralization, representative bureaucracy, collegial authority, or employee-centered, innovative or organic organizations—to mention only a few of the highly normative prescriptions that are being offered by social scientists today—is to call for a type of structure that can be realized only with a certain type of technology, unless we are willing to pay a high cost in terms of output. Given a routine technology, the much maligned Weberian bureaucracy probably constitutes the socially optimum form of organizational structure.

If all this is plausible, then existing varieties of organizational theory must be selectively applied. It is increasingly recognized that there is no "one best" theory (any more than there is "one best" organizational structure, form of leadership, or whatever) unless it be so general as to be of little utility in understanding the variety of organizations. The perspective proposed here may allow us to utilize existing theories selectively.

For example, a characteristic of thoroughly routinized organiza-

---

*Many of the frameworks for comparative analysis, such as those cited in March and Simon [2], break down because of their broad categories. The failure of some of these schemes to meaningfully order the data from a large sample of a great variety of organizations is discussed in J. Eugene Haas, Richard H. Hall, and Norman J. Johnson, "Toward an Empirically Derived Taxonomy of Organizations," in *Studies on Behavior in Organizations* (Atlanta: Univ. of Georgia Press, 1966), pp. 157-80.

†This may be a basic error in the ambitious survey conducted by Haas and his associates.

tions is the programmatic character of decisions, and perhaps the infrequency with which important decisions have to be made. A decision-making framework that attempts to simulate executive behavior would be fruitful in such cases, for decisions are programmed and routinized. There are fairly clear guidelines for decisions, and clear routing maps, flow charts, and so forth. (See the examples in the second half of the Cyert and March volume, *The Behavioral Theory of the Firm* [12, *Chaps. 7-11*].) However, a decision-making perspective which emphasizes uncertainty, such as Herbert Simon's, or that illustrated in the first part of the Cyert and March volume, would not be fruitful here [12, *Chaps. 1-4, 6*]. It would be fruitful where nonroutine tasks are involved.

The study of organizations with a moderate or high component of nonroutine activities, especially at the design and planning level, would benefit from the institutional analysis proposed by Selznick, whereas more routine organizations would not. Selznick, himself, would see them as technical tools. The Communist Party is engaged in nonroutine activities and Selznick chose to analyze the nonroutine rather than the routine aspects of the multi-organization, the Tennessee Valley Authority [13]. Except for its Bell Laboratories, the American Telephone and Telegraph Corporation is probably a rather routine organization in a stable product environment and Barnard's equilibrium analysis works well [14]. Equilibrium analysis also works well for the routine operatives at the production level in economic organizations that constitute most of the subjects for the discussion by March and Simon of the contribution-inducement model [2, *Chap. 4*]. Where nonroutine activities are involved, however, the measurement of both inducements and contributions tends to be difficult, and little is gained by this model except the unenlightening assertion that if the person stays in the organization and produces, there must be some kind of an inducement at least to match his contribution.*

There are, of course, many aspects of the general perspectives or theories of organizations that apply to all organizations, and many more will be forthcoming. What is asserted here is that we know enough about organizations in general, at this point, to suggest that more of our effort should be directed toward "middle range" theories which attempt to increase their predictive power by specifying

---

*Woodward's remarkable book offers several implicit examples of selective utility. It seems clear, for example, that firms in her middle category (large batch, assembly, and mass production) exhibit the characteristics of political science models such as Melville Dalton (*Men Who Manage* [New York: Wiley, 1959]) and the first part of Cyert and March [12]. But this view would not illuminate the other two categories in her scheme; application must be selective.

the types of organizations to which they apply. To do this we need far better classification systems than we now have. A better classification system will be based upon a basic aspect of all organizations. In this paper we have suggested that a better system would be one which conceptualizes organizations in terms of the work that they do rather than their structure or their goals.

Other Studies Utilizing Technology

If there is anything novel in the present essay it is the setting forth of an integrated and somewhat comprehensive viewpoint on technology and complex organizations. Numerous studies have dealt with specific aspects of this viewpoint and some are discussed here.

There have been a few general theoretical statements regarding technology and structure. The one closest to the perspective presented here is a seminal essay by Litwak which distinguishes uniform and nonuniform tasks [15, *pp. 177-84*]. His framework received some empirical support in an interesting essay by Hall.* One of the first attempts to specify some structural and goal concomitants of technology in general terms was by Thompson and Bates [16]. March and Simon [2], and Simon alone [17], proposed and discussed a distinction between programmed and nonprogrammed decisions in general terms. Bennis verges upon a technological conceptualization in parts of his excellent review of leadership theory and administrative behavior [18, 259-301].

There have been numerous studies of the role of technology in work groups and small groups. One of the most widely cited is that of the long-wall coaling method by Trist and Bamforth [19, 3-38]. In our terms this represents a premature attempt at rationalizing nonroutine activities. An assembly-line work layout was imposed on a craft and job-shop operation which was essentially nonroutine,

---

*Richard H. Hall, "Intraorganizational Structural Variation: Application of the Bureaucratic Model," *Admin. Sci. Quart.,* 7 (Dec. 1962), 295-308. However, the normative anti-bureaucratic tone of many of Hall's questionnaire items precludes an adequate test. An affirmative response to an item such as "I have to ask my boss before I do almost anything" probably indicates a very poor boss, rather than a situation where a bureaucratic structure is viable. A factor analysis of Hall's items was utilized to construct several discrete dimensions of some aspect of bureaucracy in connection with research reported by Aiken and Hage. It appears that the groupings are not on the basis of content, but on the evaluative wording of the items. Those stated negatively, as in the above example, group together, and those implying "good" leadership techniques (rather than bureaucratic or nonbureaucratic techniques) group together. It is doubtful that anything but good or bad leadership in a gross sense is being tested here. A valid item for degree of bureaucratization would permit respondents to approve of the necessity for close supervision, for example, as well as to indicate it is not appropriate. See Michael Aiken and Jerald Hage, "Organizational Alienation: A Comparative Analysis," *Amer. Sociological Review,* 31 (Aug. 1966), 495-507.

and the results were predictably unfortunate, as were similar attempts to impose a bureaucratic structure on the nonroutine underground mining operations described by Gouldner [20]. Those interested in human relations in organizations have increasingly toyed with technology as an independent variable, but with mixed feelings and reluctance, since it appears to jeopardize some implicit values of this school of thought. See, for example, the curious chapter in Likert where many of the central hypotheses of previous and subsequent chapters are undermined by observing that the consequences of leadership style varied with the routine and nonroutine nature of the work [21, *Chap. 7*]. More sophisticated statements of the impact of technology upon work groups can be found in Dubin [22] and in the comparative study of Turner and Lawrence [23]. The most sophisticated statement of the impact upon workers is presented by Blauner, who uses a comparative framework to great effect; he also summarizes the vast literature on this topic which need not be cited here [8]. Studies of experimental groups have provided evidence of the effect of technology upon small group structure. See the work of Bavelas, Guetzkow and Simon, and Leavitt [24].

The impact of routine technologies upon both managerial and nonmanagerial personnel is apparent, though not explicit, in Argyris' study of a bank [25], in Sudnow's study of a court system [3], and in two studies of French organizations by Crozier [11].

Technology plays an explicit and important role in a number of studies of single types of organizations, such as Janowitz's outstanding study of the military [26], and Rose Coser's contrast of two units in a long-term hospital [27]. It is implicit in her contrast of a medical and a surgical ward [28, 56-64]. It is also implicit in Rosengren's analysis of milieu therapy [29, 70-90]. It plays the key role in the author's analysis of the literature on general and mental hospitals [30], and in his longitudinal study of a maximum security institution for juveniles [31]. It plays an ambiguous role in the Street et al. study of six correctional institutions where its impact is obscured by a competing emphasis upon executive goals and behavior, and an inappropriate reliance upon a simple custodial-treatment continuum which leads to many ambiguities about the middle organizations where components of treatment vary independently [4].

Explicit contrasts of organizations have utilized technological variables. The most ambitious, of course, is Udy's analysis of simple organizations in nonindustrial societies where the emphasis upon technology is explicit [32]. Unfortunately, it is difficult to import his techniques of operationalization and his theory into the world of complex organizations in industrialized societies. As is noted in the preceding essay, technology is a relevant variable, and is sometimes made explicit, in Stinchcombe's discussion of structure and time periods [33, *Chap. 4*]. It also plays a role, though not the key one, in his discussion of craft and bureaucratic organization [34, 168-87]. The key role is reserved for market factors, and this is true of two other comparative studies—the study of two business concerns by Dill [35] and an ambitious study of two industrial firms by Lorsch [36]. In both these cases it would appear that technology is an important variable but is absorbed in the broader variable, environment. A study of several British firms by Burns and Stalker uses technology as an important variable, though in a quite nonrigorous fashion [6]; their one explicit comparison of a routine and a nonroutine firm is excellent [6, *Chap. 5*].

The most ambitious and stimulating comparative study using technology as an independent variable is Joan Woodward's survey of 100 industrial organizations [37]. Her independent variable is not, strictly speaking, technology, but is a mixture of type of production, size of production run, layout of work and type of customer order. These distinctions overlap and it is difficult to decide how a particular kind of organization might be classified in her scheme, or how she made her final classification. An examination of the actual types of organizations (bakery, electronic firm, etc.) utilized in her study, kindly provided by Miss Woodward, suggests that most of those in the general category "small batch and unit" are probably involved in nonroutine production; those in the "large batch and unit" are probably involved in routine production; those in the "large batch and mass production" category have a mixture of routine and nonroutine technologies, but are predominantly routine. If so, her findings would be consistent with our perspective. However, her analysis of continuous process firms unfortunately cannot easily be incorporated in the scheme advanced here. Efforts to do so after her book appeared floundered because of lack of crucial data.

Considering the strong empirical tradition of sociology, it is surprising that so few studies actually give details regarding the kind of work performed in organizations that permit technological generalizations. Two of the best are Gouldner's contrast of mining and manufacturing within a gypsum plant [20], and Blau's implicit contrast of a routine employment agency and a nonroutine regulatory agency [38]. The works of Argyris [25], Crozier [11], Sudnow [3], and Trist and Bamford [19] also are exceptions.

Finally, we should mention the problem of operationalizing the various concepts of technology—programmed and nonprogrammed decisions, uniform and nonuniform events, routine and nonroutine techniques, simple and complex technologies, and so forth. This has rarely been systematically handled. Udy's procedures do not seem to be applicable to complex organizations [32]. Neither Lorsch [36] nor Hall [39] indicate in detail how they make their distinctions. March and Simon provide some general guidelines [2, *pp. 142-43*], but Litwak [15] provides none. It is impossible to determine how Woodward [37] or Burns and Stalker [6] arrived at their class-ifications of companies. Street et al. provide indications of opera-tionalization, but these are not particularly applicable to other types of organizations nor are the authors particularly sensitive to the problem [4]. Only Turner and Lawrence have approached the problem systematically and fully described in an appendix the mea-surement of their variables [23]. The level of conceptualization is not general enough to apply to other types of organizations than industrial firms, and the material is limited to blue-collar workers, but it is at least encouraging that in our own study of industrial firms we arrived independently at some roughly similar measures.

Udy, in a discussion of this paper, aptly noted the difficulty of reconciling the respondent's perception of the nature of his work with the observer's perception, which is based upon a comparative view. Few organizations will characterize themselves as routine, and most employees emphasize the variability of their jobs and the discretion required. Nevertheless, contrasts between extreme ex-amples of a single type of organization appear to present no problem. It seems clear that the technology of custodial and therapeutic men-tal hospitals, or of firms producing ingot molds and those producing titanium-based metals, differ greatly. On the other hand, to say pre-cisely wherein these differences occur, and how one might compare the two routine examples, is far more difficult. Such operational-ization, however, depends first upon adequate conceptualization. That proposed in this essay—the two continua of exceptions and search procedures—hopefully can be operationalized for a variety of settings. (An attempt is made, with fair success, by Kovner in his study of nursing units [40].) But much more research and theory will be required to determine if these concepts are relevant and ade-quate. Meanwhile, we are aware of a number of other studies of technology and organization currently under way or even in press; other concepts will no doubt be formulated and perhaps will be given systematic operational definition.

Notes

1. Revision of a paper read at the 1966 Annual Meeting of the American Sociological Association. This paper was prepared during the course of research on industrial corporations supported by Grant No. GS-742, National Science Foundation. Numerous colleagues criticized an earlier version unstintingly, but I would like to single out Ernest Vargas, Geof-frey Guest, and Anthony Kovner, who transcended their graduate student roles at the University of Pittsburgh during the formulation of these ideas in sticky field situations.

2. James G. March and Herbert A. Simon, *Organizations* (New York: Wiley, 1958).
3. David Sudnow, "Normal Crimes: Sociological Features of the Penal Code in a Public Defender Office," *Social Problems,* 12 (Win. 1965).
4. For a more extensive treatment of raw material somewhat along these lines, see David Street, Robert Vinter, and Charles Perrow, *Organization for Treatment: A Comparative Study of Institutions for Delinquents* (New York: Free Press, 1966), Chap. 1.
5. Eliot Jaques, *The Measurement of Responsibility* (Cambridge: Harvard University Press, 1959).
6. Tom Burns and G. M. Stalker, *The Management of Innovation* (London: Tavistock, 1961).
7. Street, Vinter, and Perrow, op. cit., note 4, Chaps. 5, 6. The organization is called Milton.
8. Robert Blauner, *Alienation and Freedom: The Factory Worker and His Industry* (Chicago: Univ. of Chicago Press, 1964), Chap. 4. Blauner's theory, incidentally, is entirely consistent with the perspective proposed here, even though we do not concern ourselves explicitly in this article with the morale of hourly employees.
9. For a full discussion of these and three others, see Charles Perrow, "Organizational Goals," *International Encyclopedia of the Social Sciences,* rev. ed. (Draft copies, mimeo. 18 pp., can be obtained from the author.)
10. Cf. Alvin Gouldner, "Cosmopolitans and Locals: Toward an Analysis of Latent Social Roles," *Admin. Sci. Quart.,* 2 (Dec. 1957; March 1958), 281-306, 444-80; and Warren G. Bennis et al., "Reference Groups and Loyalties in the Out-Patient Department," *Admin. Sci. Quart.,* 2 (March 1958), 481-500.
11. Michel Crozier, *The Bureaucratic Phenomenon* (Chicago: Univ. of Chicago Press, 1964).
12. Richard M. Cyert and James G. March, *The Behavioral Theory of the Firm* (Englewood Cliffs: Prentice-Hall, 1963).
13. Philip Selznick, *The Organizational Weapon* (New York: McGraw, 1952) and *TVA and the Grass Roots* (Berkeley: Univ. of California Press, 1949). See also *Leadership in Administration* (Evanston: Row, 1957), Chap. 1.
14. Chester Barnard, *The Functions of the Executive* (Cambridge: Harvard University Press, 1938).
15. Eugene Litwak, "Models of Organization Which Permit Conflict," *Amer. J. Sociology,* 67 (Sept. 1961).
16. James D. Thompson and Frederick L. Bates, "Technology, Organization, and Administration," *Admin. Sci. Quart.,* 2 (Mar. 1957), 325-43.
17. Herbert Simon, *The New Science of Management Decisions* (New York: Harper, 1960).
18. Warren G. Bennis, "Leadership Theory and Administrative Behavior: The Problem of Authority," *Admin. Sci. Quart.,* 4 (Apr. 1959).
19. Eric L. Trist and E. K. Bamforth, "Some Social and Psychological Consequences of the Long-Wall Method of Coal-Getting," *Human Relations,* 4 (1951).
20. Alvin W. Gouldner, *Patterns of Industrial Bureaucracy* (Glencoe: Free Press, 1954).
21. Rensis Likert, *New Patterns of Management* (New York: McGraw, 1961).
22. Robert Dubin, "Supervision and Productivity: Empirical Findings and Theoretical Considerations," in Robert Dubin et al., *Leadership and Productivity* (San Francisco: Chandler, 1965), pp. 1-50.

23. Arthur N. Turner and Paul R. Lawrence, *Industrial Jobs and the Worker* (Cambridge: Harvard University Press, 1965).
24. Alex Bavelas, "Communication Patterns in Task-Oriented Groups," *J. Stat. Soc. Amer.*, 22 (1950), 725-30; Harold Guetzkow and Herbert Simon, "The Impact of Certain Communication Nets Upon Organization and Performance in Task-Oriented Groups," in *Some Theories of Organization*, edited by Albert H. Rubenstein and Chadwick J. Haverstroh (Homewood, Ill.: Dorsey Press, 1960), pp. 259-77; Harold J. Leavitt, "Some Effects of Certain Communication Patterns on Group Performance," in *Readings in Social Psychology* (New York: Holt, 1958), pp. 546-63.
25. Chris Argyris, *Organization of a Bank* (New Haven: Yale University Press, 1954).
26. Morris Janowitz, *The Professional Soldier* (Glencoe: Free Press, 1960).
27. Rose L. Coser, "Alienation and the Social Structure: A Case Analysis of a Hospital, in *The Hospital in Modern Society*, edited by Eliot Freidson (New York: Free Press, 1963), pp. 231-65.
28. _____ , "Authority and Decision-Making in a Hospital,"*Amer. Sociological Review* 23 (Feb. 1958).
29. William R. Rosengren, "Communication, Organization and Conduct," *Admin. Sci. Quart.*, 9 (June 1964).
30. Charles Perrow, "Hospitals: Technology Structure and Goals, in *Handbook of Organizations*, edited by James March (Chicago: Rand, 1965), Chap. 22.
31. _____ , "Reality Adjustment: A Young Organization Settles for Humane Care," *Social Problems*, 14 (Sum. 1966), 69-79.
32. Stanley Udy, *Organization of Work* (New Haven: Human Relations Area Files Press, 1959).
33. Arthur L. Stinchcombe, "Social Structure and Organization," in *Handbook of Organizations*, edited by James March (Chicago: Rand, 1965).
34. _____ , "Bureaucratic and Craft Administration of Production: A Comparative Study," *Admin. Sci. Quart.*, 4 (Sept. 1959).
35. William Dill, "Environment as an Influence on Managerial Autonomy," *Admin. Sci. Quart.*, 2 (Mar. 1958), 409-43.
36. Jay W. Lorsch, *Product Innovation and Organization* (New York: Macmillan, 1965).
37. Joan Woodward, *Industrial Organization: Theory and Practice* (London: Oxford University Press, 1965).
38. Peter Blau, *Dynamics of Bureaucracy* (Chicago: Univ. of Chicago Press, 1955).
39. Richard H. Hall, "Intraorganizational Structural Variation: Application of the Bureaucratic Model," *Admin. Sci. Quart.*, 7 (Dec. 1962)
40. Anthony Kovner, "The Nursing Unit: A Technological Perspective," unpublished Ph.D. dissertation (Univ. of Pittsburgh, 1966).

Technology
and
Organization

Raymond G. Hunt

*In order to solve practical problems of organizational design, it is
necessary initially to understand the many differences between types
of organizations and the reasons that these differences exist. The
fact that these aspects have not been considered until the mid-1960's
is reflected by the independence of developments in organizational
design and theory until this time [1]. However, recent progress in
comparative analysis of organizations, together with integrative
theory building, gives promise of altering this state of affairs, especially regarding the appreciation of technology as a main basis for
differentiating organizational varieties and explaining organizational
processes.*

*These recent developments are the foundation for this paper;
first, we will outline the ways in which organizations may be classified, and then we will appraise the current understanding of the relationship between technology and organizational design.*

Classifying Organizations

To be useful, a schema for distinguishing organizations must identify
cogent parameters or dimensions that cut across particular cases and
provide a basis for ordering those cases, even if it is only on a yes-no
basis. Different schemas will be useful for different purposes, but
since every organization can be construed as having: (1) a function
in society; (2) a pattern of input; (3) a pattern of output; (4) a set
of procedures for converting inputs into outputs (something to which
we shall apply the term "throughput") [2] ; and (5) a pattern according
to which it is put together, it follows that any organization could be

From *Academy of Management*, September, 1970, 235-252. Copyright © 1970 by Academy
of Management. Preparation of this paper was assisted by NASA Grant NGR 33=015=061.

classified on any or all of these bases. Indeed, allowing for some mixed cases and some ambiguous ones, examples of all five kinds of classification can be found.

Classification by social function. In Chapter 5 of their remarkable book, Katz and Kahn present a "typology" of organizations based on "first-order" and "second-order factors" [2]. First-order factors describe "genotypic functions" that differentiate among all kinds of organizational systems and subsystems. Thus, in Katz and Kahn's typology there are productive or economic organizations (e.g., factories); maintenance organizations (e.g., those, like schools, specialized to socialize people); adaptive organizations (e.g., research labs); and managerial or political organizations. These first-order distinctions have to do principally with the part played by the organization in the larger society; thus, they can claim kinship with Parsons' social function criteria [3]. With regard to actual organizations, of course, these categories are not mutually exclusive. A particular organization could fall into more than one class: AT&T may be mainly an economic organization, but in its research labs it contains adaptive organizations.

Defined by its contributions to the larger social system, an organization's social function, unlike the other four of its facets, has to do with its *relations* with the society as a whole, not just with its own characteristics. Talking of an organization's social functions is to treat it (the organization) not so much as an integral system, but as a subsystem of a larger system. One might therefore infer that this essentially *exogenous* criterion for classification is different from and independent of the others. Katz and Kahn obviously think so with their distinction between first- and second-order factors[4]. To be sure, an organization's social function is likely to influence its perceived social value which, in turn, may affect its access to societal resources, including technological ones which may help shape its other characteristics. But any such linkages depend entirely on the organization's embeddedness in the larger societal system. In any event, these linkages are complex and clearly not direct.

For very general purposes, classification by social function can be helpful. However, the variability within functional types is too great for them to afford much analytic power [5, 195-208]. Katz and Kahn are aware of this, of course, as their positing of second-order factors implies. These second-order factors have more to do with input, output, or conversion methods (throughput), or else with design features.

Classification by form or pattern.   Pattern denotes the discernable "phenomenology" or anatomy of an organization—its characteristics or properties *qua* organization. This aspect of organizations we shall herein reference by the term "structure," or, when construed in a purposive sense, "design."

With its functional traditions, American scholarship has tended to pay more attention to operational than to structural properties of organizations [6, 360-62]. To be sure, structure is only revealed in the functions of organizations [2, *Chap. 1*], but structure there is nevertheless. We mean by it the varied patterns of interaction, intended or otherwise, that characterize an organization. To the degree these patterns are codified or standardized, we can speak of the organization as being formal. And "formal organizational structure" can be defined in terms of prescriptions regarding lines of authority, divisions of labor, and allocations of resources that often can be found memorialized in such things as organization charts, job descriptions, and budgetary formulae [7]. Such pointers are far from infallible guides to organizational reality, but even so it is essential to recognize that the nature of the formal organization has much to do with limiting and shaping organizational life (including whatever "informal" processes may be spawned therein). Moreover, the idea of formal structure is fundamental to rational organization design.

Our concept of structure in substance and in spirit approximates Anthony's idea of "system" as distinct from "process" [8]. The latter has to do with the actual events and decisions that transpire within the organization, whereas the former represents the formal and informal framework within which these are done—the "formula," as it were, according to which the organization's tasks are specified, interrelated, performed, and controlled. Obviously this formula can be either explicit or not explicit.

As for the use of structural criteria for classifying organizations, it has long been traditional to distinguish three basic forms of organization design: (1) line organization, (2) functional organization, and (3) line-staff organization [9]. In line organizations everybody does essentially the same kind of work under the more or less immediate authority of a "man at the top." Some degree of internal specialization may lead to departmentalization of line organizations, but this does not necessarily change their fundamentals.

Pure functional organizations are scarce, apparently because they are based on the sensible but hard to implement idea that since it is difficult to combine all necessary managerial-supervisory skills in single individuals, it is wise to organize around functions—skills, activities, etc.—rather than people. The desire to include functional specialists within an organization while retaining unity of command is the basis for the widespread "compromise" development of line-staff organizations wherein supporting specialists work through particular line managers.

It is obviously possible to combine these models in various ways and mention might be made of such special cases as project organizations (which, in a sense, are temporary, special-purpose, line organizations) and matrix organizations (which are meldings of project and functional models calculated to satisfy institutional needs for permanence). Furthermore, other structural classifications are possible. Pugh et al. stress a multidimensional characterization built around performance regulation, centralization of authority, and the degree to which operations are controlled by line management rather than by impersonal records and procedures generated from staff offices [7]. Burns and Stalker's well-known distinction between "organic" and "mechanistic" management patterns is another somewhat similar example [10]. Organic organizations are characterized by less formalized definitions of jobs, by more stress on flexibility and adaptability, and by communication networks involving more consultation than command. Mechanistic organizations are more rigidly specialized functionally, and in general, define an opposite pole on an organic-mechanistic continuum. Finally, of course, distinctions between bureaucratic and nonbureaucratic organizations exemplify the classificatory use of structural or design criteria [11].

Classification by output. Classifying organizations according to their output is a common practice that may involve one of two emphases. One, the kind or type of output (i.e., the product), is a standard basis for defining industries (e.g., automobile, motion pictures, etc.) and is too familiar to require further comment. But, output can also be viewed from the standpoint of the quantity or volume of whatever it is that is produced. For example, Woodward, although she thought of it more as a direct expression of technology, used to good effect classification of industrial firms as unit, small-batch, large-batch, and mass production [9]. The immediate meaning of unit, batch, and mass production is plain: it describes a scale of production quantities ranging from one of a kind through a few to very many.

W. F. Whyte makes use of these same distinctions, but only as subcategories within a broader, more heterogeneous system of classes [12]. Whyte's primary breakdown of organizations into "office, service, manufacturing, and continuous process" varieties clearly employs criteria other than output. Indeed it makes use of just about all criteria save social function. Office and service classes, for instance, appear to be distinguishable on the basis of the nature of their outputs, but they (and surely manufacturing and continuous processing) are classifications that also make use of other bases for categorization, notably throughout processes and, possibly, input as well.

Classification by input.   Distinctions between organizations based on input rest on contrasts regarding the raw materials on which the system works. The possibilities here are at least as numerous as the vast number offered to classifications based on output. One input distinction that has received special attention in the literature, however, is that between organizations (such as prisons, schools, employment agencies) that deal mainly with people and those organizations that operate chiefly on things, objects, hardware, or the like. Erving Goffman has provided some especially exotic discussions of "people-processing" systems, and the topic is capable of generating more than a little emotion [13]. It is doubtless that such systems differ from others, if for no other reason than because their raw materials are "reactive" instead of passive. In fact, this reactivity can itself be made a basis for a distinction between organizations by focusing on the form of feedback controlling the system's operations. We shall illustrate this in the next section.

In the meantime, take notice of Thompson and Bates' use of a "ratio of mechanization to professionalization" to distinguish organizations [14, 325-42]. By this they mean the extent to which technology is represented in human or nonhuman resources. But whether this is truly a classification based on input is questionable for, if Thompson and Bates stress the *locus* of technology, the notions of mechanization and professionalization seem to link the distinction closely to technology itself.

Classification by throughput.   Conversion processes or throughput are the various things done, with or without tools and machines, to transform inputs into outputs. The term "technology" is usually applied to these processes [15]. Our own definition of technology encompasses the three facets of technology, (1) operations, (2) materials, and (3) knowledge, differentiated by Hickson et al. [15] and includes the sequencing of activities involved in the conversion process, thereby including what Whyte, among others, refers to as "work flow" [12].

A straightforward throughput classification might be exemplified by J. D. Thompson's distinction between long-linked, mediating, and intensive technologies [16]. The first of these includes conversion processes (like those found in automobile assembly plants) involving serially interdependent operations, standard products, and constant, repetitive work rates. Mediating technologies link clients who "are or wish to be interdependent (as banks link depositors and lenders)." These, too, commonly employ standardization along with bureaucratic formats. Intensive technologies are those involving application of a variety of techniques to the change of some specific object, in which actual operations are determined by feedback from the object itself. This is clearly a "custom technology," and includes such examples as hospitals, schools, research projects, and tailor shops. Obviously a single organization might include within itself multiple technologies.

We have already mentioned that Whyte's classification of organizations included an admixture of output and throughput criteria; the same was true of Woodward's classification. Along with other categories defined by output, both Whyte and Woodward include in their schemes a "continuous process" category (e.g., a fully automated oil refinery) that indexes technology rather than output [17].

It must be evident that input and output systems, as well as throughput systems, can be described in terms of the processes or technologies by which they are implemented. That is, the operations by which inputs—raw materials—are introduced into a system describe a technology, and the same is true on the output (product) side. This fact, plus the other consideration that conversion processes in an organization must be relative to the input and output to and from the system (e.g., knowledge of the raw materials and product specifications) strongly suggest that the input-conversion-output cycle represents a single basic technological sequence or organizational substrate. Thus, the crucial consideration may not be the particular properties of the inputs or the outputs *per se*, but the technologies according to which they are accomplished.* In any case, it seems clear that input, output, and technology (throughput) are inextricably joined. Taken together they constitute the basic *endogenous* operational properties of organizations and, when actualized, collectively describe what Anthony calls organizational "process" (or function) as distinguished from structure (system) [8].

There is, of course, nothing in these unifying assertions to preclude variation in technological manifestations at different points in the process cycle. Input and conversion operations might be highly routinized, for example, but output methods (e.g., marketing) might be quite nonroutine.† And certainly nothing prevents separate analyses of respective technological features of input, output, or conversion subsystems. The point here is that input and output criteria for classifying organizations may be structurally significant only insofar as they indirectly index technological phenomena.

---

* For a related discussion with different conclusions see Hickson et al., note 15, p. 380.

† Distinctions could be drawn, but throughout this discussion we shall use the basic terms "routine" (or "routinized") and "program" ("programmed") more or less interchangeably to mean the extent to which an organization's tasks can and have been specified and prescribed—formalized. Programming performance (as, to take an extreme example, in a robot) is difficult when tasks are vague, variable, or complicated, but the process can be generally regarded (with neither approval nor disapproval) as a broad organizational means of reducing operational uncertainty by eliminating operator discretion.

Another thing that may have been evident in our exposition is the difficulty one has treating technology or process without making reference to structural or design aspects of the organization (see, e.g., the allusion to bureaucratic formats in the presentation above of Thompson's "mediating" technology). This is no accident of discursive formats. Indeed, we have taken notice of Anthony's proposition that system (structure) represents the formulae for organizational processes (input-throughput-output) [8]. Certainly the two dimensions are intimately entwined, even if the nature and degree of that intimacy may not yet be altogether clear; furthermore, they are both technologies. Conversion processes, or, more generally, modes of production, constitute what Olsen has called "material technologies." He has described modes of organization as "social technologies" [18]. Thus, from Anthony's perspective, exploring relations between "technology" and "organization" resolves itself into an analysis of relations between system and process. From Olsen's standpoint, this amounts to tracing the linkages between material and social technologies. We should hardly be surprised to find a good deal of interdependence in these relationships. Indeed, the expectation is implicit in the now common characterization of organizations as sociotechnical systems. In a manner of speaking, then, describing relations between technology and organizational forms amounts to an extended definition of the meaning of the concept of the sociotechnical system. With that observation, a more explicit overview of technology and organizational patterns is in order.

Technology and Organization Design

Beginning at least with Veblen and Marx, material technology has been regularly proposed as a major influence on organizational phenomena. Indications of its broad significance can be found in Toynbee's demonstration of changing forms of English social organization as new industrial technologies emerged during the 18th and 19th centuries. Margaret Mead has provided vivid portrayals of interrelations between technological advances and social patterns [19]. More recently, Dubin has nominated technology as the single most important determinant of work behavior and Mouzelis has spoken at length of the determining effect of technological structures and processes on organizational interaction [20; 11]. Stinchcombe, too, in context with his discussion of "motives for organizing," mentions technology among the basic variables affecting organizing capacity, and Olsen lists material technology as one of four primary factors underlying forms of social organization (the other three are the natural environment, population, and the human being) [21; 18]. Finally, in his excellent review of comparative studies, Udy points out two basic "causal mechanisms" that shape organizations. One operates via people to affect structures, and the other is *ecological* and deals with how activity is limited and channeled [22, *pp. 678-710*]. Together with the "social setting," which we are disregarding here, technology can be construed as imposing ecological limits on organizational properties.

In somewhat the same way, social technology can be looked upon as constraining material technology, as in the case of cultural or organizational resistance to change [23] or as in the extent to which a system is attuned to the receipt of inputs regarding new material technologies. Burns and Stalker, to cite a pertinent instance, found that firms adapting successfully to the electronics industry were characterized by a more global task model and a different communication process for innovative information than were the less successful ones. In the adaptive firms, technological or market information was introduced to reprogram routine operations, thus enhancing flexibility in a technologically changing environment [10].

To undergird these contentions, a significant empirical literature has now emerged relating technology to various organizational matters. The most noteworthy examples are probably Woodward's seminal studies [9]. Her work and other relevant investigations have been well reviewed by Perrow, J. D. Thompson, and Hickson et al. so there is no need for repetition here [24]. It will be sufficient to observe that, although the nature, degree, and conditions of its effect remain controversial,* technology has been shown to affect structure, to shape interaction, and to influence the personal characteristics of organizational members [25].

Yet, as late as 1964, W. R. Scott felt constrained to mark the infrequency with which technological variables had been built into theory [26, *pp. 485-530*]. The reasons for this seem to reside partly in a preoccupation of organizational scholars with nonstructural human relations or "informal" processes† and partly from the fact that, although technological phenomena were widely recognized and sometimes even categorized, until recently there literally were no technological *variables* to build into theory [12, *Chap. 3*]. Perhaps what is most important in the technology-organization literature of the past few years, therefore, aside from empirical explication, is that it has begun to give form to conceptualizations of manageable technological variables or dimensions. Prominent in this connection has been the work of Bell, Harvey, Perrow, Whyte, and Pugh and Hickson.

---

*Illumination of the controversy can perhaps best be found in Hickson et al., note 15.

† See Mouzelis, note 11, for further discussion of this point.

The technology variable.   It will be recalled from our earlier discussion that productive as it was empirically, the technology variable was ambiguous in Woodward's classification scheme. She regarded her entire scheme as a direct index of technology, even as a scale of technological complexity ranging from unit to mass to process modes of production. Harvey, however, has quite reasonably pointed out that the complexity scale could equally well be the reverse [27, 247-59]. And Woodward's own finding that unit production and continuous process organizations tended to exhibit many common characteristics that contrasted sharply with other kinds of organizations could imply a "circular" interpretation of the technological dimension underlying her classification.

The precise mechanisms linking technologies with organizational forms are still problematical in the literature, but, as a generality, the critical technological element to which organizational structure must respond seems best conceptualized as *complexity*. This is something that unit production organizations, for instance, may have in at least as long a supply as their continuous process counterparts—a moment's reflection on the many esoteric one-of-a-kind products produced under the American space program vindicates that assertion. To state it simply, this view of correlation between organization and technology signifies that the concrete manifestations of technology are less important than the essential complexity underlying them. Having said that, however, it is necessary to acknowledge immediately that complexity is an elusive concept that takes many forms.

Bell, for instance, has dealt explicitly with the matter of complexity and structure in his study of spans of control (ratios of personnel to supervisors) in a large hospital [28, 90-101]. He defined complexity as:

(1)   The degree of predictability of work demands;
(2)   The discretion provided for in a position; and
(3)   The responsibility of the job-holder (construed as the time lapse between decision and its supervisory review or assessment).

Bell then showed that as complexity increased with regard to either subordinates' or supervisors' roles, the span of control decreased.

Harvey, using Woodward's work as a point of departure, prefers to speak of a complexity dimension ranging from technical diffuseness ("made to orderness') to specificity [27]. He argues that one needs to take account not only of the *form* of technology (as Woodward tried to do), but also of the amount of "changefulness" *within* a form. As he puts it: A unit production firm might produce the same thing most of the time and thus be "specific." Or, it might vary its outputs and be "diffuse." Harvey postulated that whether the organization is specific or diffuse, it will have differential implications for its structural characteristics. He conceived three "socio-technical types" (marriages of technology and internal organizational structure): (1) diffuse, (2) intermediate, and (3) specific (defined in terms of frequency of product change) and showed that when compared with specific types, diffuse types had fewer specialized sub-units, fewer levels of authority, a lower ratio of managers and supervisors to total personnel, and a lessened degree of performance program specification.

Drawing mainly on the work of Woodward, Harvey, and Bell, together with his own experience, Whyte has gone about the detailed application of technological concepts to analysis of that basic organizational element, the span of control, asking what factors are responsible for its variations [12]. He concludes that there are five factors:

(1) The complexity (in Bell's sense) of the job for the supervisor and subordinate;
(2) The visibility of results from performing the work;
(3) The interdependence and need for coordination among tasks;
(4) The degree to which interdependent activities require human rather than mechanical control; and
(5) The kinds of personnel required by the technology.

Probably the most searching attempts at conceptualizing technology and relating it to organizational processes can be found in Perrow's work with his contingent, two-dimensional model that elaborates a distinction between routine and nonroutine technologies [5]. Perrow's emphasis is on classifying technologies regarding the frequency with which exceptional cases* are encountered and with reference to the nature of the search process (for solutions) that ensues when exceptions (problems) do occur. Using this general model, he relates task-structure to analogous control/coordination processes involving variations in individual or group discretion and the nature of the feedback mechanisms controlling performance (i.e., their degree of "programming"). Perrow also distinguishes three functional areas in management: (1) design and planning, (2) technical control and support of product, and (3) the supervision of production and marketing, each of which he ties in with the technological and task dimensions described. Finally, in a tentative way, Perrow undertakes to relate nontask-related (i.e., informal) interaction to the basic model.

---

*I.e., tasks, decisions, etc., not covered, or perceived to be covered, by existing performance programs. Such exceptions define problems for which organizational solutions must be sought if the system is to function, or at least if it is to function smoothly.

In a later paper, Perrow refined his basic model and extended it to connect with the psychological processes of its human operatives [29]. He stresses a kind of "cognitive" conception of technology working as a system of cues (that may vary in clarity), which signal the initiation of performance routines (that also may vary in their degree of explicit "programming") and involve provision for handling exceptions that may be procedurally more or less routinized. The notable feature of this construction is that regardless of how complicated or elaborate, a system may be viewed as technologically routine to the extent that:

(1)   The signals that initiate its processes are unambiguous;
(2)   The performance processes so cued are programmed; and
(3)   When faced with exceptions not covered by regular performance routines, search processes and problem-solving methods are programmed.

The properties of technology emphasized by other writers (e.g., Harvey's "changefulness" or Whyte's "human" vs. "mechanical" control) can probably be treated in Perrow's formulation as either sources of cognitive complexity (exceptions) or as proxies for it.

Perrow's cognitive constructions rather closely parallel the much more general cybernetic model of human problem-solving due to Miller, Galanter, and Pribram [30]. These authors construe individual performance in relation to a cognitive Test-Operate-Test-Exit (TOTE) model which is based on the notion of "plan." A plan is defined as any hierarchical process controlling the sequence in which a set of operations is performed. They discuss a variety of ways that plans may differ (communicability, source, detail, flexibility, etc.) and also discuss plans for searching and solving, distinguishing between systematic and heuristic varieties.

Very briefly, their idea is that people have images of reality and an array of plans for dealing with it. As information in the form of environmental signals flows into a human performance system, it is "tested" for fit with existing plans which then may be put into operation. Results of action are appraised via feedback from the performance, and the system moves on either to another performance segment or, if a problem has arisen, to a more or less standardized search routine. Of course, the system could cycle into a search routine immediately if the initial "test" yielded no suitable performance program. From Miller, Galanter, and Pribram's presentation it is evident that when a search plan exists one may not even be aware of it, although it is necessary to perceive the exception—it is the function of the TOTE unit to guarantee that. Thus, regardless of how complicated it may be materially, at the behavioral level, technology can be defined in terms of an ordered set of skills or habits that differ mainly in their degree of routinization, integration, or mechanization. Complicated material technologies may be more difficult to program and they may place greater demands on human resources, but be that as it may, what counts operationally is behavioral routinization. We may say, then, that technological complexity is a function of the frequency with which problems (exceptions) confront organizational operations and the practical difficulty and degree of individual discretion or judgment required in resolving or finding solutions to them.

Performance vs. problem-solving system.   It may be concluded from the foregoing that it is not material technology, *per se*, that presents organizational challenges, but the nature of the behavioral and problem-solving tasks confronting those operating the system at all its various levels. The extent to which an organization's task systems can be programmed and operational uncertainty thereby eliminated seems to be the critical circumstance. However, no performance program can anticipate every contingency; exceptions will occur. Even if it can be reduced, operational uncertainty cannot be totally eliminated. Consequently, as Perrow has maintained, the decisive structural determinants are apt to be associated with the handling of exceptions to task programs. The frequency of such exceptions, of course, will not be unrelated to material technology, but it still may not parallel it closely—very complicated material technologies may, for instance, be highly programmed. But, in any event, the more crucial consideration would seem to be the importance of exceptions to the viability of the organization and how these exceptions can be handled by it.

If paradoxical, then, it seems nevertheless reasonable to assume that the more a system depends upon its performance programs to control its outputs, the more seriously it must view exceptions to their application or breakdowns in their operation and, hence, the more it must be geared to deal with them if and when they occur. If problem-solving processes are routinized along with task performance, one could expect a different kind of organization from the one that would result when they are not. In an unpublished paper, Perrow has presented some data consistent with such an expectation [31].

If this is sensible, a potential basis for the similarity found by Woodward between unit production and process organizations is discoverable via the simple expedient of conceiving, somewhat after the fashion of Burns and Stalker [10], of two quite different kinds of organization: one geared chiefly to performance (as in a mass production factory or a modern bank) and the other one geared to problem-solving (as in a hospital or a design and development enterprise). In a unit production firm, the system deals almost entirely with exceptions, and its problem-solving modes are likely to be un-routinized, especially if it is technologically diffuse.* In automated continuous process organizations, whether exceptions are frequent or not, they will be critical when they occur so that such systems, too, are likely to be structured as problem-solving or trouble-shooting affairs. Thus, both unit-production organizations (at any rate diffuse ones involved with complicated material technologies) and continuous-process varieties are likely to be similarly structured —as organic problem-solving systems. Other operations, facing fewer exceptions and less vitally affected by ones that occur or are equipped with simple routines for solving the problems that ensue from them, are likely to be differently structured—as mechanistic performance systems. We shall not now go into the matter further, but it does seem likely that over the long run firms may tend to organize more and more as performance systems, whether or not it is good for them to do so.†

Organization-level analysis of technology and structure. So far we have talked of relations between technology and structure mostly at the so-called level of the organization, treating the system largely as a unitary entity. Yet, we have mentioned the frequent internal technological diversity of organizations—a fact that confronts organization-level analyses with thorny problems. In addition to complicating life, it prompts serious questions about suitable units of system analysis, for there is no inherent reason to expect technologically diverse organizations to be any less diverse structurally. Therefore, assessments of technology-structure correlations might profit from being based on homogeneous organizational subsystems instead of "forcing" aggregated total systems into statistically defined "types." Or, a system-level alternative might be to devise suitable indexes of technological diversity for use either as independent variables or as "test factors."

To illustrate the force of this point: it is possible that one reason Hickson et al. found stronger relations between organizational size and structure than between technology and structure (leaving aside their definition of technology), is that size may well be correlated with diversity [15]. Small unit production firms (missing from Hickson's et al. research) are likely to be technologically more homogeneous (in the cognitive sense described above) than are very large

---

*For data regarding this point, see Harvey, note 27.

† Pertinent discussions of processes of bureaucratization can be found in Mouzelis, note 11, and Olsen, note 18, Chap. 17.

firms (which were heavily represented in the Hickson et al. investigation). While no evidence exists bearing on the matter, actually, Hickson's et al. attempts to reconcile their findings with Woodward's are not too different from the present thesis. In any event, the issue is one which deserves attention in future research.

Designing organizational structures.   The design of an organization refers to the composition of its structure; moreover, "design" implies a purposive formulation legitimized by an organization's formal authority [32, 1171-1213]. Certainly, presumptions of organizational rationality implicit in the idea of design connote a sense of organizational construction which is neatly adapted by managerial plan to the objectives and circumstances (technological or other) of a particular organization, adaptations optimized by careful analyses and the systematic application of "principles" of organization and management theory. Yet curiously enough, in her extensive studies, Woodward found firms, both successful and unsuccessful, to vary markedly in "organization consciousness." Even among firms "in which production systems were basically the same," considerable differences could be found regarding the extent to which they tried "to rationalize their production, in their awareness of technical developments, and in their use of techniques such as work study, methods engineering, and operations research" [9, *p. 42*].

Woodward was led to the view that conscious organizational planning rarely is based on technical considerations; that it amounts mostly to implicit recognition of technologically constrained situational demands; and that it represents the institutionalization of prevailing organizational realities. Woodward did find process-type firms to be successful a little more often than any other kind, but by and large she discovered that successful firms were mostly those organizations which were *typical* of their technological types. Successful large-batch firms, for instance, tended to be mechanistic (in Burns and Stalker's sense), whereas other successful firms tended to be organic. And the same organizational characteristic associated with success among large-batch firms—formalization of roles—augured failure among process types. But, in Woodward's studies, the organizational designing was so "unconscious" that most managers were not even aware of how their organizations compared structurally with others.

Findings like Woodward's suggest that planning is either absent (which it often surely is) or that it is more apparent than real (coming to little more than formalization of what already is). Undoubtedly, much ostensible organizational analysis and design does represent a sort of managerial doodling instigated by external affiliations [9,

p. 21], motivated by managers' desires to display virtuosity, or motivated by their needs to "keep up with the Joneses." This analysis
and design may also depend heavily upon having time to think about
such things—on organizational "slack," as Perrow put it [5]. Furthermore, Blau, Scott, and V. A. Thompson have suggested that
organizational elaboration often arises simply from desires on the
part of those in power either to evade unpleasant tasks or to bol-
ster the prevailing status structure [33], or from some other consideration (e.g. empire-building) quite extraneous to technical requirements of organizational tasks.

Still Woodward found, too, that "organic" firms tended as a group
to be low in organization consciousness, thus implying that these
things may not depend altogether on managerial caprice. And, while
organization consciousness was not always a mark of "mechanistic"
orientations—organization charts sometimes poorly reflected what
actually happened in the firm—consciousness did not seem to be
altogether random regarding technology. In short, some technologies
seem to prompt more concern with design than others. It follows
that they would, from arguments like Udy's: that the salience of
technology as an influence upon structure will decrease with its
flexibility and that mechanization of technology will enhance the
salience of group structure [22]—a proposition fully consistent with
Cyert and March's assertion that questions of organizational design
are meaningful only when alternative modes of performance exist [1].

These issues have been well reviewed by J. D. Thompson who
offers an array of propositions relating technology to organizational
operations and thence to rational organizational design [16]. His
book nicely illustrates both how operations depend on technology
and how various principles of organizational design implicitly assume
sustaining technologies. The latter is a matter of overarching significance highlighted by Woodward's finding that success was associated
with "textbook" management applications only among large-batch
concerns [9]; this suggests the conclusion that management theory
has been largely based on this technological model, without this fact
having been understood. If that is true, application of standard
managerial precepts in other technological contexts is likely to yield
less than salutary consequences. Miller and Rice have made this
point, commenting that classical theories of organization drew mainly on experience in industries representing only a narrow technological range [34]. They add that their own experiences support Woodward's implication that the models and principles derived do not fit
either process or unit production industries. Hickson et al. have
also argued the relativity of design precepts to technological environments, though they appear to believe this is because technology is

relevant mostly at "shop-floor levels" and, therefore, chiefly in small organizations "where nothing is far removed from the workflow itself" [15 *p. 396*]

In any case, it follows, as Perrow also has said [5], that there can probably be no "one best" organizational structure of managerial orientation—not participative management, not bureaucracy, not any single fashionable methodology. In this regard, one might call to mind Fiedler's persuasive arguments that effective leadership entails an adaptation of "style" to organizational context [35]. In the same way, organizational success depends fundamentally upon meshing design (social technology) with the material technology out of which emerges the organization's tasks. It may be, as Woodward's work suggests, that organizations tend as a "natural" process to shape themselves into at least a loose match of technologies, but that does not mean that management design activity is irrelevant or that management ought to become passive and desist from efforts to plan and enhance operational effectiveness.* What follows is only that it must acknowledge the technological imperative [15]. Social and material technology must be mutually adapted in system designs. Admittedly, until more adequately differentiated social technological models become available from comparative studies this will be hard to do. But who ever said management was easy?

Concluding Observations

We have distinguished between two fundamentally different models for organization—performance and problem-solving. Analogous in conception to Burns and Stalker's mechanistic and organic management models, this distinction has the virtue of making management methods the means to ends—e.g., problem-solving—rather than inherently good or bad things. In any event, we have also suggested that most management theories pertain to performance models, not to problem-solving models of organization but that, for various reasons, organizations tend to evolve toward performance models; i.e., they endeavor to increase routinization. It may be, as Olsen says, that such tendencies arise from the organization's continual efforts to rationalize its functioning in order to achieve its goals more effectively [18, *pp. 300-301*], but nevertheless there are many times when such

---

*I am indebted to John D. Senger for pointing out the possible analogy between this "natural" process and Darwinian evolution of form and its attendant costs. Managerial manipulation of organizational forms then might be considered an attempt to reduce the costs of evolutionary development, even if it might not always succeed.

movement is premature and dysfunctional. Consequently, it will sometimes require deliberate managerial effort to resist such evolution when it would compromise the flexibility and creativity of the system and defeat effective goal achievement.

Probably nowhere is this maxim more applicable than in research and development environments (whether in industry, universities, or wherever). Decentralized, organically operated project organizations have been effective vehicles for accomplishing goals in such contexts, but the moral of our story, paradoxically perhaps, is that centralized authority may be necessary to preserve their adaptive integrity in the face of "natural" forces toward bureaucratization. Udy, for instance, hypothesized that technological "complexity" stimulates concerns for coordination that tend to lead toward elaboration and formalization of administration [22]. Furthermore, the generation of inflexibility occasioned by predilections toward "empire building" within projects and by dispositions to assimilate project organizations to functional (or administrative) divisions are familiar experiences in research and development environments [36].

Finally, we should close by commenting that nothing in the foregoing should be interpreted to preclude various kinds of performance or information programming. Nor should it foreclose use of searching methods for systems analysis; the basic message is that these things must be employed in the service of a fundamental problem-solving model of organization. In brief, they would be means to ends and not devices for transforming the organizational design or for reducing it to some tepid least common denominator. One unfortunate (or fortunate, depending on your view) consequence of this policy, of course, is that it leaves the organization in a condition of heavy dependence on the commitment and competence of the people who run it—or at least those who manage it.

Summary

Various means of classifying organizations are reviewed and the relevance of technology to the structure of organization is discussed. Developments in the operationalization of technological variables are traced, and the implications for purposive organizational planning considered. Emphasis is placed on a "cognitive" interpretation of technological complexity and on the role of uncertainty as a basic constraint upon organizational design. Two basically distinct organizational models are differentiated: one is oriented toward problem-solving and the other toward performance. It is concluded that most management theories pertain to the latter and not the former, and various consequences of that judgment are considered.

Notes

1. R. M. Cyert and J. G. March, "Organizational Design," in *New Perspectives in Organization Research,* edited by W. W. Cooper, H. J. Leavitt, and M. W. Shelly (New York: Wiley, 1964), Chap. 29, p. 558.
2. In this usage we are following the example of D. Katz and R. Kahn, *The Social Psychology of Organizations* (New York: Wiley, 1966).
3. T[alcott] Parsons, *Structure and Process in Modern Societies* (Glencoe: Free Press, 1960).
4. D. Katz and R. Kahn, "Dimensions of Organization Structure," *Admin. Sci. Quart.,* 13 (1968), 65-105.
5. See C. A. Perrow, "A Framework for the Comparative Analysis of Organizations," *Amer. Sociological Review,* 32 (1967)
6. See R. G. Hunt, "Review of Systems of Organization" by E. J. Miller and A. K. Rice, *Admin. Sci. Quart.,* 13 (1968).
7. See D. S. Pugh et al., "Dimensions," in *Organizational Behavior: Theory and Application,* edited by W. F. Whyte (Homewood, Ill.: Irwin-Dorsey, 1969).
8. R. N. Anthony, *Planning and Control Systems* (Cambridge: Harvard University Press, 1965).
9. See Joan Woodward, *Industrial Organization: Theory and Practice* (London: Oxford University Press, 1965).
10. Tom Burns and G. M. Stalker, *The Management of Innovation* (London: Tavistock, 1961).
11. See, e.g., D. Katz and R. Kahn, op. cit., note 2, Chap. 5; N. P. Mouzelis, *Organization and Bureaucracy* (Chicago: Aldine, 1967); W. F. Whyte, op. cit., note 7, Chap. 1; W. Bennis, "Beyond Bureaucracy," *Transaction,* 2 (1965), 31-5.
12. W. F. Whyte, op. cit., note 7.
13. Erving Goffman, *Asylums* (Garden City: Doubleday, Anchor ed., 1961).
14. J. D. Thompson and F. L. Bates, "Technology, Organization, and Administration," *Admin. Sci. Quart.,* 2 (1957).
15. For a useful discussion of definitional issues, see D. J. Hickson, D.S. Pugh, and D. C. Pheysey, "Operations Technology and Organizational Structure: An Empirical Reappraisal," *Admin. Sci. Quart.,* 14 (1969), 378-97.
16. J. D. Thompson, *Organizations in Action* (New York: McGraw, 1967).
17. Whyte, op. cit., note 7; Woodward, op. cit., note 9. Notice might be taken of Hickson's et al. incorporation of this category, along with unit production, mass production, and the others, into a thoughtful scale of "production continuity" (see Hickson et al, op. cit., note 15).
18. M. E. Olsen, *The Process of Social Organization* (New York: Holt, Rinehart & Winston, 1968).
19. Arnold Toynbee, *The Industrial Revolution* (Boston: Beason, 1956); Margaret Mead, editor, *Cultural Patterns and Technological Change* (New York: New American Library, 1955).
20. R. Dubin, *The World of Work* (Englewood Cliffs: Prentice-Hall, 1958).
21. A. L. Stinchcombe, "Social Structure and Organization," in *Handbook of Organizations,* edited by James G. March (Chicago: Rand, 1965), pp. 142-94.
22. S. H. Udy, "The Comparative Analysis of Organizations," in *Handbook of Organizations,* edited by March, op. cit., note 21.
23. See, e.g., Mead, op. cit., note 19, for illustrations of such cultural disinclinations.

24. Perrow, op. cit., note 5; Thompson, op. cit., note 16.; Hickson et. al., op. cit., note 15.
25. One example of this last point, which is here mentioned only incidentally, may be found in R. Blauner's studies of alienation, e.g., *Alienation and Freedom* (Chicago: Univ. of Chicago Press, 1964).
26. W. R. Scott, "Theory of Organizations," in *Handbook of Modern Sociology,* edited by R. E. L. Faris (Chicago: Rand, 1964).
27. E. Harvey, "Technology and the Structure of Organizations," *Amer. Sociological Review,* 33 (1968).
28. G. D. Bell, "Determinants of Span of Control," *American J. Sociology,* 73 (1967).
29. C. A. Perrow, "Technology and Structural Changes in Business Firms," paper presented at First World Congress, International Industrial Relations Association, Geneva (Sept. 1967).
30. G. A. Miller, E. Galanter, and K. H. Pribram, *Plans and the Structure of Behavior* (New York: Holt, Rinehart & Winston, 1960).
31. C. A. Perrow, "Working Paper on Technology and Structure," mimeo (University of Wisconsin, 1970).
32. See C. J. Haberstroh, "Organization Design and Systems Analysis," in *Handbook of Organizations,* op. cit., note 21.
33. Peter Blau and W. R. Scott, *Formal Organizations* (San Francisco: Chandler, 1962); V. A. Thompson, *Modern Organization* (New York: Knopf, 1961).
34. E. J. Miller and A. K. Rice, *Systems of Organization* (London: Tavistock, 1967).
35. F. E. Fielder, *A Theory of Leadership Effectiveness* (New York: McGraw, 1967).
36. See Haberstroh, op. cit., note 21, pp. 1208-9, for a brief discussion of these issues.

Introduction to the Structural Design of Organizations

Jay W. Lorsch

Our purpose is to introduce you to a useful way of thinking about the structural design of organizations, and to make you aware that the structure of an organization is not an immutable given, but rather a set of complex variables about which managers can exercise considerable choice.

Definition of Structural Design

It is useful to make a distinction between the basic structure and the operating mechanisms which implement and reinforce this basic structure [1]. Design of the *basic structure* involves such central issues as how the work of the organization will be divided and assigned among positions, groups, departments, divisions, etc., and how the coordination necessary to accomplish total organizational objectives will be achieved. Choices made about these issues are usually publicized in organization charts and job descriptions. If we recognize that behavior in an organization is influenced by a system of variables (technical, individual, social, and organizational inputs), it is obvious that such formal documents are only one method of signaling to individuals what behavior is expected of them. Nevertheless, this method is important because it is so widely used by managers to define and communicate their expectations of other organization members.

Managers also can reinforce the intent of their basic structural design through what we call *operating mechanisms*. Operating mech-

Reprinted with permission from Lorsch, "Introduction to the Structural Design of Organizations," in *Organizational Structure and Design* by Dalton, Lawrence & Lorsch (Homewood, Ill.: Richard D. Irwin, Inc., 1970), pp. 1-16.

anisms include such factors as control procedures, information systems, reward and appraisal systems, standardized rules and procedures, and even spatial arrangements. These structural variables can be used to more clearly signal to organizational members what is expected of them, to motivate them toward their assigned part of the organization's goal, and, as necessary, to encourage them to undertake collaborative activity. While our central focus is on the basic structure, we shall have more to say about these operating mechanisms later.

Conventional Approaches to Structural Design

In the past, the most widely used ideas about structural design were those developed by a group of organization theorists who have been labeled the *classicists* [2]. Fayol, Gulick, Urwick, Mooney, and their colleagues and successors drew heavily on their own experience in early twentieth century organizations and on the industrial engineering ideas of Frederick J. Taylor. While a detailed review of these ideas is beyond our scope, we can briefly summarize the central features of their "principles of organization."

With regard to the division of work, most of the authors recommended dividing up the work by function (i.e., sales, manufacturing, engineering, etc.). The one exception was Gulick, who suggested that the work of an organization could be divided on several bases: by function, by product, by territory, and by time. In any case these writers emphasized economic and technical efficiency. The only human variable given major attention was the limited intellectual capacity of the individual. To cope with this limitation, division of labor was advocated. Each individual would have a narrow task which, given his limited capacity, he could accomplish in the most technically efficient manner. While these ideas are based on the simplistic assumption that man is motivated only by money and will do as he is directed, they still persist and are widely used as a basis for making decisions about organization structure.

According to these writers, coordination was not a major problem. Work was to be divided so that the subgoals of various units would add up to the overall organizational goals. Any remaining coordinating issues would be handled through the management hierarchy. Since people followed the direction of their superiors, the management hierarchy was the only coordinating device necessary.

While this approach has been widely used, it has severe limitations. First, it provides little help in designing a task with intrinsic motivation. Second, it is of limited value in dealing with the multiple levels of division of work in most large organizations. Third, managers have become more aware that the management hierarchy is not sufficient as a mechanism to achieve the coordination required in an organization. The goals of individuals and units do not automatically add up to the total goals of the organization.

Because of these shortcomings, other organizational theorists, most of whom were psychologists or social psychologists, began conducting research into these issues and have more recently come up with a second set of prescriptions which, while less widely applied, are sufficiently used to be worthy of mention. Perhaps the most concise statement of these ideas is offered by Likert [3]. This approach considers the motivational and collaborative issues left unattended by the classical theorists. While these behavioral scientists do not deal explicitly with the issue of division of labor, they do implicitly suggest that jobs should be divided to give the individual meaningful work over which he can have some feeling of control and influence. According to this view, the individual is motivated by self-actualization, and it follows that he will seek more complicated and engaging jobs. This must be taken into account in the division of work. The individual is also motivated by social needs and it is therefore important, according to Likert, to structure the organization so that each individual belongs to a cohesive work group in which participation in decision making is the accepted norm.

While this approach offers no explicit recommendation about how to divide up the work of an organization to provide self-actualizing work and group membership, it is very explicit about how to achieve collaboration or coordinated effort. This is done by linking work groups together by members who hold overlapping membership in two or more groups. This "linking pin" individual is a key figure in the organization, since it is through him that information about group objectives and decisions is transmitted and conflicting viewpoints are resolved.

One shortcoming of this approach is the implicit assumption that all individuals are motivated by similar needs. No attention is focused on the important differences in individual needs. A second problem is, because of either the needs of organization members or the nature of the task, linking pin and participative decision-making practices are often impractical. For example, some managers find it difficult because of their own predispositions to involve subordinates in all decisions. Similarly, some tasks require decisions for which the information is not available to all the members of the work group.

Both of these approaches described above are subject to a more general criticism. While each offers a particular prescription about how to design the basic structure of an organization, both approaches are offered as the one best way to organize. To the readers who have already been exposed to a systemic conceptual framework, it should be obvious that any blanket prescription is an oversimplification. As the recent title of a book on organization theory states, "It all depends" [4]. Furthermore, recent research which utilizes the systemic approach suggests that the choices made in designing a basic structure depend on the task and human inputs involved.

A Systemic Approach to the Design of Organization Structure

Two recent studies point to the validity of this conclusion. Burns and Stalker, in their pioneering study of firms in both a dynamic, changing industry and a more established, stable industry, report that there were important structural differences between the successful firms in each industry [5]. In the stable industry, successful organizations tended to what the authors called "mechanistic." There was more reliance on formal rules and procedures. Decisions were made at the higher levels of the organization. The spans of supervisory control were narrow. In the more dynamic industry, the authors characterized the effective organizations as "organic." Spans of supervisory control were wider; less attention was paid to formal procedures; and more decisions were reached at the lower levels of the organization. The second study was conducted by Joan Woodward [6]. She found that economically successful organizations in industries with different production technologies were characterized by different organization structures. For example, successful firms in industries with a unit or job-shop technology had wider spans of supervisory control and fewer hierarchical levels than did successful firms with continuous process technologies.

While both of these studies consider the structure of an organization as one variable in a system affecting behavior in organizations, they do not provide a conceptual framework which is sufficiently comprehensive for analyzing and solving structural design problems. A more recent study by Lawrence and Lorsch builds on the basic idea of Woodward, Burns and Stalker, and others, and provides a more comprehensive analytic framework for working on structural design problems [7].

Differentiation and Integration

Before describing the analytic framework which Lawrence and Lorsch have developed, it is important to emphasize three points.*

---

*A more complete statement of their findings can be found in *Organization and Environment*, note 7.

First, this conceptual scheme is based on an empirical study of ten organizations with varying levels of economic performance in three different industrial environments (plastics, consumer foods, standardized containers) and these findings have been corroborated by research in several additional settings. Second, this conceptual model does not provide a prescription for the one best way to organize. Instead, it provides a framework for thinking about structural design issues based on the demands of the organization's particular market and technological environment. Third, this set of concepts can be used to analyze the structural design which seems to best fit an organization's environment. These concepts can also be used to understand the organization's current strengths and weaknesses and to help determine what design changes will move a particular organization toward a better fit with the demands of its specific environment.

As we begin this discussion, we must first define two of the central concepts in this framework. First, *differentiation* is defined as *the differences in cognitive and emotional orientations among managers in different functional departments, and the differences in formal structure among these departments.* Rather than thinking of division of work as only affecting the economies and efficiencies of task performance, as did the classicists, Lawrence and Lorsch recognized that each unit was itself a subsystem in which members would develop particular orientations and structural patterns, depending on their task and their predispositions. Since different units were working with different parts of the organization's environment (e.g., market, scientific techno-economic [manufacturing] variables), these units would develop differentiation to some degree or other, depending upon the specific environment.

The second concept which we want to define is *integration—the quality of the state of collaboration that exists among departments that are required to achieve unity of effort by the environment.*

As we have already indicated, different environments require varying degrees of differentiation among organizational units. Basically, the extent of organizational differentiation depends upon the *certainty or uncertainty of the environment* and its *diversity or homogeneity.* Rather than being concerned with the environment as a single entity, the authors recognized that complex organizations—those with more than one unit—actually segment their environments into parts. The authors then identified the relative certainty of the parts of any environment. For example, each of the ten organizations was dealing with a market subenvironment (the task of the sales organization), a techno-economic subenvironment (the task of the manufacturing unit), and a scientific subenvironment (the task of the research or design unit). Each of these subenvironments within any one industry had a different degree of certainty of information about what needed to be done. How similar or different these parts of any environment were on the certainty—uncertainty continuum determined whether that environment was relatively homogeneous or diverse. For example, in one of the environments studied, the container industry, all parts of the environment were relatively certain and the environment was characterized as homogeneous. On the other hand, in a second environment, the plastics industry, the parts of the environment ranged from a highly certain techno-economic sector to a very uncertain scientific subenvironment and the total environment was characterized as more diverse. As suggested above, the degree of differentiation in an effective organization was found to be related to the diversity of the environment. Thus, in the economically effective container industry there was less differentiation than in an effective plastic organization. The less effective organizations in these industries did not meet the environmental demand for differentiation so well.

We can now summarize the general relationship the authors found between the certainty of the subenvironment a unit is dealing with and three of the unit characteristics along which differentiation was measured (Figure 1).

FIGURE 1

Uncertainty of environmental sector	High	Moderate	Low
Extent of formalized unit structure	Low	Medium	High
Interpersonal orientation*	Task	Social	Task
Time orientation	Long	Medium	Short

*This curvilinear relation between the members' interpersonal orientation on a task-oriented/social-oriented continuum is consistent with the work of Fred E. Fiedler, *Technical Report No. 10* (Urbana, Ill.: Group Effectiveness Research Laboratory, Department of Psychology, University of Illinois, May 1962).

The fourth characteristic of units along which differentiation was measured—goal orientation—was not related to the certainty of the environment, but instead to the goals inherent in each part of the environment—e.g., the market (customer service, competitive action, etc.); techno-economic (costs, quality, efficient schedules, etc.); science (discovery of new knowledge; utilization of technical talent, etc.).

We can quote from the original study for a more detailed picture of how the varying degrees of differentiation manifest themselves in the high-performing organizations in two of the three industries studied [7, *pp. 134-36*].

To illustrate the varying states of differentiation among these three organizations, we can use hypothetical encounters among managers in both the plastics and the container high-performing organizations. In the plastics organization we might find a sales manager discussing a potential new product with a fundamental research scientist and an integrator. In this discussion the sales manager is concerned with the needs of the customer. What performance characteristics must a new product have to perform in the customer's machinery? How much can the customer afford to pay? How long can the material be stored without deteriorating? Further, our sales manager, while talking about these matters, may be thinking about more pressing current problems. Should he lower the price on an existing product? Did the material shipped to another customer meet his specifications? Is he going to meet this quarter's sales targets?

In contrast, our fundamental scientist is concerned about a different order of problems. Will this new project provide a scientific challenge? To get the desired result, could he change the molecular structure of a known material without affecting its stability? What difficulties will he encounter in solving these problems? Will this be a more interesting project to work on than another he heard about last week? Will he receive some professional recognition if he is successful in solving the problem? Thus our sales manager and our fundamental scientist not only have quite different goal orientations, but they are thinking about different time dimensions—the sales manager about what's going on today and in the next few months; the scientist, how he will spend the next few years.

But these are not the only ways in which these two specialists are different. The sales manager may be outgoing and concerned with maintaining a warm, friendly relationship with the scientist. He may be put off because the scientist seems withdrawn and disinclined to talk about anything other than the problems in which he is interested. He may also be annoyed that the scientist seems to have such freedom in choosing what he will work on. Furthermore, the scientist is probably often late for appointments, which, from the salesman's point of view, is no way to run a business. Our scientist, for his part, may feel uncomfortable because the salesman seems to be pressing for immediate answers to technical questions that will take a long time to investigate. All these discomforts are concrete manifestations of the relatively wide differences between these two men in respect to their working and thinking styles and the departmental structures to which each is accustomed.

Between these different points of view stands our integrator. If he is effective, he will understand, and to some extent share, the viewpoints of both specialists and will be working to help them communicate with each other. We do not want to dwell on his role at this point, but the mere fact that he is present as a result of the great differences among specialists in his organization.

In the high-performing container organization we might find a research scientist meeting with a plant manager to determine how to solve a quality problem. The plant manager talks about getting the problem solved as quickly as possible, in order to reduce the spoilage rate. He is probably thinking about how this problem will affect his ability to meet the current production schedule and to operate within cost constraints. The researcher is also seeking an immediate answer to the problem. He is concerned not with its theoretical niceties, but with how he can find an immediate applied solution. (Research in this industry tended to focus on short-term process development.) What adjustments in materials or machine procedures can he suggest to get the desired effect? In fact, these specialists may share a concern with finding the most feasible solution. They also operate in a similar, short-term time dimension. The differences in their interpersonal styles are also not too large. Both are primarily

concerned with getting the job done, and neither finds the other's style of behavior strange. They are also accustomed to quite similar organizational practices. Both see that they are rewarded for quite specific short-run accomplishments, and both might be feeling similar pressures from their superiors to get
the job done. In essence, these two specialists, while somewhat different in
their thinking and behavior patterns, would not find it uncomfortable or difficult to work together in seeking a joint solution to a problem. Thus they
would need no integrator.

The authors summarize this approach as follows: "These two hypothetical examples show clearly that the differentiation in the [effec-
tive] plastics organization is much greater than in the equally effective container concern. The high-performing food organization fell
between the extremes of differentiation represented by the other
two organizations." [7, *p. 137*]

But the environment of an organization imposes requirements
other than differentiation upon the organization. One of these is
the *dominant competitive issue*. In the plastics and food environment, this was the issue of innovating new products and processes;
for the container industry the dominant issue was the scheduling
and allocation of production facilities to meet market demands.

The dominant competitive issue was also related to the final environmental characteristic of interest to the authors—the pattern
and degree of integration required among units. In all three environments the tightness of integration required was found to be identical.
However, there was an important difference in the pattern around
which this integration was occurring. In plastics and foods, where
innovative issues are dominant, the tight integration was required
between sales and research and production and research.

FIGURE 2

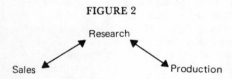

In the container industry, the tight integration was required between
production and sales and between production and research.

FIGURE 3

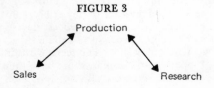

The authors report that in each industry the high-performing organizations achieved more effective integration around these critical interdependencies than their less effective competitor. Thus, the effective organization more satisfactorily met the demands of its environment for both differentiation and integration than did the less effective organization(s) in the same environment.

This finding is particularly interesting, because the authors found a strong inverse relationship between differentiation and integration within any one organization. When highly interdependent units are highly differentiated, it is more difficult to achieve integration among them than when members of the units have similar ways of thinking and behaving. This antagonistic relationship is illustrated by Figure 4, taken from the original study [7, Fig. II-2, p. 48].

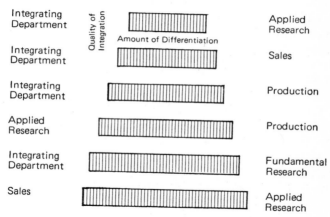

Relationship Between Differentiation and Integration

This is a schematic representation of the relationship among departments in one organization. The longer the bar, the more differentiation; the wider the bar, the better the integration. This relationship held between pairs of units in all six organizations.

FIGURE 4

Thus, we are presented with an interesting paradox: effective organizations in a given environment achieve more differentiation *and* more integration, but these two states are basically antagonistic. How does an organization get both? The authors found that two related factors made this possible.

First, when an organization is both highly differentiated and well integrated, it is necessary for the organization to develop more complicated mechanisms for achieving integration. Of course the basic organizational device for achieving integration is the management hierarchy. In an organization such as the effective container firm, with relatively low differentiation, the authors found that the hierarchy, along with formal plans and controls, was sufficient to achieve the required integration. However, the effective plastics and food organizations, faced with a requirement for both high differentiation and close integration, developed other supplemental integrating devices. These included individual coordinators (integrators), cross-unit teams, and even whole departments of integrators—individuals whose basic contribution is achieving integration among units. The integrative devices present in the high-performing organization in each environment are summarized in Figure 5.

The authors point out that while the effective organizations always had integrative devices which were sufficient to handle both the differentiation and integration required, often the less effective firm also had appropriate integrative devices. Thus, the integrative devices alone do not explain why the more effective firms were able to achieve the required states of differentiation and integration while the less effective firms did not.

A second set of factors seems to account for this difference. This is the behavior pattern used within the organization to manage intergroup conflict. As individuals with different points of view attempt to attain unity of effort, conflicts inevitably arise. How well the organization does in achieving integration in the face of differentiation is very dependent upon how the individuals involved resolve their conflicts. Lawrence and Lorsch's findings indicate that the behavior which leads to effective conflict resolution in certain respects varies with environmental demands, but in other respects shows no such variations.

Those conflict management factors which vary with environmental influence include the pattern of power or influence among groups and at various levels of the management hierarchy of each group. In the high-performing organizations where conflict was managed effectively, influence was concentrated at the level within each group where the information relevant to the decision was also present. The exact level in any unit depended upon the certainty of information in its part of the particular environment. For example, in the research units of the effective plastics organization, because of the uncertainty of knowledge, influence was concentrated at the lowest management level. In the production unit of this same plastics organization, where environmental information was more certain, influence was concentrated at a higher level of the management hierarchy. Because of the diversity of this environment, the hierarchical influence in this organization was distributed differently among different levels in each function. The same was true of the effective food organization for similar reasons. However, in the container organization, dealing with more certain and more homogeneous environment, the information could be efficiently gathered

FIGURE 5

Introduction to the Structural Design of Organizations

(environmental factors and organizational characteristics of effective organizations)

Industry	Environment Diversity	Actual Differentiation	Actual Integration	Integrative Devices		Conflict Management Variables	
				Type of Integrative Devices	Special Integrating Personnel as % of Total Management	Hierarchical Influence	Unit Having High Influence
Plastics	High	High	High	Teams, roles, departments, hierarchy, plans and procedures	22%*	Evenly distributed	Integrating unit
Foods	Moderate	Moderate	High	Roles, plans, hierarchy, procedures	17%*	Evenly distributed	Sales and research
Container	Low	Low	High	Hierarchy, plans and procedures	0%*	Top high, bottom low	Sales

*This proportion was constant for the high and low performer within these industries.

by upper levels of management in all functions. Thus, hierarchical influence in this organization was concentrated at the top in all units.

The required pattern of influence among units also varied with environmental requirements. In the effective organization the unit(s) which had the central knowledge about environmental conditions related to the dominant strategic variable was the one with the most influence. For instance, in the effective plastics organization, where a separate integrating unit had been established, this group had the highest influence because it was in a position to have information about the various parts of the environment, all of which were important in achieving innovation. In the food organization, where the dominant issue was also innovation, the situation was slightly different. Here no integrating department had been established, because the differentiation required was not as high as in the plastics environment. Also, because of the consumer products involved, the dominant knowledge was in the market and scientific sectors of the environment. Therefore, the sales and research units had similar high levels of power in relation to the production unit. In the container industry the dominant issue of customer service meant that the sales unit must call the tune, and this unit did have the highest influence.

The two factors which led to effective resolution under all environmental conditions were the mode of conflict resolution, and the basis from which high influence was derived. In high-performing organizations in all environments, it was found that conflict was managed by involved individuals who dealt openly with the conflict and worked a problem until a resolution was reached which best met total organizational goals. In the effective organizations, there was more of a tendency to *confront* conflict instead of using raw power to *force* one party's compliance or instead of *smoothing* over the conflict by agreeing to disagree.

In all the high-performing organizations, the authors also found that the individuals primarily involved in resolving conflict, whether they were a common superior in the hierarchy or persons in special integrating positions, had influence based to a large extent on their perceived competence and knowledge. This was in contrast to the less effective organizations where such persons usually drew their power solely from their position or from their control over scarce resources. The persons centrally involved in achieving integration in the high-performing organizations were followed not only because they had formal positional authority, but also because they were seen as knowledgeable about the issues which had to be resolved.

In those organizations where special integrators existed, Lawrence and Lorsch found one additional conflict management factor which seemed important. In the effective organizations, such integrators had orientations which were balanced between those of the groups whose efforts they were integrating. This made it possible for them to understand and communicate with each of the groups concerned. In the less effective organizations, these integrators tended to have one-sided orientations. They thought and acted like sales personnel or like researchers and this made it difficult for them to work with other groups.

All of these conflict management variables taken together suggest why the effective organizations in each environment were able to achieve the differentiation and integration required by the particular environment when less effective firms were not able to do so. These conflict management practices were the glue which held the differentiated units together as they worked toward integrated goals.

To summarize, then, the Lawrence and Lorsch study provides a set of research findings and concepts which enable us to understand what characteristics an organization must have to be effective in a particular set of environmental circumstances. This study directs our attention to the environmental demands placed on the organization in terms of the degree of differentiation, the pattern and degree of integration, integrative mechanisms, and conflict management behaviors. Those factors in the study which varied among high-performing organizations in the three environments studied are summarized in Figure 5.

With this summary of the findings of this study, we now want to examine briefly how these ideas can be put to use to work on the issues of structural design.

Applying Differentiation and Integration Concepts to Structural Design

As we consider these concepts as they apply to structural design decisions, we will also suggest the sequence of structural subproblems. While these subproblems are stated as discrete issues, the reader should be aware that in practice it is necessary to move back and forth among them as one thinks about the whole problem of structural design in a given organization. We will look first at the design of the basic structure and then at the necessary operating mechanisms.

Grouping activities into units is the logical first step in designing a basic structure. The differentiation and integration concepts focus our attention on two criteria for making decisions about grouping activity. First, units which will have similar orientations and tasks should be grouped together, both because they can reinforce each other's common concerns to achieve the needed differentiation and because this will simplify the coordinating task of the common boss. Second, units which are required to integrate their activities closely should be grouped together, because the common superior can then work to achieve the required integration through the management hierarchy. Therefore units which have a requirement for both low differentiation and tight integration, should be grouped together. However, when some units are low in differentiation but are not highly interdependent, or conversely, high in differentiation but also highly interdependent, the choice about grouping becomes more complex. In these cases, we must use our judgment to determine which criterion—low differentiation or high integration—we want to optimize in grouping activities.

Designing integrative devices is the second step in determining the basic structure. As we suggested above, the grouping of activities itself has an effect upon the design of integrative devices. A primary integrative device in any organization is the management hierarchy. In grouping activities, we are essentially making choices about which units we want to integrate through the hierarchy. However, as the Lawrence and Lorsch findings suggest, even after the units are grouped and decisions have been made about where the hierarchy can be used to achieve integration, we are still left with the question of what other integrating devices are desirable and necessary. Their findings suggest that as the environment requires more differentiation and tighter integration it is necessary to build supplemental integrating mechanisms such as integrating departments or cross-functional teams into the organization. This study also suggests that these special devices should be built into the organization in such a way that they facilitate the interaction of integrators with functional specialists who have the relevant knowledge to contribute to joint decisions. Alternatively, they may also need to facilitate the direct interaction among functional specialists who have the necessary knowledge to contribute to these joint decisions.

Structuring the individual units is a third step in the design process. Here the emphasis is on operating mechanisms, which will be consistent with the unit task and the needs of its members. Issues of individual motivation are particularly relevant here [8]. In addition, the Lawrence and Lorsch findings underline the importance of designing measurement and reward procedures to encourage orientations which are appropriate to the unit task. Similarly, reliance on formal rules and standardized procedures should be consistent with the task. Finally, the unit hierarchy and spans of control should be designed not only to provide the intra-unit coordination required by the task, but also to encourage involvement in decision making at the level where the relevant information is available.

Other operating mechanisms. In addition to the operating mechanisms within each unit, it is necessary to consider operating mechanisms which are applied across the whole organization. Do rewards and measurements encourage collaboration around the critical integrative issues? Do they demand consistency and conformity among units where more differentiation is required? Again, issues of individual rewards and motivation should be helpful here, but we must also realize that some operating mechanisms must be built to encourage differentiation, while others are necessary to encourage integration. We must understand the environmental demands on the organization so that reward and measurement systems can be designed to encourage both the differentiated and integrated behavior required.

Factors affecting conflict management. Finally, we should consider the effect of the basic structure and the operating mechanisms on conflict resolution. The basic structure should assign responsibility for cross-functional liaison to individuals who have the relevant knowledge. If individuals who have such knowledge are formally assigned the responsibility for joint decision making, there is the highest probability they will develop the power necessary to resolve conflict effectively. A second issue is related to operating mechanisms. Do they induce unnecessary conflict? Do they cause organization members to see conflicts as win-lose rather than integrative? If so, can they be altered to encourage more integrative problem solving?

Finally, there is the issue of training and its impact on conflict-resolving behavior. While this topic could lead into a long discussion of organizational change, it is useful to mention here that some forms of laboratory training and education may be helpful to encourage the confrontation of conflict [9]. The ideas we have been discussing may be helpful in identifying which organization members are so involved in conflict management that such training might be useful.

Summary

In this introduction we have explored the approaches available to solving structural design problems. In concluding, we offer a word of caution. Our understanding of organizations as systems is new and it is growing rapidly. The ideas which are presented here will certainly be modified and improved. But as crude as they are, they represent better tools than the principles which have been relied on in the past. These ideas clearly move us in a new and promising direction—that of tailoring the organization to its environment and to the complex needs of its members.

Notes

1. I am indebted to my colleague, Larry E. Greiner, for suggesting this conceptual distinction.
2. Henri Fayol, *Industrial and General Administration*, Part II, Chap. I, "General Principles of Organization"; Chap. II, "Elements of Administration," (Paris: Dunod, 1925); Luther Gulick, "Notes on the Theory of Organization," in *Papers on the Science of Administration*, edited by Luther Gulick and Lyndall F. Urwick (New York: Institute of Public Administration, Columbia University, 1937); Lyndall F. Urwick, "Organization as a Technical Problem," ibid.; James D. Mooney, "The Principles of Organization," ibid.
3. Rensis Likert, *The Human Organization* (New York: McGraw, 1968). See also Douglas McGregor, *The Human Side of Enterprise* (New York: McGraw, 1960).
4. Harvey Sherman, *It All Depends: A Pragmatic Approach to Organization* (Tuscaloosa: Univ. of Alabama Press, 1966).
5. T[om] Burns and G. M. Stalker, *The Management of Innovation* (London: Tavistock, 1961).
6. Joan Woodward, *Industrial Organization: Theory and Practice* (Oxford: Oxford University Press, 1965).
7. P. R. Lawrence and J. W. Lorsch, *Organization and Environment: Managing Differentiation and Integration* (Boston: Division of Research, Harvard Graduate School of Business Administration, 1967).
8. See G. W. Dalton and P. R. Lawrence, *Organizational Motivation and Control* (Homewood, Ill.: Irwin, 1970).
9. See G. W. Dalton and P. R. Lawrence, *Organizational Change and Development* (Homewood, Ill.: Irwin, 1970).

An Empirical Taxonomy of Structures of Work Organizations

D. S. Pugh   *D. J. Hickson*   *C. R. Hinings*

The taxonomy of structures of work organizations presented is based on three previously established empirical dimensions: structuring of activities, concentration of authority, and line control of workflow. On the basis of a sample of 52 organizations in the English Midlands, clusters of organizations on these three dimensions are examined and a sevenfold classification of organization structures is developed. These are identified as full bureaucracy, nascent full bureaucracy, workflow bureaucracy, nascent workflow bureaucracy, preworkflow bureaucracy, personnel bureaucracy, and implicitly structured organizations, their characteristic contextual features as to size, technology, dependence on other organizations, and ownership are demonstrated, and a possible developmental sequence is suggested. The results indicate that the concept of a single bureaucratic type is no longer useful, since bureaucracy takes different forms in different settings.

D. S. Pugh is director of research and reader in organizational behavior at the London Business School, England; D. J. Hickson is visiting professor of organizational behavior; and C. R. Hinings is associate professor in the Organizational Behavior Research Unit of the University of Alberta, Edmonton, Canada.

Classifications in organization theory have suffered from two limitations: First they have been all-embracing, basing themselves not only on the valid assumption that the context, purposes, structure, and functioning of an organization are intimately interrelated, but also on the much less valid assumption that each of these interrelationships reflects a complete one-to-one interdependence of each aspect on every other. Thus it has been thought possible to take any aspect for the basic classification and assume that the others

From *Administrative Science Quarterly*, March, 1969, 115-126. Copyright © 1969 by Graduate School of Business and Public Administration, Cornell University.

can be derived from it. Secondly, they have been *a priori* classifications, based on wide generalizations derived from common knowledge and common sense, the only concession to empirical complexities being the admission that they are in some sense pure, ideal, or archetypal.

Faced with data on real functioning organizations, the researcher has often found these classifications inadequate and has had to add types of his own. Thus Weber's classification of organizations [1] has been qualified with the addition of new types by Gerth [2], Constas [3], Gouldner [4], Presthus [5], Stinchcombe [6], and others. Blau and Scott admit in relation to certain classification problems in their scheme that "Our typology is not as unequivocal on this point as it might be." [7, *p. 43*] Hall, Haas, and Johnson, in applying the Blau-Scott and the Etzioni [8] typologies to a heterogeneous group of 75 organizations, found that many assignments had to be rather arbitrary, as inspection of their assignment lists confirms [9, *Tables 1 and 2*]. It is not surprising that in such *a priori* classifications the relationships found between classifications of prime beneficiaries or forms of compliance and classifications of contextual and structural aspects of organizations were limited.

This paper presents not a typology of organizations, but a taxonomy of organization structures derived from a correlational analysis previously reported [10]. The term "taxonomy" implies that the classification is based upon dimensions that are measurable and empirically established. Clusters of organizations found on these dimensions may well be labeled types, it being recognized that these types have been derived from the empirical data rather than postulated as *a priori* lists of discrete, discontinuous categories. A taxonomy is thus a multidimensional classification.

Haas, Hall, and Johnson developed a taxonomy from a large and heterogeneous number of characteristic variables of organizations, and the resulting classification system was based on variables that produced relatively homogeneous groupings [11, *pp. 157-80*]. The taxonomy presented here, however, is based on three previously established dimensions, and is applied to organization structures, not organizations in general. This avoids any implications about other organizational aspects, and enables their relationships to be examined empirically. The taxonomy of organization structures may be considered as a set of dependent variables in relation to their context, and as independent variables in relation to organizational performance and behavior [12, 289-315].

Haas, Hall, and Johnson list the possible uses of a taxonomy with an empirical basis: (1) it would be strategically helpful for refining hypotheses; (2) it would aid in the investigation of the validity and utility of intuitively based typologies; and (3) it could serve as a basis for predicting organizational decisions of change [11]. It might be added that it serves as a simplifying summary of complex underlying patterns. The adequacy of the present taxonomy in terms of these criteria is discussed below.

The sample and methods of investigation used in this study have already been described in detail [10; 13]. For taxonomic purposes, the whole group of 52 work organizations was used.

Dimensions of Structure

Sixty-four scales were constructed to operationalize five primary variables of structure: (1) specialization of functions, the division of labor in the organization; (2) standardization of procedures, the existence of rules purporting to cover all circumstances and applying invariably; (3) formalization of documentation, the extent to which rules, procedures, instructions, and communications are written; (4) centralization of authority, the locus of decision making; and (5) configuration of positions, the shape of the role structure. These were held to represent a large part of the concepts used in the literature on organizational structure. The variance measured by these scales was found to be largely accounted for by four underlying dimensions of structure exposed by factor analysis, each in turn accounting for more of the variance after the previous ones had been extracted. The first three of these dimensions are used as a basis for the taxonomy.

The first dimension was *structuring of activities*, the degree to which the behavior of employees was overtly defined, incorporating the degree of role specialization in task allocation, the degree of standardization of organizational routines, and the degree of formalization of written procedures.

The second dimension was *concentration of authority*, the degree to which authority for decisions rested in controlling units outside the organization and was centralized at the higher hierarchical levels within it. The measures for the dimension were developed by comparison across organizations of the different levels in the hierarchy which had the formal authority to make one of a standard list of recurrent decisions.

The third dimension was *line control of workflow*, degree to which control was exercised by line personnel as against its exercise through impersonal procedures. It accounted for differences remaining after the previous two factors had been extracted, that is, partialled out. Thus for a given degree of structuring, there are systematic differences between organizations in the extent to which this structuring is linked with a bias to line control of workflow through a smaller number of subordinates per supervisor, as against impersonal control of workflow through formalization of recording of role performance.

Clusters of organizations on two dimensions.   If the structural dimensions are plotted one against another, using the standard scores of the 52 organizations studied, clusters of organizations are found with similar characteristics. Figure 1 shows concentration of authority plotted against structuring of activities. Since these dimensions are orthogonal, there is a considerable spread, but a noticeable clustering in all but the upper right quadrant. Thus a first step towards a taxonomy could be taken by focusing on a description of those organization structures in the three quadrants showing clustering. Can the coincidence of structural clusters be explained; that is, do the organizations have anything else in common? From the previous correlational analysis some distinctive pattern of scores might be hy-

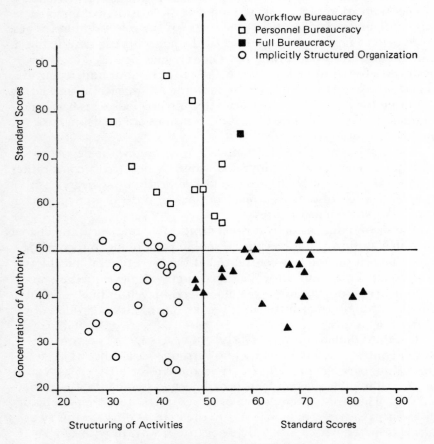

FIGURE 1. Concentration of Authority.

pothesized on contextual (that is, independent) variables such as size, ownership, dependence, technology, charter, location, and history [13].

On examination, the organizations that are highly structured and have a low concentration of authority (lower right quadrant) are found to be large, mainly independent, and to have their workflow relatively highly integrated, as in the vehicle components, standard engineering, foodstuffs, confectionery, and rubber goods factories, with their production schedules, quality inspection procedures, records of output per worker and per machine, records of maintenance, and so on. This particular structural combination is that developed by large-scale manufacturing, or big business, and such an organization is here called a *workflow bureaucracy*.

Grouped mainly in the upper left quadrant are organizations that show a high concentration of authority and low structuring of activities. The authority of these organizations is centralized, usually concentrated in a controlling committee outside and above the unit itself; and in most cases such organizations do not structure daily work activities very much. Their scores on a scale of procedures for standardization of selection, advancement, and so on, indicate that they do standardize or structure the employment activity, however. They have central recruiting, selecting, disciplining and dismissing procedures, conducted by formally constituted boards, and official establishment figures, appeal procedures, and the like. Such an organization is called a *personnel bureaucracy*, since it bureaucratizes everything related to employment, but not the daily work activity to the same degree. Personnel bureaucracies are typically local or central government departments (for example, a municipal education department or the regional division of a government ministry) and the smaller branch factories of large corporations.

In general, there is less formal structuring of activities in service organizations than in manufacturing industries. Also, when service organizations are geographically dispersed over many sites or are publicly owned, the concentration of authority increases and they become personnel bureaucracies. An example of the influence of public ownership is the difference between one omnibus organization owned by a local government authority and another, one of the largest remaining "private" transport organizations in the country. The central government, through a holding corporation, owns 50 per cent of the equity of the private company, but takes no direct part in its operations. Both have identical technologies (scores of 6 each on the scale of workflow integration) and are in the same size range (8,618 and 6,300 employees); therefore, they are very close in structural profile, *except* for the higher concentration of authority of the municipal undertaking, which is related to its high dependence on the local government framework.

A cluster of organizations can be seen in the lower left quadrant, which are low on *both* dimensions. It might be thought that this minimal structuring and dispersed authority suggests unregulated chaos. Instead this indicates that such organizations have low scores on the structural characteristics measured with the particular scales of rather overt regulation that were used. They cannot be labeled unstructured; their structure, as far as the measures used go, is probably implicit. Such an organization is here called an *implicitly structured organization*. It was hypothesized that these organizations are run not by explicit regulation but by implicitly transmitted custom, such as the traditional means usually typical of organizations of small or medium size where ownership and management still overlap. On investigation, this hypothesis was supported. These implicitly structured organizations are comparatively small factories (within the size range of the sample); they tend to be independent of external links; and they have scores on concentration of ownership that indicate that the operational control of the organization has remained with the owning directors [13].

The upper right quadrant of Figure 1 would include those organizations that are high on both structural dimensions, and therefore show the characteristics of both workflow *and* personnel bureaucracies. The few organizations in this quadrant are close to the mean on one or the other dimension and therefore would seem to be better regarded as belonging to one or the other type. In fact, only one organization is clearly above the mean (that is, more than five points of standard score above) on both dimensions [14]. This organization would thus be expected to show the characteristics of a workflow bureaucracy (for example, standardization of task control procedures), as in large manufacturing corporations, together with the characteristics of personnel bureaucracy (for example, centralized authority for decision making) as in government departments. This was in fact found to be the case. The organization is a manufacturing branch factory of a central government department, the only one of its type in the present sample. It may thus be regarded as a *full bureaucracy*.

Addition of the third dimension.   This initial attempt to identify clusters of organizations on the basis of the first two major dimensions of organization structure may now be developed by adding the third structural dimension, line control of workflow. Figure 2, which shows line control of workflow plotted against structuring of activities, will be sufficient for the purpose of this discussion, although a three-dimensional figure would be desirable, since this dimension is orthogonal to the other two. High scores on line control

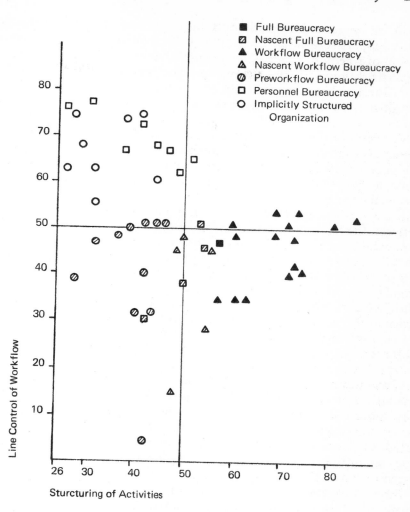

FIGURE 2. Structuring of Activities.

through controlling staff departments and role performance documents.

Again there are few organizations in the upper right quadrant, and these cluster close to the means; there is no organization with more than five points of standard score above the mean on both dimensions. High line control of workflow is not found with high structuring of activities. Organizations high on structuring, the workflow bureaucracies, are all at, or below, the mean on line control.

The personnel bureaucracies, on the other hand, with high concentration of authority but low structuring of activities are in general

found in the upper left quadrant, indicating a relatively high proportion of supervisors per direct worker and a relative absence of formalization of role performance documents. The relative lack of structuring of workflow activities but marked structuring of personnel
procedures is shown by the high scores on the scale of standardization of selection, advancement, etc.

Structure of professional organizations.   This description of personnel bureaucracies has something in common with the characteristics usually attributed in the literature to professional organizations.
Scott defined the professional organization as one in which "professional groups play the central role in the achievement of the
primary organizational objectives," and made a useful distinction
between the "autonomous professional organization" such as a law
firm, where the professional is subject only to the jurisdiction of
his fellows, and the "heteronomous professional organization," such
as a social work agency, where the professional is subject to an external (often governmental) jurisdiction [15, 65-82]. Hall added a
third category, the "professional department," such as the research
division of a manufacturing organization, where the professional
group is merely one part of a larger organization [16, 462-77]. In
all these three types, the professionals constitute the line management (though only in autonomous professional organizations are
they the top management), and they are not unduly controlled by
administrative procedures when engaged in their professional tasks.
The implication is that such organizations will be (in the present
terms) high on line control of workflow and low on structuring of
activities. The dimensions and taxonomy make it possible to treat
this assumption as a hypothesis and test it on the scores of the
organizations.

Based on the Scott-Hall classification, there are no autonomous
professional organizations in this sample; three organizations, the
Local Authority education department including the teaching staff,
the Local Authority civil engineering department, and the central
government inspection department with a staff of qualified engineers,
are clearly heteronomous professional organizations; two organizations, a civil engineering subsidiary of a large manufacturing group
and the research division of a large industrial metal organization,
are professional deparments.

How far does the structure of these organizations support the
hypothesis? The three heteronomous organizations fall completely
into the hypothesized pattern, being well above the mean on line
control of workflow and considerably below the mean on structuring
of activities. The implication is that when the hierarchy is staffed by
professionals, they exercise control directly and personally (line con-

trol) and do not develop bureaucratic control routines (low structuring of activities), since the activities of subordinate personnel are governed by professional standards. When such organizations fall within a local government framework of overall statutory control, they are very high on concentration of authority, and the control of broader policy is taken away from the professionals. In a study by Tauber it was found that using the present measures on a sample of six Birmingham hospitals within the British National Health Service, both mental and general, all six fell into this cluster [17]. The typical structural pattern of the heteronomous professional organization is therefore a particular case of personnel bureaucracy.

Neither of the two professional *departments* fits this pattern. Authority in the research division is more dispersed and it appears closer to the implicitly structured organization.

Other clusters of organizations.   Four of the organizations tentatively identified as personnel bureaucracies in Figure 1 fall at or below the mean on line control, in two cases much below; that is, they already have much of the apparatus of impersonal control. They are among the most structured personnel bureaucracies, with scores clustered about the mean (range 43-54). Since they also have high scores on concentration of authority, they could develop the characteristics of a full bureaucracy. Such an organization, like the civil engineering professional department, is considered an example of a *nascent full bureaucracy*. With the impersonal control apparatus already present, increase in size or increase in the workflow integration of the technology could result in an increase in structuring of workflow activities and make these four organizations comparable with the government manufacturing full bureaucracy. As was hypothesized in the earlier paper, the very existence of an impersonal control structure may lead to contextural changes of the sort suggested [14].

When those organizations initially classifed as implicity structured organizations (lower left quadrant of Figure 1) are considered in the light of the third structural dimension, a further distinction is immediately apparent. Just under half the organizations are high on line control of workflow, appearing in the upper left quadrant of Figure 2. These are the implicitly structured organizations combining lack of structuring and decentralization with high line control through the managerial hierarchy in a traditional manner. Over half of the implicitly structured organizations are found at or below the mean on line control (lower left quadrant of Figure 2). These organizations have much of the apparatus of impersonal control. They have relatively large numbers of subordinates per supervisor, and rely for control on the completion of role performance records (task completion, etc.). Although they are the same size as the implicitly structured organizations, they are considerably more integrated in technology (i.e., towards automated, continuous, fixed-sequence flow). So the cluster consists typically of small manufacturing firms that could develop into workflow bureaucracies as a result of further growth or technological change, and such an organization is called a *preworkflow bureaucracy.*

One final distinction can usefully be made. If workflow bureaucracies are organizations clearly above the mean on structuring of activities (scores of 55 and over) and preworkflow bureaucracies are organizations clearly below the mean (scores of 45 and below), then a group of organizations whose structuring scores cluster about the mean (range 45-55) can be distinguished. Do they have contextual features in common? They are typically subsidiary operating units of manufacturing groups, and are larger than preworkflow bureaucracies; but they resemble workflow bureaucracies in having dispersed authority and impersonal control. Such an organization is called a *nascent workflow bureaucracy.*

Types of Organizations

The taxonomy of organization structures based on a multidimensional classification thus yields seven distinctive types:

> Full bureaucracy
> > Nascent full bureaucracy
>
> Workflow bureaucracy
> > Nascent workflow bureaucracy
> > Preworkflow bureaucracy
>
> Personnel bureaucracy
> Implicitly structured organization

Table 1 lists the organizations in the sample as they are grouped by this classification.

The clusters of organization structures have been described only in general terms in the discussion, but their definitions in terms of operationally defined structural dimensions are given in Table 2. The cut-off points of these cluster definitions are arbitrary, but the dimensions themselves are not. Since they represent continuous variables and not discrete categories, they can be used as a multidimensional taxonomic tool to generate classes of organization structures that can be tested.

Organization structures in their contexts. The sevenfold classification of organization structures presented is tentative and further

TABLE 1
Taxonomy of Organizations (N = 52)

Cluster and Organization Product or Service

Full bureaucracy (N = 1)
  Repairs for government department

Nascent full bureaucracy (N = 4)
  Civil engineering firm
  Abrasives manufacturer
  Local authority transport
    department
  Paper manufacturer

Workflow bureaucracy (N = 15)
  Vehicle manufacturer
  Food manufacturer
  Confectionery manufacturer
  Tire manufacturer
  Nonferrous metal manufacturer
  Printer
  Three motor components
    manufacturers
  Commercial vehicle manufacturer
  Omnibus company
  Glass manufacturer
  Metal motor components
    manufacturer
  Heavy electrical engineering
    equipment manufacturer
  Aircraft components manufacturer

Nascent workflow bureaucracy (N = 5)
  Metal goods manufacturer
  Components manufacturer
  Brewery
  Engineering component manufac-
    turer
  Domestic appliances manufacturer

Preworkflow bureaucracy (N = 11)
  Four metal component manufac-
    turers
  Motor component manufacturer
  Two metal goods manufacturers
  Carriage manufacturer
  Engineering tool manufacturer
  Food manufacturer

Personnel bureaucracy (N = 8)
  Government inspection department
  Local authority baths department
  Cooperative chain of retail stores
  Local authority education depart-
    ment
  Savings bank
  Local authority civil engineering
    department
  Food manufacturer
  Local authority water department

Implicitly structured organizations
(N = 8)
  Component manufacturer
  Chain of retail stores
  Department store
  Insurance company
  Research division
  Chain of shoe repair shops
  Building firm
  Toy manufacturer

TABLE 2

*Definitions of Clusters (in Terms of Standard Scores on Structural Dimensions)**

Symbol used in in Figure 2	Cluster	Structuring of activities	Concentration of authority	Line control of workflow	Number of organizations
■	Full bureaucracy	above 55	above 55	below 55	1
▨	Nascent full bureaucracy	below 55	above 55	below 55	4
▲	Workflow bureaucracy	above 55	below 55	below 55	15
◬	Nascent workflow bureaucracy	45 to 55	below 55	below 55	5
◉	Preworkflow bureaucracy	below 45	below 55	below 55	11
▫	Personnel bureaucracy	below 55	above 55	above 55	8
○	Implicitly struc- tured organization	below 45	below 55	above 55	8

*D.S. Pugh et al., "Dimensions of Organizational Structure," *Admin. Sci. Quart.*, 13 (1968), 65-105.

work may lead to more useful classifications. The mean structural scores of the seven clusters are given in Table 3 (following page), together with thier standard scores on contextual variables.

The *full bureaucracy* studied has relatively high scores on both structuring of activities and concentration of authority, a high dependence score (being government owned), and a relatively low score on workflow integration of technology as a repair department. It has high scores on both standardization of procedures for selection and advancement, etc., and formalization of role definition, and is the only organization in the present sample with the characteristics of both personnel and workflow bureaucracy. A further study on a new sample of organizations using the present concepts confirms the existence of such an organizational type: government-owned organizations concerned with railways, supply of electricity and others [18]. The *nascent full bureaucracies* possess the same characteristics, but not to such a pronounced degree.

Workflow bureaucracies are characterized by high scores on structuring of activities combined with relatively low scores on the remaining two structural factors. Their use of impersonal control mechanisms is shown by the high scores on formalization of recording of role performance as well as a high percentage of nonworkflow personnel and clerks. The cluster includes the largest organizations in the sample and has the high scores of workflow integration of manufacturing industries. It includes only one service organization —an omnibus company. *Nascent workflow bureaucracies* show the same characteristics to a less pronounced degree, and are considerably smaller. *Preworkflow bureaucracies* are considerably lower on scores of structuring of activities, but have the typical workflow-bureaucracy pattern of dispersed authority and impersonal line control. They are smaller in size than nascent workflow bureaucracies, but are much more independent, with high scores on concentration of ownership with control.

Implicitly structured organizations have low structuring of activities, dispersed authority, and high line control. This cluster includes the smallest organizations in the sample, and has low scores on workflow integration, as it includes small manufacturing firms, retail stores, an insurance company, and a building firm. The organizations in this cluster are relatively independent, with high scores on concentration of ownership with control.

Personnel bureaucracies, although similar to implicitly structured organizations in having low scores on structuring and high scores on line control, differ markedly in their high scores on concentration of authority. This is associated with their characteristically high scores on dependence and low scores on concentration of ownership with control. The owning-controlling group is always outside and

TABLE 3

Mean Standard Scores of Clusters

Cluster	Structural Dimension			Structural Variables					Contextual Variables			
	Structuring of activities	Concentration of authority	Line control of workflow	Standardization of procedures for selection and advancement, etc.	Formalization of recording of performance	Subordinate ratio	Percentage nonworkflow personnel	Percentage of clerks	Size	Workflow integration of technology	Dependence	Concentration of ownership with control
Full bureaucracy	57.0	76.0	46.0	67.0	62.0	54.0	46.0	49.0	49.0	37.0	71.0	41.0
Nascent full bureaucracy	50.0	63.8	41.3	56.5	63.5	56.8	44.3	48.0	45.8	47.3	69.0	42.5
Workflow bureaucracy	69.5	44.9	45.5	54.9	62.4	49.8	60.7	56.5	65.8	57.2	47.9	47.5
Nascent workflow bureaucracy	51.4	42.8	36.2	34.4	59.6	58.8	64.0	49.2	48.4	57.6	46.4	48.0
Preworkflow bureaucracy	40.1	39.5	40.7	33.7	47.0	61.5	45.7	41.9	42.8	57.4	41.4	58.1
Personnel bureaucracy	41.4	73.0	68.8	68.1	35.9	36.0	39.8	48.4	49.3	40.8	64.4	37.6
Implicitly structured organization	34.4	42.6	67.1	49.7	30.3	37.9	44.3	42.1	40.7	32.3	41.7	65.6

* D. S. Pugh et al., "Dimensions of Organizational Structure," *Admin. Sci. Quart.*, 13 (1968), 65-105.
D. S. Pugh et al., "The Context of Organization Structures," *Admin. Sci. Quart.* 14 (1969), 91-114.

above the operating organization, being the central government or the city council. This results in high scores on centralization of decisions and standardization of procedures for selection and advancement, etc.

The spectrum of types of organization structures generated by the present taxonomy applied to the present sample is shown in the three-dimensional graphic representation of their relationships presented in Figure 3.

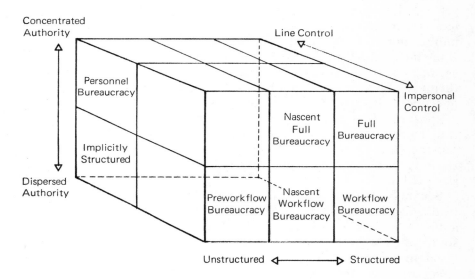

FIGURE 3. Relationships Between the Clusters.

Developmental Sequences

The terminology used to designate the various kinds of *workflow bureaucracies* implies some form of developmental sequences. The classification runs from implicitly structured organizations, through preworkflow and nascent workflow bureaucracies to the workflow bureaucracies themselves. 'Implicit," "pre-," and "nascent" imply some kind of process occurring in a movement towards workflow bureaucracy. What is this process? If in a cross-sectional design, such as this study, a classification ordered along a historical dimension can be obtained, then it is possible to hypothesize about developmental sequences.

It is possible to argue that the two dimensions that distinguish among the workflow bureaucracies are both outcomes of historical change. The first of these is structuring, the existence of role definitions and procedures. The implicitly structured organizations that have low scores on this dimension are small in size compared with the fully developed workflow bureaucracy. Increasing size of organizations is part of the process of development of the economy. Florence described the process of increasing size of plants and organizations for Britain [19]. Boulding wrote of "the organizational revolution" [20] and Gross of "the administrative revolution," saying, "This administrative revolution has been characterized by more organization, larger-scale organization, more bureaucracy, and more administrators." [21] The large organization of fifty years ago is the medium-sized or small organization of today. To quote Gross again, "The size of organizations can be measured by their assets, their use of manpower and other resources, or their output of goods or services. By any of these measuring rods, a vast and ever-increasing portion of human activity is now handled by large-scale administrative organizations." [21, *p. 40*] The correlation of 0.67 between size and structuring of activities presented in another paper strongly suggests that increasing structuring is concomitant with increasing size [13].

Secondly, the dimension of line control versus impersonal control distinguishes among organizations which are low on concentration of authority. With line control, control is exercised by workflow personnel themselves and their line superordinates rather than by impersonal procedures. Again it is possible to see that as industry has changed, so the occupational distribution in society has changed; that more and more people are engaged in controlling and recording tasks in industry instead of production tasks [22]. Woodward, Touraine, and Blauner have all outlined classifications of technology which they see as developmental, arising from a long-run trend to increasing mechanization and increasing standardization of products [23]. With these changes, there is increasing impersonality as control passes from the individual production worker and his direct supervisors to the procedures dictated by standardization and the new specialists who devise the procedures.

Thus it is possible to see developmental trends in the syndromes of contextual variables associated with the clusters of similarly structured organizations. There is the line controlled, implicitly structured organization, initially small in size (relatively speaking) with a flexible technology. In the preworkflow bureaucracy there is a change from line to staff control, shown by Bendix in his analysis of the changing role of the foreman [24]. With the nascent workflow bureaucracy there are the beginnings of structuring, the appearance of specialists and expansion of procedural control. With the workflow bureaucracy, specialists appear, producing more proce-

dures and reinforcing control by the line with impersonal bureaucratic regulation. The same sequence of arguments would apply in
regard to the development of nascent full bureaucracies into full
bureaucracies.

No such developmental sequence seems to apply in relation to the
dimension of concentration of authority. The position of the organizations with high scores on this dimension seems to be more a difference of kind, with personnel bureaucracies having the particular
contextual characteristics of government-controlled public services.
Implicitly structured organizations, such as a chain of retail stores
or an insurance company, might be expected to develop the structural characteristics of personnel bureaucracy only if acquired by central or local government authorities and administered as public
services.

Summary and Conclusions

The taxonomic use of three underlying dimensions of organization
structure previously established generated a sevenfold classification
of a sample of work organizations in the English Midlands. Each
class or cluster of organizations was associated with a typical pattern
of contextual variables, from which its occurrence might be predicted. The contextual variables were the size of the organization,
its external dependence, the extent to which its technology was
integrated, and its ownership. Tentative developmental sequences
can be seen on the basis of the assumed effects of changes in these
contextual variables on structure.

The clusters of organizations described have implications for the
concept of bureaucracy. It has been argued that the existence of
orthogonal structural dimensions demonstrates "that bureaucracy
is *not* unitary, but that organizations may be bureaucratic in any
number of ways" [10]. The cluster of personnel bureaucracies
shows that the popular stereotype of public bureaucracies is partly
accurate; they have a typical kind of bureaucracy. What the stereotype has obscured is that the workflow bureaucracies also have a
characteristic kind.

Nor did Weber suspect this. Giving examples of "rather distinctly
developed and quantitatively large bureaucracies" he cited Egypt,
China, and the Roman Catholic Church; and both "public corporations since the time of princely absolutism" and "the large modern
capitalist enterprise" [1]. His scholarly penetration saw the coming
bureaucratization of industry. What was not so apparent was that
bureaucracy takes different forms in different settings. The clusters
found here are not intended to be exhaustive; they are suggestive of
what may be learned by a multidimensional study.

Notes

1. H. H. Gerth and C. W. Mills, editors, *From Max Weber: Essays in Sociology* (London: Routledge, 1948).
2. H. H. Gerth, "The Nazi Party: Its Leadership and Composition," in *Reader in Bureaucracy*, edited by R. K. Merton et al. (Glencoe: Free Press, 1952), pp. 100-13.
3. H. Constas, "The U. S. S. R.—from Charismatic Sect to Bureaucratic Society," *Admin. Sci. Quart.*, 6 (1961), 282-98.
4. A. W. Gouldner, *Patterns of Industrial Bureaucracy* (London: Routledge and Kegan Paul, 1955).
5. R. V. Presthus, "Weberian versus Welfare Bureaucracy in Traditional Society," *Admin. Sci. Quart.*, 6 (1961), 1-24.
6. A. L. Stinchcombe, "Bureaucratic and Craft Administration of Production: A Comparative Study," *Admin. Sci. Quart.*, 4 (1959), 168-87.
7. P. M. Blau and W. R. Scott, *Formal Organizations* (San Francisco: Chandler, 1962).
8. A. Etzioni, *A Comparative Analysis of Complex Organizations* (Glencoe: Free Press, 1961).
9. R. H. Hall, J. E. Haas, and N. J. Johnson, "An Examination of the Blau-Scott and Etzioni Typologies," *Admin. Sci. Quart.*, 12 (1967), 118-39.
10. D. S. Pugh et al., "Dimensions of Organizational Structure," *Admin. Sci. Quart.*, 13 (1968), 65-105. This work was conducted when the authors were members of the Industrial Administration Research Unit, the University of Aston in Birmingham, England. Research conducted by that unit is jointly supported by the Social Science Research Council and the university.
11. J. E. Haas, R. H. Hall, and N. J. Johnson, "Toward an Empirically Derived Taxonomy of Organizations," in *Studies on Behavior in Organizations*, edited by R. V. Bowers (Athens: University of Georgia, 1966).
12. D. S. Pugh et al., "A Conceptual Scheme for Organizational Analysis," *Admin. Sci. Quart.*, 1963.
13. D. S. Pugh et al., "The Context of Organization Structures," *Admin. Sci. Quart.*, 14 (1969), 91-114.
14. Pugh et al., op. cit., note 10. The structural profile of this organization is the fourth given in fig. 2, p. 90.
15. W. R. Scott, "Reactions to Supervision in a Heteronomous Professional Organization," *Admin. Sci. Quart.*, 1965.
16. R. H. Hall, "Some Organizational Considerations in the Professional-Organizational Relationship," *Admin. Sci. Quart.*, 1967.
17. I. Tauber, *A Yardstick of Hospital Organization*, thesis for diploma in nursing administration (Birmingham: The University of Aston, 1968).
18. J. H. K. Inkson, D. J. Hickson, and D. S. Pugh, "Organization Context and Structure: An Abbreviated Replication," forthcoming [1969].
19. P. S. Florence, *Economics and Sociology in Industry* (London: Watts, 1964).
20. K. Boulding, *The Organizational Revolution* (New York, Harper, 1953).
21. B. M. Gross, *The Managing of Organizations* (Glencoe: Free Press, 1964).
22. D. C. Miller and W. H. Form, *Industrial Sociology* (New York: Harper & Row, 1964).
23. J[oan] Woodward, *Industrial Organization: Theory and Practice* (London: Oxford University Press, 1965); A. Touraine, "An Historical Theory in the Evolution of Industrial Skills," in *Modern Technology and Civilization*, edited by C. R. Walker (New York: McGraw, 1962), pp. 425-37; R. Blauner, *Alienation and Freedom* (Chicago: Univ. of Chicago Press, 1964).
24. R. Bendix, *Work and Authority in Industry* (New York, Wiley, 1959).

Organizational Characteristics and Individual Motivation

John J. Morse

Morse examines the connection between individual motivation and organization in this paper which, although preliminary, may have far-reaching implications. His basic finding is that when a functional unit has formal organizational practices and climate which fit the requirements of its particular task, the unit will be effective and the members of the unit will be more motivated. It is the latter point which is novel and intriguing, for it suggests that designing and developing an organization to fit the demands of its environment may also provide important psychological rewards for the members of the organization. The chapter reports on Morse's doctoral thesis at the Harvard Business School. Morse, who is an assistant professor at the Graduate School of Business Administration at the University of California at Los Angeles, is currently working on an extension of this study with Professor Lorsch.

In designing an organization and any functional unit within managers must decide which organizational characteristics will get the job done with the people available to do the work. Managers have been helped by a number of recent studies that focus on the relationship of organizational design and task performance. For example, Burns and Stalker give some clues to the kind of organizational design that makes sense for the effective performance of a highly structured or a highly unstructured task: they label these two patterns of organizational characteristics "mechanistic" and "organic" respectively [1]. And Argyris, among others, looks at organizational patterns that appear to be useful primarily in unstructured task settings, although his major concern seems to be providing for the needs and wants of individuals in the organization [2]. However, managers

Reprinted with permission from Morse, "Organizational Characteristics and Individual Motivation," in *Studies in Organization Design* by Lorsch and Lawrence (Homewood, Ill.: Richard D. Irwin, Inc., 1970), pp. 84-100.

have been pretty much let down in terms of studies that try to link organizational characteristics in both structured and unstructured task settings to the motivation of the individuals who do the work in them. Just as important, there is little behavioral science data available that simultaneously link organizational characteristics with both effective task performance and individual motivation. Not so surprisingly, even the well-informed manager adopts the attitude that it may be possible to build an organization to get the task done well, or to build an organization to satisfy the needs of the people in it, but that the accomplishment of either one of these two goals may require a compromise in the other.

In the field of organizational theory and practice and in the field of motivational psychology, there seem to be some ideas that could possibly begin to fill in these gaps. In the first place, the proposal of a "contingency model" of organizations made sense in terms of achieving effective task performance [3]. According to the model, an organization's characteristics or attributes should be appropriate to, or should "fit," the kind of task being done. There is no one best way to organize in all task situations: rather, a manager should analyze his task in terms of (1) its degree of predictiveness, routineness, or certainty, and (2) its dominant concern or its major competitive issue. The manager should then design his organization to reflect these dimensions of the task in order to achieve high task performance. For example, a successful manufacturing plant doing the relatively routine and certain job of turning out standardized household appliances would probably have organizational attributes that differed markedly from those of a successful research laboratory working on basic chemical research.

Some questions occurred to us after an examination of this model. When an organization pattern fits the task requirements of the task organization, what led to effective performance or behavior on the part of the individuals in the organization and, therefore, to effective performance for the organization as a whole? More specifically, could fit situations, by engaging and fulfilling certain kinds of needs and wants, motivate the managers and professionals in such settings to successful task performance? An especially useful approach to answering that specific question came from the area of motivational psychology. Here, an individual is viewed as having an active tendency or need to master and tame his external environment, including the task environment that he faces when he chooses to become a member of a particular work organization [4]. The accumulated feelings of satisfaction that come from successfully meeting and mastering an environment are called a "sense of competence." We felt that this "sense of competence" could possibly help explain how fit settings could motivate individuals toward high and successful performance. The reasoning was that an organizational fit situation motivates individuals precisely because it leads to a sense of competence from mastering a particular task environment. Another way of putting this is to say that the kind of behavior that results when organizational characteristics are appropriate to the task is the kind of behavior that leads to effective task performance, and that the individual is motivated to perform such behavior because it leads to his experiencing feelings of mastery and competence.

In summary, then, because of some gaps in the current knowledge concerning organizations and their functioning, we wanted to see if we could link organizational characteristics of both structured and unstructured tasks to individual motivation and, second, if we could point out the impact of that first link on task performance so as to tie organizational design simultaneously to both individual needs and task accomplishment. When we speak of organizational characteristics here, we speak in general in terms of their degree of appropriateness to the task according to the contingency model. And when we speak of individual motivation here, we mean an individual's sense of competence from mastering a particular task environment.

The Research Study

The study that was subsequently designed focused on measuring the feelings of competence or the sense of competence in four functional task units, two each in two very different kinds of task environments [5].* These environments posed two very different kinds of tasks and, therefore, from the contingency model, called for very different kinds of organizational characteristics for successful performance. One environment was dealing with a highly routine, predictable and certain task, producing standardized containers manufactured on high-speed, automated production lines. The other was dealing with a highly unpredictable, uncertain, rapidly changing task, communications technology research and development. Two large companies were approached, one with a number of similar containers manufacturing plants and one with a number of similar communications research laboratories. In both cases, top company executives were

---

*We should point out that while the "contingency model" deals with both the *differentiation,* or task specialization, between functional task units such as manufacturing, sales, and research departments and then the *integration* of those units into a unity of effort, we in our study decided it was wiser to focus only on the notion of differentiation in the model and correspondingly to deal only with functional task units such as manufacturing plants and research laboratories. We felt that it was in such units that the individual ultimately confronted his task environment and that it was there that the organizational characteristics might have their most potent influence on his motivation to perform effectively.

asked to select one unit that they judged to be a highly effective performer and one that they judged to be a less-successful or low performer. It was expected that such differences in performance would be preliminary clues to the differences in fit, which would allow us to test our ideas about the links between organizational characteristics, individual motivation, and task performance. Our study sites looked like this:

	Certain Manufacturing Task	*Uncertain Research Task*
High performer as initial clue to high degree of "fit"	Akron containers plant	Stockton communications research laboratory
Less successful performer as initial clue to lower degree of "fit"	Hartford containers plant	Carmel communications research laboratory

Dimensions of Fit

For all four of the functional units studied, that is, for both the high and low performer in both the certain and uncertain task environment, it was necessary to define what was meant by "fit," or to define what kinds of organizational attributes or characteristics to look at to gauge how appropriate the unit's organizational design was to its particular task. 'Fit' as used in this study was made up of two things. First, it was "formal fit," or fit between the kind of task being done and the formal practices that the unit used to get its job done. And, formal practices meant:

1. The pattern of formal relationships and duties, as signified by organization charts, position descriptions, procedural manuals, etc., and whether or not this pattern approached a high or low degree of structure;
2. The pattern of formal rules, formal operating and control procedures, formal standards and measurements, etc., and again whether or not this pattern approached a high or low degree of structure;
3. The time dimensions incorporated in the formal practices above, and if those practices stressed a long- or short-term time frame; and,
4. The goal dimensions incorporated in the formal practices, and if those practices stressed manufacturing, sales, or scientific goals.

Second, fit was "climate fit," or fit between the kind of task being worked on and the perceptions and orientations that had developed among the individuals in the functional unit. "Climate" is really the aspect of the organizational setting that is subjectively perceived or experienced by the individuals in the unit [6]. In this study, "climate" signified:

1. The structural orientation in the unit, that is, whether or not individuals in the unit perceived their behavior to be tightly controlled and structured;
2. The time orientation in the unit, that is, whether individuals were more concerned with the long- or the short-term;
3. The goal orientation in the unit, that is, whether individuals were more concerned with manufacturing, sales, or scientific goals;
4. The distribution of influence in the unit, that is, how much total influence was perceived in the unit and whether the distribution of that influence was perceived to be concentrated in the upper levels of the formal structure (hierarchical distribution) or more evenly spread out among more levels in the formal structure (egalitarian distribution);
5. The top executive's "managerial style," that is, whether individuals in the unit perceived their chief executive to be more concerned with the task and getting the work done or more concerned with people and establishing and maintaining good interpersonal relations;
6. The character of superior-subordinate relations in the unit, that is, how much "say" individuals in the unit perceived they had with their superiors in choosing the kind of task they were to work on and in doing the task on their own once it had been chosen; also, the perceptions of the type of supervision in the unit, if it was seen as being more directive or more participatory; and,
7. The character of colleague relations in the unit, that is, the perceptions of how similar colleagues were in backgrounds, education, prior work experiences, strategies for tackling job-related problems, etc., and the perceptions of the degree of coordination of effort or the unity of effort among colleagues in the unit.

We asked a cross section of about 30 managers and professionals in each of our study sites to take short tests that measured all the attributes listed above in order to determine the degree of fit between the organizational characteristics and the kind of task being worked on. We then used our measurement of the feelings of competence of the managers and professionals in the units to investigate our ideas on the link between fit and sense of competence motivation.

The Major Findings of the Study

To point up the principal findings of the study, we will compare and contrast the data collected on the high performer in the certain task environment (Akron containers manufacturing plant) with the data collected on the high performer in the uncertain environment (Stockton communications research laboratory). However, it is necessary first to recognize an important aspect of this research. Because Akron and Stockton performed tasks at the opposite ends of the spectrum of certainty and tasks with different dominant concerns, we anticipated that there would have to be major differences between them on the organizational characteristics of fit if they were to perform effectively. So, as we point out the differences in these attributes of organizational design as we found them in the two high performing units, we will also be pointing out differences that we had expected and predicted using a contingency model approach.

Differences in the Characteristics of "Formal Fit" in Akron and Stockton

The Akron and Stockton organizations fit their respective tasks better than did their less-successful counterparts in Hartford and Carmel. In the certain task environment in which Akron operated, the pattern of formal relationships and duties was highly structured and precisely defined, while in Stockton in the uncertain task environment, that pattern had a low degree of structure and was much less precisely defined. We also found that Akron's pattern of formal rules, procedures, control systems, etc., was pervasive, specific, uniform, and comprehensive. One manager in Akron went so far as to say: "Good God! We've got rules here for everything from how much powder to use in cleaning the toilet bowls to how to cart a dead body out of the plant." In contrast, Stockton's formal rules were minimal, loose, and flexible. One scientist there, when asked if he felt the rules ought to be tightened, said: "Hell, no. We produce under relaxed conditions here. Why tamper with success?"

Akron's highly structured formal practices were appropriate to its certain task because behavior there had to be rigidly defined and controlled around the automated production line. There was really only one way to accomplish Akron's very routine and programmable job, and managers there defined that way precisely and insisted that each man in the plant do what was expected of him in order to achieve the high coordination of effort that was necessary to get the job done well. On the other hand, Stockton's highly unstructured formal practices made just as much sense because behavior there simply could not be rigidly defined. In such an unpredictable, fast-changing field as communications technology research, there was more than one way to get the job done well and Stockton's managers therefore said they could not define any one and only way. They correspondingly used an unstructured pattern of formal practices that left scientists in the laboratory free to behave as the changing task situation required.

Akron's formal practices were also very much geared to short-term manufacturing concerns. For example, formal reports and review sessions were daily occurrences, consistent with the fact that the throughput time was typically a few hours for the kind of containers manufactured.

By contrast, Stockton's formal practices were geared to long-term scientific concerns. For example, formal reports and reviews ordinarily occurred only quarterly, semiannually, or annually. This was appropriate because research at Stockton often did not come to fruition for three to five years.

These differences in the characteristics of "formal fit" in the two high performers are summarized in Table 1. The two less-effective sites, the Hartford containers plant and the Carmel research laboratory, had formal organizational characteristics that were not as appropriate for their respective tasks. For example, Hartford's formal practices were much less structured and controlling than Akron's, while Carmel's were more restraining and restricting than Stockton's. It would not be too far off base to say that the organizational characteristics of formal fit in the less-successful Carmel research laboratory approached those in the high-performing Akron manufacturing plant, and that the formal practices in the low-performing Hartford plant were similar to those in the highly effective Stockton research laboratory.

TABLE 1
Differences in the Characteristics of Formal Fit in Akron and Stockton

	Akron (Certain Manufacturing Task)	Stockton (Uncertain Research Task)
1. Pattern of formal relationships and duties	Highly structured, precisely defined	Low degree of structure, less well defined
2. Pattern of formal rules, procedures, controls, measurements, etc.	Pervasive, specific, uniform, comprehensive	Minimal, loose, flexible
3. Time dimensions incorporated in formal practices	Short-term	Long-term
4. Goal dimensions incorporated in formal practices	Manufacturing	Scientific

Differences in the Characteristics of "Climate Fit" in Akron and Stockton

Concerning the differences in the characteristics of "climate fit," our findings in general showed that Akron and Stockton again fit their tasks better than Hartford and Carmel did. In the more certain manufacturing task environment, Akron's managers perceived a great deal of structure in their plant, and they were highly oriented toward the short-term and toward manufacturing goals. In contrast, Stockton's professionals perceived very little structure in their laboratory and were highly oriented toward the long-term and toward scientific goals. Appropriately, perceptions of high structure and of precisely defined behavior were just what Akron needed to ensure that each man was conforming to the uniform set of behavioral prescriptions that the automated production flow demanded. One manager said: "We can't let the lines run unattended. We lose money when they do. So we make sure each man *knows* his job, *knows* when we can take breaks, *knows* how to handle a change in shifts, etc. It's spelled out for him the day he comes to work here." And Akron's managers said that their orientations to short-term manufacturing goals meant that they tended to seek quick feedback from customers concerning the quality and service that the plant was providing—this kind of behavior is certainly conductive to high performance in this kind of environment.

In Stockton, though, the perceptions of less structure sanctioned the relaxed, individualistic, and creative behavior that the uncertain, rapidly changing research task called for. Likewise, Stockton's researchers said that their orientations to long-term scientific goals meant that they were willing to rely on long-term feedback from a research project that might take years to complete. One scientist said: "We're not the kind of people here who need a pat on the back every day. We can wait for months if necessary before we get feedback from colleagues and the profession. I've been working on one project for three months now and I'm still not sure where it's going to take me. I can live with that, though." This is the kind of behavior and attitude that tends to spell success in this kind of environment.

We also found that Akron and Stockton differed substantially on their distribution of influence and on the character of superior-subordinate and colleague relations. With the certain task, Akron's managers perceived much less total influence in their plant than Stockton's professionals did with their uncertain task. In Akron, individuals felt that their task did not require continual reworking or reformulation: the task in Akron had already been well defined and there was less need there than in Stockton's continually changing task for individuals to have a say in decisions concerning the work process. Also, in Akron influence was perceived to be concentrated in the upper levels of the formal structure (a "top-heavy" distribution), while in Stockton influence was perceived to be more evenly spread out among more of the levels in the formal structure (egalitarian distribution). Akron's managers felt they had a low degree of freedom with their superiors both to choose the tasks they were to work on and to handle the task on their own once it had been chosen. They also described the type of supervision in the plant as being relatively directive. Stockton's scientists, on the other hand, felt they had a great deal of freedom with their superiors both in the choosing and execution of tasks or projects. They also described the type of supervision in the laboratory as being very participatory. Concerning colleague relations, Akron's managers perceived a great deal of similarity among themselves in backgrounds, prior work experiences, and approaches for solving job-related problems. They also perceived the degree of coordination of effort among colleagues to be very high. Stockton's researchers perceived a great deal of differences among themselves and perceived the coordination of effort or the unity of effort among colleagues to be relatively low.

Akron's top-heavy distribution of influence and directive type of supervision meant that decision-making tended to be concentrated at the top levels in the organization. This made sense in this certain environment because the information necessary to make the critical decisions, especially decisions concerning overall scheduling of the plant, resided at the top. In fact, we attended one scheduling meeting in Akron where the plant manager informed his managers that there had been a change in the top management of one of their best customers. He said that he had decided on the basis of this information, information that no one else in the plant could as easily have had, ". . . to flood him with containers so that he'll get the message quickly that we're the best supplier he has available to him." With the requisite knowledge to make decisions at the top, the orientations of Akron's managers appropriately supported decision-making there. And, because Akron's task was so precisely defined and its behavior so rigidly controlled around the automated production lines, the high degree of coordination of effort and of colleague similarities is suitable to that unit.

In contrast, Stockton's egalitarianly distributed influence and participatory type of supervision meant that decision-making tended to be sanctioned and encouraged at all levels in the formal structure. Such orientations appropriately reflected the fact that the information and knowledge needed to make critical research decisions in such an unpredictable, fast-changing environment resided in the researchers themselves and at all levels in the laboratory. And, Stockton's perceptions of differences among colleagues and of a relatively low degree of coordination of effort among colleagues reflected the

fact that a wide variety of scientific disciplines and projects had to
be represented in a laboratory of this kind if it were to be successful.
One research manager in Stockton summed up the appropriateness
of these attributes to the research task especially well: "I don't have
the expert knowledge about astrophysics that one of our newest
researchers has. It would be plain foolish for me to try to second-
guess the kinds of projects we ought to take on in that field. So, we
expect everyone in the laboratory to have a say in the things we do.
. . . You can't run a place with as many different kinds of knowledge
represented as we have here any other way."

It is also interesting to note that the less successful Carmel research
laboratory tended to have more of the decisions made at the top of
the organization, and the researchers' particular expertises did not
give them much say in the laboratory's choice of projects.

Finally, the professionals in *both* Akron and Stockton perceived
their chief executive to have more concern for the task than for
people or relationships. This kind of managerial style seemed to us
to make sense in both kinds of task environments. In Akron, the
technology of the task was so pervasive and controlling that if top
managerial behavior relegated concern for that technology and task
to second-best, effectiveness of performance probably would have
been reduced. On the other hand, knowledge concerning Stockton's
task was rapidly changing and uncertain, and this called for more
individualistic problem-solving behavior. However, that individualistic behavior might have become totally segmented and totally un-
coordinated, causing the group to fall apart, unless the top executive
tended to focus the group's attention on the overall research task via
his high concern for that task.

These differences in the characteristics of climate fit in the two
high performers are summarized in Table 2. As with the attributes
of formal fit, the less-effective Hartford and Carmel sites measured
a lower degree of fit with their respective tasks than did Akron and
Hartford. As examples, the Hartford containers plant showed a relatively egalitarian distribution of influence, perceptions of low structure and a more participatory type of supervision. The Carmel
research laboratory showed a somewhat top-heavy distribution of
influence, perceptions of high structure, and a more directive type
of supervision.

Sense of Competence Motivation in Akron and Stockton

Akron and Stockton were obviously quite different as places to
work. In comparing and contrasting their organizational attributes,
we have been stressing two interrelated points. On the one hand,

TABLE 2
Differences in the Characteristics of "Climate Fit" in Akron and Stockton

	Akron (Certain Manufacturing Task)	Stockton (Uncertain Research Task)
1. Structural orientation	Perceptions of tightly controlled behavior and high degree of structure	Perceptions of low degree of structure
2. Time orientation	Short-term	Long-term
3. Goal orientation	Manufacturing	Scientific
4. Distribution of influence	Perceptions of low total influence, concentrated at upper levels	Perceptions of high total influence, more evenly spread out among all levels
5. Character of superior-subordinate relations	Low freedom vis-à-vis superiors to choose and handle task, directive type of supervision	High freedom vis-à-vis superiors to choose and handle task, participatory type of supervision
6. Character of colleague relations	Perceptions of much similarity among colleagues, high degree of coordination of colleague effort	Perceptions of much difference among colleagues, relatively low degree of coordination of colleague effort
7. Top executive's "managerial style"	More concerned with task than people	More concerned with task than people

although the organizational characteristics differed markedly in the two sites, such differences suited the distinctive dimensions of each task well. On the other hand, such differences in organizational characteristics led to differences in behavior in the two units, but these differences tended in both cases to result in effective task performance. Our particular concern in this study was to link the organizational characteristics that define task fit for an organization with individual motivation. What could motivate individuals in a high-fit task setting to act in a manner consistent with task unit fit, leading to effective task performance?

A partial answer was related to the sense of competence motivation of the professionals in both sites. Managers and professionals in Akron and Stockton showed higher feelings of competence or more of a sense of competence than did their counterparts in the lower fit Hartford and Carmel sites. In other words, the individuals in Akron and Stockton were more motivated by feelings of competence than were the individuals in Hartford and Carmel. The differences in the sense of competence for the managers and professionals in the certain manufacturing task environment (Akron and Hartford containers plants) are summarized in Figure 1, and these same differences in the uncertain research task environment (Stockton and Carmel communications technology laboratories) are summarized in Figure 2.* The data incorporated in these charts suggest that the individuals in Akron and Stockton were *motivated* to perform that kind of behavior that results from task unit fit and that leads to effective task performance precisely because such behavior was also leading to mastery of a particular task environment and, therefore, to a heightened sense of competence for them.

Differences in the Sense of Competence in the Containers Plant Environment

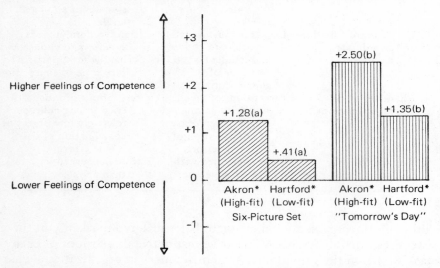

*Akron scores are the means of averages of 30 respondents. Hartford scores are the means of 32 respondents. All tests were scored and re-scored. The correlation (r) between the first score and the re-score on Part One of all the tests was .903 and on Part Two of all the tests was .882. The percent of imagery agreement between the first score and the re-score on Part One of all the tests was 91.6% and on Part Two of all the tests was 89.8%.

    (a) Statistical significance of differences in means: one-tailed probability, t = 3.84, P = < .001

    (b) Statistical significance of differences in means: one-tailed probability, t = 3.97, P = < .001

FIGURE 1

---

* The instrument we used to measure the feelings of competence in our sites contained two parts. The first asked a participant to write creative and imaginative stories in response to six ambiguous pictures, while the second asked a participant to write a creative and imaginative story about his day on the job "tomorrow," that is, what he may be doing, thinking, and feeling "tomorrow" on his job. Instruments such as these are called "projective tests" because it is assumed that the respondent projects into his stories his own attitudes, thoughts, feelings, needs, and wants, all of which can be measured from the stories.

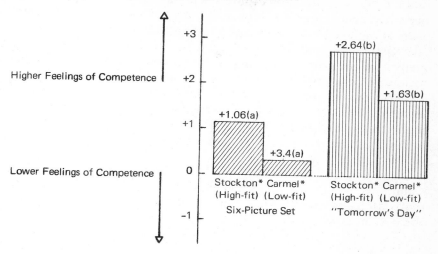

Differences in the Sense of Competence in the Communications Technology Research Environment.

*Stockton scores are the means of averages for 25 respondents. Carmel scores are the means for 24 respondents. All tests were scored and re-scored. The correlation (4) between the first score and the re-score on Part One of all the tests was .856 and on Part Two of all the tests was .877. The percent of imagery agreement between the first score and the re-score on Part One of all the tests was 90.7% and on Part Two of all the tests was 92.4%.

(a) Statistical significance of difference in means: one-tailed probability, $t = 2.83$, $P = .01$.
(b) Statistical significance of difference in means: one-tailed probability, $t = 2.71$, $P = .01$.

FIGURE 2

Summary of the Study

In its barest form, then, the major study findings seem to indicate:

1. That there is a reward in feelings of competence or a sense of competence from gaining mastery over and performing effectively in a task environment;
2. That the managers and professionals in high-fit Akron and high-fit Stockton were in task organizations whose organizational characteristics, although markedly different from each other, encouraged the kind of behavior that could lead, and in fact was leading, to effective and successful performance in each's particular task environment; and,
3. That the managers and professionals in Akron and Stockton were motivated to perform the kind of behavior that results from task unit fit and that leads to successful task performance because it was indeed leading to the reward in feelings of competence and mastery for them.

Our study suggests a link between organizational characteristics and individual motivation. More specifically, we found that when organizational characteristics suit the kind of task being performed, there is the likelihood of engaging and fulfilling needs for mastery and competence and the likelihood of an individual's attaining high feelings of competence or a high sense of competence. The organizational characteristics in Akron and Stockton, as were described earlier, were very different. Their common feature, though, was that in both sites such characteristics were appropriate to the differences in the task of the units. And this appropriateness was matched in both units by high sense of competence motivation of the individuals working there.

The study findings also suggest organizational characteristics to be simultaneously linked to, or interdependent with, *both* individual motivation *and* effective task performance. Akron and Stockton, the two units whose organizational characteristics suited their separate tasks well, had both been evaluated for us as highly successful performers.* And, we found the individuals in these high-fit, high-performing units had a high sense of competence. What our work points to, therefore, are interdependencies or links between the organizational characteristics of "fit," effective task performance, and individual sense of competence motivation. Graphically, these links can be expressed thus:

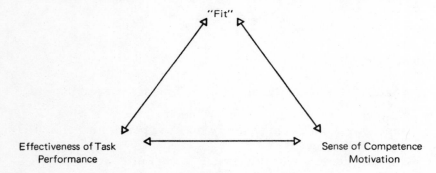

Implications of the Study for Managers

This study should help managers principally by identifying major links and interdependencies to consider in designing an organization which will accomplish its task *and* provide for the needs of individuals. Our approach therefore bridges works such as Burns' and Stalker's dealing with the effective performance of structured and unstruc-

---

*Note that this is completely consistent with the Lawrence and Lorsch theorizing and findings in *Organization and Environment,* note 3.

tured tasks and works such as Argyris' dealing with individual motivation. For example, we found in our two high-fit units, one with a structured, certain task and one with an unstructured, uncertain task, that such fit was associated at one and the same time with effective task performance and with high sense of competence motivation. And, although we did not focus here on the low-fit Hartford plant and the low-fit Carmel research laboratory, we can say that the lower degree of fit in both instances tended to be linked to less-effective task performance and to lower feelings of competence. As a result, this study suggests organizational fit to be interdependent with both task performance and sense of competence motivation, as signified by the triangle of relationships described above.

Perhaps one of the most intriguing aspects of our findings is this probable interdependency and circularity of the three variables in the triangle: each appears to be related to the other so that manipulating one can result in a change in the others. For example, by manipulating organizational characteristics so that they suit the task better or by engaging more feelings of competence in the members of the organization, a manager may be able to improve task performance. Likewise, a manager may be able to somehow independently improve performance, which we suggest would also lead to higher feelings of competence and to individual behavior that suits the task better, as members of the organization try to maintain and add to their higher sense of competence. And, finally, a manager may be able to heighten the feelings of competence in his organization by, for example, an influx of new blood that would be challenged by the task, a move our findings indicate would probably lead to more effective performance and to a higher degree of "fit" as individuals sought to reinforce their competent behavior.

Although our primary concern has been the interdependencies among our variables, our study also seems to indicate that a manager can most easily derive the benefits of all those links by initially focusing on one of the variables, organizational "fit." We have identified certain organizational characteristics that a manager can manipulate to better suit his task. As examples, we looked at the formal practices in an organization; the time and goal orientations; the perceptions of structure, of the distribution of influence, of superior-subordinate and colleague relations, and of the top manager's "managerial style." These are all aspects of an organization that a manager can change and vary according to the requirements of the task. And, as the organizational pattern becomes more appropriate to the kind of work being done, the manager may have "locked on" to the triangle of interdependencies identified in the study to raise the level of performance and the sense of competence motivation in his work unit.

Finally, we believe that sense of competence motivation itself has significant implications for managers because it seems to be important to individuals with very different patterns of predispositions and very different patterns of other needs and values. For example, the professionals we talked to in the Akron plant seemed to us to be quite different from those we talked to in the Stockton research laboratory. In Akron, people in general did not seem to mind the predictiveness, the certainty, the routineness of the task, or the highly structured, hierarchical organizational pattern that precluded the necessity of their making many of the critical decisions. In Stockton, on the other hand, individuals in general thrived on change and challenge, and felt comfortable only in an organization that put some of the burden of making critical decisions on them. But, the professionals in Akron, who were more comfortable with predictability and structure, and the professionals in Stockton, who were very comfortable with ambiguity and change, *all* showed significantly higher feelings of competence than their counterparts in the less-effective, lower "fit" units. A major contribution to managers, therefore, may be the study's identification and investigation of a particular need pattern concerning the sense of competence that appears to be a powerful motivator for individuals with either a high predisposition and need for structure or a high predisposition and need for autonomy.

So, in terms of the managerial dilemma of designing an organization or functional task unit to accomplish its task well and to provide for the needs of the individuals who do the work, this study points up a practical, empirically-based set of links that recognizes the import of task requirements and individual needs in equal and interdependent measure.

Notes

1. Tom Burns and G. M. Stalker, *The Management of Innovation* (London: Tavistock, 1961).
2. Chris Argyris, *Integrating the Individual and the Organization* (New York: Wiley, 1964).
3. See Paul R. Lawrence and Jay W. Lorsch, *Organization and Environment* (Boston: Division of Research, Harvard Business School, 1967).
4. See Robert W. White, "Ego and Reality in Psychoanalytic Theory," *Psychological Issues,* 3 (1963).
5. John J. Morse, "Internal Organizational Patterning and Sense of Competence Motivation," unpublished Ph.D. dissertation (Boston: Harvard Business School, 1969).
6. See Renato Tagiuri and George H. Litwin, editors, *Organizational Climate: Exploration of a Concept* (Boston: Division of Research, Harvard Business School, 1968).

Style or Circumstance:
The Leadership Enigma

Fred E. Fiedler

What is it that makes a person an effective leader?

We take it for granted that good leadership is essential to business, to government, and to all the myriad groups and organizations that shape the way we live, work, and play.

We spend at least several billions of dollars a year on leadership development and executive recruitment in the United States. Leaders are paid 10, 20, and 30 times the salary of ordinary workers. Thousands of books and articles on leadership have been published. Yet we still know relatively little about the factors that determine a leader's success or failure.

Psychologists have been concerned with two major questions in their research on leadership: How does a man become a leader? What kind of personality traits or behavior makes a person an *effective* leader? For the past 15 years, my own work at the University of Illinois Group-Effectiveness Research Laboratory has concentrated on the latter question.

Psychologists used to think that special personality traits would distinguish leaders from followers. Several hundred research studies have been conducted to identify these special traits. But the search has been futile.

People who become leaders tend to be somewhat more intelligent, bigger, more assertive, more talkative than other members of their group. But these traits are far less important than most people think. What most frequently distinguishes the leader from his co-workers is that he knows more about the group task or that he can do it better. A bowling team is likely to choose its captain from good rather than poor bowlers, and the foreman of a machine shop is more likely to be a good machinist than a poor one.

In many organizations, one only has to live long in order to gain experience and seniority, and with these a position of leadership.

In business and industry today, the men who attain a leadership

Reprinted from *Psychology Today* Magazine, March, 1969, 38-43. Copyright © 1969 Communications/Research/Machines, Incorporated.

position must have the requisite education and talent. Of course, as W. Lloyd Warner and James C. Abegglen of the University of Chicago have shown, it has been most useful to come from or marry into a family that owns a large slice of the company's stock.

Becoming a leader, then, depends on personality only to a limited extent. A person can become a leader by happenstance, simply by being in the right place at the right time, or because of such various factors as age, education, experience, family background, and wealth.

Almost any person in a group may be capable of rising to a leadership position if he is rewarded for actively participating in the group discussion, as Alex Bavelas and his colleagues at Stanford University have demonstrated. They used light signals to reward low-status group members for supposedly "doing the right thing." However, unknown to the people being encouraged, the light signal was turned on and off at random. Rewarded in this unspecified, undefined manner, the low-status member came to regard himself as a leader and the rest of the group accepted him in his new position.

It is commonly observed that personality and circumstances interact to determine whether a person will become a leader. While this statement is undoubtedly true, its usefulness is rather limited unless one also can specify how a personality trait will interact with a specific situation. We are as yet unable to make such predictions.

Having become a leader, how does one get to be an effective leader? Given a dozen or more similar groups and tasks, what makes one leader succeed and another fail? The answer to this question is likely to determine the philosophy of leader-training programs and the way in which men are selected for executive positions.

There are a limited number of ways in which one person can influence others to work together toward a common goal. He can coerce them or he can coax them. He can tell people what to do and how to do it, or he can share the decision-making and concentrate on his relationship with his men rather than on the execution of the job.

Of course, these two types of leadership behavior are gross oversimplifications. Most research by psychologists on leadership has focused on two clusters of behavior and attitudes, one labeled autocratic, authoritarian, and task-oriented, and the other as democratic, equalitarian, permissive, and group-oriented.

The first type of leadership behavior, frequently advocated in conventional supervisory and military systems, has its philosophical roots in Frederick W. Taylor's *Principles of Scientific Management* and other early 20th Century industrial engineering studies. The authoritarian, task-oriented leader takes all responsibility for making decisions and directing the group members. His rationale is simple: "I do the thinking and you carry out the orders."

The second type of leadership is typical of the "New Look" meth-

od of management advocated by men like Douglas McGregor of
M.I.T. and Rensis Likert of the University of Michigan. The democratic, group-oriented leader provides general rather than close supervision and his concern is the effective use of human resources through
participation. In the late 1940s, a related method of leadership training was developed based on confrontation in unstructured group situations where each participant can explore his own motivations and
reactions. Some excellent studies on this method, called T-group,
sensitivity, or laboratory training, have been made by Chris Argyris
of Yale, Warren Bennis of State University of New York at Buffalo,
and Edgar Schein of M.I.T.

Experiments comparing the performance of both types of leaders
have shown that each is successful in some situations and not in
others. No one has been able to show that one kind of leader is
always superior or more effective.

A number of researchers point out that different tasks require
different kinds of leadership. But what kind of leader? To answer
this question, I shall present a theory of leadership effectiveness
that spells out the specific circumstances under which various leadership styles are most effective.

We must first of all distinguish between leadership style and leader
behavior. Leader behavior refers to the specific acts in which a leader
engages while directing or coordinating the work of his group. For
example, the leader can praise or criticize, make helpful suggestions,
show consideration for the welfare and feelings of members of his
group.

Leadership style refers to the underlying needs of the leader that
motivate his behavior. In other words, in addition to performing
the task, what personal needs is the leader attempting to satisfy?
We have found that a leader's actions or behavior sometimes does
change as the situation or group changes, but his basic needs appear
to remain constant.

To classify leadership styles, my colleagues and I have developed
a simple questionnaire that asks the leader to describe the person
with whom he can work least well:

Least-Preferred Co-worker

Think of the person with whom you can work least well. He may be someone
you work with now, or he may be someone you knew in the past. Use an X to
describe this person as he appears to you.

helpful	: :	: :	: :	: :	: :	: :	: :	: :	frustrating
	8	7	6	5	4	3	2	1	
unenthusiastic	: :	: :	: :	: :	: :	: :	: :	: :	enthusiastic
	1	2	3	4	5	6	7	8	
efficient	: :	: :	: :	: :	: :	: :	: :	: :	inefficient
	8	7	6	5	4	3	2	1	

From the replies, a Least-Preferred-Co-Worker (LPC) score is obtained by simply summing the item scores. The LPC score does not measure perceptual accuracy, but rather reveals a person's emotional reaction to the people with whom he cannot work well.

In general, the high-scoring leader describes his least-preferred co-worker in favorable terms. The high-LPC leader tends to be "relationship-oriented." He gets his major satisfaction from establishing close personal relations with his group members. He uses the group task to gain the position of prominence he seeks.

The leader with a low score describes his least-preferred co-worker in unfavorable terms. The low-LPC leader is primarily "task-oriented." He obtains his major satisfaction by successfully completing the task, even at the risk of poor interpersonal relations with his workers.

Since a leader cannot function without a group, we must also know something about the group that the leader directs. There are many types of groups, for example, social groups which promote the enjoyment of individuals and "counteracting" groups such as labor and management at the negotiating table. But here we shall concentrate on groups that exist for the purpose of performing a task.

From our research, my associates and I have identified three major factors that can be used to classify group situations: (1) position power of the leader, (2) task structure, and (3) leader–member personal relationships. Basically, these classifications measure the kind of power and influence the group gives its leader.

We ranked group situations according to their favorableness for the leader. Favorableness here is defined as the degree to which the situation enables the leader to exert influence over the group.

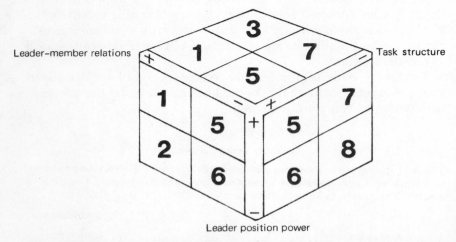

Group Situation Model. Task-oriented groups are classified in a three-dimensional model using the three major factors affecting group performance.

Based on several studies, leader–member relations emerged as the most important factor in determining the leader's influence over the group. Task structure is rated as second in importance, and position power as third.

Under most circumstances, the leader who is liked by his group and has a clear-cut task and high position power obviously has everything in his favor. The leader who has poor relationships with his group members, an unstructured task, and weak position power likely will be unable to exert much influence over the group.

The personal relationships that the leader establishes with his group members depend at least in part upon the leader's personality. The leader who is loved, admired, and trusted can influence the group regardless of his position power. The leader who is not liked or trusted cannot influence the group except through his vested authority. It should be noted that a leader's assessment of how much he is liked often differs markedly from the group's evaluation.

Task structure refers to the degree the group's assignment can be programmed and specified in a step-by-step fashion. A highly structured task does not need a leader with much position power because the leader's role is detailed by the job specifications. With a highly structured task, the leader clearly knows what to do and how to do it, and the organization can back him up at each step. Unstructured tasks tend to have more than one correct solution that may be reached by any of a variety of methods. Since there is no step-by-step method that can be programmed in advance, the leader cannot influence the group's success by ordering them to vote "right" or be creative. Tasks of committees, creative groups, and policy-making groups are typically unstructured.

Position power is the authority vested in the leader's position. It can be readily measured in most situations. An army general obviously has more power than a lieutenant, just as a department head has more power than an office manager. But our concern here is the effect this position power has on group performance. Although one would think that a leader with great power will get better performance from his group, our studies do not bear out this assumption.

However, it must be emphasized that in some situations position power may supersede task structure (the military). Or a very highly structured task (launching a moon probe) may outweigh the effects of interpersonal relations. The organization determines both the task structure and the position power of the leader.

In our search for the most effective leadership style, we went back to the studies that we had been conducting for more than a decade. These studies investigated a wide variety of groups and leadership situations, including basketball teams, business management, military units, boards of directors, creative groups, and scientists engaged in

pure research. In all of these studies, we could determine the groups
that had performed their tasks successfully or unsuccessfully and
then correlated the effectiveness of group performance with leadership style.

Now by plotting these correlations of leadership style against our
scale of group situations, we could, for the first time, find what
leadership style works best in each situation. When we connected
the median points on each column, the result was a bell-shaped curve.

The results show that a task-oriented leader performs best in situations at both extremes—those in which he has a great deal of influence and power, and also in situations where he has no influence
and power over the group members.

Relationship-oriented leaders tend to perform best in mixed situations where they have only moderate influence over the group. A
number of subsequent studies by us and others have confirmed these
findings.

The results show that we cannot talk about simply good leaders or
poor leaders. A leader who is effective in one situation may or may
not be effective in another. Therefore, we must specify the situations in which a leader performs well or badly.

This theory of leadership effectiveness by and large fits our everyday experience. Group situations in which the leader is liked, where
he has a clearly defined task and a powerful position, may make attempts at nondirective, democratic leadership detrimental or super-
fluous. For example, the captain of an airliner can hardly call a
committee meeting of the crew to share in the decision-making during a difficult landing approach. On the other hand, the chairman
of a voluntary committee cannot ask with impunity that the group
members vote or act according to his instructions.

Our studies also have shown that factors such as group-member
abilities, cultural heterogeneity, and stressfulness of the task affect
the degree to which the leader can influence members of the group.
But the important finding and the consistent finding in these studies
has been that mixed situations require relationship-oriented leadership while very favorable and very unfavorable job situations require
task-oriented leaders.

Perhaps the most important implication of this theory of leadership is that the organization for which the leader works is as responsible for his success or failure as is the leader himself.

The chances are that *anyone* who wants to become a leader can become one if he carefully chooses the situations that are favorable to
his leadership style.

The notion that a man is a "born" leader, capable of leading in all
circumstances, appears to be nothing more than a myth. If there are

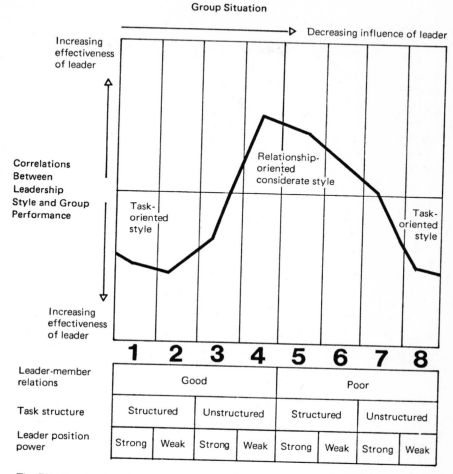

The Effective Leader. Directive leaders perform best in very favorable or in unfavorable situations. Permissive leaders are best in mixed situations. Graph is based on studies of over 800 groups.

leaders who excel under all conditions, I have not found them in my 18 years of research.

When we think of improving leadership performance, we tend to think first of training the leader. Personnel psychologists and managers typically view the executive's position as fixed and unchangeable and the applicant as highly plastic and trainable. A man's basic style of leadership depends upon his personality. Changing a man's leadership style means trying to change his personality. As we know from experiences in psychotherapy, it may take from one to several years to effect lasting changes in a personality structure. A leader's personality is not likely to change because of a few lectures or even a few weeks of intensive training.

It is doubtful that intensive training techniques can change an individual's style of leadership. However, training programs could be designed to provide the opportunity for a leader to learn in which situations he can perform well and in which he is likely to fail. Laboratory training also may provide the leader with some insights into his personal relationships with group members.

Our theory of leadership effectiveness predicts that a leader's performance can be improved by engineering or fitting the job to the leader. This is based, at least in part, on the belief that it is almost always easier to change a leader's work environment than to change his personality. The leader's authority, his task, and even his interpersonal relations within his group members can be altered, sometimes without making the leader aware that this has been done.

For example, we can change the leader's position power in either direction. He can be given a higher rank if this seems necessary. Or he can be given subordinates who are equal or nearly equal to him in rank. His assistants can be two or three ranks below him, or we can assign him men who are expert in their specialties. The leader can have sole authority for a job, or he may be required to consult with his group. All communications to group members may be channeled through the leader, making him the source of all the inside information, or all members of the group can be given the information directly, thus reducing the leader's influence.

The task structure also can be changed to suit the leader's style. Depending upon the group situation, we can give the leader explicit instructions or we can deliberately give him a vague and nebulous goal.

Finally, we can change the leader–member relations. In some situations it may be desirable to improve leader–member relations by making the group homogeneous in culture and language or in technical and educational background. Interdisciplinary groups are notoriously difficult to handle, and it is even more difficult to lead a group that is racially or culturally mixed. Likewise, we can affect leader–member relations by giving a leader subordinates who get along well with their supervisor or assign a leader to a group with a history of trouble or conflict.

It may seem that often we are proposing the sabotaging of the leader's influence over his group. Although common sense might make it seem that weakening the leader's influence will lower performance, in actuality our studies show that this rarely happens. The average group performance (in other words, the leader's effectiveness) correlates poorly with the degree of the leader's influence over the group.

In fact, the findings from several studies suggest that a particular leader's effectiveness may be improved even though the situation is made less favorable for him.

The leader himself can be taught to recognize the situations that best fit his style. A man who is able to avoid situations in which he is likely to fail, and seek out situations that fit his leadership style, will probably become a highly successful and effective leader. Also, if he is aware of his strengths and weaknesses, the leader can try to change his group situation to match his leadership style.

However, we must remember that good leadership performance depends as much upon the organization as it does upon the leader. This means that we must learn not only how to train men to be leaders, but how to build organizations in which specific types of leaders can perform well.

In view of the increasing scarcity of competent executives, it is to an organization's advantage to design jobs to fit leaders instead of attempting merely to fit a leader to the job.

Choosing the Depth of Organizational Intervention

Roger Harrison

There is a need for conceptual models which differentiate intervention strategies from one another in a way which permits rational
matching of strategies to differing organizational change problems.
A central concept in such a model could be the depth of individual
emotional involvement in the change process. By depth we mean how
deep, value-laden, emotionally charged, and central to the individual's sense of self are the issues and processes about which a consultant attempts directly to obtain information and which he seeks to
influence. In order of increasing depth are the change strategies:
operations analysis, management by objectives, the managerial grid,
the T-group, and task group therapy.

 As depth of intervention increases, so also do a number of concomitants of depth: dependence on the special competence of the
change agent, centrality of the individual as the target of the change
attempt, costs of intervention, and the risk of unintended consequences for individuals. These concomitants suggest a criterion for
the depth of intervention: to intervene at a level no deeper than
that required to produce enduring solutions to the problems at
hand. However, a countervailing trend tends to push the level of
intervention deeper as organizational systems shift from greater external control to more autonomy and internal control for members.
As the individual becomes more important, the level at which the
processes which effectively determine his behavior operate becomes
deeper, and the individual has increasing influence over the success
or failure of the intervention. A case is presented for a radical shift
of consultant orientation in the direction of accepting a client's
felt needs and presented problems as being real and of working on
them at a level where the client can serve as a competent and willing

Reproduced by special permission from *Journal of Applied Behavioral Science,* 6 (April/
May/June 1970), 2:-181-202. Copyright © 1970 by Journal of Applied Behavioral Science.

collaborator. This leads to the second criterion: to intervene at a level no deeper than that at which the energy and resources of the client can be committed to problem solving and to change [1].

Since World War II there has been a great proliferation of behavioral science-based methods by which consultants seek to facilitate growth and change in individuals, groups, and organizations. The methods range from operations analysis and manipulation of the organization chart, through the use of grid laboratories, T-groups, and nonverbal techniques. As was true in the development of clinical psychology and psychotherapy, the early stages of this developmental process tend to be accompanied by considerable competition, criticism, and argument about the relative merits of various approaches. It is my conviction that controversy over the relative goodness or badness, effectiveness or ineffectiveness, of various change strategies really accomplishes very little in the way of increased knowledge or unification of behavioral science. As long as we are arguing about what method is better than another, we tend to learn very little about how various approaches fit together or complement one another, and we certainly make more difficult and ambiguous the task of bringing these competing points of view within one overarching system of knowledge about human processes.

As our knowledge increases, it begins to be apparent that these competing change strategies are not really different ways of doing the same thing—some more effective and some less effective—but rather that they are different ways of doing *different* things. They touch the individual, the group, or the organization in different aspects of their functioning. They require differing kinds and amounts of commitment on the part of the client for them to be successful, and they demand different varieties and levels of skills and abilities on the part of the practitioner.

I believe that there is a real need for conceptual models which differentiate intervention strategies from one another in a way which permits rational matching of strategies to organizational change problems. The purpose of this paper is to present a modest beginning which I have made toward a conceptualization of strategies, and to derive from this conceptualization some criteria for choosing appropriate methods of intervention in particular applications.

The point of view of this paper is that the depth of individual emotional involvement in the change process can be a central concept for differentiating change strategies. In focusing on this dimension, we are concerned with the extent to which core areas of the personality or self are the focus of the change attempt. Strategies which touch the more deep, personal, private, and central aspects of the individual or his relationships with others fall toward the deeper end of this continuum. Strategies which deal with more external aspects of the individual and which focus upon the more formal and public aspects of role behavior tend to fall toward the surface end of the depth dimension. This dimension has the advantage that it is relatively easy to rank change strategies upon it and to get fairly close consensus as to the ranking. It is a widely discussed dimension of difference which has meaning and relevance to practitioners and their clients. I hope in this paper to promote greater flexibility and rationality in choosing appropriate depths of intervention. I shall approach this task by examining the effects of interventions at various depths. I shall also explore the ways in which two important organizational processes tend to make demands and to set limits upon the depth of intervention which can produce effective change in organizational functioning. These two processes are the autonomy of organization members and their own perception of their needs for help.

Before illustrating the concept by ranking five common intervention strategies along the dimension of depth, I should like to define the dimension somewhat more precisely. We are concerned essentially with how private, individual, and hidden are the issues and processes about which the consultant attempts directly to obtain information and which he seeks to influence. If the consultant seeks information about relatively public and observable aspects of behavior and relationships and if he tries to influence directly only these relatively surface characteristics and processes, we would then categorize his intervention strategy as being closer to the surface. If, on the other hand, the consultant seeks information about very deep and private perceptions, attitudes, or feelings and if he intervenes in a way which directly affects these processes, then we would classify his intervention strategy as one of considerable depth. To illustrate the surface end of the dimension let us look first at operations research or operations analysis. This strategy is concerned with the roles and functions to be performed within the organization, generally with little regard to the individual characteristics of persons occupying the roles. The change strategy is to manipulate role relationships; in other words, to redistribute the tasks, the resources, and the relative power attached to various roles in the organization. This is essentially a process of rational analysis in which the tasks which need to be performed are determined and specified and then sliced up into role definitions for persons and groups in the organization. The operations analyst does not ordinarily need to know much about particular people. Indeed, his function is to design the organization in such a way that its successful operation does not depend too heavily upon any uniquely individual skills, abilities, values, or attitudes of persons in various roles. He may perform this function adequately without knowing in advance who the people are who will fill these slots. Persons are assumed to be moderately interchangeable, and in order to make this approach work it is necessary to design the organization so that the capacities, needs, and values of the individual which are relevant to role performance are relatively public and observable, and are possessed by a fairly large proportion of the population from which organization members are drawn. The approach is certainly one of very modest depth.

Somewhat deeper are those strategies which are based upon evaluating individual performance and attempting to manipulate it directly. Included in this approach is much of the industrial psychologist's work in selection, placement, appraisal, and counseling of employees. The intervener is concerned with what the individual is able and likely to do and achieve rather than with processes internal to the individual. Direct attempts to influence performance may be made through the application of rewards and punishments such as promotions, salary increases, or transfers within the organization. An excellent illustration of this focus on end results is the practice of management by objectives. The intervention process is focused on establishing mutually agreed-upon goals for performance between the individual and his supervisor. The practice is considered to be particularly advantageous because it permits the supervisor to avoid a focus on personal characteristics of the subordinate, particularly those deeper, more central characteristics which managers generally have difficulty in discussing with those who work under their supervision. The process is designed to limit information exchange to that which is public and observable, such as the setting of performance goals and the success or failure of the individual in attaining them.

Because of its focus on end results, rather than on the process by which those results are achieved, management by objectives must be considered less deep than the broad area of concern with work style which I shall term instrumental process analysis. We are concerned here not only with performance but with the processes by which that performance is achieved. However, we are primarily concerned with styles and processes of work rather than with the processes of interpersonal relationships which I would classify as being deeper on the basic dimension.

In instrumental process analysis we are concerned with how a person likes to organize and conduct his work and with the impact which this style of work has on others in the organization. Principally, we are concerned with how a person perceives his role, what he values and disvalues in it, and with what he works hard on and what he chooses to ignore. We are also interested in the instrumental acts which the individual directs toward others: delegating authority or reserving decisions to himself, communicating or withholding information, collaborating or competing with others on work-related issues. The focus on instrumentality means that we are interested in the person primarily as a doer of work or a performer of functions related to the goals of the organization. We are interested in what facilitates or inhibits his effective task performance.

We are not interested per se in whether his relationships with others are happy or unhappy, whether they perceive him as too warm or too cold, too authoritarian or too laissez faire, or any other of the many interpersonal relationships which arise as people associate in organizations, However, I do not mean to imply that the line between instrumental relationships and interpersonal ones is an easy one to draw in action and practice, or even that it is desirable that this be done.

Depth Gauges: Level of Tasks and Feelings

What I am saying is that an intervention strategy can focus on instrumentality or it can focus on interpersonal relationships, and that there are important consequences of this difference in depth of intervention.

When we intervene at the level of instrumentality, it is to change work behavior and working relationships. Frequently this involves the process of bargaining or negotiation between groups and individuals. Diagnoses are made of the satisfactions or dissatisfactions of organization members with one another's work behavior. Reciprocal adjustments, bargains, and trade-offs can then be arranged in which each party gets some modification in the behavior of the other at the cost to him of some reciprocal accommodation. Much of the intervention strategy which has been developed around Blake's concept of the managerial grid is at this level and involves bargaining and negotiation of role behavior as an important change process.

At the deeper level of interpersonal relationships the focus is on feelings, attitudes, and perceptions which organization members have about others. At this level we are concerned with the quality of human relationships within the organization, with warmth and coldness of members to one another, and with the experiences of acceptance and rejection, love and hate, trust and suspicion among groups and individuals. At this level the consultant probes for normally hidden feelings, attitudes, and perceptions. He works to create relationships of openness about feelings and to help members to develop mutual understanding of one another as persons. Interventions are directed toward helping organization members to be more comfortable in being authentically themselves with one another, and the degree of mutual caring and concern is expected to increase. Sensitivity training using T-groups is a basic intervention strategy at this level. T-group educators emphasize increased personalization of relationships, the development of trust and openness, and the exchange of feelings. Interventions at this level deal directly and intensively with interpersonal emotionality. This is the first intervention strategy we have examined which is at a depth where the feelings of organization members about one another as persons are a direct focus of the intervention strategy. At the other levels, such feelings certainly exist and may be expressed, but they are not a direct concern of the intervention. The transition from the task orientation of instrumental process analysis to the feeling orientation of interpersonal process analysis seems, as I shall suggest later, to be a critical one for many organization members.

The deepest level of intervention which will be considered in this paper is that of intrapersonal analysis. Here the consultant uses a variety of methods to reveal the individual's deeper attitudes, values, and conflicts regarding his own functioning, identity, and existence. The focus is generally on increasing the range of experiences which the individual can bring into awareness and cope with. The material may be dealt with at the fantasy or symbolic level, and the intervention strategies include many which are noninterpersonal and nonverbal. Some examples of this approach are the use of marathon T-group sessions, the creative risk-taking laboratory approach of Byrd, and some aspects of the task group therapy approach of Clark [2]. These approaches all tend to bring into focus very deep and intense feelings about one's own identity and one's relationships with significant others.

Although I have characterized deeper interventions as dealing increasingly with the individual's affective life, I do not imply that issues at less deep levels may not be emotionally charged. Issues of role differentiation, reward distribution, ability and performance evaluation, for example, are frequently invested with strong feelings. The concept of depth is concerned more with the *accessibility* and *individuality* of attitudes, values, and perceptions than it is with their strength. This narrowing of the common usage of the term, *depth*, is necessary to avoid the contradictions which occur when strength and inaccessibility are confused. For instance, passionate value confrontation and bitter conflict have frequently occurred between labor and management over economic issues which are surely toward the surface end of my concept of depth.

In order to understand the importance of the concept of depth for choosing interventions in organizations, let us consider the effects upon organization members of working at different levels.

The first of the important concomitants of depth is the degree of dependence of the client on the special competence of the change agent. At the surface end of the depth dimension, the methods of intervention are easily communicated and made public. The client may reasonably expect to learn something of the change agent's skills to improve his own practice. At the deeper levels, such as interpersonal and intrapersonal process analyses, it is more difficult for the client to understand the methods of intervention. The change agent is more likely to be seen as a person of special and unusual powers not found in ordinary men. Skills of intervention and change are less frequently learned by organization members, and the change process may tend to become personalized around the change agent as leader. Programs of change which are so dependent upon personal relationships and individual expertise are difficult to institutionalize. When the change agent leaves the system, he may not only take his expertise with him but the entire change process as well.

A second aspect of the change process which varies with depth is the extent to which the benefits of an intervention are transferable to members of the organization not originally participating in the change process. At surface levels of operations analysis and performance evaluation, the effects are institutionalized in the form of procedures, policies, and practices of the organization which may have considerable permanence beyond the tenure of individuals. At the level of instrumental behavior, the continuing effects of intervention are more likely to reside in the informal norms of groups within the organization regarding such matters as delegation, communication, decision making, competition and collaboration, and conflict resolution.

At the deepest levels of intervention, the target of change is the individual's inner life; and if the intervention is successful, the permanence of individual change should be greatest. There are indeed dramatic reports of cases in which persons have changed their careers and life goals as a result of such interventions, and the persistence of such change appears to be relatively high.

One consequence, then, of the level of intervention is that with greater depth of focus the individual increasingly becomes both the target and the carrier of change. In the light of this analysis, it is not surprising to observe that deeper levels of intervention are increasingly being used at higher organizational levels and in scientific and service organizations where the contribution of the individual has greatest impact.

An important concomitant of depth is that as the level of intervention becomes deeper, the information needed to intervene effectively becomes less available. At the less personal level of operations analysis, the information is often a matter of record. At the level of performance evaluation, it is a matter of observation. On the other hand, reactions of others to a person's work style are less likely to be discussed freely, and the more personal responses to his interpersonal style are even less likely to be readily given. At the deepest levels, important information may not be available to the individual himself. Thus, as we go deeper the consultant must use more of his time and skill uncovering information which is ordinarily private and hidden. This is one reason for the greater costs of interventions at deeper levels of focus.

Another aspect of the change process which varies with the depth of intervention is the personal risk and unpredictability of outcome for the individual. At deeper levels we deal with aspects of the individual's view of himself and his relationships with others which are relatively untested by exposure to the evaluations and emotional reactions of others. If in the change process the individual's self-perceptions are strongly disconfirmed, the resulting imbalance in internal forces may produce sudden changes in behavior, attitudes, and personality integration.

Because of the private and hidden nature of the processes into which we intervene at deeper levels, it is difficult to predict the individual impact of the change process in advance. The need for clinical sensitivity and skill on the part of the practitioner thus increases, since he must be prepared to diagnose and deal with developing situations involving considerable stress upon individuals.

The foregoing analysis suggests a criterion by which to match intervention strategies to particular organizational problems. It is *to intervene at a level no deeper than that required to produce enduring solutions to the problems at hand.* This criterion derives directly from the observations above. The cost, skill demands, client dependency, and variability of outcome all increase with depth of intervention. Further, as the depth of intervention increases, the effects tend to locate more in the individual and less in the organization. The danger of losing the organization's investment in the change with the departure of the individual becomes a significant consideration.

Autonomy Increases Depth of Intervention

While this general criterion is simple and straightforward, its application is not. In particular, although the criterion should operate in the direction of less depth of intervention, there is a general trend in modern organizational life which tends to push the intervention level ever deeper. This trend is toward increased self-direction of organization members and increased independence of external pressures and incentives. I believe that there is a direct relationship between the autonomy of individuals and the depth of intervention needed to effect organizational change.

Before going on to discuss this relationship, I shall acknowledge freely that I cannot prove the existence of a trend toward a general increase in freedom of individuals within organizations. I intend only to assert the great importance of the degree of individual autonomy in determining the level of intervention which will be effective.

In order to understand the relationship between autonomy and depth of intervention, it is necessary to conceptualize a dimension which parallels and is implied by the depth dimension we have been discussing. This is the dimension of predictability and variability among persons in their responses to the different kinds of incentives which may be used to influence behavior in the organization. The key assumption in this analysis is that the more unpredictable and unique the individual's response to the particular kinds of controls and incentives one can bring to bear upon him, the more one must know about that person in order to influence his behavior.

Most predictable and least individual is the response of the person to economic and bureaucratic controls when his needs for economic income and security are high. It is not necessary to delve very deeply into a person's inner processes in order to influence his behavior if we know that he badly needs his income and his position and if we are in a position to control his access to these rewards. Responses to economic and bureaucratic controls tend to be relatively simple and on the surface.

Independence of economic incentive. If for any reason organization members become relatively uninfluenceable through the manipulation of their income and economic security, the management of performance becomes strikingly more complex; and the need for more personal information about the individual increases. Except very generally, we do not know automatically or in advance what styles of instrumental or interpersonal interaction will be responded to as negative or positive incentives by the individual. One person may appreciate close supervision and direction; another may value independence of direction. One may prefer to work alone; another may function best when he is in close communication with others. One may thrive in close, intimate, personal interaction, while others are made uncomfortable by any but cool and distant relationships with colleagues.

What I am saying is that when bureaucratic and economic incentives lose their force for whatever reason, the improvement of performance *must* involve linking organizational goals to the individual's attempts to meet his own needs for satisfying instrumental activities and interpersonal relationships. It is for this reason that I make the assertion that increases in personal autonomy dictate change interventions at deeper and more personal levels. In order to obtain the information necessary to link organizational needs to individual goals, one must probe fairly deeply into the attitudes, values, and emotions of the organization members.

If the need for deeper personal information becomes great when we intervene at the instrumental and interpersonal levels, it becomes even greater when one is dealing with organization members who are motivated less through their transactions with the environment and more in response to internal values and standards. An example is the researcher, engineer, or technical specialist whose work behavior may be influenced more by his own values and standards of creativity or professional excellence than by his relationships with others. The deepest organizational interventions at the intrapersonal level may be required in order to effect change when working with persons who are highly self-directed.

Let me summarize my position about the relationship among autonomy, influence, and level of intervention. As the individual becomes less subject to economic and bureaucratic pressures, he tends to seek more intangible rewards in the organization which come from both the instrumental and interpersonal aspects of the system. I view this as a shift from greater external to more internal control and as an increase in autonomy. Further shifts in this direction may involve increased independence of rewards and punishments mediated by others, in favor of operation in accordance with internal values and standards.

I view organizations as systems of reciprocal influence. Achievement of organization goals is facilitated when individuals can seek their own satisfactions through activity which promotes the goals of the organization. As the satisfactions which are of most value to the individual change, so must the reciprocal influence systems, if the organization goals are to continue to be met.

If the individual changes are in the direction of increased independence of external incentives, then the influence systems must change to provide opportunities for individuals to achieve more intangible, self-determined satisfactions in their work. However, people are more differentiated, complex, and unique in their intangible goals and values than in their economic needs. In order to create systems which offer a wide variety of intangible satisfactions, much more private information about individuals is needed than is required to create and maintain systems based chiefly on economic and bureaucratic controls. For this reason, deeper interventions are called for when the system which they would attempt to change contains a high proportion of relatively autonomous individuals.

There are a number of factors promoting autonomy, all tending to free the individual from dependence upon economic and bureaucratic controls, which I have observed in my work with organizations. Wherever a number of these factors obtain, it is probably an indication that deeper levels of intervention are required to effect lasting improvements in organizational functioning. I shall simply list these indicators briefly in categories to show what kinds of things might signify to the practitioner that deeper levels of intervention may be appropriate.

The first category includes anything which makes the evaluation of individual performance difficult:

> A long time span between the individual's actions and the results by which effectiveness of performance is to be judged.
> Nonrepetitive, unique tasks which cannot be evaluated by reference to the performance of others on similar tasks.
> Specialized skills and abilities possessed by an individual which cannot be evaluated by a supervisor who does not possess the skills or knowledge himself.

The second category concerns economic conditions:

> Arrangements which secure the job tenure and/or income of the individual.
> A market permitting easy transfer from one organization to another (e.g., engineers in the United States aerospace industry).
> Unique skills and knowledge of the individual which make him difficult to replace.

The third category includes characteristics of the system or its environment which lead to independence of the parts of the organization and decentralization of authority such as:

> An organization which works on a project basis instead of producing a standard line of products.
> An organization in which subparts must be given latitude to deal rapidly and flexibly with frequent environmental change.

I should like to conclude the discussion of this criterion for depth of intervention with a brief reference to the ethics of intervention, a problem which merits considerably more thorough treatment than I can give it here.

The ethics of delving deeper.   There is considerable concern in the United States about invasion of privacy by behavioral scientists. I would agree that such invasion of privacy is an actual as well as a fantasied concomitant of the use of organizational change strategies of greater depth. The recourse by organizations to such strategies has been widely viewed as an indication of greater organizational control over the most personal and private aspects of the lives of the members. The present analysis suggests, however, that recourse to these deeper interventions actually reflects the greater *freedom* of organization members from traditionally crude and impersonal means of organizational control. There is no reason to be concerned about man's attitudes or values or interpersonal relationships when his job performance can be controlled by brute force, by economic coercion, or by bureaucratic rules and regulations. The "invasion of privacy" becomes worth the cost, bother, and uncertainty of outcome only when the individual has achieved relative independence from control by other means. Put another way, it makes organizational sense to try to get a man to *want* to do something only if you cannot *make* him do it. And regardless of what intervention strategy is used, the individual still retains considerably greater control over his own behavior than he had when he could be manipulated more crudely. As long as we can maintain a high degree of voluntarism regarding the nature and extent of an individual's participation in the deeper organizational change strategies, these strategies can work toward adapting the organization to the individual quite as much as they work the other way around. Only when an individual's participation in one of the deeper change strategies is coerced by economic or bureaucratic pressures do I feel that the ethics of the intervention clearly run counter to the values of a democratic society.

Role of Client Norms and Values in Determining Depth

So far our attention to the choice of level of intervention has focused upon locating the depth at which the information exists which must be exchanged to facilitate system improvement. Unfortunately, the choice of an intervention strategy cannot practically be made with reference to this criterion alone. Even if a correct diagnosis is made of the level at which the relevant information lies, we may not be able to work effectively at the desired depth because of client norms, values, resistances, and fears.

In an attempt to develop a second criterion for depth of intervention which takes such dispositions on the part of the client into account, I have considered two approaches which represent polarized orientations to the problem. One approach is based upon analyzing and overcoming client resistance; the other is based upon discovering and joining forces with the self-articulated wants or "felt needs" of the client.

There are several ways of characterizing these approaches. To me, the simplest is to point out that when the change agent is resistance-oriented, he tends to lead or influence the client to work at a depth greater than that at which the latter feels comfortable. When resistance-oriented, the change agent tends to mistrust the client's statement of his problems and of the areas where he wants help. He suspects the client's presentation of being a smoke screen or defense against admission of his "real" problems and needs. The consultant works to expose the underlying processes and concerns and to influence the client to work at a deeper level. The resistance-oriented approach grows out of the work of clinicians and psychotherapists, and it characterizes much of the work of organizational consultants who specialize in sensitivity training and deeper intervention strategies.

On the other hand, change agents may be oriented to the self-articulated needs of clients. When so oriented, the consultant tends more to follow and facilitate the client in working at whatever level the latter sets for himself. He may assist the client in defining problems and needs and in working on solutions, but he is inclined to try to anchor his work in the norms, values, and accepted standards of behavior of the organization.

I believe that there is a tendency for change agents working at the interpersonal and deeper levels to adopt a rather consistent resistance-oriented approach. Consultants so oriented seem to take a certain quixotic pride in dramatically and self-consciously violating organizational norms. Various techniques have been developed for pressuring or seducing organization members into departing from organizational norms in the service of change. The "marathon" T-group is a case in point, where the increased irritability and fatigue of prolonged contact and lack of sleep move participants to deal with one another more emotionally, personally, and spontaneously than they would normally be willing to do.

I suspect that unless such norm-violating intervention efforts actually succeed in changing organizational norms, their effects are relatively short-lived, because the social structures and interpersonal linkages have not been created which can utilize for day-to-day problem solving the deeper information produced by the intervention. It is true that the consultant may succeed in producing information, but he is less likely to succeed in creating social structures which can continue to work in his absence. The problem is directly analogous to that of the community developer who succeeds by virtue of his personal influence in getting villagers to build a school or a community center which falls into disuse as soon as he leaves because of the lack of any integration of these achievements into the social structure and day-to-day needs and desires of the community. Community developers have had to learn through bitter failure and frustration that ignoring or subverting the standards and norms of a social system often results in temporary success followed by a reactionary increase in resistance to the influence of the change agent. On the other hand, felt needs embody those problems, issues, and difficulties which have a high conscious priority on the part of community or organization members. We can expect individuals and groups to be ready to invest time, energy, and resources in dealing with their felt needs, while they will be relatively passive or even resistant toward those who attempt to help them with externally defined needs. Community developers have found that attempts to help with felt needs are met with greater receptivity, support, and integration within the structure and life of the community than are intervention attempts which rely primarily upon the developer's value system for setting need priorities.

The emphasis of many organizational change agents on confronting and working through resistances was developed originally in the practice of individual psychoanalysis and psychotherapy, and it is also a central concept in the conduct of therapy groups and sensitivity training laboratories. In all of these situations, the change agent has a high degree of environmental control and is at least temporarily in a high status position with respect to the client. To a degree that is frequently underestimated by practitioners, we manage to create a situation in which it is more unpleasant for the client to leave than it is to stay and submit to the pressure to confront and work through resistances. I believe that the tendency is for behavioral scientists to overplay their hands when they move from the clinical and training situations where they have environmental control to the organizational consulting situation, where their control is sharply attenuated.

This attenuation derives only partially from the relative ease with which the client can terminate the relationship. Even if this most drastic step is not taken, the consultant can be tolerated, misled, and deceived in ways which are relatively difficult in the therapeutic or human relations training situations. He can also be openly defied and blocked if he runs afoul of strongly shared group norms, whereas when the consultant is dealing with a group of strangers, he can often utilize differences among the members to overcome this kind of resistance. I suspect that, in general, behavioral scientists underestimate their power in working with individuals and groups of strangers, and overestimate it when working with individuals and groups in organizations. I emphasize this point because I believe that a good many potentially fruitful and mutually satisfying consulting relationships are terminated early because of the consultant's taking the role of overcomer of resistance to change rather than that of collaborator in the client's attempts at solving his problems. It is these considerations which lead me to suggest my second criterion for the choice of organization intervention strategy: *to intervene at a level no deeper than that at which the energy and resources of the client can be committed to problem solving and to change.* These energies and resources can be mobilized through obtaining legitimation for the intervention in the norms of the organization and through devising intervention strategies which have clear relevance to consciously felt needs on the part of the organization members.

The Consultant's Dilemma: Felt Needs vs. Deeper Levels

Unfortunately, it is doubtless true that the forces which influence
the conditions we desire to change often exist at deeper levels than
can be dealt with by adhering to the criterion of working within
organization norms and meeting felt needs. The level at which an
individual or group is willing and ready to invest energy and resources
is probably always determined partly by a realistic assessment of the
problems and partly by a defensive need to avoid confrontation and
significant change. It is thus not likely that our two criteria for
selection of intervention depth will result in the same decisions when
practically applied. It is not the same to intervene at the level where
behavior-determining forces are most potent as it is to work on felt
needs as they are articulated by the client. This, it seems to me, is
the consultant's dilemma. It always has been. We are continually
faced with the choice between leading the client into areas which are
threatening, unfamiliar, and dependency-provoking for him (and
where our own expertise shows up to best advantage) or, on the
other hand, being guided by the client's own understanding of his
problems and his willingness to invest resources in particular kinds
of relatively familiar and non-threatening strategies.

When time permits, this dilemma is ideally dealt with by intervening first at a level where there is good support from the norms, power
structure, and felt needs of organizational members. The consultant
can then, over a period of time, develop trust, sophistication, and
support within the organization to explore deeper levels at which
particularly important forces may be operating. This would probably be agreed to, at least in principle, by most organizational consultants. The point at which I feel I differ from a significant number
of workers in this field is that I would advocate that interventions
should *always* be limited to the depth of the client's felt needs and
readiness to legitimize intervention. I believe we should always
avoid moving deeper at a pace which outstrips a client system's willingness to subject itself to exposure, dependency, and threat. What
I am saying is that if the dominant response of organization members
indicates that an intervention violates system norms regarding exposure, privacy, and confrontation, then one has intervened too deeply
and should pull back to a level at which organization members are
more ready to invest their own energy in the change process. This
point of view is thus in opposition to that which sees negative reactions primarily as indications of resistances which are to be brought
out into the open, confronted, and worked through as a central part
of the intervention process. I believe that behavioral scientists acting
as organizational consultants have tended to place overmuch emphasis on the overcoming of resistance to change and have underempha-

sis on the overcoming of resistance to change and have underemphasized the importance of enlisting in the service of change the energies and resources which the client can consciously direct and willingly devote to problem solving.

What is advocated here is that we in general accept the client's felt needs or the problems he presents as real and that we work on them at a level at which he can serve as a competent and willing collaborator. This position is in opposition to one which sees the presenting problem as more or less a smoke screen or barrier. I am not advocating this point of view because I value the right to privacy of organization members more highly than I value their growth and development or the solution of organizational problems. (This is an issue which concerns me, but it is enormously more complex than the ones with which I am dealing in this paper.) Rather, I place first priority on collaboration with the client, because I do not think we are frequently successful consultants without it.

In my own practice I have observed that the change in client response is frequently quite striking when I move from a resistance-oriented approach to an acceptance of the client's norms and definitions of his own needs. With quite a few organizational clients in the United States, the line of legitimacy seems to lie somewhere between interventions at the instrumental level and those focused on interpersonal relationships. Members who exhibit hostility, passivity, and dependence when I initiate intervention at the interpersonal level may become dramatically more active, collaborative, and involved when I shift the focus to the instrumental level.

If I intervene directly at the level of interpersonal relationships, I can be sure that at least some members, and often the whole group, will react with anxiety, passive resistance, and low or negative commitment to the change process. Furthermore, they express their resistance in terms of norms and value regarding the appropriateness or legitimacy of dealing at this level. They say things like, "It isn't right to force people's feelings about one another out into the open"; "I don't see what this has to do with improving organizational effectiveness"; "People are being encouraged to say things which are better left unsaid."

If I then switch to a strategy which focuses on decision making, delegation of authority, information exchange, and other instrumental questions, these complaints about illegitimacy and the inappropriateness of the intervention are usually sharply reduced. This does not mean that the clients are necessarily comfortable or free from anxiety in the discussions, nor does it mean that strong feelings may not be expressed about one another's behavior. What is different is that the clients are more likely to *work with* instead of *against* me, to feel and express some sense of ownership in the change process, that the clients are more likely to *work with* instead of *against* me, to feel and express some sense of ownership in the change process, and to see many more possibilities for carrying it on among themselves in the absence of the consultant.

What I have found is that when I am resistance-oriented in my approach to the client, I am apt to feel rather uncomfortable in "letting sleeping dogs lie." When, on the other hand, I orient myself to the client's own assessment of his needs, I am uncomfortable when I feel I am leading or pushing the client to operate very far outside the shared norms of the organization. I have tried to indicate why I believe the latter orientation is more appropriate. I realize of course that many highly sophisticated and talented practitioners will not agree with me.

In summary, I have tried to show in this paper that the dimension of depth should be central to the conceptualization of intervention strategies. I have presented what I believe are the major consequences of intervening at greater or lesser depths, and from these consequences I have suggested two criteria for choosing the appropriate depth of intervention: first, *to intervene at a level no deeper than that required to produce enduring solutions to the problems at hand;* and second, *to intervene at a level no deeper than that at which the energy and resources of the client can be committed to problem solving and to change.*

I have analyzed the tendency for increases in individual autonomy in organizations to push the appropriate level of intervention deeper when the first criterion is followed. Opposed to this is the countervailing influence of the second criterion to work closer to the surface in order to enlist the energy and support of organization members in the change process. Arguments have been presented for resolving this dilemma in favor of the second, more conservative, criterion. The dilemma remains, of course; the continuing tension under which the change agent works is between the desire to lead and push, or to collaborate and follow. The middle ground is never very stable, and I suspect we show our values and preferences by which criterion we choose to maximize when we are under the stress of difficult and ambiguous client-consultant relationships.

Notes

1. A revised version of a paper presented at the International Congress of Group Psychotherapy, Vienna, Austria, September 16, 1968. Roger Harrison is vice-president, and London-based representative, of Development Research Associates, Inc., Cambridge, Massachusetts.
2. R. E. Byrd, "Training in a Non-Group," *J. Humanistic Psychology,* 7 (1967), 18-27; J. V. Clark, *Task Group Therapy,* unpublished manuscript (Los Angeles: Univ. of California, 1966).

Relativism
in Organizations

George F. F. Lombard

*The idea that has captured the minds of men and women everywhere
can be a tool of renewal for management*

Foreword

In a popular folk song known to millions of young people, Bob Dylan writes of a
number of questions and answers that are "blowin' in the wind" around the
world today. Underlying such ideas—and underlying the approach to life taken
by many young thought leaders— is an even more basic idea: relativism. This is
the philosophy of guiding one's action in the light of multiple values and goals,
subjective as well as objective. For business and other organizations, relativism
is a revolutionary principle, for it means that traditional goals (e.g., profit, costs,
turnover) are but one set of goals to meet, and that such needs as individual
satisfactions, group norms, and social causes should also be met. This article
deals with the meaning and implications of relativism for managers. After describing it first in an educational setting, where it is most readily understood and
has been best explored, the author turns to a series of studies showing the utility
of relativism in management of corporations and other types of organizations.
   Mr. Lombard is Senior Associate Dean for Educational Affairs and Louis E.
Kirstein Professor of Human Relations at the Harvard Business School. He has
been active in a number of industrial and nonprofit organizations, has undertaken research in the aircraft, retailing, and other industries, and is the author
of books and articles on various aspects of organizational behavior.

A central theme of student protests today concerns organizations
and their administration. Some students protest the establishment
as a whole. Others act against those in positions of authority. Still
others protest inequities associated with the output of organizations,
including profits and their distribution, faulty or unsafe products,
and pollution of the environment.

There is substance to many of these criticisms. For the most part,
organizations are not dealing successfully with today's problems,
such as those concerning the cities, poverty, hunger, and race. This

lack of success is apparent around the world. The difficulties are both geographically widespread and, in many kinds of institutions, pervasive. Thus:

Business organizations, the most effective wealth-creating instruments yet devised by men, have not invented ways of distributing their products without leaving large areas of poverty in the regions where they have been most successful, to say nothing of whole continents of poverty where they have been less successful.

The medical professions and the organizations associated with them do no better in the delivery of health care.

Our religious organizations are bothered by schisms and a sense of purposelessness as perplexing as it is profound.

Though governments perhaps can prevent at least some small wars from becoming large ones, they do not end them.

Widespread, radical, revolutionary change indeed seems necessary. At the same time, numerous observers of the world scene, while recognizing the seriousness of our unsolved problems, fear change in the processes and goals of organizations as we know them. According to one magazine:

"The single-minded pursuit of profit is the discipline that reconciles conflicting interests; it is the wind of reality that blows away executive cobwebs; it achieves renewal when businesses falter. . . . Change the discipline, introduce purposes linked with broad public responsibility, however praiseworthy they may be, blur the criterion of performance, and the result is likely to be confusion." [1, *p. 95*]

The contrary views of revolutionists and defenders of the "establishment" frame the questions I wish to explore. Are today's ideas about organizations a source of our troubles? Are changes possible in them? If so, need the changes be disruptive changes, or can they be orderly? If the latter, to what agencies should we look to bring them about?

My thesis is that, especially during the last half century, an important change has taken place in the systems of knowledge and values which men use to guide their thoughts and actions. The direction of the change has been away from universals and simple, right-wrong, authoritarian formulations and toward multiple values and what I shall call *relativism*. This trend is clear in such areas as the sciences, art, music, literature, religion, and philosophy, but it has not affected men's ideas about organizations and administration, which typically are conceived in what might be called *dualistic* frameworks.

The tensions that result from these two differently structured systems of knowledge and values affect university students especially.

Just when they are learning the ideas of relativism, they must live and choose careers in organizations that are bureaucratically conceived and administered. I think this situation helps explain why their protests are so intense.

Significant leads are available from recent research for the reconception of organizations and their administration in relativistic frameworks. The development of these leads calls for new programs of research and education on the part of the universities, and for new understanding and leadership on the part of businessmen.

Revolution in Outlook

I first became aware of the worldwide nature of the breakdown in universities at a conference I attended in Rotterdam more than three years ago. The conference concerned management education in Western Europe. The occasion provided an opportunity for impromptu discussions on topics of common interest to persons who otherwise do not often see each other. I was a participant in one such conversation which produced this thought-provoking question: what conditions in world affairs led to the crises of the 1960's being expressed in universities? After all, the world has seen many crises, but none has been expressed in universities to the extent that this one has. Moreover, the disturbances in universities are universal in scope and not to be explained by local and regional causes alone.

Attitudes toward knowledge. Some valuable help in answering that question comes from a research report by William G. Perry, Jr., Director of the Bureau of Study Counsel at Harvard College, an office to which students go for help when they are having difficulty with their work [2]. In the mid-1950's Perry and his staff, who have acquired a wealth of experience in working with student problems, undertook to document the experiences of students during their college years. The interviewers asked the students who volunteered to take part in the research to think and talk about the meaning to them of what they were learning. The quality of the resulting interviews is outstanding. It quickly becomes apparent to a reader that the students are answering the questions out of their own experiences.

The report begins with an inquiry into the changes that have occurred in the questions which professors ask on examinations in courses with large enrollments. Fifty years ago, Perry says, such questions as, "When was the battle of Hastings?" or, "Who wrote such and such a poem?" or, "What did so-and-so say about a particular experiment?" were typical. Today's questions are different.

For instance:

If the examination is about a poem, the student may be asked to state the significance of the poem to its author in the light of the knowledge and circumstances of his times and situation.

A second question might well be: "What would Shakespeare, Freud, Dewey, Whitehead, and McLuhan each have said about the poem in the circumstances of his life and times?"

Perry infers from these changes in examination questions that professors' assumptions about knowledge and standards for knowledge have changed. Fifty years ago the questions showed that professors viewed knowledge as structured in ways that led to essentially simple, two-valued, right-or-wrong answers to questions and problems. Today's examinations show that professors hold knowledge to be relative, not absolute; not meaningful except in the context of the idea systems, times, and circumstances in which it was generated. Perry labels the first orientation "dualistic" and the second "relativistic." He calls the change revolutionary because it means that the professors' views of knowledge as a source of authority do change.

In the first orientation, knowledge is a unidimensional source of authority, right or wrong, not to be questioned. In the latter, the authority of knowledge is relative to the situation. Perry points out that when professors add to their examination questions, as they frequently do, an additional one: "What does the poem mean to you, Mr. Sophomore?"—then the revolution in approach is indeed extensive. For the question tells a student that his professors expect him to commit himself to his view in order that they may compare it with those of authorities. To most undergraduates this is heady stuff.

Thought processes. For the purposes of this article I do not need to go into Perry's careful analysis of the nine stages of student thought as it develops toward relativism, but I do need to comment on one intermediate stage between dualism and relativism, which Perry calls "multiplicity." I do this in an attempt to convey, albeit briefly, some sense of the signifcance of the changes of which Perry speaks. Even though we may not think about it consciously, changes we make in our assumptions about knowledge and in our ideas, values, and attitudes concerning knowledge affect deeply what we do in our everyday lives.

To characterize dualism, Perry uses the phrases, "we-right-friendly; others-wrong-hostile." He points out that such an orientation is characteristic of the knowledge with which primitives, whether aborigines or children, we view the world. Dualism also characterizes many attitudes in modern adult cultures. For example, it is associated with much that we consider "good" about competition in our society, whether the competition is between football teams or brands of automobiles or other merchandise. It is also, of course, a major theme governing the relations between various other institutions of Western societies, including religious faiths and national states.

Perry uses the statement, "Every one has a right to his own view," to characterize a middle stage in the development from dualism to relativism. In this stage the student recognizes that others' knowledge, attitudes, and views about themselves and their world may differ from his. (The student must truly believe this; it is not enough that he accept the notion on the authority of his professors.) At this middle stage, however, the student is not aware, as he is at the more advanced stage of relativism, that his views of himself and the world have an internal structure, i.e., a consistency and self-reinforcing organization based on certain experiences. Other people's views and his own remain loosely organized in his thought processes, like a pile of sticks or a heap of sand.

At the stage of relativism a student *is* aware of the internal structure of his views, and he has the capacity to examine hitherto unstated basic assumptions in his thinking and thus to change them (and his behavior). Not only does he perceive events differently from the way he did earlier, but he can also perceive the same event *from different perspectives.* Thus he has choices in respect to his actions with others that he did not have at the stage of multiplicity.

A central characteristic of a student's thought processes at the stage of relativism is a capacity for independent study and decision. Perry says that when a student, as the result of an ordered process of observation and reasoning, can state what a poem or the data of an experiment mean to him or others, he is at the stage of relativism. The student recognizes the meanings that the poem or experiment has for others in the light of their lives, times, and ideas, just as he recognizes how his circumstances shape the meaning for him. Perry describes three themes as central to the discipline of independent study and action: (1) choice among alternatives; (2) awareness of choice; and, usually later, (3) commitment to a choice.

Perry does not fall into the trap of becoming absolute about relativism. Were he to do so, he would not have escaped from an "either-or" framework, for when relativism becomes a "must," it returns to dualism. Thus, Perry classifies as being at the stage of relativism a student who elects to conduct his life by absolute values, after considering alternatives, recognizing the limits of his own situation with its particular purposes, times, circumstances, and systems of ideas,

Effect of Relativism

What difference does relativism make in decision making? Taking
a relativistic approach rather than a dualistic one, a manager
would be likely to:

* Recognize more different kinds of goals and needs for his organization, such as economic, individual, group, and social
  goals, always trying to keep them in some sort of workable
  balance.

* Consider more factors bearing on a decision, and attach different weights to them as circumstances change.

* Employ a wider variety of ways of making and carrying out
  decisions.

* Avoid following rules of thumb about administration (such as,
  "An employee should never report to more than one boss,"
  or, "An executive's span of control should not exceed six
  subordinates").

* Evaluate decisions not one by one but in relation to each
  other and to other interests, knowing that the validity of a
  decision is dependent on other decisions, actions, and events
  about which he generally has imperfect knowledge.

* Appreciate the practical necessity for having certain policies
  and standards for employees to observe but recognize that
  such rules often come at a price (e.g., resentment or uncooperative behavior on the part of those who see the problem
  differently) and that their disadvantages must therefore be
  weighed against their advantages.

and understanding that others may live equally intelligently by values different from his.

Universal questions. The idea of relativism is not, of course, limited to the campus. It is basic to twentieth century culture. Its roots go back at least to the nineteenth century, perhaps to Darwin's theory of evolution. Einstein's theories of relativity and all that has followed are part of the same stream of ideas. Further reinforcements have come in the fields of literature, arts, and music.

Recent technological advances, especially television and, in underdeveloped countries, the transistor radio, bring home to all of us that many other people live differently from the way we do. Modern decision techniques, too, abet the spread of relativism. Computers and Bayesian approaches to decision make it possible to study systematically a much greater number of alternatives for action, particularly in organizations, than ever before, thus pointing up the relativity of any particular course of action. Finally, in a still more personal sense, "the pill" raises questions about long-held moral and ethical standards and moves us in the direction of relativism.

Perry's research gives us data about the depth and extent to which this great idea of modern times is revolutionizing the outlook and decisions of college students. He reports that it is the commonplace of education in good liberal arts programs in U.S. colleges today.

If I were to seek data with which to answer the question asked at Rotterdam, I would use as a guide the hypothesis that student protest in the 1960's and early 1970's has been a function of the tension between conceptual relativism and bureaucratic behavior. That is to say, in organizations where relativism as a system of values is conceptually clear, and bureaucratic behavior is also clear, then protests will be both frequent and intense. A quick review of studies of protest at Berkeley, New York (Columbia), Cambridge (Harvard), Paris, Tokyo, New Delhi, and elsewhere indicates that systematic support for this hypothesis would not be difficult to find [3]. In these cases relativism as a value important to students conflicted with dualism as a value important in the administration of universities.

Though Joseph W. Scott and Mohamed El-Assal formulated their variables differently in a study of 70 colleges and universities, their findings support the same point. They found that demonstrations were more frequent (most of the correlation coefficients fell between .70 and .90) in the large, complex, high-quality schools than in the small, simple, low-quality ones. They explained: "Large, complex, high quality schools, being more likely to use autocratic and bureaucratic means to redress student grievances . . . encouraged and increased the likelihood of student protest demonstrations." [4]

Dualism in Management

I have indicated that relativism is stimulated and reenforced by trends and practices in many aspects of life. Let us turn our attention now from the campus to business and other organizations.

Generally speaking, the theory and practice of formal organizations is still, I believe, essentially based on unidimensional, right-wrong, dualistic approaches. The principles of organization stated by such authors as Henri Fayol, Luther Gulick, Lyndall Urwick, James Mooney, Frederick Taylor, and their colleagues and successors rest on the primacy of technical and economic efficiency. Deviations, as they see them, represent inefficiencies and disruptions of organizational processes. An important aspect of executives' work is to provide standards, preferably written, for attaining efficiency. Any situation that is not so provided for is to be referred to the central authority for decision. Thus, the right-wrong, dualistic character of standards for action is clear. The sociological and psychological consequences of this model have been described by Weber and his followers.

In important ways this model about how people in organizations are to behave characterizes today's actions and beliefs about management in large organizations in business, government, education, medicine, religion, the military, and almost every other branch of organized life. One unfortunate and unintended consequence is that undergraduates have to live and study in dualistically oriented organizations *as well as anticipate careers in them,* just when those we regard as the best among them have found the inner strength to commit themselves to relativism as a way of thinking. I believe this juxtaposition provides a source of dissonance and tension that underlies the current crisis in society.

Are organizations as we know them today doomed because of this conflict, or are there ways for executives to reduce the dissonance between value systems while keeping their organizations productive and viable? I believe that there are such ways and that we can learn to use them if we want to.

To elaborate on this belief, I shall turn now to a series of studies of organization and administration. I will limit myself to analyses of business operations because they are the ones most familiar to me. (The findings of comparable studies in other kinds of organizations are not essentially different, at least in the aspects we need to consider [5].) My intent is a limited one: not to develop a new theory of organizations—to do this, much additional, difficult work would have to be done—but to show that such an understanding is feasible.

Revolutions in Ideas

To assist us in knowing what to look for, we need a way of thinking about what happens when new systems of values and ideas displace old ones. Such a process is not familiar to most of us, who usually assume that old ideas just disappear when they are replaced. For guidance on this question in his work, Perry turns to studies in the history of science [6]. These studies make it clear that major changes in systems of ideas and values occur slowly over long periods of time and that, at least in some instances, it is not accurate to say that the old ideas disappear. Rather, they often continue to have validity in special and limited circumstances within the broad framework provided by the new ideas. To illustrate:

Neither Newton's specific ideas about motion nor the broad views of the world associated with them have disappeared since Einstein suggested relativity. Newton's ideas continue to be useful to all of us—for example, in understanding our motions and the motions of people and things around us.

On an everyday level, I recall hearing the words of a careful radio announcer as he described the increasing speed of Apollo 8 returning from the moon and approaching our world at so many miles per hour "relative to the earth." That is, of course, accurate phrasing. Nevertheless, when I drive a car, I neglect to keep in mind that its speed as shown on the speedometer is relative to that of the earth through space. The older formulation serves me well enough for any actions I need to take when I am driving.

Thus, in reviewing studies of organizations and their administration, we need not necessarily discard older, dualistic values and ways of thinking. We can seek to find ways of reconceiving them within broader frameworks.

For the exploration that follows I choose three topics: formal organization, decision making, and productivity. I select the first because of its importance in the conventional wisdom about organizations, the second because the undeniably "go—no go" character of decisions seems to lead inescapably to dualism, and the third because it is frequently assumed that an organization's contributions to society are solely purposive.

New organization patterns. Many recent writers have commented on a trend away from simple, unitary concepts of formal organization and toward increasingly complex theories [7]. The trend has several dimensions and manifestations. For instance, aerospace firms have largely given up a form of organization based on simple concepts of unified command and narrow span control. Instead, their executives speak of matrix organizations, in which both project and functional supervisors and professional workers as a team have responsibility for the same project. Again, it is said that the artists and engineers who built Pepsi-cola's pavillion for Expo '70 at Osaka "did what was required of them without supervision. There was no real chain of command." [8]

In addition, various studies suggest that there is no one best way to organize. In contrast to the bureaucratic theories referred to in a previous section, the findings of these recent studies suggest that the form of an organization depends on the context provided by its setting of individuals and purposes in society. This central theme of the conclusions is the more striking in that each researcher approached his study from a different perspective. Let me be more specific:

Alfred Chandler's approach was historical. His conclusion, stated broadly, is that conditions in the environment of a firm demand different organizational structures. He says that "Different organizational forms result from different types of growth. . ." and that "Structure follows strategy." [9]

Lawrence E. Fouraker and John M. Stopford tested Chandler's broad hypothesis with data derived from modern, complex, and large multinational enterprises. They concluded that "the question of the characteristics of the organization is a question of management's choice between sets of problems." [10, 47]

Abraham Zaleznik's focus is on authority relationships within a firm. He finds "a formal structure in the final analysis represents one design of organization, among a number of options, in which the authority figure invests his confidence." [11, *p. 163*]

Paul R. Lawrence and Jay W. Lorsch suggest "a contingency theory of organization . . . the basic assumption . . . [of which] is that organizational variables are in complex interrelationship with one another and with conditions in the environment." [12, *p. 157*]

These findings show how far modern concepts of formal organization have moved from dualistic, right-wrong approaches and toward concepts that are consistent with relativism.

Contingency in decisions. In the study just referred to, Lawrence and Lorsch suggest the idea of contingency in relation to organizations and administration. I believe that this idea helps to delineate a relativistic framework for reconceiving the seemingly inescapable dualistic aspects of decision making. Let me illustrate in terms of some personal experiences and views:

I have found it useful to classify organizational decisions into their internally and externally oriented aspects. In a large organization, particularly one with many functional line and staff departments, the internally oriented aspects are hardly ever simple and dualistic.

In my work in academic administration, I find that almost any decision I reach has not one but many consequences for action. A "single" decision suggesting, for example, a change in a professor's assignment may make it necessary for me to speak to two program chairmen and the administrative directors of their respective programs; to one or two area chairmen; to the registrar's office; and to the finance office. And that is fairly routine; a complicated decision requires even more implementation. Moreover, each interaction may produce information I had not taken into account at the time of the original decision, and I may have to extend or go back over and even reverse the communications I have already made.

Again and again this process has impressed me with the contingent and relativistic nature of the action I am taking. Though each step in the whole sequence is important in its place, it is the comprehension of the whole set of potentials, actualities, and interconnections that seems to make the difference between decisions well communicated and not well communicated.

I had long thought of investment decisions and decisions to "make or buy" as two-valued. But a few minutes' reflection shows that carefully made decisions of these kinds are reached only after alternatives, perhaps many of them, have been considered. In many situations more than one of the alternatives would be equally good, were only one or two factors in the situation to be changed a little.

Thus, even a good decision of these types is actually based on contingencies. A slight change in one or more factors would lead to decisions other than the one acted on.

In summary, a relativistic framework seems helpful in thinking of one's job as a decision maker. Whereas a dualistic framework describes only one step in the process, not necessarily even a final one, a relativistic viewpoint combines the outwardly oriented and visible steps of a decision with the internal thought processes that guide a manager. The apparent "go—no go" aspects of a decision become the limited, special instances of a broader, total, thought-and-action approach that includes alternatives considered as well as actions taken. Though the decision may appear dualistic in character, the total decision set, including both the obvious physical act and the inner subjective consideration of alternatives and contingencies, is appropriately conceived as a totality in a relativistic framework.

Complex purposes. Companies no longer limit themselves to producing products and services sold in free private markets. The outputs of business today are varied and complex. For instance, hitherto private-sector organizations are moving rapidly in the direction of providing what in the past have been thought of as public-sector goods and services. Business firms contract to provide education, welfare, rehabilitation, and urban renewal programs and services, just as public-sector enterprises in many parts of the world perform what we would call private-sector activities. Everywhere the interconnections between the two sectors are on the increase.

What is more, companies think of their missions in complex ways. A manufacturing company's purpose is no longer conceived as making, let us say, toasters for the breakfast table and electric motors for industry. The General Electric Company says, "Progress is our most important product"—and this is not just an advertising slogan. Again, the conglomerate and the multinational corporation, with all of their complexities, are ever more frequent. Other events call to our attention that the products of organizations are not all benign. We are learning to think of industries' noxious effluents as outputs.

But this is only part of the story. The modern businessman is saying that his company is more than a producer of ever-changing goods and services. One executive puts it this way:

I have never been particularly taken with the various single-thought definitions that have been offered to describe the role of as complex an institution as the American corporation.... Business discharges its true social responsibility by meeting individual and communal economic needs, to the profit of society and itself, while giving expression to the other, noneconomic values of society. [13, *pp. 4-5*]

Fritz J. Roethlisberger has suggested that an organization contributes to four needs or values: the norms of groups, the ideals of society, the personalities of individuals, and the purposes of the organization itself [14, *p. 125*]. Many studies show how employee behavior serves individual needs and group norms as well as production and profit goals. The Hawthorne works study at Western Electric Company, the first to demonstrate this phenomenon, has now been confirmed in a wide variety of organizations [15].

Unfortunately, researchers have largely ignored questions about the contributions work groups make to the attainment of the broad ideals of society. I know of a few beginnings in this direction, but they were not followed up:

In the course of the field work for his thesis a few years ago, a student at the Harvard Business School came across a situation involving the behavior of members of a work group in relation to questions of social justice. In one of these groups, the members had arranged their activities in ways that resolved their feelings and attitudes about differences in their backgrounds. (Their supervisors had paid no attention to this matter.)

The 25 or so persons in the group represented at least 8 ethnic and racial backgrounds. Instead of showing covert hostility and aggression toward each other, the employees had arranged their work and a variety of other educational and recreational activities in ways that resolved individual fears about mistreatment and persecution at the hands of the others. They read books together and discussed them. They went to concerts together and organized their own picnics, golf tournaments, card games, and fishing trips. They and others referred to their group as "The United Nations." The student did not analyze the data in terms of relativism.

In another Harvard Business School study, the researcher followed up similar leads with results that were so surprising we did not fully trust them [16]. The researcher was concerned with the pairs of individuals who "checked out" the purchases of customers in a supermarket. The tasks of the two persons in each pair were different; also, one was paid at a higher rate than the other. Moreover, there were differences among the workers with respect to sex, age, education, and ethnicity.

The study showed the workers had decided views about what combinations of persons should work together. Some combinations they felt were fair and just, some unfair and unjust. Once expressed, their views on these matters turned out to be surprisingly clear and effective in terms of worker satisfaction and productivity achieved for the store. The study showed how much arrangements at work can contribute to the attainment of social values, and it demonstrated that behavior in organizations concerns goals other than productivity, efficiency, profitability, and similar corporate aims.

Unrealized Potentials . . .

This brief review of studies of formal organization, decision making, and productivity suggests that the findings of modern research are consistent with ideas of relativism. Specific events may still be conceived in dualistic frameworks; supervisors still govern subordinates, subordinates still report to supervisors in a chain of command, a decision to do one thing is still a decision not to do another at that time, and purpose still continues as a dimension of productivity. But these matters can also appropriately be conceived in a wider framework of values and ideas that are structured relativistically.

This possibility is important, for it is sometimes argued that the inevitable consequence of the increasing size and scale of today's organizations is more bureaucracy. If this is so, we are in for difficult times indeed. We must not seek to deal with the conditions which produce disturbances and protests by repressing the ideas of relativism. Those ideas underlie too much of world society today for us to rid ourselves of them. Curbed in one area (e.g., business), they would thrive in others (e.g., science and the arts). Granted that the ideas have led to excesses in many phases of life, particularly and tragically among the young, they may still serve us well.

Today organizations are needed that can create greater equality in the distribution of wealth, more racial and social justice, and other social benefits. Civil rights associations, churches, universities, schools, and similar organizations seek to achieve such gains. Yet they typically are administered bureaucratically, like other organizations today, and in terms of dualistic values. Perhaps we need more of these kinds of organizations. If so, we are being well served, for new ones are formed every day. But perhaps what are being created are more failures.

We are not limited to creating organizations that, having single purposes such as the production of profit or power, must be managed in a dualistic manner. An alternative is available: we can reconceive our ideas about organizations and administration on a relativistic basis. The studies reviewed show that behavior in organizations can satisfy individual, group, and social needs as well as formal organizational objectives. Organizations and the leadership roles in them typically have not been conceived and designed to support such behavior—but they *could* be.

. . . and some problems. In the concluding chapter to an essay on social revolution, Brooks Adams wrote 50 years ago that administration is "possibly the highest faculty of the human mind." He went on to say:

It is precisely in this preeminent requisite for success in government that I suspect the modern capitalist class to be weak. . . . Modern capitalists appear to have been evolved under stress of an environment which demanded excessive specialization in the direction of a genius adapted to money-making under highly complex industrial decisions. . . .

Advances in administration seem to presuppose the evolution of new governing classes, since, apparently, no established type of mind can adapt itself to changes in environment, even in slow-moving civilizations, as fast as environments change. Thus a moment arrives when the minds of any given dominant type fail to meet the demands made upon them and are superseded by a younger type, which in turn is set aside by another still younger, until the limit of the administrative genius of that particular race has been reached. Then disintegration sets in, the social momentum is gradually relaxed, and society sinks back to a level at which it can cohere. [17, *p. 205*]

To avoid the disintegration of which Brooks Adams wrote, we need to comprehend, at a broad conceptual level, the depth and extent of the changes in the structure of knowledge, values, and approaches to life that the ideas of relativism have opened to us in the twentieth century. It will not be easy. If we fail, it will be a failure of the imagination, a failure to grasp the significance for administration of ideas already available in other fields.

When I have suggested to some executives what needs to be done, they have responded, "We don't want more relativism! There is too much now. If only someone would tell us what to do!" Others find the ideas I have described quite familiar. I can understand this latter reaction, for the ideas about which I have written are alive in the world today. At the same time, I do not know of an instance in which someone has designed a course for executives or has tried to run an organization with a relativistic framework explicitly in mind. In short, we have not yet tried to put these ideas to work. When we do, we will probably find ourselves wrestling with questions like these:

Are ideals consistent with relativism? I have heard it argued —and vehemently—that if there are no absolutes, there are no ethics. The view is that an ethic must be an absolute. I do not know how tomorrow's students and practitioners will answer this question, though leads for further study of the problem are easily available [18].

How relative is relativism itself? In an interesting critique of his own research, Perry suggests the need for commitment to specific values within a framework of relativism, knowing that the values are not absolute for all times, circumstances, and systems of ideas.

What about the impact on people at middle levels of organizations? It has been suggested that while relativistic frameworks for action and decision may work very well at top levels of management, they lead to insecurity and uncertainty at middle levels. Perhaps Perry's suggestion would likewise be useful in handling this problem.

Conclusion

The implementation of these ideas calls for new effort on the part of universities. There must be new research to develop ways of teaching relativism to practitioners; administrators in many kinds of organizations must develop new competence in decision making. This in turn

calls for strength in universities at a time when their internal problems make it difficult for them to attend to this work, and when
others call for them to abandon the intellectual path to engage in
direction action in society.

How will relativism affect management in the future? Its probable
impact is not easy to describe; it is visible not in individual acts but
in larger *patterns* of thought and action that give significance to what
an administrator does. Although, as earlier suggested, the acts by
themselves may seem to be two-valued—choices between alternatives
—they can still be conceived as part of a relativistic thought-and-
action approach. With this point in mind, let me outline some characteristics of administration under relativism as I think it will develop:

First, tomorrow's decision makers, more than their counterparts
today, will need to be able to conceptualize the problems they face.
They will need the ability to comprehend the appearance of the particular in the full complexity of its setting in society. To use an
example to which I have already referred, the supermarket manager
of the future will need to perceive the opportunity to take concrete
action in respect to values regarding race, sex, education, and ethnicity when he orders boys and girls to work together to serve customers during rush hours at the check-out counters.

Second, executives of the future will need the capacity to examine
problems from several different perspectives and along more than one
value dimension. They will need to be able to think effectively about
what differences will result from each of several diagnoses and actions
in specific situations. To illustrate:

It will not be news, as it is today, when a company issues a plant
location directive that stresses positive social criteria. This is what
the Quaker Oats Company has done. On top of conventional economic yardsticks, Quaker Oats managers are asked to consider two
other corporate goals: (a) decentralizing operations away from con-
gested metropolitan areas, and (b) providing job opportunities for
minorities. Management also recently decided to build a new frozen
foods plant in Jackson, Tennessee, rather than in Memphis largely
because of the availability of black labor "coming off the farms," an
integrated school system, and the community's progressive attitude.
Earlier the company had refrained from committing a new factory
to Danville, Illinois, until after the city fathers passed an open housing ordinance [19, *p. 21*].

Third, executives will evaluate situations on more than one basis.
They will continue to use such scales of evaluation as productivity,
sales, and profit—what might be called external, absolute scales because they are developed by top management for the organization
as a whole. But they will also use scales of evaluation developed by

members of a work group themselves—what might be called internal yardsticks. Examples of the latter are social codes and ideas about fair work standards. In short, just as physicists have used ideas about both mass and motion to improve their understanding of the behavior of matter, executives will use the two kinds of ideas I have mentioned to improve their understanding of behavior in organizations.

Fourth, leaders of organizations will use ideas without being bound by ideologies. Rather than acting in the situations they encounter according to stereotypes provided by their cultures (for instance, the white manager from an upper middle-class background who is repelled by what he considers the "laziness" of minority-group employees from poor homes), they will be able to work through different ideas and theories about situations to realistic and correctible diagnoses of them and of themselves. They will not be frightened by new problems and new solutions to them. More than now, they will be able to assess realistically the potentials of a situation, without distortion as a result of their personal involvement and values.

Fifth, the general manager's capacity for problem solving will be based more on his skills of *processing* information about a situation accurately than on his ability to contribute knowledge as an expert from a field such as engineering, law, or accounting. He will work in many roles—conceptualizer, negotiator, counselor, arbiter, teacher—to improve the capacity of individuals to affect their environment.

Sixth, to behave effectively in the many roles they will be called on to assume, executives will need a new capacity to assess the frameworks they use in evaluating situations. They will need an inner strength, the strength of knowing their convictions and the limits of them. Neither bound by their beliefs nor arrogant about them, they will try to know themselves and others with recognition, not denial, of the sources of their convictions. Thus they will work continually for new values and an open society.

The sooner such decision makers are trained to assume the direction of organizations in business, government, education, and other fields, the better off our society will be.

The profession of administration has been slow to develop conceptually during the twentieth century. This has contributed in no small way to the severe problems which we are experiencing in race relations, in schools, in the cities, and elsewhere. We must pay much more attention to the concepts and frameworks that we use in thinking about problems and events in our organizations. Relativism is an idea whose time has come—not only for young people but also for managers.

Notes

1. *Fortune,* Sept. 1969.
2. William G. Perry, Jr., *Forms of Intellectual and Ethical Development in the College Years* (New York: Holt, Rinehart & Winston, 1968).
3. See, e.g., *The Cox Commission Report: Crisis at Columbia* (New York: Random House, 1968).
4. "Multiuniversity, University Size, University Quality, and Student Protest: An Empirical Study," *Amer. Sociological Review,* Oct. 1969, 702; see also *Amer. Sociological Review,* June 1970, 525.
5. See, e.g., Peter M. Blau, *The Dynamics of Bureaucracy* (Chicago: Univ. of Chicago Press, 1955).
6. Thomas S. Kuhn, *The Structure of Scientific Revolutions* (Chicago: Univ. of Chicago Press, 1962).
7. See, e.g., W. G. Bennis, "Organizational Developments and the Fate of Bureaucracy," paper presented at the annual meeting of the American Psychological Association, Los Angeles, Sept. 4, 1964; see also Peter F. Drucker, *The Age of Discontinuity* (New York: Harper & Row, 1969).
8. Calvin Tomkins, "E.A.T." (Experiments in the Arts and Technology), "Onward and Upward with the Arts," *The New Yorker,* Oct. 3, 1970.
9. Alfred Chandler, *Strategy and Structure* (Cambridge: MIT Press, 1962).
10. Lawrence E. Fouraker and John M. Stopford, "Organizational Structure and the Multinational Strategy," *Admin. Sci. Quart.,* June 1968.
11. Gene W. Dalton, Louis B. Barnes, Abraham Zaleznik, *The Distribution of Authority in Formal Organizations* (Boston: Div. of Research, Harvard Business School, 1968).
12. Paul R. Lawrence and Jay W. Lorsch, *Organization and Environment* (Boston: Div. of Research, Harvard Business School, 1967).
13. Virgil B. Day, "The Social Relevance of Business," speech presented at the Annual College-Business Symposium, Dec. 3, 1969, Providence, Rhode Island; reprinted by General Electric Co., Schenectady, New York.
14. Fritz J. Roethlisberger, *Training for Human Relations* (Boston: Div. of Research, Harvard Business School, 1954).
15. _____ and W. J. Dickson, *Management and the Worker* (Cambridge: Harvard University Press, 1939).
16. J. V. Clark, *A Preliminary Investigation of Some Unconscious Assumptions Affecting Labor Efficiency in Eight Supermarkets,* unpublished doctoral thesis (Boston: Harvard Business School, 1958); see also George C. Homans, *Social Behavior* (New York: Harcourt, Brace & World, 1961), p. 255.
17. Brooks Adams, *The Theory of Social Revolutions* (New York: Macmillan, 1913).
18. Joseph F. Fletcher, *Situation Ethics* (Philadelphia: Westminster Press, 1966).
19. *The Christian Science Monitor,* Nov. 20, 1970.

The Administrative Process

James D. Thompson

Modern societies have been busier making complex organizations work, largely through trial and error, than studying them. As a result we have no clear picture of what administration is or what it does, either for organizations or society, and we have no consensus on the nature of the administrative process. Available "principles" of administration or management are essentially statements derived from rational-model assumptions, and tend to be normative rather than always realistic.

Whatever we say about administration, of course, is governed by what phenomena we refer to by the term, and that is an arbitrary matter. The approach taken in this volume, that complex purposive organizations are natural systems subject to rationality norms, permits us to suggest that the significant phenomena of administration arise precisely because of the inconsistencies of that duality. If complex organizations were simply natural systems, we might expect spontaneous processes to handle their problems. If complex organizations were simply rational-model machines, they would require designers to initiate them, but their operation thereafter would be automatic. It is because the organization is not simply either, we suggest, that administration emerges as an identifiable and important process in modern societies.

From this point of view, the available principles of administration derived from rational-model assumptions apply to those portions of organizations which are so protected from exogenous variables that the closed system of logic is practical, but it would be a mistake to assume that such principles equal administration.

While our exploration of organizations in action does not permit us to offer a new set of principles more inclusive than present ones, it does enable us to suggest some of the elements which may have to be incorporated in a new and fuller understanding of administra-

tion. For unless we have been far astray, there are important problems for complex organizations which cannot be settled spontaneously and which are not hinted at by prescriptions derived from
the rational model.

We have argued, for example, that the organization must find and
maintain a viable technology—that it must have some capacity to
satisfy demands of a task environment, and that these demands may
be changing. In the society geared to complex organizations, technologies change as cause/effect understandings change; hence a
technology that was effective yesterday may be inadequate today.
Or yesterday's viable technology may be viable again today but with
a different set of partners, a new task environment. Questions of
which technology to retain, which to expel, and which to adopt may
not be daily matters for any complex organization, but they are potential problems for every organization in a modern society, and we
see no reason to believe that they get solved spontaneously or via
the closed logic of the rational model.

We indeed have empirical reasons for believing that such problems
are experienced as knotty ones by those involved in the administrative process. Hitler's use of paratroops against enemy defenses organized for stationary warfare is an historic example, and Billy
Mitchell became a martyr while advocating air technology for military purposes. The technology question is currently symbolized
in industry by questions of what, and how fast, to automate, but it
has parallels in other fields. Hospital administrators, for example,
may worry about the merits and demerits of intensive care centers
with electronic monitoring of multiple patients, or the introduction
of self-service hotel facilities for ambulatory patients. Educational
administrators have parallel worries about teaching machines, team-
teaching techniques, and possible programs for breaking the inter-
generational perpetuation of dropouts.

In these and other fields, solutions are not easily come by, for the
adoption of new technologies reduces the value of present resources
—whether physical or human—and introduces elements of uncertainty; the alternative of finding a new task environment requires establishing new dependencies and thus new contingencies.

Protection of technical cores from overwhelming uncertainties or
contingencies in the environment was also advanced as a central
problem for the organization. We have argued that the protection
necessary to enable achievement by technical cores may be afforded
by domain maneuvering or by modifications in organizational design, but we have no reason to believe that either will happen spontaneously, and there is no closed-system solution to the alternatives
posed.

We have asserted that an organization structure must be developed
and maintained consistent with technological requirements yet at the

same time consistent with input and output requirements and the realities of the task environment. In the small and simple organization this fitting and modification of structure may be autonomous and spontaneous, but in the large and complicated organization, the conversion of uncertainties into certainties becomes something less than obvious [1] and interdependence radiates. Again, neither spontaneity nor closed-system logic can govern structure.

We have implied that every complex organization has some combination of three types of interdependence, and therefore requires some combination of three basic types of coordination. But there is no spontaneous mechanism which confines the application of rules to those areas where uniformity is needed, or which adjusts rules to the needs for scheduling flexibility or intensive judgment. The proper dovetailing of several forms of coordination is not handled by the natural-system approach, nor is it treated within the rational-model approach.

We have argued that assessment of components and of the whole is of basic importance to organizations subject to achievement norms and it seems clear that the subtle complications in assessment call for something more than automatic or closed-logic solutions. Assessment seems to be an administrative problem.

Finally, we have maintained that inducements/contributions contracts must be arranged, and at times adjusted, in order to elicit the inputs necessary for organizational action. In the small and simple organization, this too may be automatic, but in the large and complicated organization with a heterogeneous and dynamic task environment, this is a never-ending and deliberate matter, an administrative matter.

It is our view that any description of administration which ignores the kinds of problems enumerated above is insufficient. But the enumeration of administrative problems is inevitably misleading, for it casts thought into a one-matter-at-a-time framework, while the essence of administration lies in their configuration.

Co-Alignment: The Basic Administrative Function

We and others have emphasized the coalitional nature of complex organizations, but always in terms of agreements among individual members, each having something to contribute and each receiving something in exchange. There is, however, a larger sense of configuration, which we will refer to as *co-alignment.*

Perpetuation of the complex organization rests on an appropriate co-alignment in time and space not simply of human individuals but of streams of institutionalized action. Survival rests on the co-alignment of technology and task environment with a viable domain, and of organization design and structure appropriate to that domain.

The co-alignment we assert to be the basic administrative function is not a simple combination of static components. Each of the elements involved in the co-alignment has its own dynamics. Each behaves at its own rate, governed by forces external to the organization. Technology, for example, is embedded in the cause/effect belief systems of a wider environment. The rate of obsolescence and the direction of innovation in that wider environment may be predictable, but the organization can neither prevent nor command innovation or obsolescence. Personnel resources are similarly governed by institutionalized patterns. Although in modern societies the institutions of job and career, and the associated opportunity structures, result from the aggregate actions of many organizations, seldom can the organization in the short run make more than a ripple in those institutional patterns [2]. The specific organization must work within that stream of action as it finds it. Similarly, the financial acts of the organization contribute to the aggregate patterns of investment and cash flows, but at any particular time the organization must fit itself into those patterns [3]. Boundaries of legitimacy may be influenced by organizations in the aggregate, but for any specific organization at any specific time those boundaries are determined largely by legislative, executive, or judicial developments which have their own history and dynamics.

Clienteles possess demographic characteristics and trends which the individual organization may be able to project and to which it may adapt, but which it can hardly control. Age and sex distributions are subject to biological dynamics; geographic distributions, to economic, political and social forces which are bigger than any organization.

Now if the elements necessary to the co-alignment are in part influenced by powerful forces in the organization's environment, then organization survival requires *adaptive* as well as *directive* action in those areas where the organization maintains discretion. Since each of the necessary streams of institutional action moves at its own rate, the timing of both adaptive and directive action is a crucial administrative matter. As environments change, the administrative process must deal not just with which domain, but how and how fast to change the design, structure, or technology of the organization.

Thus, in our view, the central function of administration is to keep the organization at the *nexus* of several necessary streams of action; and because the several streams are variable and moving, the nexus is not only moving but sometimes quite difficult to fathom.

We must emphasize that organizations are not simply determined by their environments. Administration may innovate on any or all of the necessary dimensions, but only to the extent that the innovations are acceptable to those on whom the organization must and can depend. The organization must conform to the "rules of the game" or somehow negotiate a revised set of rules.

But if the organization is not simply the product of its environment, neither is it independent. The configuration necessary for survival comes neither from yielding to any and all pressures nor from manipulating all variables, but from finding the *strategic variables*—those which are available to the organization and can be manipulated in such a way that interaction with other elements will result in a viable co-alignment [4].

The paradox of administration. If the basic function of administration involves shooting at a moving target of co-alignment, in which the several components of that target are themselves moving, then we can expect the central characteristic of the administrative process to be a search for flexibility. Yet our theme throughout has been one of reduction of uncertainty and its conversion into relative certainty. How do we meet this apparent paradox?

The administrative hierarchy, often described as "channels," appears to be a dual-purpose mechanism, progressively eliminating or absorbing uncertainty as we move from higher to lower levels, and progressively affording flexibility as we move from lower to higher levels [5]. The first purpose has been thoroughly treated in the literature of administration, and perhaps most succinctly described by Simon as a process by which each hierarchical level establishes the premises on which the next lower level is to base its decisions [6]. The second purpose is relatively neglected in the literature, but it seems clear that if the coalition or its representatives are to be able to "contract" with elements of the task environment, the technical core and the managerial layers must afford capacity—and deliverable or unfrozen capacity [7, 89-106].

From this perspective, administration is not something done by an administrator except in the simple organization, but instead is a process flowing through the actions of various members. Also from this point of view, administration is not something done at one level in the organization, but is a process spanning and linking levels. Finally, from this viewpoint, administration is not a process which simply flows down from one level to the next, but a process related to the interaction of levels and components.

In the complex organizations, then, we cannot understand administrative behavior by studying it at one level. This can best be illustrated in terms of our decision-making scheme, as applied to the three major levels distinguished by Parsons (p. 32 of this book). Technical rationality, which we have said is the priority target at the technical core of the organization, calls basically for the computational decision strategy. Technical rationality is a sensible concept only if outcome preferences are crystallized and cause/effect relationships fairly well defined. Neither of these conditions can be satisfied within the technical core of the organization, except as higher levels provide them. We would expect the outcome preferences, or "goals of the organization," to be specified by what Parsons terms the "institutional level" of the organization. . . . But we would expect specification of cause/effect relationships to be provided by the middle or managerial level of the hierarchy. This does not imply that managers are technical inventors, but rather that they control the kinds of resources inputs obtained and the kinds of interdependence that is recognized and reflected in organization structure.

Thus our approach to organizations and administration suggests that the technical level of the administrative hierarchy is dependent on higher levels to provide the conditions necessary to approach technical rationality. But by the same token the other end of the administrative hierarchy is dependent on the technical core and the managerial level to provide the capacities and the slack which allow the organization to make demands on its environment and to take advantage of opportunities afforded by that environment [5].

The paradox of administration, the dual searches for certainty and flexibility, to a large extent revolves around the dimension of time. In the *short run*, administration seeks the reduction or elimination of uncertainty in order to score well on assessments of technical rationality. In the *long run*, however, we would expect administration to strive for flexibility through freedom from commitment—i.e., slack—for the larger the fund of uncommitted capacities, the greater the organization's assurance of self-control in an uncertain future.

Economic debates have made us well aware of the problems of determining, operationally, the difference between long run and short run, and it is this distinction that divides the desire for certainty from the desire for slack. How far into the future the administrative focus goes is a variable to be determined empirically, not by conceptual argument.

Now we are in a position to suggest that the time dimension of concern is inversely related to level in the organization's administrative hierarchy. Thus at the upper reaches, or institutional level, we would expect the short run to be relatively insignificant and the longer run to be of central concern. Here we would expect the focus to be on increasing or maintaining flexibility and command of uncommitted or easily recommittable resources. At the other extreme, the technical core, we would expect concern for certainty in the short run to drive out consideration of the longer run. The central part of the administrative hierarchy, the managerial layer, would thereby become the "translator," securing from the institutional level sufficient commitments to permit technical achievement, yet securing from the technical core sufficient capacity and slack to permit administrative discretion and, if necessary, recommitment of resources.

Variations in Administrative Process

The above discussion of administration is an idealized version, a picture of what administration is or would achieve in the perpetually healthy organization. Obviously some organizations die, and some suffer for considerable periods of time with ailments of one sort or another; the administrative process frequently departs from the ideal. Are these departures random, or can we find patterns?

Administrative styles.   Cyert and March have introduced the important concept of problemistic search, in connection with organizational decision making [8]. They define problemistic search as search that is stimulated by a problem and directed toward finding a solution to that problem. It is thus distinguished from random curiosity and from the search for understanding per se. In the Cyert and March behavioral theory of the firm—and undoubtedly in much real-life organizational behavior—search is "simple-minded," reflecting simple concepts of causality, and initially is based on two simple rules: (1) search in the neighborhood of the problem symptom and (2) search in the neighborhood of the current alternative. When these two rules do not produce an acceptable solution, they add a third: (3) search in organizationally vulnerable areas; that is, in areas where slack exists or where power is weak.

We can subscribe to these propositions as describing the empirically dominant style with which the administrative process is carried out, and yet we need to suggest that it is but one of at least two styles. It is possible to conceive of monitoring behavior which scans the environment for opportunities—which does not wait to be activated by a problem and which does not therefore stop when a problem solution has been found. We will refer to this as *opportunistic surveillance*, and suggest that it is the organizational counterpart to curiosity in the individual.

We would expect problemistic search to be predominant in complex organizations, and we would especially expect to find it in the technical core, or in the managerial layer most closely associated with the technical core, where behavior is oriented and bound within rather tight constraints, and where assessments tend to be made in terms of efficiency or instrumentality. But we have argued that finding a viable nexus is the heart of administration; and in dynamic environments this is not likely to result from problemistic search. On questions of domain, it would seem that the organization which anticipates institutional trends is in a better position to exercise self-control than the organization which waits until the domain problem arises.

Opportunistic surveillance, if it is to be found, should be associated with the institutional level of the organization, according to our reasoning. Yet in every field—education, medicine, industry, commerce, military, and government—instances are apparent where once-robust organizations decline or pass through crises because they have failed to anticipate institutional changes. What accounts for the relative scarcity of opportunistic surveillance? We have no definite answer to that question, but we can seek clues in two directions: (1) in the attributes of administrators as individuals and (2) in the structure of the situations in which they operate. These may be more easily separated conceptually than in fact.

Limitations on the administrative process.   Perhaps the most widespread limitation on the administrative process results when participants define administration as *officeholding* rather than an essential ingredient in organizational accomplishment. This is likely when rationality norms are weakly enforced.

The officeholding view of administrative positions may occur in the sheltered organization, the organization which has somehow obtained limitless resources or a monopolistic position, and thereby has achieved an unusual degree of independence. In such situations dissatisfaction with or lack of respect for the organization may be present, but the organization's lack of dependence reduces the ability of task-environment elements to make them felt.

Still another situation giving rise to the officeholding view of administration is the captive organization, where power in the organization is based on factors extraneous to organizational achievement. Where family ties, patronage, bribery, or tradition is the basis for participation in the coalition, we would expect intrigue rather than achievement to dominate in administrative circles.

Both of these conditions may be found in the modern society, but they are especially likely in the society not yet geared to complex organizations. In traditional societies, moreover, existing organizations and institutional patterns are assumed to be inevitable. It therefore appears that the individual's efforts may make a difference in his relationship to the organization, but cannot make a difference in the organization itself. This is a basic source of frustration for administrators who have been schooled in modern societies but hold administrative responsibilities in traditional societies.

A second and also widespread limitation on administration seems to be a bias toward certainty, which shows up in various forms including preference for short-term rather than long-term considerations, quantitative rather than qualitative data, and precedent rather than innovation.

At least one personality variable, intolerance for ambiguity seems to be associated with the administrative bias toward certainty [9, 108-43]. We would expect the individual who is uncomfortable with ambiguity but placed in a situation where action has future consequences, to be oriented to the short run. The consequences of causal action become less predictable as the time horizon extends, for consequences ramify into the future. Precedent, and the assumption that the future will be similar to the past should also be attractive to the administrator with low tolerance for ambiguity. We have indicated elsewhere that individuals uncomfortable with discretion might nevertheless be motivated to occupy positions where discretion resides, and under such conditions, we would expect a bias toward certainty in the administrative process.

Quite apart from the personality variable, however, we might expect the bias toward certainty to occur by default, through weakness in or absence of a definable institutional layer in the organization. If the powerful inner circle is composed solely of individuals with responsibilities in the managerial layer, we would expect problemistic search, not opportunistic surveillance, to prevail. The same result can be obtained when nonmanagerial members of the inner circle are personally intolerant of ambiguity. Default at the institutional level, however, is more likely to come because of lack of a sharp distinction, conceptually, between managerial and institutional matters. As Parsons has suggested, this functional differentiation is clouded by a tradition of a uniform chain of command which makes each successive rank different only in degree from the preceding one [10]. The conversion of administrators from managerial to institutional responsibilities is more than a promotion, for it entails a shift in attention from technical to organizational rationality, from instrumental to social assessments.

This structural bias toward certainty is especially likely when elements of the task environment lack sufficient power to challenge the assumptions on which the inner circle bases its actions. Ultimately, of course, task-environment elements do have or achieve such power, but it may be exercised only in the case of bankruptcy, economic or otherwise.

A third major limitation on the administrative process lies in the diffusion of power to the point where no inner circle emerges with sufficient stability to give direction to the organization. Although this situation is more visible at the level of national governments in various parts of the world, we believe it is approached in universities, voluntary hospitals, and local government with some frequency. Where the power base is widely diffuse and shifting we expect administrative behavior to be problem oriented, not aggressive, and to be safety oriented, not innovative.

A final limitation on the administrative process is lack of knowledge or know-how. As was made clear by Chandler's study of the development of the modern corporation in the United States, some of the spectacularly successful innovations in organization design and structure came after many years of painful trial and error [11]. The resulting rationality is clear in hindsight, but innovative solutions to basic administrative problems are not easily found.

Social Aspects of Administration

Societies geared to complex organizations lodge heavy proportions of their resources in complex organizations and thereby become dependent on such organizations. Performance errors or failures can have profound consequences for the health or safety of individuals or groups in the task environment of an organization [12], and failure of an organization to survive may have serious ramifications for careers of many individuals—indeed, for the careers of communities [13].

Modern societies thus have a stake in the welfare of complex organizations. Societies geared to complex organizations do not depend solely on the sagacity of an inner circle or on the private motives of a large coalition to ensure the survival of complex organizations. True, the modern society may permit or encourage the launching of many small organizations, knowing that they will have high mortality rates, but once an organization has become established and has demonstrated capacities, the social costs of dismantling are large, and dismantling is seldom permitted.

The commuter service, for example, may be unable to establish a domain or to defend one against superhighway competition; yet elements of the environment are reluctant to see the commuter service die, and the result is an enlarged task environment including governmental units to lend support. Business organizations in trouble frequently find it possible to go through bankruptcy, in which the task environment shares in the misfortune, to regain viability. Hospitals, schools, or universities may lose their viability and their identity, but usually not through dismantlement. Rather they are amalgamated into larger organizations.

Such solutions to troubles in organizations are often costly, however, precisely because organizations are significant instruments of modern societies. Their underuse or abuse can have wide consequences. If our thesis in this volume is correct, task environments generally act as constant tests of complex organizations, signaling errors of omission or commission, and often intervening when organizations fail to heed such signals. Yet we know of business bankruptcies which have surprised even the closest associates of the troubled organization, and governmental laxities which remain unnoticed or unspoken until a major scandal erupts. Task-environment policing is not foolproof.

The secondary defense, expansion of the task environment to influence troubled organizations, is an essential social response to the fact of increased social dependence on complex organizations. We see it in hospitals with the rise of third-party payers, who in addition to channeling insurance payments may begin to question performance standards, charges, or the quality of patient care. We see it in public education with the emergence of powerful state and national programs which can set standards and limits on formerly autonomous local boards of education. We see it in business, first with the emergence of centralized associations of firms in an industry, and also with the rise of centralized labor organizations, both with power to intervene in local activities when larger interests are challenged. A somewhat later development (in the western world) has been a tendency for government to be an active member of the task environment for complex organizations of all types, including business and industry.

The current challenge to administration. Reliance on existing or expanded task environments to salvage troubled organizations is costly. By the time these mechanisms work, the organization may be in an advanced stage of abuse, requiring years to overcome. Preventive care, in this case viable administration, is a much less costly way of keeping organizations socially useful.

Undoubtedly the administrative process works brilliantly in some of our most significant organizations as well as in some of the less significant ones. But there is no guarantee that the society which assigns such importance to complex organizations will be able to provide them with administrators equal to the task. Undoubtedly some administrators have deep insight into the nature and workings of organizations and the administrative process, but the conversion of private insight into sharable—teachable and learnable—understanding is not an automatic process. Systematic understanding of organizations and administration is scarce. Little is known about the preparation of individuals for administrative careers; and technical supervision or management is frequently equated with administration, thus ignoring the crucial institutional role in the process [14].

In American public education, hospitals, and social welfare organizations, the tendency has been to insist that competence related to the organization's technical core be an essential ingredient for the administrator; for example, in most cases, school administrators must hold teaching certificates. We have little systematic evidence of the impact of such practices on administration, but it seems likely that they (1) restrict the scope of an organization's search for administrative abilities and (2) intensify differences between professionals and lay boards in the administrative process [15].

We know that the sources of administrators, and the career preparation or experience they may receive, can differ from society to society, but we know very little about the consequences of such differences for the administrative process [16]. The societal dependence on complex organizations has led to the establishment of professional schools or departments for the training of administrators —business, public, medical, educational, social work, etc.—in American universities and in various kinds of institutes in many parts of Europe and Asia. Yet even in America, which pioneered in modern education for administration, such schools are still trying to rise out of the stage of relaying current practices and exhorting "good works." The research base which might enable such schools to mold future practice is conspicuously short.

The conclusion seems inescapable that the society which depends mightily on complex organizations is going to have to give serious attention to the administration of such organizations.

The frontier of administration. Civilization seems inescapably to bring with it the expansion of interdependencies. Complex organizations appear to be social responses to enlarged networks of cause/effect relationships, and we have suggested [elsewhere] that organizations will grow in the direction of their most crucial dependencies. But the gearing of society to complex organizations, together with the institutionalization of scientific research and the resulting expansion of interdependencies, seems to be creating needs for action on a scope even larger than the capacity of our organizations.

Bluntly speaking, social purposes in modern societies increasingly exceed the capacities of complex organizations, and call instead for action by multiorganization complexes. This may be seen, for example, in the custom construction of giant hydroelectric dams, which call for the combined efforts of several giant construction organizations. It may be seen in space exploration, which calls for the research, developmental, engineering, and production efforts of a complex of organizations, organized around a "prime contractor." It may be seen in the multistate port authority, in the combine of universities to operate jointly a costly and scarce research facility.

It appears in highly complicated form in the movement to improve the teaching of physical sciences in the secondary schools of the United States, as described by Clark [17]. The movement was spear-headed by Professor Zacharias as head of a committee of university professors and secondary school teachers. This group of professional scientists and educators was joined by the National Science Foundation, an arm of the Federal government, which financed the commit-tee's work. The resulting teaching materials were made available to the nation's school systems by being distributed through normal commercial channels. The National Science Foundation supported a program of summer institutes offered by colleges to train teachers in the use of the new materials. Within ten years from the initiation of the project, more than forty per cent of high school students studying physics were studying the new materials, in spite of the fact that adoption of the materials remains officially a matter for local school board decision.

What emerges from Clark's analysis is a marshalling of resources from diverse sources in an effective sequence to bring about a result that was beyond the ability of any single organization. A Federal agency provided the initial funds, a private nonprofit group devel-oped a new course, commercial organizations made the new materials available throughout the decentralized educational system, varied universities and colleges trained teachers to use the new materials, and local authorities adopted the new materials and permitted tea-chers to revise local courses.

Recapitulation

The basic function of administration appears to be co-alignment, not merely of people (in coalitions) but of institutionalized action—of technology and task environment into a viable domain, and of orga-nizational design and structure appropriate to it. Administration, when it works well, keeps the organization at the nexus of the several necessary streams of action. Paradoxically, the administrative pro-cess must reduce uncertainty but at the same time search for flexibility.

Administrative decision making frequently rests on problemistic search, especially in and around the technical core, but opportunistic surveillance is also needed, especially at the institutional level. It may fail to materialize if rationality norms are weak, if administra-tors are biased toward certainty, or if power is too diffuse to be mo-bilized to give stability and direction to the organization.

The administrative process may also be limited by sheer lack of knowledge and insight into new situations. The achievement of high levels of technical rationality has indeed been a major accomplishment of modern societies, and similar accomplishments by societies now in transition present important challenges. But in modern societies, it appears, we have passed from the era in which control and coordination of technological activities were the central administrative challenge, into an era in which organizational rationality is the core of administration, and the administration of multiorganization projects and activities is the central challenge. Whether we have or will gain the knowledge about the organizations that it takes to use and control them under conditions of extreme interdependence remains to be seen.

Notes

1. James D. Thompson, "Decision-making, the Firm, and the Market," in *New Perspectives in Organization Research,* edited by W. W. Cooper et al. (New York: Wiley, 1964).
2. Wilbert E. Moore and Arnold S. Feldman, *Labor Commitment and Social Change in Developing Areas* (New York: Social Science Research Council, 1960).
3. Talcott Parsons and Neil J. Smelser, *Economy and Society* (New York: Free Press of Glencoe, 1956).
4. Chester I. Barnard, *The Functions of the Executive* (Cambridge: Harvard University Press, 1938).
5. James G. March and Herbert A. Simon, *Organizations* (New York: Wiley, 1958).
6. Herbert A. Simon, *Administrative Behavior,* 2d ed. (New York: Macmillan, 1957).
7. Robert W. Hawkes, "The Role of the Psychiatric Administrator," *Admin. Sci. Quart.,* 6 (June 1961).
8. Richard M. Cyert and James G. March, *A Behavioral Theory of the Firm* (Englewood Cliffs, N.J.: Prentice-Hall, 1963).
9. Else Frenkel-Brunswik, "Intolerance of Ambiguity as an Emotional and Perceptual Personality Variable," *J. Personality,* 18 (Sept. 1949).
10. Talcott Parsons, *Structure and Process in Modern Societies* (New York: Free Press of Glencoe, 1960).
11. Alfred D. Chandler, Jr., *Strategy and Structure* (Cambridge: MIT Press, 1962).
12. Kenneth E. Boulding, *The Organizational Revolution* (New York: Harper & Row, 1953).
13. W. Fred Cottrell, "Death by Dieselization: A Case Study in the Reaction to Technological Change," *Amer. Soc. Rev.,* 16 (June 1951), 358-65; See also Cottrell, *Energy and Society* (New York: McGraw, 1955).
14. Philip Selznick, *Leadership in Administration* (Evanston: Row, 1957).
15. James D. Thompson, "Common and Uncommon Elements in Administration," in *The Social Welfare Forum, 1962* (New York: Columbia University Press, 1962).
16. Frederick H. Harbison and Charles A. Myers, *Management in the Industrial World: An International Analysis* (New York: McGraw, 1959).
17. Burton R. Clark, "Interorganizational Patterns in Education," *Admin. Sci. Quart.,* 10 (Sept. 1965), 224-37.

Strategy
and Management
Structure

William H. Newman

How is corporate strategy influenced by the management structure and the technological environment within which it is developed? In this article Professor Newman argues that technology is the intervening variable by means of which strategy can be matched with a total management design. He also suggests some practical guidance for managers who wish to change their corporate strategy. [1]

The matching of strategy and management design presents a challenging opportunity to scholars of management. It calls for skill in building a viable, integrated system; it draws upon insights on many facets of management; and it plunges us into a highly dynamic set of relationships. Both synthesis and refinement of theory are involved.

Moreover, as A. D. Chandler demonstrates in his classic study, *Strategy and Structure,* keeping managerial arrangements in tune with strategy plays a vital role in enterprise survival and growth [2]. The accelerating pace of change in economic, technological, political, and social forces will lead companies to adjust their strategies more often in the future than has been typical in the past. And with each shift in strategy the appropriateness of existing management design should be examined anew. Consequently, the issues we explore in this paper hold practical as well as theoretical significance.

Our discussion is divided into four parts: (1) strategy is defined; 2) the concept of a coherent management design is set forth, with particular attention to those features most likely to be affected by strategy; (3) then an analytical approach for matching strategy and management design is examined; and (4) implications for heterogeneous as well as homogeneous enterprises are identified.

From *Journal of Business Policy,* 2 (Winter 1971/72), 1:56-66. Copyright © 1971 by Mercury House Business Publications Ltd.

Scope of Master Strategy

Strategy, as the term is used in this paper, sets the basic purposes of an enterprise in terms of the services it will render to society and the way it will create these services. More specifically, master strategy involves (a) picking particular product market niches that are propitious in view of society's needs and the company's resources, (b) selecting the underlying technologies and the ways of attracting inputs, (c) combining the various niches and resource bases to obtain synergistic effects, (d) expressing these plans in terms of targets, and (e) setting up sequences and timing of steps toward these objectives that reflect company capabilities and external conditions.

Obviously, the formulation of strategy calls for diagnostic skills and keen judgment. A great deal of analysis and theorizing remains to be done on this frontier. It is an area of study in itself. The present paper, however, focuses on another task of central management—the interrelation between master strategy and management design [3]. Here we assume that strategy does get formulated and periodically revised. Such strategy will become effective only when it is linked to a mutually supporting management design.

Integrated Management Design

Discussions of "strategy and structure" often focus on organization structure only. If the match between strategy and management design is to be fully effective, however, more than organization must be harmonized. The nature of the planning process, the leadership style and the form and location of control mechanisms are also intimately involved. This more inclusive view of management arrangements—planning, organizing, leading and controlling—we call management design.

Management designs differ. Every university is, and should be, managed in ways that are different from those used to manage the bus system that brings students to its doors. Likewise, within the university, the managerial design best suited to research laboratories is inappropriate to the cafeteria. To be sure, several common processes—organizing, planning, leading and controlling—are essential for each of these units, but as we adapt various concepts to the unique needs of each venture refinement is vital [4]. Management sophistication is revealed in this adapting and refining of the design.

Need for Coherent Management Design

In each particular situation the phases of management should be synergistic. That is, organization structure should facilitate control,

control should generate useful data for planning, planning should be conducted in a way that assists in leading, and so forth. These mutually supporting effects are a vital feature of a good management design. Yet in practice a surprising number of instances arise where just the opposite pull occurs. Tensions mount instead of reinforcements.

A striking lack of synergy arose when one of the nation's leading railroads undertook a sweeping decentralization. According to the plan, regional managers were to replace a highly centralized headquarters as the focus for operating decisions, and these regional managers were given significantly increased authority. Unfortunately the control mechanisms did not change with the organization design. Detailed reports continued to flow to the vice-presidents at headquarters, and these men continued their previous practice of stepping into trouble spots and issuing orders. Confusion resulted. The fact that legal and technological reasons prevented regional managers from making their own plans regarding prices, train schedules, new equipment, wage rates, and other important matters merely aggravated the situation. So the actual planning mechanism did not line up with the announced organization. It soon became obvious that the total management design had not been thought through.

The chief executive of a computer company, to cite another example, decided that participative leadership would stimulate the engineers and other technical people in his firm. He arranged for all managers and vice-presidents to first-line supervisors to have T-group training so that everyone would understand the new leadership style. The results were not entirely happy. Competition forced the president himself to make several key decisions, specifications had to be frozen, pressure was placed on production people to meet tough deadlines, and budgetary-control limits were stipulated by headquarters. This top-down planning was a well-established pattern within the company. But to many managers who had just got the message about participative leadership, the former planning procedures suddenly became oppressive. Their morale was hurt rather than helped because their expectations, which had been raised by the leadership training, were soon undermined by use of the old planning mechanisms. Here again we see that a change in one phase of management was not matched by necessary adjustments in other phases.

Prominent Features of a Management Design

Recognition of need for a coherent management design raises a question of what is embraced in such a design. What features do we need to consider?

It is not very helpful to suggest that elements in the management design for a particular situation can be selected from the many concepts covered in management literature, even though this statement is true. Such guidance is too broad. In order to narrow the focus a bit, let us concentrate on those managerial arrangements most likely to be affected by choice of strategy. In other words, which features probably will need adjustment when we fit a structure to new requirements?

Analysis of a wide variety of management designs points to the elements listed in the accompanying tables as distinguishing features. In any single design only a few of these features will dominate, and others may be insignificant. In addition, for unusual circumstances a feature not listed here may be critical. Nevertheless careful consideration of the features listed will enable us to comprehend and to deal with the management designs of most enterprises.

1) Distinguishing organizational features. Organization is widely acknowledged as a prime vehicle for adapting a management design to new needs. In fact organization often is overemphasized. Some managers make a change in their formal organization and then assume everything else will fall in place. To be fully effective, however, several compatible changes in formal organization are frequently necessary. These changes must be incorporated into informal behaviour, and supporting adjustments must be made in other facets of management.

Key personnel, the last feature listed in Table 1, warrants special emphasis. It is always involved in a change in management design, and it may be as vital to the success of a change as any other feature. Men capable of functioning in new jobs should be carefully selected and should be given time to learn new patterns of behaviour.

2) Distinguishing forms of plans. The need to think carefully about forms of plans is illustrated sharply in any international airline. Preparation of tickets in Vienna that will be understood in Nairobi and Seattle, that can be reissued in Baghdad and cancelled in Tahiti, and that provide the basis for allocating the fare collected among a dozen different airlines, requires an impressive use of standing operating procedures. Nor can equipment maintenance be left to local ingenuity. On the other hand, company-wide policies relating to sales promotion and pay-rates for baggage handlers must be cast in broad terms or shunned entirely. Then if the airline enters the local hotel business in several countries, the appropriateness of world-wide policies and procedures must be examined anew. For each subject, either too little or too much planning can lead to great confusion.

Questions about the kinds of plans suitable for a specific situation typically centre around the topics listed in Table 2. Planning, in contrast to organizing, often receives scant attention during the prep-

TABLE 1	TABLE 2
Organizational features that are likely to vary with a change in strategy	*Planning features that are likely to vary with a change in strategy*

Centralization versus decentralization	*Use of standing plans*
	Comprehensiveness of coverage
Degree of division of labour	Specificity
Size of self-sufficient operating units	
	Use of single-use plans
Mechanisms for coordination	Comprehensiveness of coverage
Nature and location of staff	Specificity
Management information system	Planning horizon
Characteristics of key personnel	Intermediate versus final objectives
	"How" versus results

aration of a management design. This disregard of planning arises from two confusions. First, the substance of specific plans may be so engrossing that little thought is given to the more basic issue of the form in which guidance will be most useful. Second, the process of arriving at a decision is confused with the mechanisms introduced to guide decision-making activities throughout the enterprise. When shaping a management design, we are primarily concerned with these mechanisms (standing plans, project planning, intermediate objectives, and the like) because they help pull the entire managerial effort into a coherent thrust.*

3) Distinguishing elements in leadership style. The leadership features listed in Table 3 are aspects of leading that should be adjusted to fit the total management design.† Many guides to good leadership practice that emerge from behavioural research apply to virtually all settings, and so they are not included in this particular list.

Leadership style is intimately tied to the temperament and beliefs of each manager. Consequently this style is more difficult to change than, say, departmentation or control reports. Nevertheless, all of us can modify our behaviour to some degree, especially when the environment in which we work reinforces our new behaviour. If a man-

---

* Good decisions on specific problems are vital, of course. But the elements of decision-making are similar in all sorts of situations, whereas the forms of plans and the organizational assignment of planning tasks differ widely. Consequently it is the latter arrangements that deserve prime attention when we prepare a management design.

† R. J. House in "Leader Behavior and Subordinate Satisfaction and Performance: A Motivational Theory of Leadership," *Admin. Sci. Quart.*, forthcoming, shows that the character of work has a significant bearing on the impact of various leadership styles. He cites several studies where role ambiguity, reflecting routine versus non-routine work, is an important variable in the kind of leadership action that is effective. J. J. Morse and J. W. Lorsch also stress the effect of the nature of work on leadership in "Beyond Theory Y," *Harv. Bus. Rev.* (May 1960). The influence of technology is at least implicit in W. Hill, "The Validation and Extension of Fiedler's Theory of Leadership Effectiveness," *Acad. Management J.* (Mar. 1969).

TABLE 3
Leadership features that are likely to vary with changes in strategy
Participation in planning
Permissiveness
Closeness of supervision
Sharing of information
Emphasis on on-the-job satisfactions

TABLE 4
Control features that are likely to vary with changes in strategy
Performance criteria emphasized
Location of control points
Frequency of checks
Who initiates corrective action
Stress on reliability versus learning
Punitive versus reward motivation

ager cannot provide the kind of leadership needed in a given situation, replacing him is an alternative. So even though leadership style is not easy to change, it should be included in the total process of matching management design to strategy.

4) Distinguishing features of the control process.   The design of controls all too often lags behind shifts in other aspects of management. The railroad reorganization mentioned earlier revealed a failure to revise controls so that they would reinforce major moves in related areas. Over-reliance on short-run, quantitative measurements shows a similar tendency to pay too little attention to control structure. Yet controls can provide the synergy we seek in an effective management design.

The features of control most likely to need adjustment when changes are made in other phases of management are listed in Table 4. Closely associated with changes in these features should be a refinement of the management information system, which has already been listed under organization. Although the preparation of a total management design rarely starts with control, no plan is complete until provision is made for control.

Weaving the various features of organizing, planning, leading and controlling that have been singled out in this section into a coherent management design calls for great skill. Each enterprise needs its own unique system. Fortunately, synergistic benefits are usually possible if we are ingenious enough to make reinforcing combinations, such as those suggested under "Nature of Technology" in Table 5. A company's design is effective, however, only when it fits neatly with the company strategy, as pointed out in the next section.

Influence of Strategy on Design

The idea of a management design is a useful concept because it turns our focus from analytical refinements to reinforcing integration. The preceding section identified an array of variable features that should

TABLE 5

Typical features of management structures for three types of technology

Features that distinguish management structures	Nature of technology		
	Stable	Regulated flexibility	Adaptive

Organizing

Centralization versus decentralization	Centralized	Mostly centralized	Decentralized
Degree of division of labour	Narrow specialization	Specialized or crafts	Scope may vary
Size of self-sufficient operating units	Large	Medium	Small, if equipment permits
Mechanisms for coordination	Built-in, programmed	Separate planning unit	Face-to-face, within unit
Nature and location of staff	Narrow functions; headquarters	Narrow functions; headquarters and operating unit	Generalists at headquarters; specialists in operating units
Management information system	Heavy upward flow	Flow to headquarters and to operating unit	Flow mostly to, and within, operating unit
Characteristics of key personnel	Strong operators	Functional experts in line and staff	Analytical, adaptive

Planning

Use of standing plans

Comprehensiveness of coverage	Broad coverage	All main areas covered	Mostly "local," self-imposed
Specificity	Detail specified	Detail in interlocking activities	Main points only

Use of single-use plans

Comprehensiveness of coverage	Fully planned	Fully planned	Main steps covered
Specificity	Detail specified	Schedules and specs. detailed	Adjusted to feedback
Planning horizon	Weekly to quarterly	Weekly to annually	Monthly to three years or more
Intermediate versus final objectives	Intermediate goals sharp	Intermediate goals sharp	Emphasis on objectives
"How" versus results	"How" is specified	Results at each step specified	End results stressed

Leading

Participation in planning	Very limited	Restricted to own tasks	High participation
Permissiveness	Stick to instructions	Variation in own tasks only	High permissiveness, if results OK
Closeness of supervision	Follow operations closely	Output and quality closely watched	General supervision
Sharing of information	Circumspect	Job information shared	Full project information shared
Emphasis on on-the-job satisfactions	Limited scope	Craftsmanship and professionalism encouraged	Opportunity for involvement

TABLE 5 (Continued   )

Controlling

Performance criteria emphasized	Efficiency, dependability	Quality, punctuality, efficiency	Results, within resource limits
Location of control points	Within process; intermediate stages	Focus on each processing unit	Overall "milestones"
Frequency of checks	Frequent	Frequent	Infrequent
Who initiates corrective action	Often central managers	"Production control" and other staff	Men in operating unit
Stress on reliability versus learning	Reliability stressed	Reliability stressed	Learning stressed
Punitive versus reward motivation	Few mistakes tolerated	Few mistakes tolerated	High reward for success

be considered in building such an integrated design, and indicated how some combinations of these features tend to be destructive whereas other combinations promote coherence. We can now tackle the tougher task—relating management design and company strategy.

Technology: the intervening variable.   The best bridge between strategy and design is "technology." Here we use technology in a very broad sense to include all sorts of methods for converting resource inputs into products and service the consumers. The inputs can be labour, knowledge and capital as well as raw materials [5]. Thus an insurance company has its technology for converting money, ideas, and labour into insurance service just as an oil company has its technology for converting crude oil and other resources into petroleum products. By extending our thinking from strategy to the technology necessary to execute that strategy, we move to *work to be done.* Once we comprehend the work to be done—both managerial and operating work—we are on familiar ground. Most of our management concepts relate directly to getting work done, and so preparing a management design to fit a particular kind of work falls within the recognized "state of the art."

The use of technology as an intervening variable produces the arrangement shown in Figure 1. To maintain perspective and to highlight key influences, strategy should focus on only a few basic ideas. Its formulation is by necessity in broad terms. We cannot jump directly from strategy to management design because we have not yet classified the array of actions that will be necessary to execute the strategy. Thinking of technology helps us to elaborate the work implications of the strategy and thereby provides us with the inputs for shaping a management design.

Types of technology.   Technology, especially in the broad sense in which we are using the term here, deals with all sorts of situations

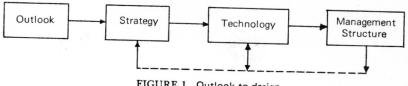

FIGURE 1   Outlook to design

and methods. For purposes of relating technology to management, however, we can concentrate on only a few characteristics of the technology. For instance, the way a technology deals with change is very significant for our purpose.

In a company with a given strategy and technology, the need for change will fall somewhere along a continuum of infrequent to frequent. Similarly, the kinds of changes the company typically faces will fall somewhere along another continuum ranging from brand new, unprecedented problems to familiar, precedented problems; in the case of the familiar problems, the company will have a well-established pattern for resolving them.

Using these two characteristics of a firm's technology, we can set up the matrix shown in Figure 2. Of course, many technologies will fit around the middle of one or both dimensions, but by thinking about technologies toward the ends of the scales we arrive at three well-known types of businesses.

Enterprises confronted with familiar problems rather infrequently are basically *stable*. Paper mills and other firms processing large volumes of raw materials fall into this category. When the need for change moves from infrequent to frequent, and the problems remain precedented, we encounter businesses that display *regulated flexi-*

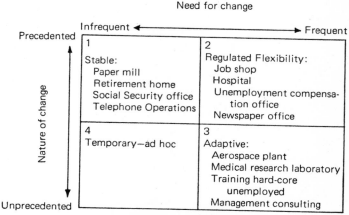

FIGURE 2   Change matrix

bility. Job shops—used by management writers since Frederick
Taylor to illustrate management concepts—fit this category. But
when the need for change is frequent and the problems are unprecedented, as often occurs in the aerospace industry, we face a sharply
different situation. Here technology requires an *adaptive* structure.

These three technology types—stable, regulated flexibility, and
adaptive—are found in many lines of endeavour. In the health field
there are retirement homes, hospitals, and medical research labs. In
government, offices for Social Security (old-age pensions), for unemployment compensation, and for the training of hard-core unemployed illustrate the types. In the service industries examples are
telephone operations, newspaper publications, and management
consulting.

In contrast to the first three types, the fourth division in the
change matrix does not point to a clear type of technology or management design. Unprecedented problems that arise only infrequently are handled by some temporary arrangement. This *ad hoc*
setup does not exist long enough to modify the underlying structure.

From technology to management design.   An intriguing aspect of
the three technology types just identified is that each leads to a well-
known management design. The usual relationships between technology and design are shown in Table 5. For each of the distinguishing features of a management design, discussed earlier in this paper,
we can see the typical response to a stable technology, a regulated-
flexibility technology, and an adaptive technology.

The primary features of each design remain substantially the same
even though the companies come from different industries. For instance, when the work situation is stable—as it usually is in a paper
mill, retirement home, Social Security office, and telephone exchange—then planning tends to be comprehensive and detailed,
intermediate goals are sharply defined, decision-making is centralized
and central staff is strong. In addition we find limited participation
and close supervision. Controls are focused on dependability and
efficiency, checks are made frequently and few mistakes are tolerated. These and other management features indicated in Table 5
enable an executive working in a stable situation to convert resource
inputs into the maximum output of consumer services.

Actually, in our modern world regulated flexibility is much more
common than the stable technology just described. A job shop,
hospital, unemployment compensation office, and newspaper all
face a continuing procession of new situations, most of which can
be handled by well-developed techniques for resolving such problems. For this kind of technology the typical management design
introduces flexibility by the use of craftsmen and professionals, by
separate scheduling units, by careful programming of workloads,

by close control of work passing from one stage to the next, by prompt information on the status of work at each stage, and so on. The kind of flexibility needed is anticipated, and provisions for dealing with it are built into the system. Each person understands the limits of his discretion, and other conditions are fully planned and controlled so that reliability of the total system is not lost.

Adaptive technology calls for quite a different management design. The research laboratory, consulting firm, and hard-core unemployed training project all face unprecedented problems frequently. Here operating units become smaller, greater reliance is placed on face-to-face contacts, authority is decentralized, planning tends to focus on objectives and broad programs, leaders use participation and expect high personal involvement, control checks are less frequent and concern results rather than methods. These and other features listed in Table 5 are often called "organic," or sometimes "democratic."

This adaptive type of situation is what many human relations advocates dream about. It provides ample opportunity for employee participation and self-actualization. However, the fact that only a small portion of all work involves frequent, unprecedented problems explains why a lot of human relations training has failed to find practical application.

Of course, no company will fit exactly into any one of the technology-management design types we have described. But the examples do suggest how thoughtful analysis of technology provides a basis for designing a suitable structure [6].

Related influences on design. Although the analysis of technology in terms of the frequency and uniqueness of the problems it faces is a fruitful first step, we should not overlook other influences. For instance, technology will also be affected by complexity and the need for speed. When several interrelated variables affect the work, as in building a communications satellite, more thorough planning and control will be necessary. The need for speedy action usually has an opposite effect. Here the urgency to get prompt action reduces the opportunity for thorough planning and control; quick results now may have a higher value than somewhat improved results a month later.

Size and uncertainty should also be taken into account. A larger volume of work will support the expense of more division of labour, mechanization, and specialized staff, and greater size complicates communication and coordination. For both these reasons an increase in size tends to add to the planning and control.

Uncertainty permeates many activities. Because of an unknown environment or unpredictable responses to our own actions, we are confronted with uncertainty. If time permits we may try to reduce this uncertainty by further tests and experiments, and this will probably add staff to our organization and reduce the permissiveness in the structure. On the other hand, if such attempts to reduce uncertainty are impractical we may hire men with the best intuitive judgment we can find, get rid of our staff, and decentralize authority to the experts. This latter response to uncertainty, which is favoured by the managers of some conglomerates, creates a simple, lean management design.

Management design, then, must be developed in light of a variety of influences. However, the added dimensions just cited still fit into our basic proposal of moving first from strategy to character of work, and then from work to management design.

Compound Design Within a Company

Thus far we have discussed the management design for a whole company. We have assumed that one technology and one design predominates, and for a single-function company this holds true. Most enterprises, however, are more complex. Within the corporate scope quite different activities may take place. So if we are correct in urging that management design reflect technology, the concepts should be applied to parts of a complex company as well as to the whole.

Diverse technologies of departments.   Consider the Greenfield Company, which has a strategy of performing the complete job of providing new, low-cost housing, from land acquisition to planting shrubbery in the play yard. Separate departments deal with architecture, real estate and finance, component manufacturer and building. The architects are the planners who conceive of types of construction, space utilization, layouts, and specifications that will create good housing at low cost; their work ranges from the highly unique and creative to the painstaking preparation of specifications for actual construction. The real estate and finance people spend a lot of their time negotiating with government agencies and other outsiders; their problems are technical and often unique. In contrast, manufacture of components (standard wall-sections, bathroom and kitchen modules, and the like) is standardized, routinized, and mechanized as much as possible. Actual building construction, necessarily, is "job order" in character, and requires the synchronization of various craftsmen.

In this one company, two of the major departments, architecture and real estate and finance, come close to the adaptive type described in the preceding section. The building department clearly displays regulated flexibility, and the component manufacturing department is moving as close to the stable type as volume permits.

A university is as heterogeneous as the Greenfield Company. Although the suitability of the same technique for teaching biology, logic, and fine arts is debatable, everyone will agree that managing a controller's office and the buildings and grounds department is in a different category. Other enterprises may not have as much diversity as the Greenfield Company or a university, but mixed activities are very common.

This diversity has serious implications for management design. Many executives who have had successful careers in one type of design believe their style of managing should be extended to all parts of the company. We often find that the managerial practices that are well suited to the dominant department of a company are automatically applied throughout. Such consistency in managerial methods does have benefits, but the astute manager will at least consider the possibility of using different administrative styles for diverse departments.

Composite design.   Generally, when a department is both large and important to the strategy of the company it should be managed with a design suited to its own activity. This means that companies embracing diverse technologies should use several different managerial styles. The justification for this mixture of managerial styles lies, of course, in the improved performance of the respective departments.

Such diversity has its costs:

1) *Cooperation between departments becomes increasingly difficult.* Voluntary cooperation between groups with different values, time orientations and willingness to take risks is inevitably strained [7]. Divergent management designs add to this "cultural barrier." Because the departments are so different, we may even separate them geographically—remove research laboratories from the plants, separate mills designed for long production runs from those for short runs, and so on. When management designs of departments differ sharply, special liaison staff or other formal means for coordination is often needed. Having deliberately accentuated the difference between departments, we then add a "diplomatic corps" to serve as a communication link between them.

2) *Company-wide services drop in value.* With a composite design, the rotation of key personnel is impeded, budgeting is complicated, training programs fit only parts of the company, capital allocation procedures have to be tailored to different inputs and criteria. In other words, synergy arising from pooled services and reinforcing features of a management design is lacking for the company as a whole.

3) *The task of central managers is complicated.*   Understanding the subtleties of the several management designs and personally adjusting one's leadership style to each calls for unusual skill and sophistication. Most managers, often unconsciously, favour departments whose management design they find congenial.

Blended designs.   Because of the drawbacks of a composite design, and because dissimilar departments may be too small to support their own distinct management structure, we often try to blend two or more systems. Some types of designs are compatible. For instance, both the stable and the regulated-flexibility designs used as examples earlier call for a high degree of central planning, strong staff, limited permissiveness, and control at intermediate points. The chief difference lies in frequent adjustment by one system to variations in client requirements; nevertheless, these adjustments normally occur within anticipated limits and often follow rules. Consequently a combined arrangement that accommodates both technologies (for example, the component manufacturer and building construction in the Greenfield Company) can be devised. The blended design is not just what each department would do for its own purposes, but the modification can be tolerated.

Another common arrangement is to build one strong structure and then recognize that exceptions must be made for some segments of the total operation. For instance, accounting usually gets special treatment in a research laboratory, just as members of the advertising group are accepted as "oddballs" in a manufacturing firm. If the people in the exception spots have enough missionary zeal for their specialty to withstand the normal pressure to conform with the majority, the mismatch can function reasonably well.*

The fact that many companies need a composite, or blended, management design does not detract from the major theme of this paper. Coherence in each management design is vital whether the design be simple or complex. The springboard for shaping each design is the character of the work to be managed; the character of the work, in turn, is a function of the company strategy. Diversity of work and the resulting complexity of designs only multiply the components that we have to take into account. The combined result, of course, is a whole mosaic of planning instruments, organizational relationships, leadership influences, and control mechanisms [8].

---

* A variation of making exceptions from the major pattern within the enterprise is to use outsiders for the deviant activity. Thus consultants may be called into a "stable" company to provide creative ideas. Brokerage firms subcontract janitorial and equipment maintenance work. Dress manufacturers often obtain designs from free-lance designers. Although volume of work and flexibility are also factors in such subcontracting, simplification of the management design is a prime benefit.

A final check, after arranging the many parts, involves going back to the master strategy of the enterprise, identifying the elements that are keys to success, and then asking whether the management design promises to emphasize these elements. In thinking through the necessary refinements of a design we are always in danger of losing perspective on the major mission.

Summary

1) The interaction of two areas of management thought—master strategy and management design—offers an unusual opportunity for fruitful synthesis.

2) The "strategy and structure" approach to this synthesis should be expanded. More than organization structure is involved. Adjustments in planning, leading, and controlling, as well as organizing, are often needed to execute a new strategy; and the integration of these subprocesses into a total *management design* is vital.

3) Of course, a particular change in strategy will affect some facets of management more than others. Several facets likely to need adjustment are listed in Tables 1 to 4. Note that controllable variables are identified within each of the subprocesses of management.

4) Matching management design and strategy directly is difficult. A useful bridge is to focus on "technology" as the intervening variable. Here "technology" is used broadly to embrace the conversion of all sorts of resources—human and financial as well as physical —into services and goods for consumers. Fortunately, we can relate technology both to *strategy* and to *manageable* tasks.

5) One characteristic of a technology is its accommodation to changes. A matrix based on frequency of changes and their novelty helps us understand three common types of technologies: stable, regulated flexibility, and adaptive. Figure 2 gives both business and non-business examples of each type. And for each type we can identify likely features of an appropriate management design. For instance:

Stable technology fits well with detailed planning, intermediate goals, centralization, close supervision, tight control.

Regulated flexibility fits well with separate planning and scheduling staff, controlled information flows, circumscribed decentralization, limited use of participative, and permissive leadership.

Adaptive technology fits well with planning by objective, decentralization, high personal involvement, control focused on results. (For further elaboration see Table 5.)

6) A corollary of the proposition that management design should

be varied so that it is (a) integrated within its parts, and (b) matched to specific company strategy is that no single management design is ideal for all circumstances. We cannot say, for example, that management by objectives, decentralization, participative management, or tight control are desirable in all situations. Company strategy is one of the important factors determining what managerial arrangement is optimal.

7) Turning from a total company to its constituent parts, if the preferred technologies of various departments *within* the company differ sharply, their optimal management structure will also differ. Central management is then confronted with a dilemma of either having a mismatch of technology and management design in some departments or coordinating diverse management designs.

While much refinement and amplification remains to be done, the foregoing approach to synthesizing diverse management concepts has exciting possibilities: it provides a vehicle for putting content into a "total systems" treatment of management; it helps reconcile conflicting research findings and experience about particular managerial techniques; and it suggests some very practical guidance for managers who wish to implement changes in their company strategy.

Notes

1. This paper has been adapted from a concluding chapter in W. H. Newman, C. E. Summer, and E. K. Warren, *The Process of Management,* 3rd ed. (Englewood Cliffs, N. J.: Prentice-Hall, 1972). Explanations of concepts treated tersely in this paper—such as strategy, planning, organizing, leading, and controlling—will be found in that source.
2. A. D. Chandler, *Strategy and Structure* (Cambridge: MIT Press, 1962).
3. For recent discussions of strategy formulation, see H. I. Ansoff, *Corporate Strategy* (New York: McGraw, 1965); R. L. Katz, *Cases and Concepts in Corporate Strategy* (Englewood Cliffs, N.J.: Prentice-Hall, 1970); E. P. Learned et al., *Business Policy: Text and Cases* (Homewood, Ill.: Irwin, 1969), text portions; and W. H. Newman and J. P. Logan, *Strategy, Policy, and Central Management* (Cincinnati: Southwestern, 1971).
4. See R. J. Mockler, "Situational Theory of Management," *Harv. Bus. Rev.,* (May 1971), for references to literature stressing need to adjust management to specific situations.
5. For an expansion of this concept of technology see C[harles] Perrow, "A Framework for the Comparative Analysis of Organizations," *Amer. Sociological Rev.* (Apr. 1967). Other writers have explored the relation between technology and structure, but they have concentrated on the narrower concept of physical conversion of materials. See T[om] Burns and G. M. Stalker, *The Management of Innovation,* 2d ed. (London: Tavistock, 1966); J[oan] Woodward, *Industrial Organization* (London:

Oxford University Press, 1965); D. H. Hickson, D. S. Pugh, and D. C. Pheysey, "Operations Technology and Organization Structure: An Empirical Appraisal," *Admin. Sci. Quart.* (Sept. 1969).

6. For a more generalized discussion of the impact of technology and goals on organization, see C[harles] Perrow, *Organizational Analysis: A Sociological View* (Belmont, Cal.: Wadsworth Publishing, 1970), Chaps. 3 and 5.

7. See P. R. Lawrence and J. W. Lorsch, *Organization and Environment* (Boston: Harvard Graduate School of Business Administration, 1967), for an insightful study of coordination difficulties between dissimilar activities.

8. Interrelationships between planning, organizing, leading, and controlling are examined explicitly in Chapters 15, 21, and 27 of W. H. Newman, C. E. Summer, and E. K. Warren, *The Process of Management,* 3rd ed. (Englewood Cliffs, N. J.: Prentice-Hall, 1972).

Part **3**

Relevance of Contingency Views to Organization Theory

We have traced the evolution of organization and management theory from traditional views, through modifications of the behavioral and quantitative sciences, to the development of systems concepts, and finally to the emergence of contingency views. This evolution has significantly broadened the perspective for the study and design of organizations and has provided new insights into management practice. The field has moved away from closed-system, simplistic views toward recognition of the rich complexities of modern organizations—systems of psychological, sociological, technical, and economic variables.

System concepts and contingency views provide a basis for understanding, designing, and managing organizations. General systems theory provides the macro paradigm for the study of social organizations. But it involves a relatively high level of abstraction. Contingency views tend to be more concrete and to emphasize more specific characteristics unique to social organizations, as well as patterns of relationships among subsystems. This trend toward more explicit understanding of patterns of relationships among organizational variables is essential if the theory is to facilitate and improve management practice. For example, there is evidence that different technical subsystems require certain types of structure if the organization is to operate efficiently. Further, the most appropriate technical subsystem and matching structure may create predictable problems in the psychosocial subsystem. A routine technology may require a high degree of structure which in turn may lead to certain dissatisfactions among the human participants.* If organization theory can provide a better understanding of these interrelationships (at least in terms of probabilities), it should lead to important insights for organization design and management practice.

The readings presented in Part 2 stress a contingency view of organizations and their management. Here we will develop a more precise definition of the contingency view; discuss its essence as expressed by a number of writers; abstract common themes which describe key characteristics and dimensions; and set forth a conceptual model for more detailed analysis and understanding.

Common Themes in Contingency Views

Traditional management theory emphasized the development of principles which were appropriate and applicable to all organizations and all managerial tasks. These universal principles were quite prescriptive—there was only one appropriate way to design and manage organizations. Although the quantitative and behavioral sciences have introduced new concepts to the study of organizations, they too have tended toward prescribing the "one best way." The quantitative sciences have emphasized a normative approach and stressed a logical, rational, algorithmic view of management and decision making. Many behavioral scientists have also emphasized a particular approach to management. For example, it is easy to recognize that McGregor considered his Theory X (man is basically lazy and irresponsible) to be less appropriate, in general, than his Theory Y (man is basically industrious and responsible) [1]. Similarly, Likert downgraded his highly-structured, autocratic System 1 and stressed the functionality and merit of the more democratic, participative System 4 for all organizational situations [2].

Systems concepts emphasize that organizations are composed of many subsystems whose interrelationships have to be recognized. Once we accept a systems view, it becomes apparent that it is impossible to prescribe polar positions or principles which are appro-

---

*There is increasing evidence of employee dissatisfaction in mass production industries. "Inevitably, the monotony issue will play a bigger part in labor relations in the future. . . . The UAW is talking of making 'alternatives to the assembly line' an issue in 1973 bargaining." "Productivity: Our Biggest Undeveloped Resource," *Business Week,* Sept. 9, 1972, p. 108.

priate to all organizations. There are so many relevant variables that it is impossible for a simplistic model to depict reality. A simple view is appropriate only when the system under consideration is stable, mechanistic, and effectively closed to intervening external variables. Once we begin to consider organizations as open systems with inter-active components, we find it impossible to think in simplistic, unidimensional terms.

The readings presented in Part 2 reflect the rejection of simplified approaches to organizations and their management and express the need for developing contingency views. Most of these readings em-phasize that there is *no one best way* for designing and managing all types of organizations. There are a wide variety of appropriate organizational designs, relationships between variables and subsystems, and management practices. *It all depends* on the particular circum-stances in a specific situation.

The excerpts in figure 3-1 suggest the essence of the contingency view and indicate each author's rejection of universal principles appro-priate to all situations. Moreover, many of the readings go further than simply indicating the necessity for a multivariate or systems view. Some themes suggest certain broad perspectives concerning different types of organizational systems. Figure 3-2 sets forth these common themes on contingency views. For sake of presentation we have indicated the overall perspective of each author in terms of two polar descriptions of organization systems or types: closed/stable/ mechanistic and open/adaptive/organic. The various authors indicate distinctive characteristics based upon these two different types of organizational systems. In developing this terminology, we were influenced by the dichotomization presented by Burns and Stalker— mechanistic versus organic managerial systems. We were also influ-enced by the general systems literature and in particular by the con-cept of closed and open systems. (Thompson, pp. 26-36) While these sources provide the fundamental basis for classification into two system types, the other authors use similar dimensions or characteristics which fit this classification.

FIGURE 3-1: ESSENCE OF THE CONTINGENCY VIEW

James D. Thompson: Most of our beliefs about complex organizations follow from one or the other of two distinct strategies. The closed-system strategy seeks certainty by incorporating only those variables positively associated with goal achievement and subjecting them to a monolithic control network. The open-system strategy shifts attention from goal achievement to survival, and incorporates uncertainty by recognizing organizational interdependence with environment. A newer tradition enables us to conceive of the organization as an open system, indeterminate and faced with uncertainty, but subject to criteria of rationality and hence needing certainty.

Fremont E. Kast and James E. Rosenzweig: The contingency view of organizations and their management suggests that an organization is a system composed of subsystems and delineated by identifiable boundaries from its environmental suprasystem. The contingency view seeks to understand the interrelationships within and among subsystems as well as between the organization and its environment and to define patterns of relationships or configurations of variables. . . . Contingency views are ultimately directed toward suggesting organizational designs and managerial actions most appropriate for specific situations.

Harold J. Leavitt: If we view organizations as systems of interaction among task, structural, technical and human variables, several different classes of effort to change organizational behavior can be grossly mapped.

Such a view provides several entry points for efforts to effect change. One can try to change aspects of task solution, task definition, or task performance by introducing new tools, new structures, or new or modified people or machines. On occasion we have tried to manipulate only one of these variables and discovered that all the others move in unforeseen and often costly directions.

Tom Burns and G. M. Stalker: We have endeavored to stress the appropriateness of each system to its own specific set of conditions. Equally, we desire to avoid the suggestion that either system [mechanistic or organic] is superior under all circumstances to the other. In particular, nothing in our experience justifies the assumption that mechanistic systems should be superseded by organic in conditions of stability. The beginning of administrative wisdom is the awareness that there is no one optimum type of management system.

Shirley Terreberry: It is our thesis that the selective advantage of one intra- or inter-organizational configuration over another cannot be assessed apart from an understanding of the dynamics of the environment itself. It is the environment which exerts selective pressure. 'Survival of the fittest' is a function of the fitness of the environment.

Henry P. Knowles and Borje O. Saxberg: The quality of human relations in any organization, from the political state to the business enterprise, reflects first of all its members', and particularly its leaders', views of the essential character of humanity itself. It makes a great deal of difference in systems of social control whether those involved tend to view man, in general, as good or evil. . . . The underlying human value which predominates is readily perceived in (1) the way social relationships are structured, (b) the kinds of rewards and penalties that are used, (c) the character of the communication process which links people together, and (d) the other elements of social control that characterize a relationship or an organization.

Herbert A. Simon: In the decision-making situations of real life, a course of action, to be acceptable, must satisfy a whole set of requirements, or constraints. Sometimes one of these requirements is singled out and referred to as the goal of the action. But the choice of one of the constraints, from many, is to a large extent arbitrary. For many purposes it is more meaningful to refer to the whole set of requirements as the (complex) goal of the action. This conclusion applies both to individual and organizational decision making.

Charles Perrow: Finally, to call for decentralization, representative bureaucracy, collegial authority, or employee-centered, innovative or organic organizations—to mention only a few of the highly normative prescriptions that are being offered by social scientists today—is to call for a type of structure that can be realized only with a certain type of technology, unless we are willing to pay a high cost in terms of output. Given a routine technology, the much maligned Weberian bureaucracy probably constitutes the socially optimum form of organizational structure.

If all this is plausible, then existing varieties of organizational theory must be selectively applied. It is increasingly recognized that there is no 'one best' theory (any more than there is 'one best' organizational structure, form of

Raymond G. Hunt: In order to solve practical problems of organizational design, it is necessary initially to understand the many differences between types of organizations and the reasons that these differences exist. The fact that these aspects have not been considered until the mid-1960's is reflected by the independence of developments in organizational design and theory until this time. However, recent progress in comparative analysis of organizations, together with integrative theory building, gives promise of altering this state of affairs, especially regarding the appreciation of technology as a main basis for differentiating organizational varieties and explaining organizational processes.

Jay W. Lorsch: The structure of an organization is not an immutable given, but rather a set of complex variables about which managers can exercise considerable choice.

. . . Our understanding of organizations as systems is new and it is growing rapidly. The ideas which are presented here will certainly be modified and improved. But as crude as they are, they represent better tools than the principles which have been relied on in the past. These ideas clearly move us in a new and promising direction—that of tailoring the organization to its environment and to the complex needs of its members.

D. S. Pugh, D. J. Hickson, and C. R. Hinings: The clusters of organizations described have implications for the concept of bureaucracy. It has been argued that the existence of orthogonal structural dimensions demonstrates 'that bureaucracy is *not* unitary, but that organizations may be bureaucratic in any of a number of ways.'

. . . *Bureaucracy takes different forms in different settings.* The clusters found here are not intended to be exhaustive; there are suggestive of what may be learned by a multidimensional study.

John J. Morse: Our study suggests a link between organizational characteristics and individual motivation.

. . . The study findings also suggest organizational characteristics to be simultaneously linked to, or interdependent with, *both* individual motivation *and* effective job performance.

. . . So, in terms of the managerial dilemma of designing an organization or functional task unit to accomplish its task well and to provide for the needs of the individuals who do the work, this study points up a practical, empirically based set of links that recognizes the import of task requirements and the individual needs in equal and interdependent measure.

Fred E. Fiedler: The results show that a task-oriented leader performs best in situations at both extremes—those in which he has a great deal of influence and power, and also in situations where he has no influence or power over the group members.

Relationship-oriented leaders tend to perform best in mixed situations where they have only moderate influence over the group. A number of subsequent studies by us and others have confirmed these findings.

The results show that we cannot talk about simply good leaders or poor leaders. A leader who is effective in one situation may or may not be effective in another. Therefore, we must specify the situations in which a leader performs well or badly.

George F. F. Lombard: A relativistic framework seems helpful in thinking of one's job as a decision maker. Whereas a dualistic framework describes only one step in the process, not necessarily even a final one, a relativistic viewpoint combines the outwardly oriented and visible steps of a decision with the internal thought processes that guide a manager. The apparent "go-no-go" aspects of a decision become the limited, special instances of a broader, total, thought-and-action approach that includes alternatives considered as well as actions taken. Though the decision may appear dualistic in character, the total decision set, including both the obvious physical act and the inner subjective consideration of alternatives and contingencies, is appropriately conceived as a totality in a relativistic framework.

Roger Harrison: As our knowledge increases, it begins to be apparent that these competing change strategies are not really different ways of doing the same thing—some more effective and some less effective—but rather they are different ways of doing *different* things. They touch the individual, the group, or the organization in different aspects of their functioning. They required differing kinds and amounts of commitment on the part of the client for them to be successful, and they demand different varieties and levels of skills and ability on the part of the practitioner.

. . . There is a real need for conceptual models which differentiate intervention strategies from one another in a way which permits rational matching of strategies to organizational change problems.

William H. Newman: The matching of strategy and management design presents a challenging opportunity to scholars of management. It calls for skill in building a viable, integrated system; it draws upon insights on many facets of management; and it plunges us into a highly dynamic set of relationships. Both synthesis and refinement of theory are involved.

. . . A corollary of the proposition that management design should be varied so that it is (a) integrated within its parts, and (b) matched to specific company strategy is that no single management design is ideal for all circumstances. We cannot say, for example, that management by objectives, decentralization, participative management or tight control are desirable in all situations. Company strategy is one of the important factors determining what managerial arrangement is optimal.

FIGURE 3-2: COMMON THEMES IN CONTINGENCY VIEWS

Characteristics of Organizational Systems

Author	*Closed/Stable/Mechanistic*	*Open/Adaptive/Organic*
James D. Thompson	Closed system Certain, deterministic, rational	Open system Uncertain, indeterministic, natural
Fremont E. Kast and James E. Rosenzweig	Closed-system principles Concentration on individual subsystem	Open-system concepts Concentration on interdependence and integration of subsystems
Harold J. Leavitt	Power concentration Combination of relatively independent parts or components	Power equalization Multivariate systems of interacting variables: task, structural, technical, and human variables
Tom Burns and G. M. Stalker	Mechanistic	Organic
Shirley Terreberry	Placid environment	Turbulent environment
Henry P. Knowles and Borje O. Saxberg	Pessimistic View (Man as Robot) System emphasizes competition and relies upon imposed organization controls	Optimistic View (Man as Pilot) System emphasizes cooperation and relies upon individual self-control
Herbert A. Simon	One goal, one criterion Decision-making strategy to achieve *a* goal	Multiple goals, multiple criteria Decision-making strategy to satisfy a *set* of constraints.
Charles Perrow	Routine technology Analyzable search procedures, few exceptions, programmable decisions	Nonroutine technology Unanalyzable search procedures, numerous exceptions, nonprogrammable decisions
Raymond G. Hunt	Performance	Problem solving
Jay W. Lorsch	Certain, homogeneous	Uncertain, diverse
D. S. Pugh, D. J. Hickson and C. R. Hinings	Full bureaucracy: structured, concentrated authority, impersonal control	Implicitly structured organizations: unstructured, dispersed authority, line control

FIGURE 3-2 (Continued)

John J. Morse	Certain, predictable, routine, unchanging, structured	Uncertain, unpredictable, nonroutine, changing, unstructured
Fred E. Fiedler	Leadership style: task oriented, low tolerance for ambiguity	Leadership style: relationship oriented, high tolerance for ambiguity
George F. F. Lombard	Undimensional Dualism (right-wrong)	Multidimensional Relativism (multiple values; "It all depends")
	Closed, rationalistic decision processes	Open, contingent, satisficing, heuristic decision processes
Roger Harrison	"Surface" interventions Low emotional involvement in organization change	"In-depth" interventions High emotional involvement in organization change
	Emphasis on instrumental relationships	Emphasis on interpersonal relationships
William H. Newman	Management design for stable technology	Management design for adaptive technology

In formulating the contents of figures 3-1 and 3-2, we have presented a contraction of the authors' ideas. It is, of course, very important for the reader to gain a fuller understanding of their concepts by reading the complete selections in this book. However, these figures do provide a broad overview of contingency views, as well as common themes from the perspective of closed/stable/mechanistic and open/adaptive/organic organizational systems.

A word of caution. Most of the authors are clear in emphasizing that any polarization is not characteristic of modern organizations. Total organizations simply cannot be described as being closed/stable/mechanistic or open/adaptive/organic. They have characteristics which fit somewhere between these extremes. A production line typically is not completely closed/stable/mechanistic nor is a research laboratory completely open/adaptive/organic. Conceptually we prefer to think of these characteristics on a dimensional basis rather than as polar positions. Moreover, different departments of a single organization may fall on different points of what we view as a continuum.

Sales departments tend to be more open and adaptive than production departments. Practically, however, we have great difficulty in presenting these characteristics as dimensions. We can describe the polar positions but it is much more difficult, if not impossible, to typify each of the possible intermediate positions (theoretically infinite) of certain characteristics—for example, between closed and open systems. Further refinements in contingency views are necessary in order to develop these characteristics into definable dimensions and to allow us to describe and analyze points along the continuum.

A Conceptual Model

We have extended the themes summarized in figure 3-2 to develop a conceptual model of contingency views for organization theory and management practice. This model reflects many contributions from a large number of researchers/writers and is not restricted to the seventeen readings presented in Part 2. (See the Bibliography for additional references.)

As background for the conceptual model we need a more explicit statement of systems concepts and contingency views. In Part 1 we defined a system as *an organized, unitary whole composed of two or more interdependent parts, components, or subsystems and delineated by identifiable boundaries from its environmental suprasystem.* We defined an organization as (1) a *subsystem* of its broader environment, and (2) *goal oriented*; comprised of (3) a *technical subsystem*, (4) a *structural subsystem,* (5) a *psychosocial subsystem*; and coordinated by (6) a *managerial subsystem.* Using these ideas we can provide a more precise definition of the contingency view:

The contingency view seeks to understand the interrelationships within and among subsystems as well as between the organization and its environment and to define patterns of relationships or configurations of variables. It emphasizes the multivariate nature of organizations and attempts to understand how organizations operate under varying conditions and in specific circumstances. Contingency views are ultimately directed toward suggesting organizational designs and managerial actions most appropriate for specific situations.

The contingency view can serve as the general model or paradigm for the investigation of important organizational and environmental variables and their interactions. Ideally, the empirical research should include models of the multivariate relationships among all of the organizational subsystems or variables. Although this objective is conceptually enticing, analyses of the interrelationships are very difficult. The current state of our knowledge about any single variable, such as technology or structure or the psychosocial system, is still very limited. How do we meet this dilemma of needing a more thorough understanding of the subsystems and their interrelationships for the appropriate design and management of organizations?

Practically, it will be a slow, painstaking process of trying to analyze the interrelationships and linking the numerous variables together; the contributions of many researchers will be needed to develop a more substantial body of knowledge concerning dual relationships. We may then be able to introduce additional factors in order to understand multivariate relationships. Through such an approach, we will be better able to define certain patterns of interaction between organizational variables and/or subsystems which will ultimately facilitate the generation of meaningful suggestions for appropriate organization designs and managerial practices.

Substantial progress has already been made in looking at the relationships between various organizational subsystems. So far, most of the empirical studies have considered the relationship between a limited number of organizational variables. For example, there has been substantial research concerning the impact of technology and/or environment on organizational structure. (Perrow, pp. 138-59; Hunt, pp. 160-78; Lorsch, pp. 179-94; Burns and Stalker, pp. 74-80; and Terreberry, pp. 81-100) These are obviously multivariate studies in that they include the interrelationships between at least two of the most important subsystems. Some progress has been made in researching systems with more than two variables. Morse, for example, studied the relation of individual motivation to the general organizational climate as defined by technology, structure, and environmental influences. His research was designed specifically to build on earlier works by Lawrence and Lorsch. (Morse, pp. 213-28) Similarly, Fiedler has investigated the relations among position power, task structure, and leader-member relations in his studies of leadership. (Fiedler, pp. 229-327)

In spite of limitations of our current knowledge, it is possible to develop a tentative model of the present status of contingency views of organization and management. Figure 3-3 represents such a conceptual model. It includes the environmental suprasystem as well as the overall organizational system and its important subsystems—goals and values, technical, structural, psychosocial, and managerial. A number of key dimensions for each are also included. These dimensions are interpreted in terms of the polar positions illustrated in figure 3-2, closed/stable/mechanistic and open/adaptive/organic organizational systems. We have used word descriptions to characterize the extremes of these key dimensions.

The analysis of the key subsystems and their important dimensions provides a pattern for the relatively closed/stable/mechanistic organi-

FIGURE 3-3
A CONCEPTUAL MODEL OF CONTINGENCY
VIEWS OF ORGANIZATION AND MANAGEMENT

Systems and Their Key Dimensions	Characteristics of Organizational Systems	
	Closed/Stable/ Mechanistic	Open/Adaptive/Organic
Environmental Suprasystem		
General nature	Placid	Turbulent
Predictability	Certain, Determinate	Uncertain, Indeterminate
Degree of environmental influence on organization	Low	High
Control of task environment by organization	High	Low
Technology	Stable	Dynamic
Input	Homogeneous	Heterogeneous
Boundary relationships	Relatively closed. Limited to few participants (sales, purchasing, etc.). Fixed and well defined.	Relatively open. Many participants have external relationships. Varied and not clearly defined.
Organization means for interfacing with environment	Routine, standardized procedures	Nonroutine, flexible arrangements
Interorganizational relationships	Few organizations and/or Organization types with well-defined, fixed relationships	Many diverse organizations with changing relationships
Overall Organizational System		
Boundary	Relatively closed	Relatively open
Goal structure	Organization as a single goal maximizer	Organization as a searching, adapting, learning system which continually adjusts its multiple goals and aspirations
Predictability of actions	Relatively certain, determinate	Relatively uncertain, indeterminate
Decision-making processes	Programmable, computational	Nonprogrammable, judgmental
Organization emphasis	On performance	On problem solving
Goals and Values		
Organizational goals in general	Efficient performance, stability, maintenance	Effective problem solving, innovation, growth
Pervasive values	Efficiency, predictability, security, risk aversion	Effectiveness, adaptability, responsiveness, risk taking
Ideological orientation	Undimensional and dualism	Multidimensional and relativism

Systems and Their Key Dimensions	Characteristics of Organizational Systems	
	Closed/Stable/ Mechanistic	Open/Adaptive/Organic
Overall Organizational System (Cont)		
Goal set	Single, clear-cut	Multiple, determined by necessity to satisfy a variety of constraints
Involvement in goal-setting process	Managerial hierarchy primarily (top down)	Widespread participation (bottom up as well as top down)
Means-ends orientation of participants	Emphasis on means (processes)	Emphasis on ends (objectives)
Number	Few	Many
Stability	Stable	Changing (over time)
Flexibility	Inflexible	Flexible
Clarity	Well defined	General (vague at times)
Specificity	High	Low
Technical System		
General nature of tasks	Repetitive, routine	Varied, nonroutine
Input to transformation process	Homogeneous	Heterogeneous
Output of transformation process	Standardized, fixed	Nonstandardized, variable
Knowledge	Specialized (narrow base)	Generalized (broad base)
Facilities	Special purpose	General purpose
Methods	Programmed, algorithmic	Nonprogrammed, heuristic
Propensity to change	Stable	Dynamic
Diversity	Low	High
Task interdependence	Low	High
Task rigidity	High	Low
Time perspective	Short term	Long term
Effect on participants	Task and technology define participant roles precisely. Difficult to adapt to individual needs and abilities. Limited discretion in carrying out tasks.	Technology is more tool than master. Considerable discretion in carrying out tasks.
Structural System		
Organizational formalization	High	Low
Differentiation and specialization of activities	Highly specific by function	More general, overlapping of activities
Specificity of tasks and functions	High	Low
Specificity of tasks and roles	High	Low

Systems and Their Key Dimensions	Characteristics of Organizational Systems	
	Closed/Stable/ Mechanistic	Open/Adaptive/Organic
Structural System (Cont)		
Procedures and rules	Many and specific, usually formal and written.	Few and general, usually informal and unwritten.
Number of levels in hierarchy	Many	Few
Authority structure	Concentrated, hierarchic	Dispersed, network
Source of authority	Authority based on position	Authority based on knowledge
Responsibility	Attached to position and/ or role	Assumed by individual participants
Interdependence of individual, group, and departmental activities	Low	High
Psychosocial System		
Interpersonal relationships	Formal	Informal
Status structure	Clearly delineated by formal hierarchy	More diffuse. Based upon expertise and profes- sional norms.
Role definitions	Specific and fixed	General and dynamic. Change with tasks
Motivational factors	Emphasis on extrinsic rewards, security, and lower level need satis- faction. Theory X view.	Emphasis on intrinsic rewards, esteem, and self-actualization. Theory Y view.
Interaction-influence patterns	Superior → Subordinate Hierarchical	Superior ⇌ Subordinate Horizontal and diagonal
Distribution of influence	Narrow, top of hierarchy	Wide, egalitarian distribution
Degree of autonomy for individual	Tightly controlled and structured	Relatively free and autonomous
Basis of organization influence upon individual	Manipulation of income and economic security	Adapting influence to higher level and internalized needs. Linking individual and organization goals.
Personal involvement	Low	High
Power system	Power concentration	Power equalization
Interpersonal collaboration	Low, discouraged	High, encouraged
Perspective of participants	Limited, parochial	Broad, systemic
Control of individual participants	Externally imposed	Self-imposed
Leadership style	Autocratic, task oriented desire for certainty	Democratic, relationship oriented, tolerance for ambiguity
Orientation of individuals	Local, institutional orientation	Cosmopolitan, environ- mental orientation

Systems and Their Key Dimensions	Characteristics of Organizational Systems	
	Closed/Stable/ Mechanistic	Open/Adaptive/Organic
Psychosocial System (Cont)		
Degree of participant commitment to organization	Low, conflicting values and goals	High, shared values and goals
Degree of participant uncertainty	Low	High
Managerial System		
General nature	Hierarchical structure of control, authority, and communications; Combination of independent, static components	A network structure of control, authority, and communications; Co-alignment of interdependent, dynamic components
Specificity of managerial role	High	Low
Problem solving	Algorithmic, systematic, optimizing models	Heuristic, "disjointed incrementalism," satisficing models
Decision-making techniques	Autocratic, programmed, computational	Participative, nonprogrammed, judgmental
Information flow	Quantitative data	Qualitative data
Content of communications	Decisions and instructions	Advice and information
Planning process	Repetitive, fixed, and specific	Changing, flexible, and general
Planning horizon	Short term	Long term
Types of plans	Standing plans, specific policies	Single-use plans, general policies
Control structure	Hierarchic, specific, short term. External control of participants	Reciprocal, general, long term. Self-control of participants
Control process	Control through impersonal means (rules, regulations, e.g.)	Control through interpersonal contacts (suggestion, persuasion, e.g.)
Position-based authority	High	Low
Knowledge-based authority	Low	High
Formality of authority	High	Low
Degree of professionalization	Low	High
Reaction to individual differences	Disallow, or at best tolerate	Recognize and value
Means of conflict resolution	Resolved by superior (refer to "book") Compromise and smoothing Keep below the surface	Resolved by group ("situational ethics") Confrontation Bring out in open
Management development	Orientation and training to fit the organization	Personal growth leading to organizational adjustments

zational system which is significantly different from that of the relatively open/adaptive/organic organizational system. Hypotheses about these relationships have not been "proven" via substantial empirical research. In fact, it is doubtful whether or not they can ever be proven conclusively. Organizations and their environments are much too dynamic to allow us to set forth "laws" about relationships. Rather, we can only expect to identify tentative patterns of relationships among the organizational variables.

However, this initial step of identifying patterns of relationships can be of major importance. We can apply this model to the study of many different types of organizations. For example, the research literature suggests that there are significant differences among correctional institutions which could be better understood by using a contingency view. These institutions which have *confinement* of inmates as a primary goal tend to exhibit characteristics set forth under "closed/stable/mechanistic" in figure 3-3. Those organizations which emphasize the goal of *rehabilitation* of participants tend to exhibit characteristics set forth under "open/adaptive/organic." The maximum security prison is very closed, highly structured, and exercises tight control (externally imposed) over inmates. The rehabilitation-oriented correctional institution is more open to society (for example, work-release programs), has a more flexible structure, and tries to develop self-control within each participant.

Even within the military differences exist which depend on the nature of specific activities. The organization utilized for basic military training displays characteristics of the closed/stable/mechanistic system. However, in the design, development, and procurement of advanced weapon systems, the military organization can be described as relatively open/adaptive/organic. New approaches, such as program management and matrix organizations, have emerged to meet changing requirements.

This model may also be useful in looking at the historical evolution of an organization or an industry. For example, our school systems have had to become more open/adaptive/organic in response to social pressures and individual participants' needs, particularly in the past two decades. The airline industry provides a unique illustration of changing organizational characteristics since it exhibits several patterns of relationship over time. In their early days the airlines were faced with a turbulent environment—accelerating technology, increasing consumer affluence, growing acceptance of a new mode of travel, and changing government regulations. During this period they could be characterized by the open/adaptive/organic form. However, as the industry became more stable and operations more routine, they moved toward a more closed/stable/mechanistic form. Within the total organization the primary task of the airline—the individual flight—became very routine, programmed, and tightly controlled by specific rules and regulations. Individual tasks became much more specific and routinized. (We can remember earlier days when stewardesses were not programmed to greet passengers, to check them for guns or bombs, to serve drinks and prepared meals; they did have time to fraternize with passengers.) However, at the coordinative level above that of individual flights—the planning, organizing, and controlling of overall flight operations—the airlines must still operate in a more open/adaptive/organic mode. The system must cope with changes in schedules, high rates of employee turnover, and new mixes of personnel for each flight. And even the routine characteristics of the individual flight may change abruptly when the hijacker suddenly says, "Give me $500,000, three parachutes, and let's fly to Tahiti." The operation moves very rapidly to a more open, adaptive system which cannot utilize procedures programmed for routine flights.

We can use this model to investigate even more subtle differences within organizations. For example, the university is typically thought of as an open/adaptive/organic system. However, within the university various subunits, departments, or programs may have different characteristics. The typical university graduate program (particularly doctoral programs) is more likely to exhibit open/adaptive/organic characteristics than the typical undergraduate program. This hypothesis leads to the suggestion that undergraduate and graduate programs should be organized and administered differently—an approach which is not always carried out in practice.

We recognize that these are merely tentative hypotheses concerning organizations and that a great deal more research needs to be undertaken using contingency views. However, in spite of the difficulty in making this conceptual matrix comprehensive, the endeavor has practical significance. Sophistication in the study of organizations will come when we have a more complete understanding of organizations as total systems (configurations of subsystems) so that we can suggest more appropriate organization designs. Ultimately, organization theory should serve as the foundation for more effective management practice.

Notes

1. Douglas McGregor, *The Human Side of Enterprise* (New York: McGraw-Hill, 1960).
2. Rensis Likert, *The Human Organization* (New York: McGraw-Hill, 1967).

Part 4

Application of Contingency Views to Management Practice

Organization theory is the body of knowledge (including hypotheses and propositions) stemming from a definable field of study or endeavor which can be termed organization science. Theory provides a useful framework for research, teaching, and practice. The study of organizations is an applied science because the resulting knowledge is relevant to problem solving in on-going enterprises or institutions. Contributions to organization theory come from many sources. Deductive and inductive research in a variety of disciplines provide a theoretical base of propositions which are useful for understanding organizations and for managing them. Experience gained in management practice is also an important input to organization theory. In short, the art of management is based on a body of knowledge generated by practical experience *and* eclectic scientific research concerning organizations.

The pervasiveness of organizations and management argues for considerable latitude with regard to the organizations studied and the methods used. Moreover, since the value systems of researchers, teachers, and practitioners are quite diverse, the evaluation of what is relevant may vary considerably. On the other hand, the concerted effort toward the development of organization theory during the mid-twentieth century has resulted in useful dialogue, cross-fertilization, and mutual understanding among participants. While no well-defined consensus has yet appeared, there are consistent threads of inquiry and agreement with regard to the general scope of organization theory.

Early management concepts came from practitioners. Writing was often the distillation of experience in on-going enterprises. Such contributions are important and valuable additions to the body of knowledge comprising organization theory. We need continued observation and conceptualization from astute practicing managers. Meanwhile, scientists have become more involved in research related to organizations but carried on in the context of basic disciplines. Other scholars have been engaged in integrating findings from basic disciplines and translating the results into meaningful concepts or propositions.

Many of the ideas expressed in the readings in Part 2 stem from large-scale research of on-going organizations. The focus has been on *describing* and *understanding* why some organizations have been more successful than others. Contingency views have been developed by observing patterns of relations among variables as well as what organization design or managerial style seems to be most effective in a given situation.

This approach to building a body of knowledge should facilitate translation of theory into practice because normative statements or propositions are developed from observing what successful managers have done in contemporary organizations. Such propositions should be more readily applicable than general principles because the manager can relate the theory to his specific situation. How often have we heard the response, "the theory may be appropriate in general, but our organization is different." The thrust of contingency views in organization theory is an attempt to bridge this gap and make the theory more readily applicable.

Do systems concepts and contingency views provide a panacea for solving problems in organizations? The answer is an emphatic *no*; this approach does *not* provide "ten easy steps" to success in management. Cookbook approaches, while seemingly applicable and easy to grasp, are usually short-sighted, narrow in perspective, and superficial—in short they are unrealistic. Fundamental concepts, such as systems and contingency views, are much more difficult to comprehend. However, they do facilitate a more thorough understanding of complex situations and increase the likelihood that appropriate action will be taken.

This approach requires a reasonable amount of conceptual skill on the part of the manager. This aptitude distinguishes the truly effective manager at any level—particularly the one who progresses to the top. (Lombard, pp. 255-72) It involves the ability to "see the forest for the trees," to discern key interrelationships, and to attach degrees of importance to the various factors bearing on a problem. As indicated by Schein in the excerpt on Complex Man (page 324), *"The success-*

ful manager must be a good diagnostician and must value a spirit of inquiry." This approach is obviously more difficult than reliance on general principles and rules. It requires heuristic problem solving rather than indiscriminate application of algorithms. And it requires a pragmatic approach with heavy emphasis on situational analysis, as described by Sherman (page 325).

The dimensions of closed/stable/mechanistic and open/adaptive/ organic can be related to individual managerial behavior. By closing the system to additional information, the decision maker can react rather quickly. By opening the system to new inputs, the decision-making process becomes more complex and time consuming. In psychological terms a direct connection between stimulus and response $(S \rightarrow R)$ suggests instinctive or habitual behavior. This could represent reliance on simplistic interpretations and the imposition of principles or rules.

In an organizational setting this involves standard operation procedures. The open-system view includes a more elaborate mediating mechanism between stimulus and response $(S \rightarrow D \rightarrow R)$. The intervening activity, diagnosis, involves situational analysis in order to ascertain the most appropriate response. It must be emphasized that neither of these approaches is either right or wrong. Highly programmed responses may be appropriate under some conditions but not in all. Prolonged diagnosis may result in paralysis by analysis. Conceptual skills (systems and contingency views) facilitate responses which are appropriate in particular situations.

As we proceed to look at the managerial task in more detail and assess the applicability of contingency views, it is important to recognize that many managers do and will continue to use such an approach intuitively and implicitly. Without much knowledge of the underlying body of organization theory, they have an intuitive grasp of the situation, are flexible diagnosticians, and adjust plans and procedures accordingly. In this sense, systems concepts and contingency views are not new. However, if this approach to organization theory and management practice can be made more explicit, we can facilitate better management and more effective and efficient organizations. As noted by Sherman, "there is nothing as practical as a theory that works."

The Managerial Task and Organizational Subsystems

In previous sections (figure 3-3, for example), we have described the managerial subsystem in relation to polar organizational character-

Complex Man

Organization and management theory has tended toward simplified and generalized conceptions of man. Empirical research has consistently found some suppo: for the simple generalized conception, but only some. Consequently, the major impact of many decades of research has been to vastly complicate our models of man, of organizations, and of management strategies. Man is a more complex individual than rational-economic, social, or self-actualizing man. Not only is he more complex within himself, being possessed of many needs and potentials, but he is also likely to differ from his neighbor in the patterns of his own complexity It has always been difficult to generalize about man, and it is becoming more difficult as society and organizations within society are themselves becoming more complex and differentiated.

. . . Man can respond to many different kinds of managerial strategies, depending on his own motives and abilities and the nature of the task; in other words, there is no one correct managerial strategy that will work for all men at all times.

. . . *The successful manager must be a good diagnostician and must value a spirit of inquiry.* If the abilities and motives of the people under him are so variable, he must have the sensitivity and diagnostic ability to be able to sense and appreciate the differences. Second, rather than regard the existence of differences as a painful truth to be wished away, he must also learn to value difference and to value the diagnostic process which reveals differences. Finally, he must have the personal flexibility and the range of skills necessary to vary his own behavior. If the needs and motives of his subordinates are different, they must be treated differently.

It is important to recognize that these points do not contradict any of the strategies previously cited. I am not saying that adhering to traditional principles of organization, or being employee-centered, or facilitating the work of subordinates is wrong. What I am saying is that any of these approaches may be wrong in some situations and with some people. Where we have erred is in oversimplifying and overgeneralizing. As empirical evidence mounts, it is becoming apparent that the frame of reference and value system which will help the manager most in utilizing people effectively is that of science and of systems theory. If the manager adopts these values toward man, he will test his assumptions and seek a better diagnosis, and if he does that he will act more appropriately to whatever the demands of the situations are. He may be highly directive at one time and with one employee but very nondirective at another time and with another employee. He may use pure engineering criteria in the design of some jobs, but let a worker group completely design another set of jobs. In other words, he will be flexible, and will be prepared to accept a variety of interpersonal relationships, patterns of authority, and psychological contracts.

Edgar H. Schein, *Organizational Psychology,* 2nd ed. (Englewood Cliffs, N.J.: Prentice-Hall, 1970), pp. 69-71.

The Pragmatic Approach

This brings me to the approach which, in the present state of the art, seems to me to be the only realistic one available—that is, pragmatism, or doing what "works" in the particular situation, with due regard to both short and long range objectives.

I include long range objectives because pragmatism that focuses only on short range objectives, degenerates into expediency. I would like to emphasize that pragmatism does not mean (to me, at least) throwing out theory. It means, rather, knowing and using theory to the extent that it works, but not using it when it doesn't. Otherwise, pragmatism degenerates into nothing more than trial and error. (This may in itself have great advantages in creativity and innovation, but at enormous cost in time and money.) Someone once said—and I agree—that there is nothing as practical as a theory that works. . . .

Organizational decisions are usually more or less rational responses to an interplay of ever-changing forces within the enterprise, in the environment, and between the enterprise and its environment. Effective organization involves continuous adaptation to a dynamic situation, and changes in the organization can be viewed as responses to actual or anticipated changes in the relationship among these forces. The study of organization, therefore, should concern itself with an understanding of those forces which are relevant and of their dynamic interplay.

Some of the most important of these forces are:

1. The enterprise's objectives and purposes, stated and implied.
2. The nature of the work to be done.
3. Technology, technological change, and the level of technological skills available to the enterprise.
4. The technological and formal interrelationships within the enterprise.
5. The psychology, values, and attitudes that prevail within the enterprise, particularly those of top management.
6. The interpersonal and sociological relationships within the enterprise.
7. Outside forces, such as changes in the economy, in competition, in technology, in laws, in labor relations, in the political situation and in broad sociological and cultural patterns.

Since all of these forces are in constant flux, it is well to reassess the organization pattern periodically. The very design of the organization structure is a significant force in the total situation, and changes in it can alter the total situation.

But there can be no ideal design or ideal arrangement that will fit all times, all situations, all objectives, and all values. The principles of both the "scientific management" and the "human relation" schools represent attempts to define such ideal arrangements. Both schools have suffered from a view of organization as an essentially static phenomenon or, if it is in motion, as moving in a straight line, and from the selection of one or another of the forces in the situation as being the only relevant one to be considered.

I suggest that the task of organization theory is not to lay down "principles," but to determine as precisely as possible what effects different arrangements of structure or process will have for a particular enterprise, staffed with real people, over a specified time period.

Harvey Sherman, *It All Depends: A Pragmatic Approach to Organization (University, Ala: University of Alabama Press, 1966), pp. 55-57.*

istics: closed/stable/mechanistic and open/adaptive/organic. This
approach suggests that the most appropriate means for carrying out
the managerial task varies according to the organization type.
Problem-solving processes and decision-making techniques, as well
as planning and control methods, should be adjusted to fit specific
organization types. The general management functions of organizing,
planning, leading, and controlling apply to all situations but the
particular means used (degree of participation, for example) varies
with differences in organization type—perhaps based on the nature of
technology. (Newman, pp. 287-303)

Another way to help understand the managerial task is to look
within organizations at various levels or subsystems. The model
shown in figure 4-1 is an extension of the work of Parsons, Thompson,
and Petit [1]. By differentiating sections of the organization into
operating, coordinative, and strategic subsystems, we can see that the
criteria cited previously—closed/stable/mechanistic and open/adaptive/
organic—can be applied to activities within an organization. For any
task and technology the operating subsystem is relatively more closed
than the strategic subsystem. In fact, part of the role of top
management is to buffer the intrusion of environmental forces so that
the operating core can concentrate on its task. (Thompson, pp. 26-
36) Differentiating by subsystems or levels as well as by organization
types compounds the difficulties in identifying patterns of relationships and/or configurations among subsystems.

A contingency view of the managerial task is illustrated in figure
4-2. In general, the categories presented can be applied to organizations of any size. The smaller the enterprise, the more probable that
the various aspects of the managerial task will be carried out by one

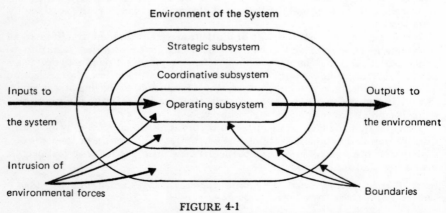

FIGURE 4-1
The Organization: A Composite of Strategic, Coordinative, and Operating Subsystems

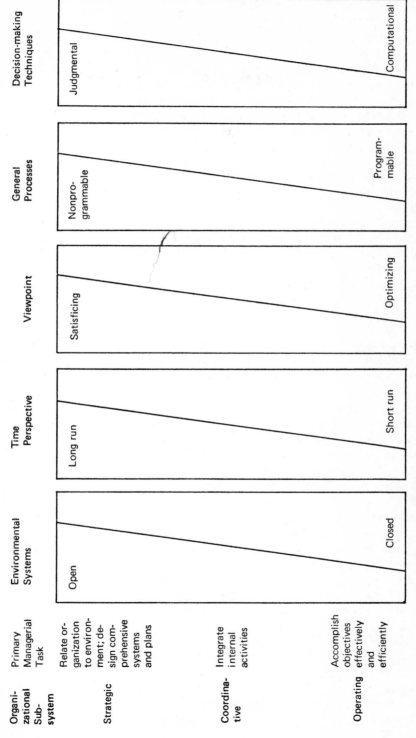

FIGURE 4-2: The Managerial Task: Strategic, Coordinative, and Operating Subsystems

individual. Obviously, the owner-manager of a proprietorship is involved in all the activities set forth in figure 4-2. He must define his task in relation to his environment, plan his activities over the short and long run, and then carry them out in order to achieve his objectives.

In larger, more complex organizations it is likely that these subsystems are separable. Top management is involved in relating the organization to its environment—identifying the goals which it must fulfill in order to survive and grow. Strategy formulation also involves designing comprehensive systems and plans. A systems philosophy is useful in conceptualizing the long-run nature of the organization and assembling the appropriate resources for achieving desired goals. The environmental system is relatively open; general processes are typically nonprogrammable; the viewpoint is essentially one of satisficing—finding workable solutions to complex, ill-structured, novel problems. Decision making is largely judgmental and cogitative—reasoned evaluation of all relevant inputs to the problem-solving process.

In the operating subsystem the primary aim is to accomplish stated objectives effectively and efficiently. It is here that the organization "does its thing"—producing bicycles or toothpaste, providing health care or fire protection. The system is relatively closed and general processes within the organization can be programmed; for example, standard operating procedures can be developed and applied. Systems analysis provides a framework for a short-run, optimizing outlook and computational decision making through the use of quantitative techniques.

In the coordinative subsystem—ranging between the strategic and operating activities—the primary concern is the integration of internal activities which have been specialized by function and/or level. Middle management translates comprehensive plans into operation procedures. It is involved in interpreting the results of the operating system and in focusing existing resources in appropriate directions. Systems management facilitates coordination of several functions, projects, or programs within an overall organization. A pragmatic point of view is essential in integrating short- and long-run considerations. Compromise is often necessary in decision making at this level in order to achieve a practical or utilitarian outcome via analysis and synthesis of problems.

The terms used in the various dimensions shown in figure 4-2 are illustrative of general tendencies; i.e., most likely activities or approaches. It is not to say that judgment is not important in the operating system or that computational techniques are never used in developing comprehensive plans. However, the terms do provide the basic flavor for the managerial task in three relatively distinct organizational subsystems.

The Task of the General Manager

In order to explore the application of systems concepts and contingency views to management practice, it may be helpful to describe the overall task of the general manager in more detail (see figure 4-3). The primary managerial task at the strategic level involves relating the organization to its environment as well as designing comprehensive systems and plans. Within that role we can choose several areas of activity (such as strategy formulation, organization design, information-decision systems, influence systems and leadership, and organization improvement) and then illustrate the application of contingency views in each of these particular functions. The single arrows in figure 4-3 indicate an appropriate sequence of activities if

FIGURE 4-3: The Task of the General Manager

Maintain a Total System View Coupled
with a Situational Perspective
  External environmental suprasystem
    Conditions
    Trends
  Internal subsystems (strengths and limitations)
    Technical
    Structural
    Psychosocial

Encourage Organization
Improvement Endeavors
  Operations analysis
  Feedback from organiza-
    tional participants
  Management development
  Organization development

Develop Objectives and
Strategies for the Organiza-
tion as a Whole
  Short-, medium-, and long-range plans
  Determine approach to goal
    setting (Degree of involvement
    throughout the organization.
    Top down and/or bottom up.)

Shape Influence Systems and
Leadership
  Reinforce desired behavior
  Intrinsic rewards
  Extrinsic rewards
  Flexible leadership styles
  Matching leaders-followers-
    situations

Dynamic
Equilibrium

Organize Technical and
Structural Subsystems
  Task specialization ("do-able"
    jobs) by levels and functions
  Methods of coordinating
    specialized jobs
  Differentiation
  Integration

Design Information-Decision Systems
  Operational measures of performance
  Planning and controlling decisions
    by levels and functions
  Data relevant to operating,
    coordinative, and strategic
    decisions

an organization were being established for the first time to achieve an objective. It would also be an appropriate sequence for re-thinking and re-designing activity in on-going organizations. In most situations, however, it is obvious that the various activities will frequently be going on simultaneously and that there are cross-currents generated by interaction between them. The manager sits in the middle of a patterned swirl of events, planning and controlling organizational endeavors in order to maintain a dynamic equilibrium.

Strategy formulation. One of the key tasks of the general manager is the development and continual refinement of a strategic, comprehensive plan for the organization. This involves understanding as much of the total situation as possible—environmental conditions and trends, as well as internal strengths and limitations (whether they are of a financial, technical, structural, or psychosocial nature). All too often this task is approached by identification of narrow, short-sighted, single-purposed objectives.* In discussing strategy formulation, Learned and his colleagues set forth a contingency view comprised of four major components: (1) market opportunity—what the organization *might do;* (2) competence and resources—what the organization *can do* realistically; (3) managerial interests and desires—what the organization *wants to do;* and (4) responsibility to society—what the organization *should do.* [2, pp. 17-32] Consideration of each and all of these components should lead to a viable strategic plan—one which has a reasonable probability of success.

This approach reflects systems concepts and a contingency view because it recognizes the interrelationships between the various components. An organization may not be able to capitalize on market opportunity if, in fact, it does not have the competence or resources to do so. Similarly, an organization is unlikely to succeed if its strategic plan is based on managerial interests, without reference to competence, market opportunity, or societal responsibilities. Balancing the four components of strategy formulation is a complex and delicate task. While the contingency approach does not simplify the problems involved, it does facilitate understanding the complexity of the interrelationships and help the general manager cope with the problem realistically.

Organization design. When the objectives and comprehensive strategy for the organization are defined, the next step is determining key operating and coordinating tasks. The basic technical system must be

---

* More realistic approaches to goal setting and strategy formulation have been described in Part 2. (Simon, pp. 120-37; Newman, pp. 287-303)

identified, as well as structural relationships among people. This typically involves specialization by level and/or function plus coordination of specialized jobs in order to focus activity on organizational goals. We have isolated organization design for purposes of illustration, though it is obviously related to planning, leadership, and control. (Newman, pp. 287-303) Newman cites a number of organizational features that are likely to vary with a change in strategy:

Centralization vs. decentralization
Degree of division of labor
Size of self-sufficient operating units
Mechanisms for coordination
Nature and location of staff
Management information systems
Characteristics of key personnel

Early examples of organization design were rather simplistic, hierarchical structures based on experience in relatively stable organizations such as the church, the military, or mass-production industries (all closed/stable/mechanistic systems). As the external environment became more turbulent, and as internal relationships became more dynamic and complex, the hierarchical model needed elaboration and modification in order to depict reality with any degree of fidelity. For example, dotted lines were introduced to identify staff (advisory) rather than line (command) relationships, or to specify lateral relationships. Informal systems were not included since they cannot be depicted on a typical organization chart.

Structure cannot be considered in isolation; it should be designed with various combinations of factors in mind. As shown in figure 3-3 two relatively general conclusions are in order:

1. The *closed/stable/mechanistic* organizational form is more appropriate for routine activities where productivity is a major objective, and/or technology is relatively uniform and stable; where decision making is programmable; and where environmental forces are relatively stable and certain.

2. The *open/adaptive/organic* organizational form is more appropriate for nonroutine activities where creativity and innovation are important; where heuristic decision-making processes are ncesssary; and where the environment is relatively uncertain and turbulent.

These conclusions emphasize a contingency view of organization design; each situation should be analyzed in order to determine the most appropriate form. What is the most useful way to divide the work—product, function, or geographic? Will a narrow or wide span of control be most appropriate?

In addition, attention must be given to designing other aspects of organizational systems, such as planning processes, control procedures, the reward system, and information-decision systems. Managers should devote explicit attention to both structure and process in organizational systems.

A basic consideration in the design of organizations is the differentiation and integration of activities. (Lorsch, pp. 174-94) The process involves differentiating the necessary activities of an organization both horizontally and vertically—dividing up the work into "do-able" tasks. At the same time attention should be given to coordinating these activities and integrating the results into a meaningful composite result.

The degree of differentiation can vary from relatively homogeneous to extremely heterogeneous. Research findings suggest that organizations operating in a changing environment and with complex and dynamic technology need a high degree of differentiation in order to function effectively. Obviously, the amount and sophistication of integrative activity must increase with the degree of differentiation and the need for integration.

Simple, less differentiated organizations (for example, a grocery chain) may rely upon the formal hierarchy, plans and procedures, and role specifications to achieve integration. More complex, highly differentiated organizations having characteristics of the open/adaptive/organic form frequently require more elaborate forms of integration. For example, in the aerospace industries many new structural means for achieving integration have evolved, such as project teams, program management, and matrix organizations. Examples of integrating units might be applied research (between fundamental research and production), production planning (between engineering and production), or market research (between fundamental research and sales). These organizations may also develop specific behaviorally-oriented programs aimed at achieving collaboration, teamwork, and integration among participants. Much of the work in organization development (OD) is aimed at achieving better collaboration in open/adaptive/organic systems. (Harrison, pp. 238-54)

A key factor for management to recognize in organization design is that greater differentiation and diversity often lead to conflict. Therefore, most effective organizations emphasize creative conflict management as a way to facilitate the integration of activities.

In high-performing organizations in all environments, it was found that conflict was managed by involved individuals who dealt openly with the conflict and worked a problem until a resolution was reached which best met total organizational goals. In the effective organization, there was more of a tendency to *confront* conflict instead of using raw power to *force* one party's compliance or instead of *smoothing* over the conflict by agreeing to disagree. (Lorsch, p. 190)

These views have important practical implications for management in the design of organizations. The need for substantial differentiation in response to environmental and technological forces requires the organization to develop more elaborate means for integration and to devote more human resources to conflict resolution. This may result in a complex and elaborate managerial system. Alternatively, it may be advisable to consider structural changes in order to offset these complexities. One means is to separate activities so as to minimize the need for integration and conflict resolution. For example, divisionalization of the organization structure along product lines may reduce the need for elaborate overall integration. This is the approach which most of the large, diversified corporations such as General Electric, General Motors, and Du Pont have taken [3]. Each separate product division has substantial autonomy and requires only nominal integration with other divisions and with corporate headquarters.

Conglomerates have grown dramatically through acquisition and merger and are examples of highly diversified and differentiated organizations which do not attempt to achieve operational integration among the various organizational units. In these organizations, integration is attempted primarily through allocation of financial resources—and not at the technical or operational levels. The various divisions have very little market or technological interdependence with other divisions. Allen suggests that conglomerates attempt to achieve *financial synergy* through their ability to obtain external funds and in the allocation of capital to various divisions. But they have achieved only limited *managerial synergy* (integrated planning and control of divisional activities) and little or no *operational synergy* (significant market or technological interdependence among divisions). [4, pp. 16-35] This approach has important advantages for the conglomerate: it makes it much easier to acquire new firms and to divest existing divisions. Substantial integration at the managerial and operational levels would make this process exceedingly difficult.

The foregoing discussion suggests that the managerial task of organization design cannot be approached on a fixed-formula basis. It requires the effective matching of the overall strategy with environmental and technological requirements as well as internal constraints, including the capabilities, needs, and aspirations of the human participants.

Information-decision systems. The phrase *information-decision system* is in itself a contingency view—information is relevant only as it pertains to managerial decision making. Therefore, it is important to begin the process by identifying the types of decisions made in various parts of the organization. As indicated earlier (figure 4-3), the system should provide data which is meaningful to the planned tasks and measures of performance.

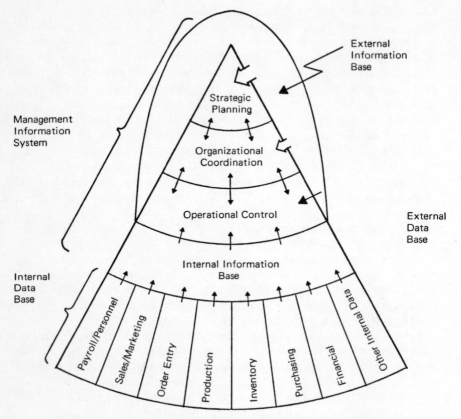

FIGURE 4-4   Relationship of Data and Management Information Systems

Developing operational measures of performance is crucial because we tend to "get what we measure" in the way of individual and organizational behavior. If quantity is the only yardstick, quality may suffer. If only short-run profitability for a unit is considered, long-run viability may be endangered because of deterioration in physical and human resources. For complex systems, sophisticated measures of performance need to be developed so that planning and control processes can be functional.

The relationship of data and management information systems is shown in figure 4-4. While all data could conceivably be considered part of an organizational information base, it is obvious that for any fairly large and complex organization such an approach would be impossible. Therefore, most systems include exception reporting wherein pertinent information from the various internal data-processing activities becomes part of the organizational information base when it is brought to the attention of appropriate decision makers.

As illustrated, a considerable amount of such information is used in planning and controlling the operating subsystem of the organization. Some of the internal information is used for strategic planning and controlling. Such information is coupled with that gathered from external sources in order to provide appropriate information for decision making at the top level. Most of the relevant external information flows into the organization through the strategic subsystem. However, some of it comes in via the coordinative and operating subsystems as well. Information used in the coordinative subsystem comes from both operations and strategic planning activities.

Much attention has been focused on computerized management information systems (MIS). However, it is important to recognize that managerial decision making typically requires the input of much information—opinions, for example—that cannot be computerized. Thus, overall management information-decision systems should be designed to include explicit attention to nonquantifiable inputs as well as those which result from computerized data-processing applications.

Application of contingency views to the development of management information-decision systems involves recognition of different kinds of decisions made in different organizational subsystems. In the operating subsystem the environment generally is closed and stable, and the process is relatively mechanistic. A short-run time perspective and an optimizing point of view allows us to use computational decision-making techniques which can be programmed. In contrast, the environment generally is relatively open and turbulent in the strategic subsystem. A long-run time perspective plus a satisficing point of view (within a set of diverse constraints) suggest that decision-making techniques will be largely judgmental and non-programmable. The management information-decision system should be tailored to the specific situation and hence may vary considerably in form and intent for different levels or functions in the organization. However, the overall system should provide for interaction between and integration of the various subsystem modules.

Influence systems and leadership. Another key function of the general manager involves nurturing the psychosocial system. Of particular importance is the development of a reward-penalty system to reinforce desired behavior on the part of organizational participants. Lorsch, pp. 174-94; Leavitt, pp. 57-73) The reward system fits into the overall spectrum of means for influencing behavior shown in figure 4-5. It is a form of inducement and blends into coercion if there is a threat of demotion or firing. The basic "flavor" of the reward system will depend on the manager's view of the nature of man. (Knowles and Saxberg, pp. 101-19) If he is relatively pessimistic (considering man basically lazy and irresponsible), he will rely on coercion and extrinsic rewards (higher wages, for instance). If he is relatively optimistic (considering man basically industrious and responsible), he will rely more on emulation of his own behavior, suggestion, and intrinsic rewards (the work itself).

These two views coincide with McGregor's Theory X and Theory Y [5]. They can also be related to Maslow's hierarchy of needs (physiological, safety, love, esteem, and self-actualization) [6, 370-96]. Herzberg's hygiene (dissatisfiers) and motivator (satisfiers) dimensions also parallel these basic assumptions. Major hygiene factors (necessary to prevent dissatisfaction but not sufficient to elicit high job satisfaction) include company policy and administration, supervision, salary, interpersonal relations, and working conditions. Key motivators include achievement, recognition, work itself, responsibility, and advancement [7].

A contingency view suggests that reward systems based entirely on a pessimistic or optimistic perception of man will not bring the desired results in all departments of an organization. Concentrating on intrinsic rewards (job enrichment) can be effective in some situations. However, *adequate* monetary rewards are usually necessary to ensure continued participation. What is the potential balance between effort and reward? If the reward system is well designed and implemented, performance should lead to satisfaction.

A company which takes this kind of view of job satisfaction adopts an approach which is different from the usual one. Its aim is not necessarily to increase everyone's satisfaction, and thereby to make "everyone happy," but rather to

| *Emulation:* striving to equal or excel; imitating with effort to equal or surpass; approaching or attaining equality | *Suggestion:* placing or bringing (an idea, proposition, plan, etc.) before a person's mind for consideration or possible action. | *Persuasion:* prevailing on a person by advice, urging, reason, or inducements to do something (rather than force). | *Coercion:* forcing constr compulsion; physical pr or compression |

FIGURE 4-5
Spectrum of Means for Influencing Behavior*

*Fremont E. Kast and James E. Rosenzweig, *Organization and Management: A Systems Approach* (New York: McGraw-Hill Book Company, 1970), p. 309.

make sure that the best performing employees are the most satisfied employees. Its goal, in other words, is not to maximize satisfaction, but to maximize the *relationship* between satisfaction and performance. [8, 122]

In designing a reward system management should keep the various theories of motivation in mind and apply them where appropriate. Piece rates for individuals may be effective in one department, whereas a group bonus might be better in another situation. Nonmonetary rewards (praise as positive reinforcement, e.g.) can be used effectively in many cases. As conditions change—across subunits and/or over time—the reward system should be adapted to the specific situation.

A basic part of management is the leadership function—coordinating group activities and eliciting behavioral responses which are more than routine. This connotation suggests the "tapping" of latent human capability in achieving group objectives. The relationship between leadership and influence systems is summarized by defining leadership as:

Interpersonal influence, exercised in situations and directed through the communication process, toward the attainment of a specified goal or goals. Leadership always involves attempts on the part of a *leader* (influencer) to affect (influence) the behavior of a *follower* (influencee) or followers in situation. [9, 3]

In applying contingency views, the manager is interested in what leadership style is appropriate for a given organizational situation. Often, the person who best satisfies the needs of the individuals in the group will emerge as the leader. However, more specific guidelines can be developed by considering the various forces that are involved in any group: (1) within the leader, (2) within the follower(s), and (3) in the situation itself. For example, Tannenbaum and Schmidt [10, 95-101] suggest that in assessing the degree of participation which might be appropriate, it would be useful to consider such factors as:

Leader:

Value system
Confidence in his subordinates
Own leadership inclinations
Feelings of security in an uncertain situation

Follower(s):

Independence-dependence needs
Willingness to assume responsibility for decision making
Tolerance for ambiguity
Degree of interest in participating

Degree of identification with organizational goals
Knowledge and experience (or growth potential)
Expectations concerning participation

Situation:
Values and traditions in the organization
Group effectiveness
Nature of the problem
Pressure of time

By considering these variables explicitly the manager will be more aware of the nature of the situation and his relationship in and to the group. If his leadership style is based on this kind of analysis, his probability of success should increase.

A key to effective leadership is clarification of expectations between the leader and his followers in order to reach a mutual understanding which sets the tone for the entire relationship. This situational approach to leadership effectiveness certainly involves contingency views. If the leader is a good diagnostician, he can ascertain the most appropriate leadership style to employ according to the circumstances. An autocratic style might be most appropriate if organizational participants expect it; for example, in times of crisis. In a military combat situation, subordinates typically rely on the decision making of their group leader. The crew of a ship hit by a torpedo would not be inclined to discuss the alternatives and then vote. If the captain announces, "Abandon ship," the order would be carried out immediately.

On the other hand, in situations where time permits, a democratic approach which includes subordinates in the decision-making process may be extremely useful. In still other situations, a bureaucratic approach may be most effective and efficient. For relatively routine decisions, standard operating procedures might be entirely appropriate. But referring to the rules when in fact there is an extraordinary set of circumstances might be dysfunctional for the organization. The manager should be as flexible as possible, gearing his style to the specific situation and the individuals involved.

Another approach to more effective leadership is to match particular skills with specific situations (Fiedler, pp. 229-37). Based on Fiedler's dimensions of position power, task structure, and leader-member relations, individuals can be reassigned to fit the proper niche, and/or groups can be restructured in order to facilitate better leader-member relations. We can change an individual's title and/or adjust the degree of authority delegated to him. For example, his position power would be reduced if his signature had to be counter-signed by another executive. Detailed instructions concerning the task reduce the leadership ability needed. Adding a subgroup of more experienced, well-qualified employees to the work group would very likely affect the leader-member relations significantly.

This matching approach, when coupled with training and coaching, provides the means by which leadership talent can be developed while at the same time available skills are used more effectively. Concerted attention in both directions—adjusting situations to fit various managers and developing managers flexible enough to fit into various situations—can result in long-term benefits for the system as a whole.

Organization improvement. As indicated in figure 4-3 the task of the general manager includes encouraging organization improvement endeavors. In the broadest sense this involves changing the organization to make it more effective and efficient, as well as more satisfying for its participants. These three objectives have a contingency flavor because a balance must be maintained in order to ensure long-run viability. Effective solutions to organizational problems must be tempered with cost considerations (cost/benefit analysis) in order to be realistic. For example, new equipment might increase output but increase cost per unit simultaneously. Overemphasis on efficiency at the expense of employee satisfaction might result in slowdown tactics, high turnover rates, and an atmosphere of tension and conflict.

Because the area of organization improvement is so broad, there are obviously many approaches, methods, or techniques which managers might utilize. For example, Leavitt discusses three areas in which techniques can be applied to bring about organizational change: (1) structure, (2) technology, and (3) human. (Leavitt, pp. 57-73) And Harrison stuggests a number of approaches which vary in the depth of emotional involvement on the part of participants: operations analysis, management by objectives, managerial grid, T-group, and task group therapy. (Harrison, pp. 238-54) Operations analysis includes operations research techniques such as queuing theory and linear programming as well as work simplification methods and other descendants of scientific management. The results of such analysis might include optimal assignment of personnel to work stations (for example, tellers in a bank) or optimal location of warehouses in a distribution system. Such organization improvement efforts can be carried out without reference to personalities; emphasis is on arrangement of functions or tasks.

The essence of management by objectives (MBO) is mutual agreement between supervisor and subordinate on goals for improvement over some future period of time. Here again, the emphasis tends to be on task issues rather than personal qualities. The managerial grid approach involves the development of individual managers as well as work teams within the organization. The essence of the grid approach is a two-dimensional model of (1) concern for people and (2) concern for production. The ultimate goal is 9,9 management—work is accomplished by committed people with a "common stake" in the organization [11, p. 10]. T-group (sensitivity training) and task-group therapy are other approaches to organizational change. They involve a much deeper emotional involvement on the part of the participants and emphasize more individual behavioral change than the methods outlined above.

Organization improvement includes management development, organization development, and feedback from organizational participants. Feedback is an essential ingredient to all such endeavors because it provides a picture of the current condition—for an individual, a small work group, or the organization as a whole. If there is a gap between the current condition and a desired condition, some form of planned change can be designed to bridge the gap. In general the process involves four phases: (1) diagnosis, (2) problem solving, (3) action steps, and (4) follow-up (re-diagnosis). Diagnosis typically involves feedback from organization members and the use of such information by participants in refining problems, analyzing alternative courses of action, and implementing planned change.

Organization improvement through management development assumes that better managers will lead to better organizational performance. Management development can be carried out as a separate and distinct activity through in-company training programs and coaching, as well as the use of off-site courses, conferences, or workshops. However, synergistic effects can be obtained if it is approached within the context of an overall organization improvement program. "Management development is a program of developing managers who will be able to contribute more to their organization: OD is a continual process of developing social conditions so that the manager can make these contributions. Although these strategies have different objectives, they are complementary and not incompatible." [12, 574]

Organization development (OD) has become one of the most widely used terms in the management literature. It has numerous connotations because of the variety of specific methods used by its practitioners. To some it is nearly synonymous with the more general term organization improvement. For example, the brochure describing the Western Organization Development Conference in San Francisco in April, 1970, refers to OD as "systematic efforts to improve organization performance—to change the way in which organizations operate by modifying the structure and processes of the management systems that guide their behavior." Others stress the psychosocial subsystem by defining OD as "an effort (which is) (1) planned, (2) organization-wide, and (3) managed from the top, to (4) increase organization effectiveness and health through (5) planned interventions in the organization's 'processes,' using behavioral-science knowledge." [13, p. 9]

Figure 4-6 provides a comparison of organization development and management development based on several dimensions: (1) reasons for use, (2) typical goals, (3) interventions for producing change, (4) time frame, (5) staff requirements, and (6) values. A contingency approach to planned change would involve diagnosing a particular need in a specific organizational situation. The manager can then determine which combination of management development and/or organization development strategies, if any, would be most appropriate. For example, if the problem were lack of knowledge on the part of some managers about the technical aspects of other units in the organizaton, "job rotation of managers" would be an appropriate strategy. Similarly, an "intergroup confrontation" meeting would be appropriate if the problem were diagnosed as misunderstanding or conflict between the engineering and production departments.

An important consideration in strategy formulation for organization improvement is the depth of emotional involvement on the part of participants. (Harrison, pp. 238-54) Intensive emotional involvement—such as sensitivity training— may be appropriate in some situations. However, sensitivity training is not synonymous with OD and certainly not synonymous with organization improvement in general. Technical or structural changes stemming from operations analysis are often more relevant than T-group sessions.

Another dimension for management to consider is the skill and interest of internal and/or external change agents. The manager should have enough of a sense of the situation so that the consultant is not allowed to "lay on" a technique just because it is available in his "trainer kit."

Figure 4-7 provides a three-dimensional view of the OD process. Here again, a contingency view is emphasized. Based on the results of problem diagnosis and the specific focus of attention, a particular mode of intervention (technique for facilitating change) can be designed. The sequence of the process is critical. Problem diagnosis must come first in order to understand the specific situation. If the OD process is technique-oriented (applying a "canned" approach to any and all situations), there is considerable danger of dysfunctional consequences—for example, wasting substantial amounts of energy on solving the wrong problem. This is a continuing dilemma in the interface between managers and scientists/consultants/change agents. Quantitative and behavioral scientists should tailor their analyses and recommendations to the specific needs of the situation. This approach coupled with systems concepts and contingency views can result in significant contributions and improved management practice.

FIGURE 4-6: A Comparison of Organization Development and Management Development*

Category	Organization Development	Management Development
Reasons for Use	Need to improve overall organizational effectiveness	Need to improve overall effectiveness of manager
	Typical examples of tough problems to be solved:	Managers do not know company policy or philosophy
	• Interunit conflict	Managers are void in certain skills
	• Confusion stemming from recent management change	Managers seem to be unable to act decisively
	• Loss of effectiveness due to inefficient organizational structure	
	• Lack of teamwork	
Typical Goals	To increase the effectiveness of the organization by—	To teach company values and philosophy
	• Creating a sense of "ownership" of organization objectives throughout the work force	To provide practice in management skills which lead to improved organizational effectiveness
	• Planning and implementing changes more systematically	To increase ability to plan, coordinate, measure, and control efforts of company units
	• Facilitating more systematic problem solving on the job	
	To reduce wasted energy and effort by creating conditions where conflict among people is managed openly rather than handled indirectly or unilaterally	To gain a better understanding of how the company functions to accomplish its goals
	To improve the quality of decisions by establishing conditions where decisions are made on the basis of competence rather than organizational role or status	
	To integrate the organization's objectives with the individual's goals by developing a reward system which supports achievement of the organization's mission as well as individual efforts toward personal development and achievement	

* W. Warner Burke, "A Comparison of Management Development and Organization Development," *J. Applied Behavioral Science*, Sept.-Oct. 1971, pp. 572-73.

Category	Organization Development	Management Development
Interventions for Producing Change	Education and problem solving is on the job; learning while problem solving and solving problems while learning	Sending of manager to some educational program
		Job rotation of managers
	Following a diagnosis, utilization of one or more of the following techniques:	Specialized training "packages"
	• Team building	Courses and/or conferences
	• Training programs	Counseling
	• Intergroup confrontations	
	• Data feedback	Reading of books and articles

	• Technostructural interventions
	   Change in organizational structure
	   Job enrichment
	   Change in physical environment
	   (social architecture)	

Time Frame	Prolonged	Short, intense
Staff Requirements	Diagnostician Catalyst/Facilitator Consultant/Helper	Teacher/Trainer Program Manager Designer of training programs
	Knowledge and skill in the dynamics of planned change	Knowledge in the processes of human learning
	Experience in the laboratory method of learning	
Values	Humane and nonexploitative treatment of people in organizations Theory Y assumptions Collaboration Sharing of power Rationality of behavior Openness/candor/honesty Importance of surfacing and utilizing conflict Right of persons and organizations to seek a full realization of their potential Explicitness of values as a value in itself	Competition Belief that "education is progress" Belief that managers need challenging periodically Manager's right to have time for reflection and renewal Belief that individual should "fit" organization's needs Right of person to seek full realization of his potential

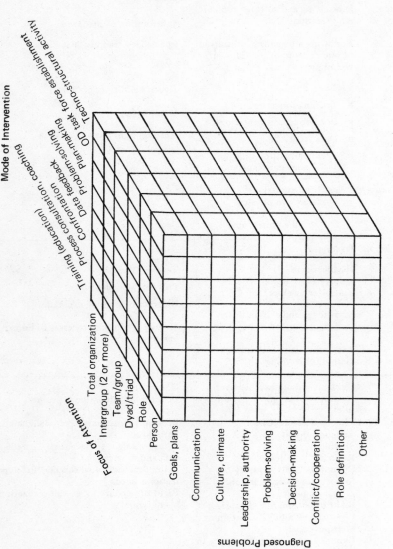

Mode of Intervention

Activity establishment

Techno-structural activity

OD Plan-making force

Problem task

Data feedback

Confrontation

Process consultation)

Training (education), coaching

Focus of Attention

Total organization

Intergroup (2 or more)

Team/group

Dyad/triad

Role

Person

Diagnosed Problems

Goals, plans

Communication

Culture, climate

Leadership, authority

Problem-solving

Decision-making

Conflict/cooperation

Role definition

Other

FIGURE 4-7   The OD Cube: A Scheme for Classifying OD Interventions

Figure 4-7 is from Richard A. Schmuck and Matthew B. Miles, "Improving Schools Through Organization Development: An Overview" in *Organization Development in Schools*, edited by Richard A. Schmuck and Matthew B. Miles (Palo Alto, Cal.: National Press Books, 1971), p. 8.

Sophistication vis-à-vis *Pragmatism*

Some effort should be devoted to introspection about organization theory and its evolution. Researchers, teachers, and practitioners should be aware of the body of knowledge that now exists and is still growing. In addition, they should be concerned about new directions of inquiry. In other words, what should organization science encompass and what should be its thrust? These considerations provide a framework within which the field of study is developing.

There is the danger at times that a scientific discipline may begin to exist for its own sake and emphasize esoteric concepts intelligible to only a few insiders. It is true that there is a gradation from applied to pure research. However, there is no absolute "pure" research. In the long run, everything is applied; hence, a discipline must keep in touch with the real world. An important step in this process is the inclusion of practitioners in the search for new knowledge because they control access to an essential ingredient—organizational data. Mutual understanding among managers, teachers, and researchers will facilitate the development of a relevant body of knowledge.

Organization theory includes many tentative conclusions and propositions which should be thoroughly tested in many different settings. However, modern organizations cannot wait for the *ultimate* body of knowledge (there is none!). Practicing managers in business firms, hospitals, and government agencies continue to function on a day-to-day basis. They must use whatever theory is available.

We have stated a number of times that much work needs to be done to refine contingency views of organizations and their management. We are interested in both descriptive findings and normative considerations. There is a great need for empirical research concerning organization and management. We have just begun to scratch the surface in this direction and to develop propositions framed in such a way that they can be applied in specific situations. Herein lies a danger—that too much energy may be spent on refining the theory and not enough on translating it into practice. It is ironic that over-sophistication can result even though much research is focused on distinguishing effective management practice in existing organizations. In short, the field may be over-emphasizing sophistication of theory at the expense of pragmatism.

We can use examples to illustrate the problem. We spend much time and money developing computerized information systems without really ascertaining what information is useful for managers. And, in an era of ultrasophisticated communications equipment, we still have difficulty in transmitting *meaning* from one person to another in a face-to-face conversation. Elegant mathematical models are developed for solving the wrong problems. More attention devoted to the application of long division (ratio analysis) in the right circumstances would have higher payoff than a more elaborate simplex method of linear programming applied to the wrong problem.

There is a need to understand clearly how individuals and organizations behave in a variety of circumstances. Once we have more complete understanding of what *is* and what happens, we can begin to consider normative propositions of what managers *ought to do or seek*. Such an approach facilitates the development of conceptual schemes that will provide useful frames of reference for managers in organizations.

While we are working on refinements of the theory, a concerted effort should be directed toward applying what we do know. We need ways of making contingency views more usable. Without oversimplification, we need relevant guidelines for practicing managers. Two- or three-dimensional matrices or models would be helpful in this regard. Managers might then be able to estimate the potential success of different approaches in given situations.

The general tenor of the contingency view is somewhere in between simplistic, universal principles and complex, vague notions ("it all depends"). It is a mid-range concept that recognizes the complexity involved in managing modern organizations but uses patterns of relationships and/or configurations of subsystems in order to facilitate improved practice. The art of management depends on a reasonable success rate for actions in a probabilistic environment. Our hope is that contingency views, while continually being refined by scientists/researchers/theorists, will also be made more applicable. Explicit attention to this endeavor should result in increased organizational effectiveness and efficiency in the future.

Notes

1. Thomas A. Petit, "A Behavioral Theory of Management," *Academy of Management Journal,* Dec. 1967, pp. 341-50; James D. Thompson, *Organizations in Action* (New York: McGraw-Hill, 1967); and Talcott Parsons, *Structure and Process in Modern Societies* (New York: Free Press, 1960), pp. 60-96.
2. Edmund P. Learned, C. Roland Christensen, Kenneth R. Andrews, and William D. Guth, *Business Policy: Text and Cases,* rev. edition (Homewood, Ill.: Richard D. Irwin, 1969).
3. For a discussion of this development, see Alfred D. Chandler, Jr., *Strategy and Structure* (Cambridge, Mass.: M.I.T. Press, 1962).
4. Stephen A. Allen, III, "Corporate-Division Relationships in Highly Diversified Firms, in *Studies in Organization Design,* edited by Jay W. Lorsch and Paul R. Lawrence (Homewood, Ill.: Richard D. Irwin and Dorsey Press, 1970).

5. Douglas M. McGregor, *The Human Side of Enterprise* (New York: McGraw-Hill, 1960).
6. Abraham H. Maslow, "A Theory of Human Motivation," *Psychological Review*, July 1943.
7. Frederick Herzberg, *Work and the Nature of Man* (Cleveland, Ohio: World, 1966).
8. Lyman W. Porter and Edward E. Lawler, III, "What Job Attributes Tell About Motivation," *Harvard Business Review*, Jan.-Feb. 1968.
9. Robert Tannenbaum and Fred Massarik, "Leadership: A Frame of Reference," *Management Science*, Oct. 1957.
10. _____ and Warren H. Schmidt, "How to Choose a Leadership Pattern," *Harvard Business Review*, Mar.-Apr. 1958.
11. Robert R. Blake and Jane S. Mouton, *The Managerial Grid* (Houston, Texas: Gulf, 1964).
12. W. Warner Burke, "A Comparison of Management Development and Organization Development," *J. Applied Behavioral Science*, Sept.-Oct. 1971.
13. Richard Beckhard, *Organization Development: Strategies and Models* (Reading, Mass.: Addison-Wesley, 1969). See also Wendell L. French and Cecil H. Bell, Jr., *Organization Development* (Englewood Cliffs, N.J.: Prentice-Hall, 1973), p. 15.

Bibliography

Ackoff, Russell L., "Towards A System of Systems Concepts," *Management Science*, July 1971, 661–71.

Aiken, Michael, and Hage, Jerald. "Organizational Interdependence and Intra-organizational Structure," *Amer. Sociological Review*, Dec. 1968, 912–29.

Aldrich, Howard. "Organizational Boundaries and Inter-organizational Conflict," *Human Relations*, Aug. 1971, 279–93.

Alexis, Marcus, and Wilson, Charles Z. *Organizational Decision Making* (Englewood Cliffs, N.J.: Prentice-Hall, 1967).

Andrew, Gwen. "An Analytic System Model for Organization Theory," *Academy of Management Journal*, Sept. 1965, 190–98.

Anthony, Robert N. *Planning and Control Systems: A Framework for Analysis* (Boston, Mass.: Harvard Graduate School of Business Administration, 1965).

Argyris, Chris. *Management and Organizational Development* (New York: McGraw-Hill, 1971).

Back, Kurt W. "Biological Models of Social Change," *Amer. Sociological Review*, Aug. 1971, 660–67.

Barnard, Chester I. *The Functions of the Executive* (Cambridge, Mass.: Harvard University Press, 1938).

Bassett, Glenn A. "The Qualifications of a Manager," *Calif. Management Review*, Winter, 1969, 34–44.

Beckett, John A. *Management Dynamics: A New Synthesis* (New York: McGraw-Hill, 1971).

Beckhard, Richard. *Organization Development: Strategies and Models* (Reading, Mass.: Addison-Wesley, 1969).

Beer, Michael, and Huse, Edgar F. "A Systems Approach to Organization Development," *J. Applied Behavioral Science*, Jan.–Feb. 1972, 79–101.

Bennis, Warren G., editor. *American Bureaucracy* (Chicago, Ill.: Aldine, 1970).

____. *Changing Organizations* (New York: McGraw-Hill, 1966).

____; Benne, Kenneth D.; and Chin, Robert, editors. *The Planning of Change*, 2d ed. (New York: Holt, Rinehart & Winston, 1969).

Berrien, F. Kenneth. *General and Social Systems* (New Brunswick, N.J.: Rutgers University Press, 1968).

Blake, Robert R., and Mouton, Jane S. *Corporate Excellence through Grid Organization Development: A Systems Approach* (Houston, Texas: Gulf, 1968).

Blau, Peter M. "The Comparative Study of Organizations," *Industrial and Labor Relations Review,* April 1965, 323-38.

____, and Scott, W. Richard. *Formal Organizations* (San Francisco, Calif.: Chandler, 1962).

____, and Schoenherr, Richard A. *The Structure of Organizations* (New York: Basic Books, 1971).

Boulding, Kenneth E. "General Systems Theory: The Skeleton of Science," *Management Science,* April 1956, 197-208.

Brown, Ray E. *Judgment in Administration* (New York: McGraw-Hill, 1966).

Brown, Warren B. "Systems, Boundaries, and Information Flow," *Academy of Management Journal,* Dec. 1966, 318-27.

Buckley, Walter, editor. *Modern Systems Research for the Behavioral Scientist* (Chicago, Ill.: Aldine, 1968).

Burke, W. Warner. "A Comparison of Management Development and Organization Development," *J. Applied Behavioral Science,* Sept.-Oct. 1971, 569-79.

Burns, Tom, and Stalker, G.M. *The Management of Innovation* (London: Tavistock, 1961).

Campbell, John P.; Dunnette, Marvin D.; Lawler, III, Edward E.; and Weick, Jr., Karl E. *Managerial Behavior, Performance, and Effectiveness* (New York: McGraw-Hill, 1970).

Carlisle, Howard M. "Measuring the Situational Nature of Management," *Calif. Management Review,* Winter 1968, 45-52.

Chamberlain, Neil W. *Enterprise and Environment: The Firm in Time and Place* (New York: McGraw-Hill, 1968).

Chandler, Alfred E., Jr. *Strategy and Structure* (Cambridge, Mass.: M.I.T. Press, 1962).

Churchman, C. West. *The Systems Approach* (New York: Dell, 1968).

Cleland, David I., and King, William R. *Systems Analysis and Project Management* (New York: McGraw-Hill, 1968).

Crozier, Michel. *The Bureaucratic Phenomenon* (Chicago: Univ. of Chicago Press, 1964).

Cyert, R. M., and March, James G. *A Behavioral Theory of the Firm* (Englewood Cliffs, N.J.: Prentice-Hall, 1963).

Dalton, Gene W.; Lawrence, Paul R.; and Lorsch, Jay W. *Organizational Structure and Design* (Homewood, Ill.: Richard D. Irwin and Dorsey Press, 1970).

DeGreene, Kenyon B., editor. *Systems Psychology* (New York: McGraw-Hill, 1970).

Delbecq, Andre L. "The Management of Decision-making within the Firm: Three Strategies for Three Types of Decision-making," *Academy of Management Journal,* Dec. 1967, 329-339.

Deutsch, Karl W. "Toward a Cybernetic Model of Man and Society," in *Modern Systems Research for the Behavioral Scientist,* edited by Walter Buckley (Chicago: Aldine, 1968), pp. 387-400.

Drucker, Peter F. *Technology, Management and Society* (New York: Harper & Row, 1970).

Easton, David. *A Systems Analysis of Political Life* (New York: Wiley, 1965).

Ellis, David O., and Ludwig, Fred J. *Systems Philosophy* (Englewood Cliffs, N.J.: Prentice-Hall, 1962).

Emery, F. E., editor. *Systems Thinking* (Harmondsworth, Middlesex, England: Penguin Books, 1969).

____, and Trist, E. L. "The Causal Texture of Organizational Environments," *Human Relations,* Feb. 1965, 21-31.

____, and ____. "Socio-technical Systems," in *Management Sciences: Models and Techniques,* edited by C. West Churchman and Michel Verhulst, Vol. 2 (New York: Pergamon Press, 1960), pp. 83-97.

Emshoff, James R. *Analysis of Behavioral Systems* (New York: Macmillan, 1971).

Etzioni, Amitai. *A Comparative Analysis of Complex Organizations* (New York: Free Press of Glencoe, 1961).

____. *Modern Organizations* (Englewood Cliffs, N.J.: Prentice-Hall, 1964).

Fiedler, Fred E. "Style or Circumstance: The Leadership Enigma," *Psychology Today,* March 1969, 38-43.

____. *A Theory of Leadership Effectiveness* (New York: McGraw-Hill, 1967).

Filley, Alan C., and House, Robert J. "Management and the Future," *Business Horizons,* April 1970, 7-20.

Fouraker, Lawrence E., and Stopford, John M. "Organizational Structure and Multinational Strategy," *Admin. Science Quarterly,* June 1968, 47-64.

French, Wendell. "Organization Development Objectives, Assumptions and Strategies," *Calif. Management Review,* Winter 1969, 23-34.

Gore, William J. *Administrative Decision-Making* (New York: Wiley, 1964).

Grimes, A. J.; Klein, S. M.; and Shull, F. A. "Matrix Model: A Selective Empirical Test," *Academy of Management Journal,* March 1972, 8-32.

Gross, Bertram M. "The Coming General Systems Models of Social Systems," *Human Relations,* Nov. 1967, 357-74.

____. *Organizations and Their Managing* (New York: Free Press of Glencoe, 1968).

Grusky, Oscar, and Miller, George A., editors. *The Sociology of Organizations* (New York: Free Press, 1970).

Guest, Robert H. *Organizational Change: The Effect of Successful Leadership* (Homewood, Ill.: Richard D. Irwin and Dorsey Press, 1962).

Guth, William T., and Tagiuri, Renato. "Personal Values and Corporate Strategies," *Harvard Business Review,* Sept.-Oct. 1965, pp. 123-32.

Hage, Jerald. "An Axiomatic Theory of Organizations," *Admin. Science Quarterly,* Dec. 1965, 289-320.

____, and Aiken, Michael. *Social Change in Complex Organizations* (New York: Random House, 1970).

Hall, A. D., and Fagen, R. E. "Definition of System," *General Systems.* Yearbook for the Society for the Advancement of General System Theory, Vol. 1 (1956).

Hall, Richard H. "The Concept of Bureaucracy: An Empirical Assessment," *Amer. J. Sociology,* July 1963, 32-41.

____. *Organizations: Structure and Process* (Englewood Cliffs, N.J.: Prentice-Hall, 1972).

Harrison, Roger. "Choosing the Depth of Organizational Intervention," *J. Applied Behavioral Science,* April-May-June 1970, 181-202.

____. "Understanding Your Organization's Character," *Harvard Business Review,* May-June 1972, 119-128.

Harvey, Edward. "Technology and the Structure of Organizations," *Amer. Sociological Review,* April 1968, 247-259.

Hauser, Philip M. "The Chaotic Society: Product of the Social Morphological Revolution," *Amer. Sociological Review,* Feb. 1969, 1-19.

Herbst, P.G. "Problems of Theory and Method in the Integration of the Behavioural Sciences," *Human Relations,* Nov. 1965, 351-59.

Hickson, D. J. "A Convergence in Organization Theory," *Admin. Science Quarterly*, Sept. 1966, 224–37.

____ ; Pugh, D. S.; and Pheysey, Diana C. "Operations Technology and Organizational Structure: An Empirical Reappraisal," *Admin. Science Quarterly*, Sept. 1969, 378–97.

Horvath, William J. "The Systems Approach to the National Health Problem," *Management Science*, June 1966, pp. B-391–95

Hunt, Raymond G. "Technology and Organization," *Academy of Management Journal*, Sept. 1970, 235–52.

Johnson, Richard A.; Kast, Fremont E.; and Rosenzweig, James E. *The Theory and Management of Systems*, 3d ed. (New York: McGraw-Hill, 1973).

Kast, Fremont E., and Rosenzweig, James E. "General Systems Theory: Applications for Organization and Management," *Academy of Management Journal*, Dec. 1972, 447-465.

____, and ____. *Organizations and Management: A Systems Approach* (New York: McGraw-Hill, 1970).

Katz, Daniel, and Georgopoulos, Basil S. "Organizations in a Changing World," *J. Applied Behavioral Science*, May–June 1971, 342–75.

____, and Kahn, Robert L. *The Social Psychology of Organizations* (New York: Wiley, 1966).

Knowles, Henry P., and Saxberg, Borje O. "Human Relations and the Nature of Man," *Harvard Business Review*, March–April 1967, 22–40ff.

Koontz, Harold, editor. *Toward a Unified Theory of Management* (New York: McGraw-Hill, 1964).

Kuhn, Thomas S. *The Structure of Scientific Revolutions* (Chicago, Ill.: Univ. of Chicago Press, 1962).

Lawrence, Paul R., and Lorsch, Jay W. "Differentiation and Integration in Complex Organizations," *Admin. Science Quarterly*, June 1967, 1–47.

____, and ____. *Organization and Environment* (Boston, Mass.: Harvard Graduate School of Business Administration, 1967).

Leavitt, Harold J. "Applied Organization Change in Industry: Structural, Technical, and Human Approaches," in *New Perspectives in Organizational Research*, edited by W. W. Cooper, H. J. Leavitt, and M. W. Shelly, II (New York: Wiley, 1964), pp. 55–71.

Levinson, Harry. *The Exceptional Executive: A Psychological Conception* (Cambridge, Mass.: Harvard University Press, 1968).

____. "Reciprocation: The Relationship between Man and Organization," *Admin. Science Quarterly*, March 1965, 370–90.

Leys, Wayne A. R. "The Value Framework of Decision-making," in *Concepts and Issues in Administration Behavior*, edited by Sidney Mailick and Edward H. Van Ness (Englewood Cliffs, N.J.: Prentice-Hall, 1962), pp. 81-93.

Likert, Rensis. *The Human Organization* (New York: McGraw-Hill, 1967).

Lippitt, Gordon L. *Organization Renewal* (New York: Appleton–Century–Crofts, 1969).

Litterer, Joseph A. *The Analysis of Organizations* (New York: Wiley, 1965).

____. *Organizations: Structure and Behavior*, Vol. 1 (New York: Wiley, 1969).

____. *Organizations: Systems, Control and Adaptation*, Vol. 2 (New York: Wiley, 1969).

Litwak, Eugene. "Models of Bureaucracy Which Permit Conflict," *Amer. J. Sociology*, Sept. 1961, 177–84.

Litwin, George H., and Stringer, Jr., Robert A. *Motivation and Organizational Climate* (Boston, Mass.: Division of Research, Graduate School of Business Administration, Harvard University, 1968).

Lombard, George F. F. "Relativism in Organizations," *Harvard Business Review,* March–April 1971, 55–65.

Lorsch, Jay W. "Introduction to the Structural Design of Organizations," in *Organizational Structure and Design,* edited by Gene W. Dalton, Paul R. Lawrence, and Jay W. Lorsch (Homewood, Ill.: Richard D. Irwin and Dorsey Press, 1970), pp. 1–16.

____, and Lawrence, Paul R., editors. *Studies in Organizational Design* (Homewood, Ill.: Richard D. Irwin and Dorsey Press, 1970).

March, James G., editor. *Handbook of Organizations* (Chicago, Ill.: Rand McNally, 1965).

____, and Simon, Herbert A. *Organizations* (New York: Wiley, 1958),

Maurer, John G. *Readings in Organization Theory: Open-System Approaches* (New York: Random House, 1971).

McGregor, Douglas. *The Human Side of Enterprise* (New York: McGraw-Hill, 1960).

Mesarovic, Mihajlo D., editor. *Views on General Systems Theory* (New York: Wiley, 1964).

Miller, E. J., and Rice, A. K. *Systems of Organization* (London: Tavistock, 1967).

Miller, James G. "Living Systems: Basic Concepts," *Behavioral Science,* July 1965, 193–237.

____. "Living Systems: Cross-Level Hypotheses," *Behavioral Science,* Oct. 1965, 380–411.

Miller, Robert F. "The New Science of Administration in the USSR," *Admin. Science Quarterly,* Sept. 1971, 247–57.

Mockler, Robert J. "Situational Theory of Management," *Harvard Business Review,* May–June 1971, 146–55.

Mohr, Lawrence B. "Organizational Technology and Organizational Structure," *Admin. Science Quarterly,* Dec. 1971, 444–59.

Morse, John J. "Organizational Characteristics and Individual Motivation," in *Studies in Organization Design,* edited by Jay W. Lorsch and Paul R. Lawrence (Homewood, Ill.: Richard D. Irwin and Dorsey Press, 1970), pp. 84–100.

Mott, Paul E. *The Characteristics of Effective Organizations* (New York: Harper & Row, 1972).

Mouzelis, Nicos P. *Organization and Bureaucracy* (Chicago, Ill.: Aldine, 1968).

Myers, M. Scott. "The Human Factor in Management Systems," *Calif. Management Review,* Fall 1971, 5–10.

Negandhi, Anant R., and Schwitter, Joseph P., editors. *Organizational Behavioral Models* (Kent, Ohio: Comparative Administration Research Institute of the Bureau of Economics and Business Research, Kent State University, 1970).

Newman, William H. "Strategy and Management Structure," *J. Business Policy,* Winter 1971/72, 56–66.

____; Summer, Charles E.; and Warren, E. Kirby. *The Process of Management,* 3d edition (Englewood Cliffs, N.J.: Prentice-Hall, 1972).

Parsons, Talcott. *The Social System* (New York: Free Press of Glencoe, 1951).

____. *Structure and Process in Modern Societies* (New York: Free Press of Glencoe, 1960).

Perrow, Charles. "The Analysis of Goals in Complex Organizations," *Amer. Sociological Review,* Dec. 1961, 854–65.

____. "A Framework for the Comparative Analysis of Organizations," *Amer. Sociological Review,* April 1967, 194–208.

____. *Organizational Analysis: A Sociological View* (Belmont, Calif.: Wadsworth, 1970).

Petit, Thomas A. "A Behavioral Theory of Management," *Academy of Management Journal*, Dec. 1967, 341–50;

Phillips, D. C. "Systems Theory—A Discredited Philosophy," *Management Systems*, 2d ed. edited by Peter P. Schoderbek (New York: Wiley, 1971), pp. 55–64.

Porter, Lyman W., and Lawler, III, Edward E. *Managerial Attitudes and Performance* (Homewood, Ill.: Richard D. Irwin, 1968).

Presthus, Robert. *The Organizational Society*. (New York: Alfred A. Knopf, 1962).

Price, James L. *Organizational Effectiveness: An Inventory of Propositions* (Homewood, Ill.: Richard D. Irwin, 1968).

Pugh, Derek S. "Modern Organization Theory: A Psychological and Sociological Study," *Psychological Bulletin*, Oct. 1966, 235–51.

____; Hickson, D. J.; and Hinings, C. R. "An Empirical Taxonomy of Structure of Work Organizations," *Admin. Science Quarterly*, March 1969, 115–26.

Rapoport, Anatol, and Horvath, William J. "Thoughts on Organization Theory," *Modern Systems Research for the Behavioral Scientist*, edited by Walter Buckley (Chicago: Aldine, 1968), pp. 71–5.

Reddin, W. J. *Managerial Effectiveness* (New York: McGraw-Hill, 1970).

Rice, A. K. *The Enterprise and Its Environment* (London: Tavistock, 1963).

____. *The Modern University* (London: Tavistock, 1970).

Rosenzweig, Jim. "Managers and Management Scientists: Two Cultures," *Business Horizons*, Fall 1967, 79–86.

Rushing, William A. "The Effects of Industry Size and Division of Labor on Administration," *Admin. Science Quarterly*, Sept. 1967, 273–95.

Sayles, Leonard R., and Chandler, Margaret K. *Managing Large Systems* (New York: Harper & Row, 1971).

Schein, Edgar. *Organizational Psychology*, 2d ed. (Englewood Cliffs, N.J.: Prentice-Hall, 1970).

Schoderbek, Peter P., editor. *Management Systems*, 2d ed. (New York: Wiley, 1971).

Scott, William G. "Organizational Theory: An Overview and an Appraisal," *Academy of Management Journal*, April 1961, 7–26.

Seiler, John A. *Systems Analysis in Organizational Behavior* (Homewood, Ill.: Richard D. Irwin and Dorsey Press, 1967).

Shakun, Melvin F. "Management Science and Management: Implementing Management Science via Situational Normativism," *Management Science*, April 1972, B-367–77.

Sherman, Harvey. *It All Depends* (University, Ala.: Univ. of Alabama Press, 1966).

Silverman, David. *The Theory of Organizations* (New York: Basic Books, 1971).

Simon, Herbert A. *Administrative Behavior* (New York: Macmillan, 1959).

____. "The Architecture of Complexity," in Joseph A. Litterer, *Organizations: Systems, Control and Adaptation*, Vol. 2 (New York: Wiley, 1969), pp. 98–114.

____. "On the Concept of Organizational Goal," *Admin. Science Quarterly*, June 1964, 1–22.

Souder, William E. "A Scoring Methodology for Assessing the Suitability of Management Science Models," *Management Science*, June 1972, pp. B-526–43.

Stinchcombe, Arthur L. "Social Structure and Organizations," in *Handbook of Organizations*, edited by James G. March (Chicago: Rand McNally, 1965), pp. 142–93.

Tannenbaum, Arnold. *Control in Organizations* (New York: McGraw-Hill, 1968).

Terreberry, Shirley. "The Evolution of Organizational Environments," *Admin. Science Quarterly*, March 1968, 590–613.

Thompson, James D., editor. *Approaches to Organizational Design* (Pittsburgh, Pa.: Univ. of Pittsburgh Press, 1966).

____. *Organizations in Action* (New York: McGraw-Hill, 1967).

____, and McEwen, William J. "Organizational Goals and Environment," *Amer. Sociological Review*, Feb. 1958, 23–31.

____, and Bates, Frederick L. "Technology, Organization, and Administration," *Admin. Science Quarterly*, Dec. 1957, 325–44.

Thompson, Victor A. "Bureaucracy and Innovation," *Admin. Science Quarterly*, June 1965, 1–20.

Von Bertalanffy, Ludwig. *General System Theory* (New York: George Braziller, 1968).

____. "The Theory of Open Systems in Physics and Biology," *Science*, Jan. 13, 1950, 23–9.

Warner, W. Lloyd, editor. *The Emergent American Society*, Vol. 1. (New Haven, Conn.: Yale University Press, 1967).

Webb, James E. *Space Age Management* (New York: McGraw-Hill, 1969).

Whisler, Thomas L. *Information Technology and Organizational Change* (Belmont, Calif.: Wadsworth, 1970).

Wilensky, Harold L. *Organizational Intelligence* (New York: Basic Books, 1967).

Wilson, Robert N. "The Social Structure of a General Hospital," *Annals of the American Academy of Political and Social Science*, March 1963, 67–76.

Woodward, Joan. *Industrial Organization: Theory and Practice* (Fair Lawn, N.J.: Oxford University Press, 1965).

Yuchtman, Ephraim, and Seashore, Stanley E. "A System Resource Approach to Organizational Effectiveness," *Amer. Sociological Review*, Dec. 1967, 891–903.

Contingency Views of Organization and Management was set in Baskerville body and display type by Editorial Associates, Los Altos, California, and printed and bound by the George Banta Company, Menasha, Wisconsin. The book and cover were designed by Joseph di Chiarro. Robert D. Bovenschulte was the sponsoring editor, and Sue Oudyn the project editor.

345/4321